DSE232
Applying Psychology

This publication forms part of an Open University course DSE232 *Applying Psychology*. Details of this and other Open University courses can be obtained from the Student Registration and Enquiry Service, The Open University, PO Box 197, Milton Keynes MK7 6BJ, United Kingdom: tel. +44 (0)845 300 60 90; email general-enquiries@open.ac.uk

Alternatively, you may visit the Open University website at http://www.open.ac.uk where you can learn more about the wide range of courses and packs offered at all levels by The Open University.

To purchase a selection of Open University course materials visit http://www.ouw.co.uk, or contact Open University Worldwide, Walton Hall, Milton Keynes MK7 6AA, United Kingdom for a brochure: tel. +44 (0)1908 858793; fax +44 (0)1908 858787; email ouw-customer-services@open.ac.uk

The Open University
Walton Hall, Milton Keynes
MK7 6AA

First published 2002. Second edition 2008

Edited and designed by The Open University.

Typeset by Pam Callow, S&P Enterprises (rfod) Ltd.

Printed and bound in Malta by Gutenberg Press.

ISBN 978 0 7492 1633 7

2.1

Contents

This book, *Applying Psychology*, was originally part of the Open University course DSE212 *Exploring Psychology*.

Original DSE212 course team

Open University staff

Dr Dorothy Miell, Senior Lecturer in Psychology, Faculty of Social Sciences (Course Team Chair)

Dr Paul Anand, Lecturer in Economics, Faculty of Social Sciences

Peter Barnes, Senior Lecturer in Centre for Childhood, Development and Learning, Faculty of Education and Language Studies

Pam Berry, Key Compositor

Dr Nicola Brace, Lecturer in Psychology, Faculty of Social Sciences

Dr Nick Braisby, Lecturer in Psychology, Faculty of Social Sciences

Maurice Brown, Software Designer

Sue Carter, Staff Tutor, Faculty of Social Sciences

Annabel Caulfield, Course Manager, Faculty of Social Sciences

Lydia Chant, Course Manager, Faculty of Social Sciences

Dr Troy Cooper, Staff Tutor, Faculty of Social Sciences

Crystal Cunningham, Researcher, BBC/OU

Shanti Dass, Editor

Sue Dobson, Graphic Artist

Alison Edwards, Editor

Marion Edwards, Software Designer

Jayne Ellery, Production Assistant, BBC/OU

Dr Linda Finlay, Associate Lecturer, Faculty of Social Sciences, co-opted member of course team

Alison Goslin, Designer

Professor Judith Greene, Professor of Psychology (retired), Faculty of Social Sciences

Celia Hart, Picture Researcher

Professor Wendy Hollway, Professor of Psychology, Faculty of Social Sciences

Silvana Ioannou, Researcher, BBC/OU

Dr Amy Johnston, Lecturer in Behavioural Neuroscience, Faculty of Science

Dr Adam Joinson, Lecturer in Educational Technology, Institute of Educational Technology

Sally Kynan, Research Associate in Psychology

Andrew Law, Executive Producer, BBC/OU

Dr Martin Le Voi, Senior Lecturer in Psychology, Faculty of Social Sciences

Dr Karen Littleton, Senior Lecturer in Centre for Childhood, Development and Learning, Faculty of Education and Language Studies

Dr Bundy Mackintosh, Lecturer in Psychology, Faculty of Social Sciences

Marie Morris, Course Secretary

Dr Peter Naish, Lecturer in Psychology, Faculty of Social Sciences

Daniel Nettle, Lecturer in Biological Psychology, Departments of Biological Sciences and Psychology

John Oates, Senior Lecturer in Centre for Childhood, Development and Learning, Faculty of Education and Language Studies

Michael Peet, Producer, BBC/OU

Dr Ann Phoenix, Senior Lecturer in Psychology, Faculty of Social Sciences

Dr Graham Pike, Lecturer in Psychology, Faculty of Social Sciences

Dr Ilona Roth, Senior Lecturer in Psychology, Faculty of Social Sciences

Brenda Smith, Staff Tutor, Faculty of Social Sciences

Dr Richard Stevens, Senior Lecturer in Psychology, Faculty of Social Sciences

Colin Thomas, Lead Software Designer

Dr Kerry Thomas, Senior Lecturer in Psychology, Faculty of Social Sciences

Dr Frederick Toates, Reader in Psychobiology, Faculty of Science

Jenny Walker, Production Director, BBC/OU

Dr Helen Westcott, Lecturer in Psychology, Faculty of Social Sciences

Dr Clare Wood, Lecturer in Centre for Childhood, Development and Learning, Faculty of Education and Language Studies

Christopher Wooldridge, Editor

External authors and critical readers

Dr Koula Asimakopoulou, Tutor Panel

Debbie Balchin, Tutor Panel

Dr Peter Banister, Head of Psychology and Speech Pathology Department, Manchester Metropolitan University

Clive Barrett, Tutor Panel

Dr Kevin Buchanan, Senior Lecturer in Psychology, University College, Northampton

Dr Richard Cains, Tutor Panel

Professor Stephen Clift, Tutor Panel

Linda Corlett, Associate Lecturer, Faculty of Social Sciences

Victoria Culpin, Tutor Panel

Dr Tim Dalgleish, Research Clinical Psychologist, Brain Sciences Unit, Cambridge

Dr Graham Edgar, Tutor Panel, Research Scientist, BAE SYSTEMS

Patricia Fisher, Equal Opportunities critical reader

David Goddard, Tutor Panel

Dr Dan Goodley, Lecturer in Inclusive Education, University of Sheffield

Victoria Green, Student Panel

Dr Mary Hanley, Senior Lecturer in Psychology, University College, Northampton

Dr Jarrod Hollis, Associate Lecturer, Faculty of Social Sciences

Rob Jarman, Tutor Panel

Dr Hélène Joffe, Lecturer in Psychology, University College London

Dr Helen Kaye, Associate Lecturer, Faculty of Social Sciences

Professor Matt Lambon-Ralph, Professor of Cognitive Neuroscience, University of Manchester

Rebecca Lawthom, Senior Lecturer in Psychology, Manchester Metropolitan University

Kim Lock, Student Panel

Patricia Matthews, Tutor Panel

Dr Elizabeth Ockleford, Tutor Panel

Penelope Quest, Student Panel

Susan Ram, Student Panel

Dr Alex Richardson, Senior Research Fellow in Psychology and Neuroscience, Imperial College of Medicine, London, also Research Affiliate, University Laboratory of Physiology, Oxford

Dr Carol Sweeney, Tutor Panel

Dr Annette Thomson, Associate Lecturer, Faculty of Social Sciences

Dr Stella Tickle, Tutor Panel

Carol Tindall, Senior Lecturer in Psychology, Manchester Metropolitan University

Jane Tobbell, Senior Lecturer in Psychology, Manchester Metropolitan University

Martin Treacy, Associate Lecturer, Faculty of Social Sciences

Professor Aldert Vrij, Professor in Applied Social Psychology, University of Portsmouth

External assessors

Professor Martin Conway, Professor of Psychology, Durham University

Professor Anne Woollet, Professor of Psychology, University of East London

DSE232 course team

Open University staff

Volker Patent, Innovations Fellow, Lecturer in Psychology, Faculty of Social Sciences, Course Team Chair

Dr Lesley Allinson, Consultant

John Berriman, Service Administrator, Learning & Teaching Solutions

Dr Gemma Briggs, Lecturer in Psychology, Faculty of Social Sciences

Kathleen Calder, Media Project Manager, Learning & Teaching Solutions

Richard Golden, Faculty Administrator, Faculty of Social Sciences

Graham Healing, Learning and Teaching Development Officer, Institute of Educational Technology

Paul Hillery, Graphic Design Media Developer, Learning & Teaching Solutions

Dr Helen Kaye, Staff Tutor, Faculty of Social Sciences

Mr Andy McBurnie, Consultant

Joanna Mack, Producer Sound and Vision, Learning & Teaching Solutions

Marie Morris, Course Secretary, Faculty of Social Sciences

Jason Platts, Interactive Media Developer, Learning & Teaching Solutions

Sarah Pelosi, Course Secretary, Faculty of Social Sciences

Dr Susan Rattray, Consultant

Elaine Richardson, Course Secretary, Faculty of Social Sciences

Emma Sadera, Editor, Learning & Teaching Solutions

Dr Jim Turner, Lecturer, Faculty of Social Sciences

Dr Dan Weinbren, Course Manager, Faculty of Social Sciences

Dr Helen Westcott, Senior Lecturer in Psychology, Faculty of Social Sciences

Angela Whicker, Course Secretary, Faculty of Social Sciences

External assessor

Hugh Coolican, Principal Lecturer in Psychology within the Faculty of Health and Life Sciences

Introduction

Andy McBurnie

DSE232 *Applying Psychology* covers some of the areas in applied psychology, and seeks to answer some relevant questions: What is applied psychology? What are its uses? How is it different from other 'kinds' of psychology? These are questions that you may have asked yourself about applied psychology. In basic terms, applying psychology is about putting research evidence and psychological ideas into practice. However, as you will see, this is an over-simplified definition. Instead, psychology can be applied in almost all the different fields of psychology, such as developmental, clinical, cognitive and social psychology to name but a few.

The question about the nature of the relationship between different fields of psychology and the applications within each of these fields is rather complex and not answerable in an introduction. However, you will find that there is a degree of overlap between different applied areas (for example occupational and clinical psychology) and that the boundary between fields and applications is somewhat fuzzy (for example social psychology of work and occupational psychology). Rather than being a limitation, this creates interesting tensions in the field and is also a source for cross-fertilisation between different psychologies. You may encounter this in your reading, but it is not something to be too concerned over. Instead, try to get a more global appreciation of the diversity of applied psychology and the advantages this provides to using psychology in the real world.

The key points to remember are that:

- psychologists who focus on applying psychology utilise research findings in a practical manner to solve real-life issues and problems, and
- research is often informed and driven by real-life issues and problems, so studies are conducted to investigate those issues and explore what they can tell us about human psychology.

Sometimes, when considering the findings of research or the theories presented in psychology, there can be a feeling of 'so what?' What does it actually tell us? How does psychology relate to the problems and issues that we face in life? What can we actually *do* with this knowledge? This course aims to answer the 'so what?' question and show how psychological theories and research methods can be applied in a practical manner to real-life issues and problems. You may be surprised at the extent to which psychology has permeated our lives, and the societies and environments in which we live, learn and work.

Some of the questions that this book will address are:

- How do we assess workplace bullying and what kind of intervention can we adopt to deal with it effectively?
- Who is better at detecting lies: police officers or the general public?
- Why is it that, given the same circumstances, some people will experience stress and others will not?
- What factors can enhance – or prevent – effective teamwork?
- How has learning theory, originally developed in a laboratory, been applied to treatment for post-traumatic stress disorder (PTSD) in real cases?
- What are some of the problems encountered when the police question witnesses to crimes, and can psychological research help to overcome these?
- What social psychological theories are there that explain aspects of computer-mediated communication, such as 'flaming'?
- How is autism defined, diagnosed and treated?

In seeking to answer these questions, DSE232 *Applying Psychology* looks at some of the classic studies that have been carried out in each of several topic areas. It also covers several types of therapies and other interventions that are designed and applied by professional psychologists in their respective fields. You will see that it is not sufficient to present anecdotal or 'common-sense' applications of psychology, or to advocate interventions that are not backed up by sound theory and research. You will also learn how to consider theory, research, explanations and interventions in light of the strengths and limitations of the methodology used, including practical and ethical aspects of researching and applying psychology. Throughout this course you will see that we must always be rigorous and adhere to best practice in applying psychology. For example, in Chapter 5 'The autistic spectrum', Ilona Roth considers what constitutes good and bad research and theory, and offers some criteria for evaluating practical treatment interventions.

Bridging academic and vocational psychology

One of the key aspects of DSE232 is that it acts as a 'bridge' between psychology as an academic subject and psychology as a professional vocation. It may well be that you have chosen to study this course because of personal experience of one of the issues covered on the course, or because you have a vocational interest in a particular area of psychology such as clinical, forensic or occupational psychology. It is easy to get drawn into the fascinating world of psychology and to discover how relevant it is to our everyday lives and experiences. However, it is unusual for any single theory, perspective or research finding to map directly onto a real-life problem or issue (unless the research has been carried out specifically in response to an issue – you will encounter examples of this at various points throughout the course). The 'bridge' provided by *Applying Psychology* will hopefully allow you to see not only *how* professional psychologists apply their knowledge, and what knowledge they apply, but also *what* they do in their work.

Applied psychologists have to draw very widely from the whole range of psychological knowledge and skills – and sometimes even from other disciplines, such as psychiatry or information technology. As you read through this book you will notice that the chapters' authors have differing expertise, perspectives on research, and even different writing styles – although they share the common goal of applying psychology to explain and solve real-world problems. Many of the contributors are also practising psychologists in one or more of the applied professions and the course team have deliberately not imposed a similar writing style or tone for all chapters. This reflects the fact that original source material within psychology is presented in a variety of formats, and for a variety of audiences. Similarly, you will also notice that the material is extensively referenced, again reflecting good practice when presenting psychological material. Familiarity with a variety of writing styles and formats will hopefully stand you in good stead when reading material from other sources, as well as helping you to consider your own writing. We hope that being exposed to different styles of writing will be beneficial both in your work on DSE232 and beyond, should you go on to study psychology further, whether with The Open University or elsewhere.

Research and theories

DSE232 *Applying Psychology* will show how research and theoretical work in various fields can inform, change and formulate policy and procedure in many different areas. For example, Chapter 7 'Psychological factors in witness evidence and identification' highlights how court proceedings have been changed, particularly with regard to child witnesses, as a direct result of psychological research in the forensic psychology field. Other examples include providing guidance on the formation of teams in the workplace (Chapter 6) and informing the design of controls and machinery and the way in which they are operated (Chapter 3).

Psychology is theory-based and there is a requirement for research to provide evidence for (or against) theories as well as to inform and add to the overall knowledge base of psychology. However, some psychological research tends to focus on specific theories, using specific methodologies and operating from specific perspectives. When applying psychology the aim is to use elements of knowledge, derived from research, to address real-life problems or issues. During this course you will see that professional psychologists often adopt an eclectic and pragmatic approach, drawing upon different research and theories rather than limiting themselves to one particular area, approach, specialism or research method. When looking at a particular issue or problem, an applied psychologist has to consider alternative explanations, weighing up the evidence presented and making a judgement about the most appropriate way to proceed. In practice, this means that applied psychologists often approach research as an investigation and testing of a situation rather than for the specific purpose of knowledge building.

You will also learn that psychologists need to utilise a range of different perspectives, data and methodologies in order to address certain problems or issues. This is because real-life problems and issues are often complex and require approaches that draw on different knowledge bases to be able to capture such complexity. For example, Chapter 7 'Psychological factors in witness evidence and identification' demonstrates how psychologists working in this field have used theories of, and research on, the nature of memory, stereotyping and perception as well as aspects such as automatic and controlled processing of information. In Chapter 6 'Relationships at work', it can be seen that psychologists working in this field have drawn on theory and research from personality, memory, identity, learning and unconscious processes and from perspectives that include social constructionism and psychoanalysis. (Note: throughout this course 'theory' generally refers to a specific explanation for a particular psychological phenomenon, whilst 'perspective' generally refers to an overall approach to psychology and psychological phenomena.) It is important to note that applying psychology is not simply a case of looking at how it has been applied previously and replicating what has been done. It is necessary to analyse each unique situation and to apply the psychological theories and research that are appropriate to that particular situation. Psychology is being actively applied every day and throughout the course we highlight this active application. Indeed, this is a key feature of the assessment for this course, as you will discover if you follow the course closely.

Just as important to note is that, although applied psychology uses findings from research, this is a transactional relationship; in other words, the practical application of psychology leads to further research, for instance to build on previous findings or to influence the direction that new psychological research takes. There are many examples of this throughout the course, and it is vital to acknowledge the interaction between theory, research and real-life issues. For example, Chapter 5 'The autistic spectrum' looks at how theory of mind research has both informed research on autism and has been informed by research and issues within the topic of autism. Similarly, Chapter 6 'Relationships at work' illustrates how one of the classic programmes of research in occupational psychology, the Hawthorne Studies, was instigated in response to the real-life issue of workplace motivation.

The topics

DSE232 *Applying Psychology* covers a wide range of areas, but it is not possible in this course to cover all of the fields in which psychology is applied – or even all of the topics within any specific field. The topics selected demonstrate some of the forms of the application of psychology, and these look at very different subjects or areas. This, almost inevitably, leads to the use of different methodologies and the discussion of different viewpoints, not only between topics but often within similar subject areas. For example, Chapter 5 'The autistic spectrum' contains several very different approaches to autism, each of which draws on different perspectives, theories and methodologies, resulting in different interventions or treatments. A similar diversity of approaches can be found in all of the chapters and reflects the eclectic nature of applied psychology. The four applied fields that are covered in the course are: health psychology, forensic psychology, clinical psychology and occupational psychology. Some of the main features of each are outlined below:

Health psychology

This is a relatively new field of psychology and involves using psychological principles to promote changes in attitudes, behaviour and thinking about health and illness. It also explores the effects that psychological well-being can have on physical well-being and vice versa.

Forensic psychology

This field looks at the psychological aspects of legal processes in court, and at applying psychological theory to policing and criminal investigations. It is also concerned with the treatment of criminal offenders and the psychological factors associated with criminal behaviour.

Clinical psychology

The work in this field aims to reduce psychological distress and enhance and promote psychological well-being. Practitioners assess the needs of clients and can provide treatments, interventions and therapy based on psychological theory and research.

Occupational psychology

This applied field is concerned with how organisations function and the behaviour and performance of individuals and groups at work. It is a wide-ranging area of applied psychology and also touches on aspects such as ergonomics (e.g. human–workplace interaction, personnel management, training, and time management).

(Source: adapted from the British Psychological Society (BPS) website, 2007)

A quick glance at the contents page of this book will show you that the course is not set out explicitly in terms of these applied fields. Instead it is based around seven specific topics and, as you will see, this has resulted in seven very different, but equally informative, chapters. Some of the topics have applications in more than one field of applied psychology and research has been carried out by researchers from different fields, with each contributing to the overall knowledge base of the topic. The table below gives an indication of which chapters relate to which fields. It is important to note that these topics do not constitute the whole of any of the applied fields (as you will see in the Epilogue to this book).

Clinical/Health	Occupational	Forensic
Stress (Chapter 1)	Stress (Chapter 1)	Witness evidence and identification (Chapter 7)
PTSD (Chapter 2)	Computer-mediated communication (Chapter 3)	Telling and detecting lies (Chapter 4)
Autistic spectrum (Chapter 5)	Relationships at work (Chapter 6)	PTSD (Chapter 2)

Whilst it has not been possible to represent all strands of applied psychology, or to cover the complete range of topics that professional psychologists are concerned with, the topics presented have been selected so that they not only provide thought-provoking, self-contained chapters, but also complement each other in different ways, for instance by contributing to the same profession as shown in the table above. As you work through the course you will see that some issues crop up in several chapters, for example issues of diagnosis and labelling occur in the chapters on stress, PTSD and the autistic spectrum. An outline of each chapter is given below.

The chapters

Chapter 1 - Stress

In Chapter 1, Mary Hanley discusses the topic of stress, an area that most people will feel some affinity with: just about everyone will feel 'stressed' at times, to a greater or lesser extent. However, the term is often used in an almost casual manner, which does not do justice to the complexities that lie beneath the topic. This chapter seeks to offer a psychological definition of stress and to look at some of the different factors involved in the topic. It outlines some of the key sources of stress and discusses the consequences of stress in terms of how it may affect sufferers at work and in their health.

Chapter 2 - Post-traumatic stress disorder

The topic of stress is also explored in Chapter 2 by Tim Dalgleish. However, the focus is rather different from the previous chapter, as stress is looked at in the specific and clinical sense of post-traumatic stress disorder (PTSD). On reading the two chapters, you will quickly see that PTSD raises some very different theoretical and treatment issues from those raised in the stress chapter. Drawing as it does on psychometrics, the theory of conditioning and psychoanalysis, the chapter discusses the definition and assessment of PTSD, considers different theoretical approaches to it and looks at differing therapies that are applied in its treatment of PTSD.

Chapter 3 - Computer-mediated communication: living, learning and working with computers

Chapter 3, by Adam Joinson and Karen Littleton, looks at how psychology relates to relatively modern developments in computer-mediated communication, such as the internet and email, and considers the potential use of computers in education. This chapter examines various theories which suggest that we communicate differently online compared to face-to-face, and considers the impact of computer-mediated communication on issues such as group dynamics, communities and identity. Social psychological processes, for example social identity theory, are looked at in terms of how much they can be drawn upon to explain differences in communications brought about by the use of, and interaction with, technology, especially computers.

Chapter 4 - Telling and detecting lies

In Chapter 4, Aldert Vrij discusses telling and detecting lies. He argues that there are no real differences in the underlying psychological processes of 'professional' liars (such as serial criminals) and the 'ordinary' man or woman. It may surprise you to learn the extent to which people are revealed to lie on a daily basis. Various psychological approaches, including cognitive, behavioural and social constructionist, are discussed regarding their contribution to an explanation of telling and detecting lies. This chapter also gives an insight into some of the difficulties that may be experienced when conducting applied research into lying.

Chapter 5 - The autistic spectrum: from theory to practice

In Chapter 5, Ilona Roth looks at the autistic spectrum, which includes psychological disorders that you may have read about or perhaps have experience of yourself or from contact with a person who has autism. The complexities underlying its origins are considered, as are other aspects such as issues of diagnosis and the various treatment programmes that have been devised. The issues covered in the chapter draw on a multitude of psychological theories and research, such as lifespan development, language, consciousness, biological psychology, memory, evolutionary psychology and learning theory.

Chapter 6 - Relationships at work

Rebecca Lawthom considers relationships at work in Chapter 6, offering an historical analysis of how the focus of research in this area has changed over the years, from early work on motivation and leadership to more recent research on workplace bullying. The formation of teams and their impact on organisations are discussed, with various psychological theories and research being brought to bear on the subject.

Chapter 7 - Psychological factors in witness evidence and identification

In Chapter 7, Helen Westcott and Nicola Brace discuss psychological factors in witness evidence and identification. Many people will have witnessed a crime or been asked to make an identification – even if only when watching a television programme aimed at obtaining assistance from viewers in the detection and investigation of crimes. This chapter looks at how people react when witnessing a crime, how they perform in subsequent interviews, and at the merits of using identification parades. It also considers how psychology can assist witnesses in court and how it can inform best practice in this area. Links between cognitive and social psychological theories and common, everyday experiences are highlighted.

Research ethics

Similar to conducting psychological research, applying treatments, therapy or other interventions requires very careful consideration. Applied psychologists often deal with vulnerable people and, as such, safeguards need to be in place. Even when the people involved are not necessarily seen as vulnerable, consideration has to be given to their continued well-being. It is vitally important for students of psychology to appreciate the importance of such issues. The British Psychological Society has published a *Code of Ethics and Conduct* which outlines the ethical principles that underpin all psychological work within the UK and by which psychologists must abide (other countries' psychological societies and associations have their own ethical codes and guidelines, which are generally based on the same underlying ethical standards). In brief, the BPS code is based on four ethical principles:

Respect: psychologists should show respect for individual, cultural and role differences and value the dignity and worth of all persons, with particular regard to people's rights, including those of privacy and self-determination.

Competence: psychologists must recognise the limits of their own knowledge, skill, training, education and experience and must work within them.

Responsibility: psychologists should avoid harming clients or research participants, and should also take care to avoid putting themselves in a position where they could be harmed. They should also strive to prevent misuse or abuse of psychological knowledge.

Integrity: psychologists should strive to be fair, honest, clear and accurate and to maintain integrity in all of their professional dealings.

Key aspects specific to research include: obtaining informed consent from all involved in the research; maintaining anonymity or obtaining consent for disclosure; eliminating (or at least reducing to the greatest extent) risks to the participants; and debriefing the participants to ensure that they are unharmed and have suffered no discomfort.

(Source: adapted from The British Psychological Society Code of Ethics and Conduct, 2007)

Research design

Whilst ethics are obviously very important to the individuals involved when applying psychology, they also throw up practical issues in research and interventions. For example, how do psychologists carry out research into workplace bullying or PTSD? Obviously, it is not ethical to subject people to workplace bullying in order to ascertain what the effects are. Nor can people be deliberately exposed to a traumatic event in order to investigate the factors that result in some people suffering from PTSD and others being seemingly unaffected. However, as you will see, with care and consideration it is possible to conduct research in these areas, and interventions, treatments and therapy are based on such research.

Psychologists constantly strive to improve on research design and to use innovative methodologies in order to overcome ethical difficulties – although occasionally these new methodologies give rise to new criticisms. Nonetheless, the decision to proceed with practical applications is almost always dependent on evaluating the practical impact of research findings. The topics covered in DSE232 *Applying Psychology* are often associated with complex methodological and ethical concerns, and throughout the chapters these are discussed together, reflecting the interrelationship between methodology and ethics in applied psychology. Throughout the chapters you will see that there is a focus on methodologies and ethics. Often there has to be compromise, or an unusual approach, when carrying out research and you may find yourself at odds with some of the approaches taken by applied psychologists. For example, some of the studies in Chapter 7 'Psychological factors in witness evidence and identification' involved psychologists experimentally investigating children's reports of painful or intimate experiences and you may find yourself feeling uncomfortable with that. Although this kind of research would seem to require particular care, the principles also apply to seemingly 'normal' situations. For example, Chapter 6 'Relationships at work' highlights some of the difficulties of studying workplace bullying without running the risk of ostracising people or of affecting participants' career prospects. You may find that some topics seem to be difficult to research within ethical and practical considerations, but, this leaves a dilemma – should psychologists ignore such topics or apply less rigour to these matters in order to comply with ethical guidelines?

This is one reason why psychologists are constantly looking to implement different methodologies and approaches to their fields. It is also important to note that any objections to carrying out research or interventions may be mitigated by the benefits of such applications and that this itself may justify the approach taken by psychologists. For example, the studies on children's intimate or painful experiences referred to in Chapter 7 have led to the implementation of best practice guidelines for interviewing allegedly abused children – a clear benefit arising from the research.

Sensitive issues

Inevitably, in a course of this nature, which focuses on applied areas of research and addresses several types of psychological problems, there is the possibility that the material will address areas that are particularly sensitive for certain people. It may be that the research will be focused on explaining difficult personal problems or on issues that some people may personally identify with. Obviously, it is not possible to judge what material may be sensitive for every individual, but care has been taken to include a comprehensive contents page as well as a box at the beginning of each chapter that identifies issues that may be particularly sensitive. It is recommended that you read these introductory sections carefully, so that you are aware of what will be covered. An awareness of the possible sensitivity of the material will enable you to engage with the material in a way that is suitable for you.

As a final note, the knowledge and skills that you will develop throughout DSE232 *Applying Psychology* have links to employability, and we hope that you find much here that will be of benefit to you and your future career. The Epilogue to this book revisits this notion, explores further topics and fields in applied psychology and highlights some career areas to which psychology links.

 # References

BPS (2007) *The British Psychological Society website* [online], http://www.bps.org.uk/home-page.cfm (Accessed 21 November 2007).

Stress

Mary Hanley

Contents

This chapter offers a review of issues relating to the concept of stress. You may find some personal resonance with the concept of stress as a whole, or with the examples that are discussed. These include being a student, work and bereavement as stressors, and cardiovascular disease as a response to stress.

Aims

This chapter aims to:

- consider what psychologists mean by the term 'stress'
- examine what happens to the physiological processes in the body when someone becomes stressed
- outline key sources of stress and factors which might mediate the experience of stress
- discuss some of the main consequences of stress on work and on health
- explore the contribution of work by health and occupational psychologists to the study of stress.

1 Introduction

Debbie is 22 years of age and lives in Leeds. She is currently living in a tiny flat which is damp and has no private bathroom or toilet, and is waiting to be placed in permanent accommodation by the Social Services Department. Debbie is eight months pregnant and already has a child of four years. She is no longer with either of the fathers and does not receive any financial assistance other than that provided by the government. She does not drive or have access to a car and the bus service is poor in the area she lives in; she is unsure how she will manage when the new baby arrives in four weeks time. Debbie believes that there is a great deal of stress in her life.

Nancy is a singer in an internationally famous pop group. She recently married her long-term partner who is a successful film actor. Nancy and her husband are regularly seen at society parties and entertain frequently with the assistance of a wide range of domestic staff. The couple own houses in London and New York and often travel between the two. Nancy said in a recent magazine interview that she found her lifestyle very stressful.

Of all the concepts examined within the discipline of psychology, stress is possibly the one with which most people in the general public will be familiar. In fact, no less than 17,000 research papers were published on stress between 1988 and 1999 (Cassidy, 1999). The popularity of the concept is also reflected in everyday life, and people will often talk about 'suffering from stress' or 'being put under stress at work'. Indeed, some people would argue that 'stress' is referred to much too readily as an 'excuse' for failure to fulfil responsibilities. However, despite the wide recognition and use of the term, a common understanding of what exactly is meant by stress is less readily available, with the same term meaning different things to different people. As you can see from the two examples above, Debbie and Nancy are two women whose lives have taken very different directions; however, they both believe that there are characteristics of their particular lifestyles which are stressful for them.

Activity 1.1

Make a list of any events or situations that you have found stressful in the last two weeks. Looking at your list of stressful events, which items do you believe that most people would find stressful? Have you included any items in your list that you think other people might not find particularly stressful, or might even enjoy?

Clearly stress is a very individual concept. While there are certain events that are generally considered stressful (e.g. the death of a partner or close friend), the things that you find stressful may not affect others in that way. Similarly, you might feel quite relaxed about situations in life that other people find to be a considerable source of stress. However, when a person does experience stress, it does not only have an effect on their performance in the short term. Research suggests that ongoing minor stress can have a significant impact on a person's health more generally, with people who experience ongoing high levels of stress being at increased risk for illness such as coronary heart disease, hypertension and ulcers. Therefore, stress and its consequences are important issues in both public and academic consciousness. As a result of its impact on health, stress is considered to be a central concept in the field of **health psychology** (Friedman, 1992). However, stress research is not only confined to this field and psychologists from other fields contribute to our understanding and management of stress and its consequences. For example, **occupational psychologists** are increasingly involved in the study of stress, particularly where the source of stress is work-based or when the effects of stress impact on the quality or the efficiency of a person's work performance. We are now starting to see health and occupational psychologists working together to understand stress more fully at both the individual and the organisational level.

This chapter will describe some of the findings of the research conducted by health and occupational psychologists. We shall see that in order to understand stress and its consequences more fully, we need to be able to answer questions such as: What makes an event stressful? Why do some people become stressed by a particular event while others take it in their stride? How does stress affect our work and our health? How can we use this information to deal with stress more effectively?

Health psychology
Health psychology is the area of psychology concerned with the application of psychological theories and findings to health and healthcare.

Occupational psychology
Occupational psychology is a branch of psychology concerned with organisational issues within the workplace, including the performance of people at work.

2   What is stress?

2.1   What is meant by the term 'stress'?

While many people feel that stress is very much a phenomenon associated with modern life, there is evidence that the term has been used, often in similar ways, for over 600 years (Cassidy, 1999). Recorded use of the term 'stress' dates back to the fourteenth century when it was used to refer to hardship, straits, adversity or conflict (Lazarus and Folkman, 1984). In the late seventeenth century, it was more commonly used in the physical sciences and engineering to describe the degree to which a structure (e.g. a bridge) could withstand pressure. The impact of this pressure on the structure was considered to be a stress-related outcome. Stress was incorporated into medicine in the modern sense in the 1920s by Walter Cannon and his successor Hans Selye, a Canadian endocrinologist, who, as you will see later in this chapter, used the term to help explain the physiological response to negative life events. Indeed, it was Selye who helped establish stress research within the domain of the social sciences by giving an invited address to the American Psychological Association in 1955 (Lazarus and Folkman, 1984).

However, as noted earlier, despite the fact that stress is a widely recognised concept with a long history, when you ask people to define the term the answers you get may be very different.

Activity 1.2

How would you define stress?

Look at the types of definitions given below and decide which one is closest to your definition of stress.

In general, definitions of stress fall into one of three categories.

For some people, stress refers to something that happens in the environment or in a person's life, such as work-overload, failing an exam, moving house, or studying for a degree, which makes more demands than the individual feels that they can comfortably meet. This type of event is often referred to as a stressor. Although a wide range of life events can be considered to be potential stressors, the important factor in determining whether an event is stressful or not for a particular individual is their perception of their ability to meet the demands of the life event.

Alternatively, people may think about stress as the response they feel as a result of coping with demanding life events, such as being over-tired, lacking energy, having sleeping problems, or feeling depressed, and this is what is usually meant when people say they are suffering from stress. For these people stress may be defined as the response a person has to the challenges of life (e.g. distress).

The third way in which people may describe stress, and this is the approach currently used by most psychologists in this area, refers to an interaction between the first and second definition. Specifically, stress refers to a process in which some event occurs in your life (i.e. a stressor) that you fear you do not have the ability to cope with. As a result, you exhibit a range of behavioural responses that cause you distress. This approach is evident in a *transactional model of stress* which considers:

- factors associated with the individual and their environment
- the source of stress
- the response to the situation.

A transactional model is the most popular current understanding of what psychologists mean by stress. This is because it takes into consideration the wide range of factors that may influence how a person copes with the demands of everyday life. So, instead of saying that a particular event is universally stressful (and this is rarely the case), it considers that any event is potentially stressful; whether or not it is ultimately stressful for any one individual is likely to be mediated by a range of factors in the person's own life.

The model shown in Figure 1.1 may help you to appreciate the wide range of factors that can play a role in mediating our response to a stressor.

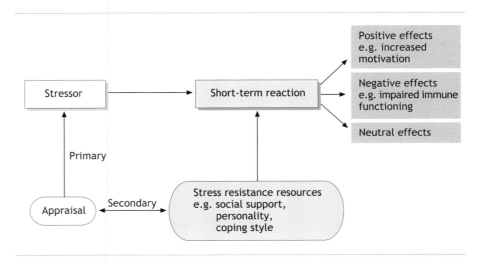

Figure 1.1　A transactional model of stress (Source: adapted from Sheridan and Radmacher, 1992, p.149)

In a transactional model of stress, there is no suggestion that any life event is inevitably stressful; rather it suggests that when an event occurs your reaction to it will depend on your appraisal of the situation. When confronted with an event you make a primary appraisal; i.e. 'does this event present a threat to me at this time?' If you conclude that it does not then you will not experience stress. If it does, however, whether you will experience stress or not depends on your secondary appraisal: that is, 'what resources do I have to cope with this situation?'. For many people, the resources that they have available (e.g. personality characteristics, social support, financial resources) will be sufficient to allow them to cope effectively with the stressor. However, some people may not perceive themselves to have sufficient resources available to deal with the problem and as a result they experience a response that we would typically refer to as a 'stress response' (Sheridan and Radmacher, 1992). Thus, no event can be identified as a stressor outside of a person's appraisal of the event. We will return to the important subject of **cognitive appraisal** later in the chapter.

On the basis of your appraisals you will then experience a short-term reaction. This may be: no overall change in state; a positive effect such as increased motivation; or, what we most commonly associate with a stressful life event, a negative effect which may result in short- and/or long-term consequences.

Looking at stress using the transactional model can help to explain why two people undergoing the same event may have very different responses. Just as no two people are the same, no two people will have exactly the same response to a stressor. Think again about the list you made earlier of the things that caused you stress during the past two weeks. You probably noticed that some of the things you mentioned may not have been a source of stress for everybody. In fact, for some people, some of the events that you have listed may be a positive experience and may act as a strong source of motivation. Therefore, it is important to recognise that the relationship between a negative life event and stress is not direct: rather it is moderated by a range of individual and contextual factors. It is these factors that will determine whether you experience stress, have a positive or negative response to the event, or, indeed, decide that the event has no effect on you in any direction.

Cognitive appraisal
The subjective judgements a person makes about a situation in order to understand it.

2.2 The physiology of stress

What impact does stress have on the physical processes of the body? To address this question we can look back at prehistoric humans. When humans first evolved, their lifestyle was obviously very different from the lifestyles that we have today.

Activity 1.3

Make a list of the kind of things that you think might have been stressful for early humans living in the prehistoric period.

Comment

You probably said something like being chased by a predator or trying to find shelter or warmth. How does this list compare to the one you made earlier about your life now? Prehistoric stressors were often very different from stressors typical in today's life, such as worrying whether there is a conspiracy against you at work, sitting in a traffic jam, or trying to juggle the various demands of family life, work and childcare on a daily basis. In Western societies we are rarely in extreme physical danger or need – our stress is typically psychological in origin. However, despite the fact that the causes of stress are very different for modern humans, the physiological reactions of the body are the same as in the prehistoric period.

The Attack by William Strutt

Let us consider what might have happened when a prehistoric human was being chased by a predator. When the body detects an emergency or a source of stress the sympathetic branch of the autonomic nervous system is activated. This stimulates a number of changes to the normal functioning of the body in a way that would have helped the prehistoric human to adapt to the source of stress. These changes include:

- increase in heart rate and blood pressure
- constriction of blood vessels in some areas of the body
- increase in blood sugar level
- redirection of blood flow away from extremities towards major organs
- breathing changes to become faster and deeper
- digestion stops or slows
- sweating increases.

(Carlson et al., 1997, p.565; Toates, 2001, pp.348–9)

These changes take place because the body is starting to prepare itself to respond to the threat. They are mediated by neurohormonal changes, including the production of two hormones, termed adrenalin and noradrenalin, from the adrenal glands. These glands are located just above the kidneys. The two hormones circulate in the bloodstream and target such organs as the heart, in this case increasing its beating. This process was described by the physiologist Walter Cannon as the **fight-or-flight response** because it physically prepares the body to stay and respond to the threat or to evade it – fight or run away (Cannon, 1929). In addition to this response by the sympathetic nervous system, there is another neurohormonal system involved. Detection by the brain of a challenge or threat causes a sequence of actions that leads to the increased secretion, also by the adrenal glands, of a class of hormones termed 'corticosteroids'. In humans, an important member of this class is **cortisol**. These hormones help to prepare the body for action and conflict by increasing the release of fuels (e.g. glucose) from stores in the body. These fuels can be used by the cells as a source of energy.

What actually happens in the body to make this response occur? Cannon believed that anything which upsets the homeostatic balance of the body may be regarded as a stressor. Homeostasis is the tendency of certain parameters of the body, such as temperature or hydration, to remain more or less constant. If one of those parameters changes, for example if the body becomes hot or dehydrated, then a 'homeostatic behaviour' will occur, such as seeking shade or drinking water. These behaviours are adaptive, as they promote survival. Similarly, the fight-or-flight response is highly adaptive in some stressful situations because it mobilises the organism to respond quickly to danger; for our prehistoric ancestors, therefore, it was associated with survival. The degree to which such a response is adaptive in modern society, however, is questionable. While this response may be useful in the short term, the body cannot sustain it for long

Fight-or-flight response
Physiological response to a stressor which causes changes in the body to prepare it for physical attack or to evade the threat.

Cortisol
Cortisol is a stress hormone released by the adrenal gland.

without harming your health. In many cases this does not pose a significant problem, as illustrated by the following example. A source of stress presents itself (e.g. you see your bus about to leave the bus stop 10 metres away) and you take advantage of the physiological changes taking place in your body to respond to the threat (i.e. you start running to catch the bus). As a result, the threat is eradicated (you manage to catch the bus) and your physiology returns to normal.

However, what happens when the source of stress is chronic or ongoing (e.g. unreasonable boss at work; frequent arguments with your partner)?

Have you argued with someone and found your heartbeat increasing (as a result of an increase in adrenalin)? This is a typical stress response, which may be useful if you have to run away, but you may find it far less helpful when trying to present a reasoned argument.

In such cases, the physiological changes associated with the stress are, in general, no longer adaptive, and they can in fact have a significant negative impact on your health. These effects were demonstrated quite clearly by Hans Selye (1956) in a series of animal experiments which examined the health consequences of prolonged exposure to stress. Based on a series of studies of rats who were exposed over a prolonged period of time to a wide variety of stressors (e.g. hormone injections, exposure to heat and cold, electric shocks, X-radiation), Selye found that the rats had developed a range of physical disorders including peptic ulcers, enlarged adrenal glands and shrunken immune tissue. Selye argued that a similar result could be seen in humans.

There are ethical issues surrounding the use of animals for such research. It is important to remember that these studies were carried out in the 1950s, and were not constrained by the ethical guidelines in operation in psychology today. While they are useful in helping us to understand how animals respond to physical stressors, there is some question as to whether we can generalise these findings to explain the human response to psychological stress. It is also highly unlikely that such experiments would be replicated today, given the current guidelines that researchers have to adhere to.

When confronted with a stressor the body's response can be divided into three stages. The first stage, alarm, corresponds to the initial response to stress in which the body's defences are mobilised, preparing the body for fight-or-flight. In the second stage – resistance – the body starts to adapt to the stressor, but some of the physical changes are maintained. It is the maintenance of such physical changes that are thought to lead to the development of diseases such as coronary heart disease or hypertension – Selye termed them 'diseases of adaptation'. The final stage of adaptation is exhaustion, in which, confronted by prolonged stress, the body's ability to resist eventually breaks down and a person may become ill. Selye termed this process the *general adaptation syndrome* (GAS).

The GAS is probably easier to understand if you think about what happens when someone moves into a job that causes stress (see Figure 1.2). As you can see, while becoming a 'workaholic' may help them adjust to the high workload in the short term, as a technique for managing stress in the longer term it can, in fact, be counterproductive.

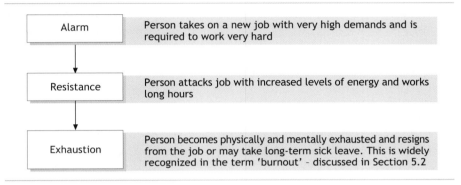

Figure 1.2   An example of the general adaptation syndrome

While the physical responses that accompany stress may be adaptive and may have been useful for prehistoric humans or any other animal that may experience being attacked by a predator, they are less useful for a modern human who has the same physiological response but who is now sitting in an office having been reprimanded by his/her manager. Similarly, prehistoric stress is more likely to have been short term, whereas modern day stress is much more likely to be ongoing, and not linked to a physical threat but rather a psychological one (e.g. fear of failure, relationship problems, performance anxiety). Such threats do not respond well to a racing heart or high blood pressure. Understanding the body's response to stress helps to explain why zebras don't get ulcers but people do (Sapolsky, 1998)!

2.3 Criticisms of Selye's work

While the basic premise of Selye's theory has been highly influential in our understanding of stress, specific aspects of the GAS have been heavily criticised. A primary criticism has surrounded the issue of the commonality of the stress response. Mason (1971, 1975) has argued that the body does not have a uniform response. It has also been suggested that in the model there is a lack of appreciation of the psychological elements which mediate the *cognitive* appraisal of a threat. Specifically, the model does not account for why two people may react in very different ways to the same stressor – with one person becoming ill and another appearing to flourish. Basically, the model in its current form lacks a recognition of psychological variability and ignores the role of cognitive appraisal in mediating the stress response. In other words, we need to understand the subjective judgements someone makes about a situation in order to understand whether or not that particular individual will find it stressful. Consequently, as we shall see in more detail later, any full understanding of stress needs to consider the interaction between the thought processes of the individual and contextual factors in moderating potentially stressful events.

Summary Section 2

- The concept of stress is now part of everyday life and most people have some understanding of what it signifies.
- The psychological changes that accompany stress are underpinned by a range of physiological changes, orchestrated by the autonomic nervous system, which adapt the body to respond efficiently to the perceived threat in the short term.
- While such physical changes may have had evolutionary importance they are less useful in helping us to adapt to the stressors in our lives today and as a result the physical reaction to ongoing stress may lead to problems with physical health.
- Cognitive appraisal is a key factor in understanding individual variability in response to a potential stressor.

3   Some sources of stress

Since stress can have such a major impact on a person's life, careful consideration should be given to identifying sources of potential stress. However, this sounds easier than it is in practice, since stress is a highly individual experience. Consequently, when we are trying to identify sources of stress in a person's life, it is important to recognise that this will be highly influenced by factors such as the person's point in their life cycle, their personal circumstances, their personality and coping mechanisms.

Lazarus and Cohen (1977) identified three classes of stressors that may influence a person's life. First there are *cataclysmic stressors* – major life events which happen to several people or whole neighbourhoods at the same time, for example a bomb, flooding, or major violent attack (see Chapter 2, Post-traumatic stress disorder, for an account of how such traumatic events may impact upon an individual). Such stressors typically have a low incidence rate but for those who are affected they are a particularly acute source of stress. These events are characterised by their unpredictability and the powerful impact they have on the community. Coming to terms with such stressors may be difficult but can be facilitated by high levels of social support through community or government intervention.

Cataclysmic stressors are typically a less common source of stress for most people than are the second class – *personal stressors*. Personal stressors typically affect individuals or small groups of people at any one time (e.g. families) and include things such as a death, loss of job, bankruptcy, unemployment, divorce or breakup of a long-term relationship. The extent to which this type of stressor is predictable varies and this will have an impact on the consequences of the event. For example, the death of an elderly relative after a long illness will not necessarily have the same consequences as the sudden and unexpected death of a young mother. The coping efforts which are required as a result of personal stressors are mediated by background factors such as the predictability of the event and the support mechanisms available to the people involved (Sheridan and Radmacher, 1992).

The final type of stressors identified by Lazarus and Cohen are *background stressors* or daily hassles. These refer to the small but persistent problems that irritate and distress people (Lazarus and Folkman, 1984). Such stressors typically have a high incidence and can affect many people: a noisy workplace, a bullying or inconsiderate manager, lack of appropriate facilities at work, children leaving clothes lying around the house, someone not washing up their dirty dishes, children kicking a football endlessly outside the door, always being in a hurry because of having too many things to do, regularly driving in heavy traffic, noisy neighbours – the list is endless. It is important to recognise that if these background stressors are not satisfactorily resolved (i.e. they become chronic) they may lead to a range of stress-related problems.

In order to understand more fully how everyday experiences may result in stress, the following subsections will examine in greater detail three areas which you may have listed as a source of stress to you – being a student, work, and bereavement. You will see that individuals do not respond to these in the same way; later in the chapter we will explore how individual differences are an important consideration.

3.1 Being a student

While the opportunity to study for a degree is an exciting challenge for many students, for some the process can also be a potential source of great stress (Stone and Archer, 1990). This may be the case particularly for mature students. Compared with their younger counterparts, who come into higher education directly from school or sixth-form colleges, mature students are more likely to have additional responsibilities and commitments such as an ongoing stable relationship, a mortgage, or family responsibilities, which will probably place greater demands on them. Mature students do not necessarily experience *more* stress than younger students and the sources of stress may be different – for example, mature students have reported enjoying going to classes and doing homework more than traditional students – but their greater responsibilities at home are potentially a significant source of additional stress (Dill and Henley, 1998; Harris and Brooks, 1998).

Are you finding studying for a degree stressful? Which factors do you find to be a particular source of stress, and how have you adapted your lifestyle to help manage such stressors?

In addition to the stressors outside of academic life (e.g. health problems, managing family life), research indicates that some students find a range of activities associated with higher education study a source of stress. Areas of potential stress for students typically fall into a number of categories: academic (e.g. feeling overwhelmed by coursework); vocational (e.g. identifying a future career path); personal–social (e.g. problems making friends, loneliness, emotional problems); and financial (e.g. working part time outside of college) (Dunkel-Schetter and Lobel, 1990). Not surprisingly, academic concerns and emotional state would appear to be a particular source of stress for many students (Monk and Mahmood, 1999). Between one-third and one-half of students in another study said they experienced stress 'often' or 'very often' during their time at university (Dunkel-Schetter and Lobel, 1990).

In order to manage stress when studying for a degree, it is recommended that students actively develop their coping strategies in order to deal more effectively with academic pressure. This can be achieved in a number of ways and support mechanisms are often available from the institution (see Box 1.1).

1.1 Ways to manage stress

Advice given as part of a student support package at one institution in the UK (University College, Northampton, 2000):

- Balance work and play.
- Relax and pamper yourself on a regular basis.
- Avoid sugary foods and caffeine (fizzy drinks, coffee, tea, 'energy' drinks) as these can impair concentration, leave you jittery and keep you awake too long.
- Eat healthily, e.g. fresh fruit, vegetables and pasta.
- Cut down on alcohol, which can interfere with sleep patterns, and cigarettes, which speed up the heart and increase blood pressure.

- Take regular exercise two to three times a week; this promotes feelings of well-being.
- Talk with someone you can trust. Together generate solutions to tackle problems.
- Get a good night's sleep. Ensure that you stop work half an hour before bedtime.
- Talk with your personal tutor if you are concerned about academic work.

3.2 Work and the workplace

Work and the characteristics of the working environment can be among the most potent stressors in a person's everyday life. Often this stress can be a result of minor, short-term problems (e.g. a relocation of office, technology failure, a busy period of the year), but sometimes the stressor can be more enduring (e.g. poor relationship with line manager/co-workers, job insecurity, very demanding job, too much responsibility or a perception that you are being passed over for promotion). Occupational stress occurs when the demands of a person's job tax or exceed the person's adaptive resources (Lazarus and Folkman, 1984). Cary Cooper has extensively investigated the sources of stress in people's lives, and has focused in particular on the sources of such stress within the work environment. He and colleague Valerie Sutherland have concluded that there are five major categories of stress at work (see Table 1.1). The exact type of stress that a person may experience will be determined by the nature of their job.

Table 1.1   Sources of stress at work

Source of stress	Examples
Stress in the job itself	Workload, physical conditions (e.g. noise, vibration, temperature, lighting, hygiene), low decision latitude, shift work, working long hours, new technology, repetitiveness/monotony, travel, exposure to risk.
Role-based stress	Role conflict (e.g. having conflicting demands from different people in the company, doing tasks that you do not consider to be part of your job, or being involved with a job that conflicts with personal values or beliefs), role ambiguity (e.g. when you do not have adequate information to carry out your tasks, or you do not understand or realise the expectations associated with that particular role), responsibility (i.e. for people or resources).
Relationships with others (e.g. supervisors or colleagues)	May include factors such as: abrasive personalities, leadership style, group pressure, social density (e.g. overcrowding), or status incongruence.
Career development	Over-promotion, under-promotion, lack of job security, career status.
Organisation structure and climate	Restrictions on behaviour, political and cultural climate of the organisation (e.g. a 'blame' culture).

Source: Sutherland and Cooper, 1990, p.25

Activity 1.4

Do the categories in Table 1.1 also apply to you? What about the sources of stress you may be experiencing as a result of your studies? Indicate below the categories that apply to you.

Source	YES/NO
Stress in the work itself	
Role-based stress	
Relationships with others	
Career development	
Organisation structure and climate	

The fact that there are so many potential sources of stress at work does not, however, explain why some people seem to cope very well when other people seem overwhelmed very easily. To explain such individual differences in response to stress at work we need to think again about the transactional model of stress presented in Section 2.1. Stress at work, like stress in any other domain of life, can only be understood from an individual perspective. Therefore, characteristics of the work environment are often made stressful by the way in which we appraise them.

In addition to the characteristics of the job itself, there are other factors associated with working life that may cause a person to experience stress. For example, shift work, which includes working during the evening or night-time hours, can be a potential source of stress (Violanti and Aron, 1994). For many occupations (e.g. healthcare, police work, air-traffic control) it is essential that personnel are available 24 hours per day and, consequently, for such workers shift work is an inevitable part of the job. However, work-related stress would appear to have a significant impact on the lives of these individuals. For example, a review of research examining the health consequences of shift work indicated that shift workers were found to have a 40 per cent increase in the risk of cardiovascular disease compared to non-shift workers (Boggild and Knutsson, 1999). Clearly for at least some individuals, the timetable of employment may act as an additional stressor to the type of work being carried out.

For some people stress may result from the multiple roles they have to fulfil, of which their job is only one aspect (see Box 1.2).

1.2 Fulfilling multiple roles

Tingey and colleagues (1996) examined stress experienced by women who were attempting to combine the role of mother and worker. In this study 72 women aged between 19 and 58 years were interviewed. Women were selected on the basis of having multiple roles – as a worker and as a caregiver of a child under the age of 18 years. All the women in the study had a partner who was also in employment. The women completed a rating scale that looked at their perceived stress levels and answered questions on a range of topics including: satisfaction with childcare arrangements; household duties; employment status; and overlap between working and family life (such as taking work home). Results from the study suggested that high levels of stress were associated with dissatisfaction with childcare arrangements and an overlap between a partner's work and family life. Furthermore, having a sense of control over the situation was a key determinant of whether these working mothers experienced stress: those who felt they had more control over their situation were less likely to report high levels of perceived stress. This finding is not unique to women – working fathers also experience stress as a result of conflicts between the needs of the individual, the family and the workplace (Berry and Rao, 1997).

Finally, it is important to remember that while being a worker can be a source of stress, so can being unemployed or retired, with the changes that extra spare time and a likely decrease in income can bring to a person's life (e.g. Cohen *et al.*, 1998).

3.3 Bereavement

The death of a spouse, partner, parent or child is commonly recognised as one of the most stressful of life events. The first six months of adjustment are perhaps the most difficult for the bereaved, with research indicating that rates of depression increase substantially during this period. There is also evidence of a slight increase in the rates of both death and disease among people who are grieving (e.g. Stroebe *et al.*, 1993). The mechanisms through which bereavement affects health are, however, less clear. It may be the case that people who are in the process of grieving are more likely to engage in a range of behaviours which put their health at risk, such as not eating properly, having poor sleeping patterns, or increasing their alcohol and drug consumption. Alternatively, it may be the case that the increase in mortality and morbidity is linked to the decrease in social support available to the person who is grieving. We shall see in Section 4 how social support is a key factor in helping someone deal with stress.

For most individuals, short-term distress is normal following bereavement, and longer-term adjustment to their new life situation is predicated on experiencing most or all of the stages of the grieving process (Cassidy, 1999). While a number of theoretical models have described the process of bereavement, one of the most influential is the integrative theory of bereavement proposed by Sanders (1999). Sanders' model describes five key phases of grief and bereavement (see Table 1.2).

Table 1.2   Integrative theory of bereavement

Phase	General description
Shock	The bereaved person moves in a confused state of disbelief, characterised by a numbness which protects the individual against the intense pain of loss. It is this response which allows people to make the necessary arrangements following the death of a loved one.
Awareness of loss	Eventually the numbness of the first phase wears off and the reality of loss must be faced. The bereaved person must face the physical and mental agony associated with the death. Separation anxiety becomes apparent, and is accompanied by strong emotional outbursts: yearning, crying, anger, guilt, shame, and sleep disturbances.
Conservation/ withdrawal	This phase is an important time to conserve what energy remains after the previous phase. Grievers often report high levels of fatigue and have difficulty in completing even very simple tasks. This phase is filled with a sense of despair, helplessness and loss of control over life, desires, hopes or dreams. This is a significant stage, however, in adjusting to loss since it gives the bereaved person the opportunity to work through their grief (e.g. rumination and preoccupation with the deceased, acceptance of loss and consequent inevitable changes in one's life). This is an important turning point to potentially start the process of healing.
Healing	Increasing strength enables the bereaved person to start building a new life. Typically this occurs in small stages with increasing perception of personal control. This phase is characterised by forgiving oneself for survival, and subsidence of rage and anger at having been left alone, along with 'letting go' of the deceased. This is the stage at which the bereaved person can reflect on memories of the dead person and recall happy memories and joyful times.
Renewal	By and large this phase is not characterised by the pain of loss. The bereaved person starts to establish a new life, accepting alternative life roles and taking new responsibilities. They typically have increased self-confidence and report a renewed level of functional stability.

Source: adapted from Sanders, 1999

This theory provides an excellent illustration of Selye's GAS as described in the previous section. The initial phase of shock *is characterised by the physical response to stress, which gives the bereaved person the increased energy to deal with the immediate consequences of the death and suppress the emotional response, which would be counterproductive at this stage. The second phase of* awareness of loss *is when the person starts to adjust to the death, but high levels of arousal remain which result in the intense emotional responses that characterise this phase. The third phase of* conservation/withdrawal *is an inevitable consequence of the intense emotional expenditure of the previous phase. These phases clearly reflect Selye's model:* alarm – *shock;* resistance – *response to awareness of loss; and* exhaustion – *withdrawal.*

While phases in the process of grieving are widely recognised, there is less agreement about the time sequence such a process must follow. Similarly, rather than following the grieving process in a predestined and directional manner, it is likely that these phases of grief describe types of responses that most people will move between at some time during the grieving process. Consequently, while bereavement is stressful, there is no *one* right way to grieve. In fact, it has been argued that high levels of distress are neither an inevitable nor a necessary aspect of the grieving process. Like other sources of stress, the response of a particular individual to death is likely to be mediated by a wide range of individual factors such as age, gender, personality, health, feelings towards the deceased, and level of dependency, as well as contextual factors including levels of available social support, who the deceased person was, how anticipated the death was, religious beliefs, and other life stressors. In general, most adults seem to adjust to the death of a close family member without significant long-term problems. In the short term, however, bereaved people are typically higher in depression, lower in life satisfaction, and at greater risk for illness than are the non-bereaved (Bee, 1998).

3.4 Measuring stress

With so many factors in life being potentially stressful, how do researchers identify who is under most stress or who is likely to suffer negative effects as a result? While stress may have been difficult to define, it is even more difficult to measure. In order to assess stress in general, three approaches are typically used: self-report measures, structured interviews, and physiological measures.

Self-report measures

Self-report measures are the most commonly used approach to assessing stress. Such methods typically involve identifying a list of life events which may be considered stressful and ranking them in an agreed order of 'stressfulness'. The basic assumption is that the higher the score a person generates on the scale (based on the frequency of stressful life events) the more likely it is that he/she will experience stress-related problems.

The original and most commonly used of such scales is the Social Readjustment Rating Scale, or SRRS (Holmes and Rahe, 1967 – see Box 1.3). This scale has been around for quite some time but it is still important in stress research since it was the first instrument which attempted to assess objectively the amount of stress in people's lives. It did this by creating a catalogue of potentially stressful events which were rated according to their impact on the individual.

Since stress would seem to be individually perceived and experienced, do you think it is possible or even desirable to try to assess it objectively?

Stress research prior to 1967 had typically focused on the number and type of stressors which occurred in people's lives, with little appreciation of the significance or magnitude of such events. The SRRS was developed largely in an attempt to address these issues.

1.3 The Holmes and Rahe (1967) study

To construct the SRRS scale, Holmes and Rahe asked 394 participants to rate 43 different life events which may be considered stressful. These events included things such as divorce, death and pregnancy and were generated from the clinical experience of the researchers. Participants were then asked to rate each of the 43 items in terms of its demands for social readjustment – where social readjustment was defined as 'the intensity and length of time necessary to accommodate to a life event' (Holmes and Rahe, 1967, p.213). Ratings were based on the average amount of social readjustment required, as judged from the participants' personal experience, and their observations of how other people coped with such life events. The score awarded to each event on the published scale was based on the mean social readjustment score reported by the sample. For example, the event which the assessment panel considered would require the most readjustment was 'death of spouse' which was subsequently given a value of 100; in the same way, 'marriage' was awarded 50 points while 'retirement' was given 45 points (see Table 1.3).

Table 1.3　**The Social Readjustment Rating Scale (top 10 items only)**

Rank	Life event	Mean value
1	Death of spouse	100
2	Divorce	73
3	Marital separation	65
4	Jail term	63
5	Death of close family member	63
6	Personal injury or illness	53
7	Marriage	50
8	Fired at work	47
9	Marital reconciliation	45
10	Retirement	45

Source: Holmes and Rahe, 1967, p.216

The SRRS has been used widely in research studies of stress and stress-related outcomes. Participants tick the events they have experienced and the researcher then calculates their stress score, which is the total of the mean values for all the items ticked. The success of this scale has led to the development of a range of similar instruments such as the Hassles Scale (Kanner *et al.*, 1981), which assesses the extent to which stress may be a result of daily hassles rather than major life events, and the College Adjustment Rating Scale (Zitzow, 1984), which measures students' self-assessment of stress within the academic, social, personal, and family-home environments (see Table 1.4).

Table 1.4　**The College Adjustment Rating Scale (top 10 items only)**

Rank	Life event	Median value (ranked on a scale from 1–9)
1	Death of a brother or sister	8.56
2	Being suspended or placed on academic probation	7.68
3	Death of a parent	7.50
4	Responsibility for unwanted pregnancy	7.50
5	Death of a friend	7.33
6	Giving a class presentation	7.28
7	Parental separation or divorce	6.83
8	Receiving a D or F on a test	6.76
9	Personal pressure to get good grades	5.81
10	Having something stolen	5.76

Source: Zitzow, 1984, p.163

The main appeal in using such scales to quantify the experience of stress is the simplicity and ease with which they are completed. Furthermore, there is an intuitive appeal in ranking a range of events that may happen in anyone's life and quantifying them in terms of their potential to generate stress.

Activity 1.5

Based on your experience of stress, write down any problems that you think might be associated with using these scales to assess stress.

One of the key problems associated with this approach to assessing stress is that there is, as we have already argued, no evidence that any two people will respond to the same life stressor in exactly the same way. For example, one person may respond to the death of a spouse with tremendous grief and may continue the process of grieving for a period of years. Another person may not have had the same quality of relationship with their spouse, or the death may have been expected following a long illness, and as a result the person may not grieve to the same extent. Despite such variations, the death of a spouse will be assessed on this scale as generating the same amount of stress. Thus, the main criticism of such scales is that they do not allow for individual variations as a result of the person's appraisal of the life event, or the change in an individual's perception of an event over time. Therefore, if you look back at the transactional model (Section 2.1) you can now understand more fully why cognitive appraisals and stress resistance resources are shown as moderating the stress-response relationship. How we respond to a potential stressor will depend on a wide variety of factors, the nature of the event itself being only one.

A further problem with stress rating scales is that they tend to be highly *culturally specific*. In other words, the sources of stress identified are often very Western in nature, reflecting the countries in which the research was initially conducted. There is a general assumption when using such scales that these events will also be a potential source of stress to people from other countries and social backgrounds. However, without evidence that these scales continue to be valid with different test populations, results from such research should be treated with caution.

Other problems include the fact that events included within the scale are often quite arbitrary and things that may be an important source of stress for you may not appear. Finally, there is a fundamental question about what exactly it is that these scales are measuring. For example, items such as 'having too many things to do' could be measuring neuroticism, depression or anxiety rather than stress per se (Marks *et al.*, 2000). Consequently, people who *feel* that they are experiencing stress are likely to identify with more of the items on the list, whether or not this is a true and accurate representation of their current life status.

As we shall see below, there are alternative methods that overcome some of these problems. However, despite their many drawbacks, rating scales can be a useful research tool – they provide a means by which stress can be measured quickly, they are easy to administer, and, as they yield quantitative data, statistical analysis can be performed and levels of stress in populations can be compared against published norms and/or other research findings.

Structured interviews

More recently, there has been an increasing trend toward using structured interviews as a means of assessing stress. One such interview, the Life Events and Difficulties Schedule or LEDS (Brown and Harris, 1989), is often used to assess, clarify, and rate the severity of stressors in a person's life. The LEDS was designed to address many of the criticisms that had been levelled at self-report measures. The main aim of conducting an interview with a person in order to assess their level of stress is to allow the researcher to define the stressfulness of life events in terms of the emotional significance for the individual. For each potentially stressful event identified by the interviewee, the researcher facilitates a discussion about how the person felt about the event, how they responded to it and what the consequences and outcomes were. Since the LEDS is an interview (and therefore more flexible in terms of data collection than the self-report questionnaires discussed above), it allows for variations in administration depending on the circumstances of the individual (Marks *et al.*, 2000). Using the LEDS the researcher will gather a vast amount of information about the life experiences of the interviewee. However, it is much more time consuming than a self-report questionnaire and, as with any form of assessment interview, a certain degree of training is required before it can be employed effectively. Although such a method has the disadvantage of reducing comparability between research studies, since each interview will be quite unique, using this technique does offer the possibility of individualising the assessment and subsequent management of stress.

Physiological measures

The final method of assessing stress is through the use of physiological measures. This approach operates on the premise that because stress results in a number of physical changes in the body – increases in blood pressure, heart rate and respiration, for example – the researcher can use such changes as an objective indicator of the level of stress a person is experiencing. Similarly, researchers can directly monitor the physiological changes in the chemical balance of the body resulting from the stress response by analysing samples of blood, saliva or urine for increased levels of cortisol. You may recall from Section 2.2 that cortisol is a stress hormone released by the adrenal gland. This approach has a number of advantages in that it is direct, reliable and easily quantifiable, and allows comparisons to be made between different people. However, as a method of collecting data it is quite intrusive and expensive. It may also rely on highly artificial methods to provoke a stress response – for example, completing difficult mathematical problems under extreme time pressure, or exposure of part of the body to an unpleasant physical stimulus such as dipping a hand in iced water. It also assumes that there are common physiological responses to stressors, and does not take account of the fact that data collection (e.g. the process of taking a blood sample) may itself contaminate the findings anyway by making the participant even more anxious! This phenomenon is sometimes referred to as the 'white coat syndrome'.

In order to assess stress more meaningfully, perhaps we should change the question we ask. In other words, instead of asking 'what is stressful?' we should be asking 'what is it about an event that makes it stressful for a particular individual?' Cassidy (1999) argues that the key factor in determining if something is stressful is the issue of control. He suggests that researchers will never be able to predict if an event will be stressful purely on the basis of objective analysis. Rather, it is the element of personal meaning, or cognitive appraisal, that is the key factor in determining the stress impact of any event. Since any event has the potential to be stressful, it is the uniqueness of the individual or their circumstances that determines whether or not it will be. In view of the complex nature of stress, the best way to assess stress may involve the **triangulation** of a range of methods including self-report measures, structured interviews and physiological measures, thereby combining the strengths of both qualitative and quantitative research methodologies to investigate this highly individualised area.

Triangulation
Using a number of different research methods to collect data, in order to combine their strengths and compensate for the weaknesses of the individual methods.

Summary Section 3

- This section has reviewed a range of sources of stress in people's lives, from cataclysmic stressors to daily hassles, which if left unmanaged can have a significant impact on a person's well-being.
- Three possible sources of stress – studying, work and bereavement – were considered, and factors which play a role in determining variations in responses were discussed.
- It is clear that stress is not only a difficult term to define, but also difficult to assess, with some methods of assessment, such as rating scales and physiological measures, failing to take into consideration the importance of individual interpretation in defining what is stressful.

- If we are to understand the stress process fully, we need to give further consideration to the moderators of a stressful event and understand why some people deal well with life events and others suffer as a result.

4 Moderators of stress

It is clear from the previous section that a wide range of life events, both large and small, can potentially be a source of stress. How then do we explain the fact that, despite the wide range of stressors in their lives, most people tend to cope very well on a day-to-day basis? Some people seem to manage, even when under what appears to others to be an insurmountable burden of stress. Based on a purely biological model of stress we would never be able to understand and explain such individual variability in response to life stressors. Therefore we need to pay attention to the other parts of the model outlined earlier – cognitive appraisal and stress resistance resources – the moderators of stress. These are the factors that help explain the individual differences in coping with stress.

Activity 1.6

Looking back to the start of this chapter (Section 1), you will remember that you made a list of the events that you have found stressful during the last two weeks. Thinking about these events, make a second list – of the factors that helped you cope with and manage these sources of stress. From this list identify the factors which are:

1   about you, e.g. aspects of your personality

2   related to external factors, such as support from friends or money.

Moderators of stress can occur at an individual level (i.e. they are something to do with the kind of person we are) and at a social/environmental level (i.e. something to do with the wider environment in which we live). Some of these areas will now be explored in more detail.

4.1 Cognitive appraisal

The essential factor which would seem to explain why we see individual variations in the experience of stress lies in the concept of cognitive appraisal, which we have already seen in the transactional model of stress. The influential work of Lazarus (Lazarus, 1966; Lazarus and Folkman, 1984) argued that an event is not in and of itself stressful, rather it is made so as a result of the cognitive interpretation of the event by the individual. Therefore, by definition, *any* event has the potential to be stressful. If this is the case, then why do we manage to cope relatively well on a daily basis? Lazarus would argue that an event becomes stressful through the interaction of both primary and secondary appraisal mechanisms. You will recall from Section 2.1 (see Figure 1.1) that a *primary appraisal* involves asking yourself 'does this event present a threat to me?' *Secondary appraisal* refers to your perception of the resources you have available to help you cope in this situation. While primary and secondary appraisals are typically described separately, in reality both processes occur concurrently (Sheridan and Radmacher, 1992). For example, at the same time that you realise your car has broken down and you can't use it to get to work for an important meeting, you are thinking of alternative strategies to solve the problem (e.g. call a friend or partner for a lift, telephone work and postpone the meeting, or call a taxi). So the outcome of the appraisal process will be the identification of a strategy to deal with or cope with the problem. Consequently, when Lazarus and Folkman (1984) describe stress they typically refer to a particular relationship between the person and the environment, one that is appraised by the person as taxing or exceeding his/her resources and endangering his/her well-being. Stress occurs when there is a mismatch between the perceived threat to a person and their perceived ability to cope (Marks *et al.*, 2000).

4.2 What factors determine a person's appraisal of a life event?

In order to understand the variability in response to negative life events, a range of factors associated with the individual have been proposed. This work will be examined under the headings of personal control (e.g. locus of control, self-efficacy, optimism/pessimism), personality characteristics (e.g. type A behaviour pattern, hardiness) and coping style.

Personal control

Personal control is increasingly recognised as a central concept in the understanding of relationships between stressful experiences, behaviour and health (Steptoe, 1989). People like to believe that they have some control over the things that happen to them in life and, as a result, they can produce desirable outcomes and/or avoid undesirable outcomes. In general, people who have a strong sense of personal control typically report experiencing less strain from a range of stressors (e.g. Regehr *et al.*, 2000).

A considerable body of research exists which points to a wide range of individual differences in people's perception of their level of control. This is very apparent with respect to **locus of control**. Locus of control is a construct proposed by Rotter (1966) to describe the extent to which individuals feel they have control over success and failure in life. Specifically, it refers to the extent to which you believe that the things that happen to you are controlled by internal factors (e.g. determination, effort) or by external and environmental factors (e.g. luck, powerful others). For example, when you get favourable feedback about your performance at work do you consider that the positive appraisal is a product of your having worked hard and been conscientious in your duties (internal locus of control), or do you think the praise is a reflection of external factors beyond your control, such as your manager happening to be in a particularly good mood that day (external locus of control)? People who have a higher internal locus of control are less likely to interpret negative life events as stressful, primarily because they have, or at least believe that they have, access to more personal resources in order to alleviate the effects of the stressor. Conversely, people who have a higher external locus of control are more likely to have an adverse response to stressful events, largely because they do not believe that it is within their power to manage the stressor. In fact, people who have a particularly extreme external locus of control are at a higher risk for developing psychological disorders associated with stress, such as depression.

Another dimension of control which appears to be important in determining an individual's response to stress is that of **self-efficacy**. Self-efficacy is a concept described by Bandura (1977) and refers to the belief that we can succeed at something we want to do. For example, say I ask you how certain you are that you could successfully learn a second language. Your answer would probably be based on a number of factors, such as whether you want to do it, whether you have any interest in acquiring the skill, and whether you have successfully learned to speak a foreign language in the past. I know that I am not particularly good at languages and do not enjoy studying them, I have no interest in engaging in further study at this time, and I do not have any plans to use another language in the near future. Therefore, I do not believe I would be able to successfully learn a second language. In other words, I would consider my self-efficacy for being able to successfully learn a second language as very low.

We use similar strategies to decide how likely it is that we will be successful in a wide range of other activities in life and we make judgements about our ability on factors like previous experience, feedback and support from family and friends, and judgements about our general interests, motivation, skills and competencies. The judgements a person makes regarding their perceived self-efficacy in response to a potential stressor will have a significant impact on

Locus of control
The extent to which individuals feel they have control over success and failure in life.

Self-efficacy
An individual's personal sense of control over actions or events.

whether or not they experience stress. For example, when you are asked to complete an assignment for a university course (a potentially stressful event) you will make judgements about your ability to complete the assignment successfully. Your judgement will be based on a range of information such as how good you are at the subject generally, how you have performed in such assignments in the past and how well you have prepared for the piece of work. Research suggests that people who have a high self-efficacy for a particular task will typically show less stress when confronted with this type of stressor (Bandura, 1977). Conversely, people who have a low self-efficacy with respect to a particular task are more likely to experience stress when completing the work, a factor that in itself may make their performance poorer.

The theme that is emerging here is that people who cope with stress more effectively share a common characteristic in that they typically try to exert some control over life. Control can be exerted in a number of ways (see Box 1.4).

1.4   Types of control

- **Behavioural control:** Ability to take concrete action to reduce the impact of a stressor (e.g. delegate some of your workload to others).
- **Cognitive control:** Ability to use thought processes or strategies to modify the impact of a stressor (e.g. don't panic when you have coursework to do but reduce your anxiety by focusing on the success you have had with other assignments in the past). This method of control is the one most consistently associated with positive outcomes.
- **Decisional control:** Taking the opportunity to choose between alternative procedures or courses of action (e.g. whether to manage an illness using medication or elect to have surgery). Often this decision will be made with the advice of others.
- **Informational control:** Finding out as much as possible about a stressful event – what will happen, when, why and what will the outcomes be (e.g. preparation for childbirth).
- **Retrospective control:** Reflection on what caused a stressful event to occur, and searching for a meaning or lesson in the event (e.g. reflecting on the lessons to be learned after a car accident).

Source: adapted from Sarafino, 1994, p.109

In order to understand how control can help to deal with stress, think about someone you know who has been affected by a serious illness. Often people who cope well with illness use techniques to exert control over their condition. This may be in the form of finding out as much about the illness, treatments and potential outcomes as possible (informational control), becoming actively involved in treatment decisions (decisional control), or trying to cope more effectively with the treatment involved by focusing not on the discomfort or inconvenience it may cause but on the positive effect it will have on their well-being (cognitive control). These are techniques that we can all use in everyday life in order to reduce the potentially negative effect of stressors.

Personality characteristics

While personal control would seem to be an important factor in determining variations in response to a stressor, some researchers would argue that it is only part of the stress story (e.g. Kobasa and Maddi, 1977). Characteristics of the individual's personality also appear to have a significant role to play in explaining variations in response to stress. If we reflect on how people who are close to us cope with life stressors, many of us can identify someone who seems to cope well in almost any situation. For example, this is the type of person who seems to be able to take on additional tasks and perform them admirably, despite seeming to have an already unmanageable workload. The reason why people in this situation show few signs of stress may be because they have what is termed a **hardy personality**.

Hardy personality
A type of personality characterised by three dimensions: commitment, control and challenge.

Kobasa (1979) used the term 'hardiness' to describe a cluster of three dimensions: commitment (i.e. sense of purpose or involvement in the events, activities and people in their lives); control (i.e. beliefs about locus of control); and challenge (i.e. the tendency to view changes as incentives or opportunities for growth rather than threats to security). Kobasa argued that when exposed to a potentially stressful situation, people who had a hardy personality were less likely to experience stress. This may be a result of having a wider range of personal and interpersonal resources to call on when appraising the potential stressor, or it may be that the beliefs a 'hardy' person holds lead them to cope with potential stressors in more effective ways (Cassidy, 1999). Research suggests that a hardy personality results from a combination of factors such as genetic predisposition, social skills and networks, and past life experiences, rather than simply being a response to current influences (e.g. Werner, 1987).

One additional perspective on personality that has attracted considerable attention with respect to understanding stress responses is that of the **type A behaviour pattern (TABP)**. TABP refers to a behavioural response identified by two cardiologists Friedman and Rosenman (1974). It is characterised by an exaggerated sense of time urgency, an excessive competitiveness, a drive for achievement, and hostility or aggression. This is sometimes referred to as 'hurry-sickness' (Bartlett, 1998). Someone who would be considered a type A individual would typically answer yes to the following questions:

Type A behaviour pattern (TABP)
A behavioural response characterised by an exaggerated sense of time urgency, an excessive competitiveness, a drive for achievement, and hostility or aggression.

Do you find that you eat more rapidly than most other people?

When someone is talking do you often try to hurry them to get to the point?

Do you find it difficult to wait in a queue?

(Selected items adapted from Jenkins Activity Survey – Jenkins et al., 1979, p.19)

When faced with a potentially stressful situation a person who is prone to TABP will respond in a stereotypic way that is not necessarily adaptive. For example, when confronted with a challenging situation at work, a type A individual might become quite aggressive with his/her work colleagues, and/or rush around the office attempting to complete a number of tasks at once rather than calmly decide on a plan of action to complete the work. The converse of TABP is called type B behaviour, and is usually defined as an absence of the behaviours that characterise TABP. As we will see later, there is clear evidence that people who have TABP have a maladaptive response to stress which places them at increased risk for negative health consequences, most notably coronary heart disease.

Coping style

People may also differ in how they respond to stress as a result of the coping strategies they employ. Coping has been defined as the person's 'cognitive and behavioural efforts to manage specific external and/or internal demands that are appraised as taxing or exceeding the resources of the person' (Folkman and Lazarus, 1988, p.310). In other words, coping refers to the types of thought processes and behaviours we engage in to try to modify the effects of a potential stressor. This is probably easier to understand by using an example.

Activity 1.7

Imagine that you have just returned from a holiday and after having looked at your budget you realise that you have spent much more money than you could afford. In addition, when you arrived home you found a number of unexpected bills and expenses that you must also now pay. What do you do? Make a list of any options you would consider in this situation.

In order to investigate the ways in which people try to cope with stress in their lives, psychologists have developed a number of questionnaires which examine coping styles. One of the most common and widely used of these questionnaires is the COPE scale (Carver *et al.*, 1989). In this scale, the authors have identified 14 different subscales, each one representing a different method of coping with potential stress (see Table 1.5).

Table 1.5   **The COPE subscales**

COPE subscale	Sample item
Active coping	'I take additional action to get rid of the problem'
Planning	'I try to come up with a strategy about what to do'
Suppression of competing activities	'I put aside other activities in order to concentrate on this'
Restraint coping	'I force myself to wait until the right time to do something'
Seeking social support for instrumental reasons	'I ask people who have had similar experiences what they did'
Seeking social support for emotional reasons	'I talk to someone about how I feel'
Positive reinterpretation and growth	'I look for something good in what is happening'
Acceptance	'I learn to live with it'
Turning to religion	'I seek God's help'
Focus on and venting of emotions	'I get upset and let my emotions out'
Denial	'I refuse to believe that it has happened'
Behavioural disengagement	'I give up the attempt to get what I want'
Mental disengagement	'I turn to work or other substitute activities to take my mind off things'
Alcohol–drug disengagement	'I drink alcohol, or take drugs, in order to think about it less'

Source: taken from Marks et al., 2000, p.113

Activity 1.8

People vary in the coping strategies they adopt, some being more appropriate and useful than others depending on the situation. Revisit your answers to Activity 1.7 and see how they fit in with the COPE subscales.

While coping questionnaires have been very popular in stress research, they have often been criticised for implying that people have a typical coping style that they employ regardless of the situation. In reality, we probably use a combination of different coping strategies that are aimed at both solving the problem in hand and helping to moderate our immediate emotional response to the stressor, and these will vary depending on the situation we are in. The key to successful coping lies in identifying and employing useful strategies that work well for you as an individual.

4.3   Social support

While the characteristics of the individual are very important in determining their response to a stressor, it is also important to remember that a person does not live in isolation. Rather, he/she deals with life stress within a social context, and this social context also has an important role to play in managing life stressors. One of the most important factors in the social environment that has an impact on how well we cope with stress is the level of social support available to us. Social support refers to the perceived comfort, caring, esteem or help a person receives from others (Cobb, 1976; Wallston *et al.*, 1983). In general, social support is studied from two perspectives – either from the perspective of the structure of social relations (i.e. number and type of interpersonal relationships), or from a functional perspective, focusing on what is actually provided by social support.

There is general consensus that social support is not a unitary phenomenon, but rather comprises a range of dimensions which contribute to perceived support (e.g. Cutrona and Russell, 1990; House, 1984; Weiss, 1986). Typically, models of social support emphasise:

- emotional support (expression of empathy, caring and concern toward the person)
- esteem support (expression of positive regard, encouragement or agreement)
- instrumental support (direct assistance)
- informational support (advice/guidance)
- network support (membership of groups etc.).

A considerable amount of research suggests that the amount and quality of social support that a person has available in their environment has an important role to play in helping them cope with life events. As discussed in Section 3.3, bereavement is a common source of stress in many people's lives. However, there would appear to be significant gender differences in coping with this stressor. After the death of a spouse, men are more likely to report increased levels of stress than are women. This is thought to reflect the fact that widowers typically have lower levels of social support available compared with that available to widows (Helsing *et al.*, 1981; Stroebe and Stroebe, 1983).

When we experience stress in the workplace, we often draw on social support from key others in our social network as a method of moderating the effects of such stress. Social support may come from a number of areas: managers, supervisors or co-workers; trade unions; family and/or friends. Indeed, it has been suggested that stress at work is best predicted by the combination of high job demands, low control and poor social support (Payne, 1999). In order to gain social support we often bring our work problems home and as a result there is an overlap between work and home life. In many cases, this strategy may help us deal more effectively with work-based stressors. However, in some cases stress at work may only act to exacerbate an already stressful situation at home, with the result that problems at home and work both become more pronounced. One of the most influential pieces of research in the area of social support is the work of Brown and Harris (see Box 1.5).

1.5 The Brown and Harris (1978) study

Brown and Harris conducted a major study in which a large number of women living in South London were interviewed about recent events in their lives and their emotional state. Between 20 and 40 per cent of the women interviewed reported having experienced a serious psychological problem during the previous year. For most of the women, the problem was depression related to a particular stressful event such as bereavement. There were some women, however, who had experienced a similar stressful event but who had not developed mental health problems. This posed a very interesting research question: what factors were operating to protect some women from the negative psychological effects of their life stressors? Brown and Harris concluded that although a number of factors distinguished the two groups of women, the most important one seemed to be whether or not the woman had a close and supportive relationship. Carroll (1992) concluded from the findings of Brown and Harris that having an intimate and confiding partner or friend served a protective function, reducing these women's vulnerability to stress, and decreasing the likelihood that stress would lead to mental health problems.

Exactly *how* social support facilitates coping with stressful life events is less clear. It has been suggested that social support may help to buffer the impact of psychological stressors either directly (e.g. by providing tangible support such as money or assistance), or by altering the cognitive appraisal of the stressful events (Fontana *et al.*, 1989; Shumaker and Hill, 1991). Similarly, social support may have its effect through facilitating the use of more effective coping strategies (e.g. problem-focused coping) or by promoting healthy behaviours (Cohen, 1988; Holahan and Moos, 1991; Shumaker and Hill, 1991).

The mechanism by which social support improves well-being is an important research question which investigators continue to explore.

Finally, it is important to note that it is not only the amount of social support that is important – the *quality* of such relationships is also an important determinant in the response to stress. Indeed the negative features of social relationships appear to be more strongly related to the presence of psychological **symptoms** than are the positive features of social support to the absence of such symptoms (Coyne and Bolger, 1990; Hann *et al.*, 1995; Kiecolt-Glaser *et al.*, 1988; Pagel *et al.*, 1987). Consequently, in terms of stress reduction it is probably better to have a few good trusted friends who will provide support, rather than to have a very extensive friendship group, few of whom could be relied on in a crisis.

Symptoms
Characteristic manifestations of a psychological or medical condition that are observable to others and/or can be described by the person who experiences them.

Summary Section 4

- In order to understand why someone has a negative response to a potential stressor, it should be recognised that there is an important interaction taking place between: (i) the event, (ii) the appraisal and response of the individual and (iii) the integration of a range of individual and social/environmental factors.
- Personal control would appear to be a key factor in adjusting to stress, with research suggesting that people who perceive that they have more control in their lives typically report a more positive response to potential stressors.
- Personality characteristics may also mediate the individual's response to stress: people who are 'hardy' typically tend to cope better.
- It is important to recognise that the individual does not exist in isolation. Social support (both practical and emotional) can be an important buffer of life stressors.

5 Consequences of stress

If you were to ask someone in the general population 'what do you believe are the consequences of stress?' you would probably be told that stress can have very severe consequences in at least two areas of your life: (1) it is damaging to your health; and (2) it interferes with your ability to work properly. How much evidence is there to support either of these responses?

5.1 Health-related outcomes

Coronary heart disease

Coronary heart disease (CHD) is the main cause of premature mortality in many countries today, and is caused by a build-up of fatty deposits within the arteries that carry blood to the heart muscle. This process is commonly referred to as **atherosclerosis**, which means hardening of the arteries. When the arteries of the heart become hardened in this way, the walls of the artery lose their normal elasticity and their diameter becomes reduced. Consequently, the muscles of the heart may not receive all the oxygenated blood they require to function effectively. This may result in angina (chest pain) or a myocardial infarction (heart attack).

Atherosclerosis
A build-up of fatty deposits within the arteries that carry blood to the heart resulting in decreased blood flow.

There is an established lay understanding that stress *causes* CHD, but what research evidence is there to support this proposition? In general, the evidence for a causal link between stress and CHD is mixed. For example, a number of studies have failed to establish that a major life stressor such as a bereavement leads to increased CHD-related mortality (Levav *et al.*, 1988; Avis *et al.*, 1991). Other researchers, however, have reported a positive link between stressful life and heart disease (e.g. Rahe, 1974). Rosengren *et al.* (1991) conducted a 12-year follow-up study of 2,000 men who were considered healthy at the start of the study. Results indicated that men who had initially reported high levels of stress were more likely to have developed symptoms of CHD on follow-up. This effect remained even when the potentially confounding effects of behaviours such as smoking and lack of exercise were taken into consideration.

If we concede that stress *does* play a role in the development of CHD, in order to facilitate the design of appropriate intervention programmes it is necessary to explore the mechanisms through which stress may influence the biology of the heart. Johnston (1992) argued that stress may exert this influence through acting on more clearly established biological risk factors such as raising blood pressure or cholesterol, or through increasing engagement in risk behaviours such as smoking. Much research into the way in which stress may increase someone's risk for CHD has concentrated on its relationship with the type A behaviour pattern (TABP), which was outlined in Section 4.

Research investigating the causal link between TABP and CHD has had a chequered and interesting history. Initial studies which examined these factors seemed to provide convincing evidence that TABP was an important independent risk factor for CHD. In fact, at one time the evidence was considered so uncontroversial that TABP was considered to be as great a risk for heart disease as biological factors such as raised blood pressure and increased cholesterol levels (Review Panel on Coronary-Prone Behaviour and Coronary Heart Disease, 1981). This conclusion was based primarily on the findings of a number of key studies, the most important of which was arguably the Western Collaborative Group Study (Rosenman *et al.*, 1975) – see Box 1.6.

1.6   *Conflicting findings over the role of TABP*

Longitudinal study
A programme of research which takes place over an extended period of time, often many years.

The Western Collaborative Group Study (WCGS) was an 8½-year **longitudinal study** that was conducted in order to identify factors which placed people at risk for developing CHD. A sample of 3454 men aged between 39 and 59 years, who had no previous history of heart disease, were recruited to the study. Data concerning a range of factors which might predict CHD were gathered, including information on TABP and medical risk factors such as a tendency for the blood to clot and blood serum cholesterol levels. When the men were followed up 8½ years later, results showed that 7 per cent of the entire sample had developed some sign of CHD and two-thirds of these were classified as being type As. Furthermore, the importance of TABP as an independent predictor of CHD remained even when the researchers carried out statistical tests which controlled for the effects of health risk behaviours such as smoking and lack of exercise.

More recent findings from a longer-term follow-up of this population, however, are more controversial. A follow-on study of the same group of participants, 22 years after they were initially tested, failed to find a reliable relationship between TABP and death from CHD (Ragland and Brand, 1988). However, this finding endorses another major longitudinal study in this area – the Multiple Risk Factors Intervention Trial (MRFIT) (Shekelle *et al.*, 1985). This study was slightly different in that it included a sample of more than 12,000 middle-aged men, who, although disease free at the start of the study, were considered to be at high risk for developing CHD as a result of their lifestyle and behaviour. The sample was then followed up for seven years, when no relationship could be found between TABP and subsequent development of CHD.

Have you noticed that the two key studies detailed in Box 1.6 have not included women in their samples? This is not untypical of healthcare research. Women are often excluded from study samples because it is considered that their normal hormonal fluctuations may contaminate the results of studies which measure biological responses. In cardiac studies, women are often excluded because CHD is a greater health risk for men than women (Niven and Carroll, 1993). However, despite the exclusion of women from the research, the findings of such work are often used to inform the treatment of female as well as male patients. This may not be appropriate, because there is often little evidence that women and men experience the same problems during rehabilitation.

In view of the mixed findings in this area a number of reviews of the literature have been conducted. These have generally concluded that much of the controversy may be attributed to methodological differences between studies, such as design (longitudinal versus **cross-sectional studies**) and how TABP was defined and assessed (Booth-Kewley and Friedman, 1987; Evans, 1990; Matthews, 1988). What does seem to be the case, however, is that one particular element of TABP, hostility (see Box 1.7), would appear to be a critical factor in explaining the link between stress and subsequent CHD (Miller *et al.*, 1996). Consequently, throughout the 1990s there has been a decrease in interest in the relationship between TABP and CHD and an increase in research on the role played by hostility in this disease (Marks *et al.*, 2000).

Cross-sectional study
A piece of research which takes a snapshot view of an issue by studying a sample of people at a given point in time (in contrast with a longitudinal study, which follows its sample over a prolonged period).

1.7 Hostility

Hostility is a broad concept that incorporates feelings of anger, aggression and a negative outlook on life, and may include feelings, overt actions, thoughts and attitudes (Barefoot, 1992). The components of hostility include behaviours such as cynicism, mistrust, and verbal and/or physical aggression (Smith, 1992; Miller *et al.*, 1996). There are a number of studies which would seem to provide good evidence that hostility, and in particular the 'cynicism' sub-component of hostility, places an individual at increased risk for CHD. For example, in the Coronary Artery Risk Development in Young Adults (CARDIA) study, Iribarren and colleagues (2000) adopted a 10-year longitudinal design in order to investigate whether hostility played a role in the development of coronary calcification (an indicator of atherosclerosis that is not sufficiently severe to be referred for clinical treatment). The sample comprised 374 white and black, male and female participants who were aged between 18 and 30 years at the start of the study. At the 10-year follow-up, the participants were screened for the presence of any detectable coronary artery calcification. Results indicated that participants who had a higher than average hostility score at the start of the study were more likely to show evidence of coronary artery calcification at the 10-year follow-up.

It is important here to note that although (unlike many other studies) the sample was not restricted to white male participants, it was not possible for the researchers to perform sex- or race-specific analyses, so the findings were not broken down by white and black, male and female participants.

Exactly why hostility should be so pathological for the heart is, however, unclear. It may be the case that hostility operates through more general lifestyle factors, such that people who have high levels of hostility also engage in more risky health behaviours such as smoking, increased alcohol consumption or lack of exercise (Everson *et al.*, 1997; Smith, 1992; Lee, 1997). It could also be argued that hostile individuals may be placed at increased risk for illness because they lack social support networks, which you will recall from the previous section are an important component in mediating the effects of life stressors.

While the link between hostility and CHD is not without controversy (O'Malley *et al.*, 2000), there does appear to be some relationship between this area of personality and CHD. However, it may be wise to take heed of the warning of Marks *et al.* in this area:

> *it remains an open question whether researchers in this field are engaged on an exciting search for the truly toxic dimension of personality as far as CHD is concerned, a dimension with demonstrable physiological pathways to heart disease, or whether they are on a wild goose chase.*

> *(Marks* et al., *2000, p.93)*

Whichever is the case, investigations into the relationship between hostility and CHD will no doubt be a dominant topic in the health psychology literature over the years to come.

Stress and immune functioning

There is now an accumulating body of research evidence suggesting that psychological stress may impair health by compromising the immune system. This area of research is often referred to as *psychoneuroimmunology* (PNI). PNI has been defined as the 'study of the interrelations between the central nervous system and the immune system' (Cohen and Herbert, 1996, p.114), and consequently research in this field typically involves researchers from a wide range of traditionally distinct academic backgrounds including psychology, physiology, immunology, biology and epidemiology.

The basic premise underlying PNI is the belief that psychological stress can have a direct effect on the immune system. The exact nature of this relationship, however, is less clear. While there is some evidence that increased levels of stress can lead to improvements or no detectable change in immune functioning, the vast majority of published research tends to focus on how the immune system may be impaired by stress. Consequently, that will also be the focus of this section.

Interest in the role of stress in the disease process arose primarily out of general observations that when a number of individuals were exposed to infection (e.g. the common cold) only some went on to develop the illness whereas others stayed well. Such individual variations led to an increased interest in identifying factors that may place a person at increased risk for developing a disease. While there is a clear range of biological factors that might influence immunity (e.g. genetic predisposition, immunisation, nutrition, etc.), psychological factors, in particular stress, were also considered to play a role (Evans *et al.*, 1997). However, in order to understand exactly how stress can influence immunity we must look first at how the body protects itself from infection and disease.

The key role of the immune system is essentially to identify foreign material in the body such as bacteria, viruses, tumour cells, and toxins – so-called *antigens* – and destroy them. The process of finding and destroying these antigens is carried out by the white blood cells (lymphocytes) of the body. Lymphocytes can be subdivided into different groups depending on the role they play in defending the body against antigens (see Table 1.6 below). Consequently when researchers are interested in assessing immune functioning they typically assess the presence and/or concentration of lymphocytes or their derivatives in the blood or saliva.

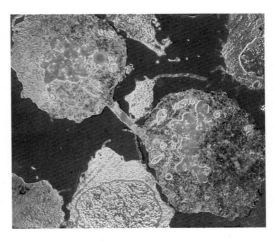

A human lymphocyte cell undergoing division to produce two daughter cells

Table 1.6   **Types of lymphocytes**

Type	Function
B cells	Produce antibodies which proliferate quickly and control infections.
NK (Natural Killer) cells	Destroy virus-infected and tumour cells.
T cells:	
(1) T helper cells	Enhance immune responses by stimulating the replication of immune system cells and antibodies.
(2) Cytotoxic T cells	Destroy virus, parasite and tumour-infected cells.
(3) T suppressor cells	Inhibit immune responses.

Source: adapted from Marks et al., *2000, p.107*

A number of reviews of the literature have been carried out in the area of PNI and they have generally concluded that there is an association between psychological stress and impaired immune functioning (Bachen *et al.*, 1997; Evans *et al.*, 1997; Herbert and Cohen, 1993; O'Leary, 1990). Although short-term stress such as examinations (Lacey *et al.*, 2000) can lead to an increased susceptibility to illness and infection, so can chronic stress, such as marital conflict (Kiecolt-Glaser *et al.*, 1997, 1998), unemployment (Arnetz *et al.*, 1987), or acting as a long-term carer (Kiecolt-Glaser *et al.*, 1991). In one study which examined immunological function in married women, results indicated that the poorer the self-reported quality of the marriage the greater the level of psychological distress and the lower the immune reaction to an introduced antigen (Kiecolt-Glaser *et al.*, 1987). The results from these studies point to a fairly consistent picture that psychological stress can suppress the immune system with changes typically noted in: (1) the number of NK cells; (2) the total number of T cells; or (3) an abnormality in the proportion of T helper cells to T suppressor cells (Marks *et al.*, 2000).

That stress can play an independent role in 'causing' illness in an otherwise healthy individual, however, is less clearly established. While there is some evidence that stressful life events may increase a person's susceptibility to disease, this is an area which needs further research before definitive conclusions can be drawn (Cohen and Herbert, 1996). Furthermore, it is necessary to examine the mechanisms by which stress may operate to influence disease. For example, does your immune system become impaired because you are experiencing stress at work, or is the suppressed immune functioning a result of the exhaustion and lack of sleep which are associated with the stress at work? Thus, rather than making general claims that 'stress causes illness', it is probably more realistic to conclude that stress is only one of a multitude of factors that influence the immune system and may cause illness (Toates, 2001). Clearly this is an important area that will also feature heavily in future research.

5.2 Work-related outcomes

From the above section it is clear that there is a relationship between stress and health. But what about the relationship between stress and work? In other words, what factors in the work environment are most likely to cause the worker stress, and when levels of stress are high, what impact does this have on job performance and the feelings a person has about their job? Because research in this area is often looking at the characteristics of the work environment, and the impact on factors such as productivity and output, it is most likely to fall within the domain of occupational psychology rather than health psychology. You should remember, however, that there is a considerable overlap between the two areas. For example, if as a result of working in a highly stressful job, an employee develops coronary heart disease resulting in a heart attack, he or she is likely to be off work for at least a few months and this will inevitably impact not only on their health but also obviously on their productivity.

What, then, are the consequences of stress in the workplace? When people experience stress at work they often engage in a range of behaviours that may impair the quality of their work output. Summers *et al.* (1995) argue that work may be affected through attitudinal factors or behavioural factors – see Figure 1.3, which is a very simplistic model. The two consequences are detailed more fully below.

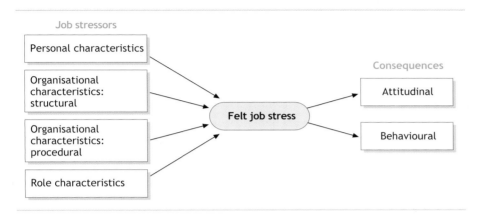

Figure 1.3   The causes and consequences of job stress (Source: Summers *et al.*, 1995, p.116)

With respect to attitudinal factors, Summers *et al.* (1995) argue that high levels of stress at work may result in:

- decreased satisfaction with one's job (both intrinsically and extrinsically)
- decreased motivation
- decreased production
- decreased organisational commitment
- increased intention to leave the organisation
- increased absenteeism.

Regarding the second category, people may manage their high levels of stress at work through the behaviours they adopt to help them cope, such as increased consumption of cigarettes, alcohol or other drugs. While engaging in such behaviours may have negative consequences for the health of the worker in the form of increased risk for lung cancer and other chronic illnesses, they may also have more direct consequences on work through an increase in accident rates and performance impairment. We will now look in more detail at the effects of alcohol use on work.

Alcohol and work

Research suggests that in the UK in the early 1990s, 90–95 per cent of the adult population consumed alcoholic drinks on an occasional or a regular basis (Goddard, 1991), with the level of consumption varying according to occupational group. A key study providing evidence for differences in level of alcohol consumption was reported by Marmot *et al.* (1993). In this study a group of over 10,000 civil servants provided self-report information about their drinking habits and a number of other relevant factors (e.g. psychological well-being), which were then linked to subsequent sickness absence from work. Marmot and colleagues reported that almost 10 per cent of male and 5 per cent of female civil servants were classed as heavy drinkers within this sample.

Consider the problem of accuracy in self-report data. Can you remember how much alcohol, if any, you drank in the last month or even in the last week, and would you be willing to state this amount to a stranger? Non-drinkers and light drinkers may be more willing (and able) to provide accurate, honest reports than heavy drinkers.

Within the working environment, alcohol use can have profound effects on the safety and effectiveness of the worker. Judgement and coordination are likely to be impaired and reactions slowed, increasing the likelihood of accidents (Sutherland and Cooper, 1990). Research suggests that between 5 and 10 per cent of serious work-related accidents can be associated with alcohol use (Guppy and Marsden, 1996). Alcohol consumption has also been linked to both short and long spells of absence from work (Marmot *et al.*, 1993). In one study of British transportation employees, those who had a problem with alcohol had an absence rate of 23 per cent compared to just 4 per cent for a matched group. For those individuals with consumption patterns indicative of abuse or dependency, the level of sick leave could be as much as 200–500 per cent higher than matched groups of employees who did not have a dependency on alcohol (Guppy and Marsden, 1996).

It is not only accident rates and absenteeism that are affected by alcohol consumption. One interesting study conducted by Mangione *et al.* (1999) looked at the impact of drinking behaviour on self-reported work performance. They concluded that, not surprisingly, work performance problems tended to increase with alcohol consumption, with moderate–heavy and heavy drinkers reporting more problems than very light, light or moderate drinkers. However, because there were more light–moderate drinkers in the sample, their overall effect was greater and they accounted for a larger proportion of work performance problems than did the heavier drinking group. Therefore, when employers are hoping to minimise the effects of alcohol on work performance, they must consider the impact of their employees' 'social drinking' as well as 'problem drinking'.

Burnout

When levels of stress become so acute that the worker can no longer deal with the pressure, the worker experiences what is commonly referred to as 'burnout'. Despite its relatively recent introduction into the realms of psychological research surrounding stress, the concept of burnout has attracted a considerable amount of research attention. Burnout can be defined as 'a syndrome of *emotional exhaustion, depersonalisation, and reduced personal accomplishment* that can occur among individuals who work with people in some capacity' (Maslach *et al.*, 1996, p.4). Table 1.7 gives an explanation of these characteristics.

Table 1.7   **Characteristics of burnout**

Emotional exhaustion	The depletion or draining of emotional resources.
Depersonalisation	Development of negative, callous, indifferent and cynical attitudes towards the recipients of one's service.
Lack of personal accomplishment	Tendency to evaluate one's work with recipients negatively.

Source: Schaufeli, 1999, p.19

People who are experiencing burnout typically show a range of behaviours. For example, they are subject to increased absenteeism, minor ailments, and lack of enthusiasm; they become overwhelmed in their reaction to new demands; they have an inability to be motivated; they have problems in initiating new plans of action; and they generally lack enthusiasm and commitment. In general, five symptom clusters may be distinguished (Schaufeli and Enzmann, 1998):

1   affective (e.g. depressed mood, emotional exhaustion)
2   behavioural (e.g. poor work performance, avoidance, alcohol use)
3   cognitive (e.g. poor concentration)
4   physical (e.g. headaches, sleep disturbances)
5   motivational (e.g. loss of idealism).

While these symptom clusters would appear to be remarkably similar to the kind of responses that anyone who is experiencing stress may report, the thing that makes burnout different from 'normal stress' is the interpersonal aspect of the condition. This is evident in all five symptom clusters to some extent, but manifests itself most predominantly in the affective and behavioural clusters. A person with burnout typically responds to the individuals they work with in a different way from someone experiencing other forms of stress. For example, people with burnout will treat patients/clients/co-workers as objects rather than as people and display a callous or cynical approach to their welfare (Jackson *et al.*, 1986). People who are burned out typically display such dysfunctional attitudes and behaviours not just towards others at work (e.g. patients on a hospital ward), but also towards the job (e.g. nursing) and the organisation (e.g. the hospital or the National Health Service), whereas general job stress is not necessarily accompanied by such attitudes and behaviours (Maslach, 1993; Schaufeli, 1999).

If you are currently in employment, are there any resources available in your organisation to help staff manage stress more effectively?

It is important to recognise that when someone says that they are experiencing stress, a wide variety of factors will be interacting to influence that person's response. The complexity of such factors should be reflected in stress management programmes, to fully address the unique needs of the individual.

Summary Section 5

- There is a general lay belief that stress can have a substantial impact on at least two areas of functioning: health and work.
- While there has been a substantial amount of research into the relationship between type A behaviour pattern and coronary heart disease, recent evidence would seem to suggest that hostility (in particular the sub-component area of cynicism) is an important factor in the development of cardiac illness.
- There is good evidence that increased levels of stress impair the immune system and can slow recovery following illness.
- Stress can have a significant impact on working life, with negative effects on both attitude and behaviour.
- People who are exposed to chronic high levels of stress in a working environment are at increased risk for burnout.

6   Stress, health and work: the future

The development of more coherent programmes of research and a clearer understanding of stress as a process, rather than a stimulus or an outcome per se, have meant that it is no longer appropriate to consider stress in isolation from its apparent consequences with respect to health and working life.

Activity 1.9

Based on what you now know about stress, what do you think may be the main causes of stress for each of the women described at the start of this chapter? Spend a few minutes thinking about this before reading on.

Burnout can be considered to be 'an extreme state of psychological strain and depletion of energy resources arising from prolonged exposure to stressors that exceed the person's resources to cope' (Cooper *et al.*, 2001, p.84). Consequently, someone who might have started a job with high level of enthusiasm and motivation may end up being emotionally blunt in response to their work and the people with whom they interact. This has obvious implications for both the individual and the organisation, such as increased job dissatisfaction, increased job turnover, and low morale.

Research indicates that not all professions are equally susceptible to burnout. Occupations that involve the worker interacting with people in some sort of caring or supportive role seem to be at a particularly increased risk. Teaching and working in healthcare have therefore been extensively studied in this area. Research indicates, though, that not all healthcare professionals are equally at risk from burnout, with nurses and physicians reporting particularly high rates (Schaufeli, 1999). Again, however, not everyone in each of these professions experiences burnout.

So which factors can help to predict who is, and who is not, at increased risk? Research indicates that a range of individual characteristics (e.g. gender, age, social class, personality, work-related attitudes, individual health) and contextual factors (e.g. general job stressors, specific job stressors, organisational behaviour) combine to place certain individuals at increased risk for burnout. A list of such factors is summarised in Table 1.8.

Not everyone falling into these categories goes on to become burned out, so the coping mechanisms employed by people at risk are a key moderator in determining the emergence of burnout as a result of job stress. Again this is a good illustration of the individual nature of stress and the important role played by cognition and the perceived availability of stress resistance resources.

Table 1.8   **Correlates of burnout in healthcare**

Biographic characteristics	Young age Little work experience
Personality	Less 'hardy' personality External locus of control Poor self-esteem Non-confronting coping style Neuroticism 'Feeling type'*
Work-related attitudes	High (unrealistic) expectations Job dissatisfaction Poor organisational commitment Intention to quit
General job stressors	High workload Time pressure Role conflict and ambiguity Lack of social support Lack of feedback Lack of participation in decision making Lack of autonomy
Specific job stressors	Much direct patient contact Severe patient problems
Individual health	Depression Psychosomatic complaints Frequency of illness
Organisational behaviour	Absenteeism Job turnover Impaired performance

* A 'feeling type' tends to be 'sympathetic, appreciative and tactful and to give great weight, when making any decisions, to the personal values that are involved, including those of other people' (Briggs Myers, 1976, p.2).
Source: Schaufeli, 1999, p.23

Although people differ in how they respond to work it would appear that, if left unmanaged, chronic occupational stress can have a very negative impact on the quality of people's lives. Furthermore, the potential exists for people in occupations with intrinsically high levels of stress to have a very extreme stress response and become burned out. Such an outcome will not only have substantial negative consequences for the individual (e.g. decreased health), but also for the organisation (e.g. decreased production, poor treatment of clients, increased absenteeism). Clearly, when developing staffing policies, organisations need to give careful consideration to the strategies they employ to help employees manage stress and aim to reduce the incidence of potential sources of stress as much as possible.

For Debbie, the main sources of stress might include: lack of money to buy essential items for herself and her children; concerns about the welfare of her children; lack of control regarding her living environment (remember she is in temporary poor quality accommodation); and lack of social support from her partners. For Nancy, however, the sources of stress might be quite different, including: lack of privacy through working in the 'public eye'; career issues, with demands to maintain continuous high levels of creative output in a competitive industry; social demands imposed through her lifestyle; and the physical and personal challenges associated with regular long-distance travel.

We don't know enough about the women's lives to speculate fully on the moderators of such stress in their lives. It may be the case that despite a generally difficult lifestyle, Debbie draws immense support from her relationship with her children. Similarly, Nancy might find that being with a partner who shares a similar lifestyle gives her the opportunity to talk about her problems with someone who understands and who can empathise. The interesting thing to note is that it is only by understanding people's lives in great detail that we can really start to understand the causes and mediators of personal stress.

What then might be the long-term consequences of stress for Debbie and Nancy? While we can't make any firm predictions, we might speculate that Debbie may find that over the coming months she is increasingly susceptible to health problems such as colds and viral infections, resulting from a depressed immune system. Nancy may also experience health problems, and may have difficulties with her career including decreased interest, motivation and satisfaction.

It is important to note that a negative outcome associated with stress is rarely inevitable. Whether a person who is experiencing stress has a positive or a negative outcome will be determined by the myriad of individual, interpersonal and environmental factors in which he or she lives their life.

But what can psychology offer by way of ameliorating the effects of stress? Initially, psychologists need to be much more critical in the way in which they conceptualise the stress relationship. For example, rather than focusing on causes of stress, moderators of stress or consequences of stress in isolation, research programmes need to reflect more clearly the dynamic and transactional nature of the phenomenon. Stressful events have a cognitive, behavioural, affective and biological component and their effects are mediated by social factors. Only by examining stress from the full range of these perspectives are we likely to appreciate its complexity. It is likely, therefore, that given the multidisciplinary nature of stress, these questions will be best addressed by psychologists working as part of a multidisciplinary team of researchers including biologists, geneticists, epidemiologists and sociologists.

Even within the discipline of psychology, stress research is not limited to one area of enquiry, and overlaps a number of areas including clinical, health, occupational, environmental and biological psychology. One area in which psychology may play an important role in the future is that of reducing workplace stress. As a profession, psychologists are uniquely placed to understand work environments in terms of their potential to explain worker stress (Raymond *et al.*, 1990). By drawing on the skills of occupational and health psychologists we can now design work environments which are less likely to cause stress, and provide individual and organisational interventions aimed at reducing the effects of any stress which may occur. Through developing such collaborative intervention programmes, psychology has a real opportunity to manage the modern epidemic of stress.

Further reading

Cassidy, T. (1999) *Stress, Cognition and Health*, London, Routledge.

This is a very interesting text which is highly readable. It is particularly useful for greater discussion of the role of cognition and its relationship with stress and health.

Bartlett, D. (1998) *Stress: Perspectives and Processes*, Milton Keynes, Open University Press.

This is a general (and more challenging) text which will appeal to the student who wants to explore the topic of stress in much more detail.

Sapolsky, R.M. (1998) *Why Zebras Don't Get Ulcers: An Updated Guide to Stress, Stress-Related Diseases and Coping*, New York, W.H. Freeman & Co.

This is a very popular book which explores the area of the biology of stress in greater detail. Although it is quite complex in places, the writing style is highly accessible and the author uses many imaginative examples to illustrate the points made.

Martin, P. (1997) *The Sickening Mind: Brain, Behaviour, Immunity and Disease*, London, HarperCollins Publishers.

This is a useful text for those who want to explore the relationship between stress and health in greater detail.

References

Arnetz, B.B., Wasserman, J., Petrini, B., Brenner, S.O., Levi, L., Eneroth, P., Salovaara, H., Hjelm, R., Salovaara, L., Theorell, T. and Petterson, I.L. (1987) 'Immune function in unemployed women', *Psychosomatic Medicine*, vol. 49, pp. 3–11.

Avis, N.E., Brambilla, J., Vass, K. and McKinlay, J.B. (1991) 'The effect of widowhood on health: a prospective analysis from the Massachusetts Women's Health Study', *Social Science and Medicine*, vol. 33, pp. 1063–70.

Bachen, E., Cohen, S. and Marsland, A.L. (1997) 'Psychoneuroimmunology', in Baum, A., Newman, S., Weinman, J., West, R. and McManus, C. (eds) *Cambridge Handbook of Psychology, Health and Medicine*, Cambridge, Cambridge University Press.

Bandura, A. (1977) 'Self-efficacy: toward a unifying theory of behaviour change', *Psychological Review*, vol. 84, pp. 191–215.

Barefoot, J. (1992) 'Developments in the measurement of hostility', in Friedman, H. (ed.) *Hostility, Coping and Health*, Washington, DC, APA.

Bartlett, D. (1998) *Stress: Perspective and Processes*, Milton Keynes, Open University Press.

Bee, H. (1998) *Lifespan Development*, New York, HarperCollins.

Berry, J.O. and Rao, J.M. (1997) 'Balancing employment and fatherhood: a systems perspective', *Journal of Family Issues*, vol. 18, no. 4, pp. 386–402.

Boggild, H. and Knutsson, A. (1999) 'Shift work, risk factors and cardiovascular disease', *Scandinavian Journal of Work, Environment and Health*, vol. 25, pp. 85–99.

Booth-Kewley, S. and Friedman, H.S. (1987) 'Psychological predictors of heart disease: a quantitative review', *Psychological Bulletin*, vol. 101, pp. 343–62.

Briggs Myers, I. (1976) *Introduction to Type* (2nd edn), FL, Centre for Applications of Psychological Type.

Brown, G.W. and Harris, T. (1978) *Social Origins of Depression: A Study of Psychiatric Disorder in Women*, London, Tavistock.

Brown, G.W. and Harris, T. (eds) (1989) *Life Events and Illness*, London, Unwin.

Cannon, W.B. (1929) *Bodily Changes in Pain, Hunger, Fear, and Rage*, New York, Appleton.

Carlson, N.R., Buskist, W. and Martin, G.N. (1997) *Psychology: The Science of Behaviour*, Boston, IL, Allyn & Bacon.

Carroll, D. (1992) *Health Psychology: Stress, Behaviour and Disease*, London, Falmer Press.

Carver, C.S., Scheier, M.F. and Weintraub, J.K. (1989) 'Assessing coping strategies: a theoretically based approach', *Journal of Personality and Social Psychology*, vol. 56, pp. 267–83.

Cassidy, T. (1999) *Stress, Cognition and Health*, London, Routledge.

Cobb, S. (1976) 'Social support as a moderator of life stress', *Psychosomatic Medicine*, vol. 38, pp. 300–14.

Cohen, S. (1988) 'Psychological models of the role of social support in the etiology of physical disease', *Health Psychology*, vol. 7, pp. 269–97.

Cohen, S., Frank, E., Doyle, W.J., Skoner, D.P., Rabin, B.S. and Gwaltney, J.M. (1998) 'Types of stressors that increase susceptibility to the common cold in healthy adults', *Health Psychology*, vol. 17, pp. 214–23.

Cohen, S. and Herbert, T.B. (1996) 'Health psychology: psychological factors and physical disease from the perspective of human psychoneuroimmunology', *Annual Review of Psychology*, vol. 47, pp. 113–42.

Cooper, C.L., Dewe, P.J. and O'Driscoll, M.P. (2001) *Organisational Stress: A Review and Critique of Theory, Research and Applications*, London, Sage.

Coyne, J.C. and Bolger, N. (1990) 'Doing without social support as an explanatory concept', *Journal of Social and Clinical Psychology*, vol. 9, pp. 148–58.

Cutrona, C.E. and Russell, D.W. (1990) 'Type of social support and specific stress: toward a theory of optimal matching' in Sarason, B.A., Sarason, I.G. and Pierce, G.R. (eds) *Social Support: An Interactional View*, New York, Wiley.

Dill, P.L. and Henley, T.B. (1998) 'Stressors of college: a comparison of traditional and non-traditional students', *Journal of Psychology*, vol. 132, pp. 25–32.

Dunkel-Schetter, C. and Lobel, M. (1990) 'Stress among students', *New Directions for Student Services*, vol. 49, pp. 17–34.

Evans, P., Clow, A. and Hucklebridge, F. (1997) 'Stress and the immune system', *The Psychologist*, vol. 10, pp. 303–7.

Evans, P.D. (1990) 'Type A behaviour and coronary heart disease: when will the jury return?', *British Journal of Psychology*, vol. 81, pp. 147–57.

Everson, S., Kauhanen, J., Kaplan, G.A., Goldberg, D.E., Julkunen, J., Tuomilehto, J. and Salonen, J.T. (1997) 'Hostility and increased risk of mortality and acute myocardial infarction', *American Journal of Epidemiology*, vol. 146, pp. 142–52.

Firth-Cozens, J. and Payne, R.L. (eds) (1999) *Stress in Health Professionals: Psychological and Organisational Causes and Interventions*, Chichester, Wiley.

Folkman, S. and Lazarus, R.S. (1988) 'The relationship between coping and emotion: implications for theory and research', *Social Science and Medicine*, vol. 26, pp. 309–17.

Fontana, A.F., Kerns, R.D., Rosenberg, R.L. and Colonese, K.L. (1989) 'Support, stress and recovery from coronary heart disease: a longitudinal causal model', *Health Psychology*, vol. 8, pp. 175–93.

Friedman, H.S. (1992) *The Self-Healing Personality: Why Some People Achieve Health and Others Succumb to Illness*, New York, Academic Press.

Friedman, M. and Rosenman, R.H. (1974) *Type A Behaviour and Your Heart*, New York, Knopf.

Goddard, E. (1991) *Drinking in England and Wales in the late 1980s*, Office of Population Censuses and Survey, London, HMSO.

Guppy, A. and Marsden, J. (1996) 'Alcohol and drug misuse and the organisation' in Schabracq, M.J., Winnubst, J.A.M. and Cooper, C.L. (eds) *Handbook of Work and Health Psychology*, Chichester, Wiley.

Hann, D.M., Oxman, T.E., Ahles, T.A., Furstenberg, C.T. and Stuke, T.A. (1995) 'Social support adequacy and depression in older patients with metastatic cancer', *Psycho-oncology,* vol. 4, pp. 213–21.

Harris, M.B. and Brooks, L.J. (1998) 'Challenges for older students in higher education', *Journal of Research and Development in Education*, vol. 31, pp. 226–35.

Helsing, K., Szklo, M. and Comstock, G. (1981) 'Factors associated with mortality after widowhood', *American Journal of Public Health*, vol. 71, pp. 802–9.

Herbert, T.B. and Cohen, S. (1993) 'Stress and immunity in humans: a meta-analytic review', *Psychosomatic Medicine*, vol. 55, pp. 364–79.

Holahan, C.J. and Moos, R.H. (1991) 'Life stressors, personal and social resources, and depression: a four year structural model', *Journal of Abnormal Psychology*, vol. 100, pp. 31–8.

Holmes, T.H. and Rahe, R.H. (1967) 'The social readjustment rating scale', *Journal of Psychosomatic Research*, vol. 11, pp. 213–18.

House, J.S. (1984) 'Barriers to work stress: 1. Social support', in Gentry, W.D., Benson, H. and DeWolff, C. (eds) *Behavioral Medicine: Work, Stress and Health*, The Hague, Martinus Nijhoff.

Iribarren, C., Sidney, S., Bild, D.E., Liv, K., Markovitz, J.H., Roseman, J.M. and Matthews, K. (2000) 'Association of hostility with coronary artery calcification in young adults – the CARDIA study', *Journal of the American Medical Association*, vol. 283, no. 19, pp. 2546–51.

Jackson, S., Schwab, R. and Schuler, R. (1986) 'Toward an understanding of the burnout phenomenon', *Journal of Applied Psychology*, vol. 71, pp. 630–40.

Jenkins, C.D., Zyzanski, S.J. and Rosenman, R.H. (1979) *Jenkins Activity Survey, Manual*, TX, The Psychological Corporation.

Johnston, D.W. (1992) 'The management of stress in the prevention of coronary heart disease' in Maes, S., Leventhal, H. and Johnston, M. (eds) *International Review of Health Psychology*, Chichester, Wiley.

Kanner, A.D., Coyne, J.C., Schaefer, C. and Lazarus, R.S. (1981) 'Comparison of two modes of stress measurement: daily hassles and uplifts versus major life events', *Journal of Behavioral Medicine*, vol. 4, pp. 1–39.

Kiecolt-Glaser, J.K., Dura, J.R., Speicher, C.E., Trask, O.J. and Glaser, R. (1991) 'Spousal caregivers of dementia victims: longitudinal changes in immunity and health', *Psychosomatic Medicine*, vol. 53, pp. 345–62.

Kiecolt-Glaser, J.K., Dyer, C.S. and Shuttleworth, E.C. (1988) 'Upsetting social interactions and distress among Alzheimer-disease family caregivers – a replication and extension', *American Journal of Community Psychology*, vol. 16, pp. 825–37.

Kiecolt-Glaser, J.K., Fisher, L.D., Ogrocki, P., Stout, J.C., Speicher, C.E. and Glaser, R. (1987) 'Marital quality, marital disruption, and immune function', *Psychosomatic Medicine*, vol. 49, pp. 13–34.

Kiecolt-Glaser, J.K., Glaser, R., Cacioppo, J.T., MacCallum, R.C., Snydersmith, M., Kim, C. and Malarkey, W.B. (1997) 'Marital conflict in older adults: endocrine and immunological correlates', *Psychosomatic Medicine*, vol. 59, pp. 339–49.

Kiecolt-Glaser, J.K., Glaser, R., Cacioppo, J.T. and Malarkey, W.B. (1998) 'Marital stress: immunologic, neuroendocrine, and autonomic correlates', *Neuroimmunomodulation*, vol. 840, pp. 656–63.

Kobasa, S.C. (1979) 'Stressful life events, personality and health: an inquiry into hardiness', *Journal of Personality and Social Psychology*, vol. 37, pp. 1–11.

Kobasa, S.C. and Maddi, S.R. (1977) 'Existential personality theory', in Corsini, R. (ed.) *Current Personality Theories*, Itasca, IL, Peacock.

Lacey, K., Zaharia, M.D., Griffiths, J., Ravindran, A.V., Merali, Z. and Anisman, H. (2000) 'A prospective study of neuroendocrine and immune alterations associated with the stress of oral academic examination among graduate students', *Psychoneuroendocrinology*, vol. 25, pp. 339–56.

Lazarus, R.S. (1966) *Psychological Stress and the Coping Process*, New York, McGraw-Hill.

Lazarus, R.S. and Cohen, J.B. (1977) 'Environmental stress' in Altman, L. and Wohlwill, J.F. (eds) *Human Behaviour and the Environment: Current Theory and Research*, vol.2, New York, Plenum Publishing Co.

Lazarus, R.S. and Folkman, S. (1984) *Stress, Appraisal and Coping*, New York, Springer.

Lee, A. (1997) 'Hostility, cigarette smoking and alcohol consumption in the general population', *Social Science and Medicine*, vol. 44, pp. 1089–96.

Levav, I., Friedlander, Y., Kark, J.D. and Peritz, E. (1988) 'An epidemiological study of mortality among bereaved parents', *New England Journal of Medicine*, vol. 319, pp. 457–61.

Mangione, T.W., Howland, J., Amick, B., Cote, J., Lee, M., Bell, N. and Levine, S. (1999) 'Employee drinking practices and work performance', *Journal of Studies on Alcohol*, vol. 60, no. 2, pp. 261–70.

Marks, D.F., Murray, M., Evans, B. and Willig, C. (2000) *Health Psychology: Theory, Research and Practice*, London, Sage.

Marmot, M.G., North, F., Feeney, A. and Head, J. (1993) 'Alcohol consumption and sickness absence: from the Whitehall II study', *Addiction*, vol. 88, pp. 369–82.

Maslach, C. (1993) 'Burnout: a multidimensional perspective' in Schaufeli, W.B., Maslach, C. and Marek, T. (eds) *Professional Burnout: Recent Developments in Theory and Research*, Washington, DC, Taylor and Francis.

Maslach, C., Jackson, S.E. and Leiter, M. (1996) *Maslach Burnout Inventory Manual* (3rd edn), Palo Alto, CA, Consulting Psychologists Press.

Mason, J.W. (1971) 'A re-evaluation of the concept of "non-specificity" in stress theory', *Journal of Psychiatric Research*, vol. 8, pp. 323-33.

Mason, J.W. (1975) 'A historical view of the stress field: Parts 1 and 2', *Journal of Human Stress*, vol. 1, pp. 6–12, 22–36.

Matthews, K.A. (1988) 'Coronary heart disease and Type A behaviours: update on and alternative to the Booth-Kewley and Friedman (1987) quantitative review', *Psychological Bulletin*, vol. 104, pp. 373–80.

Miller, T.Q., Smith, T.W., Turner, C.W., Guijarro, M.L. and Hallet, A.J. (1996) 'A meta-analytic review of research on hostility and physical health', *Psychological Bulletin*, vol. 119, pp. 322–48.

Monk, E.M. and Mahmood, Z. (1999) 'Student mental health: a pilot study', *Counselling Psychology Quarterly*, vol. 12, pp. 199–210.

Niven, C. and Carroll, D. (1993) *The Health Psychology of Women*, Chur, Switzerland, Harwood.

O'Leary, A.(1990) 'Stress, emotion and human immune function', *Psychological Bulletin*, vol. 108, pp. 363–82.

O'Malley, P.G., Jones, D.L., Feuerstein, I.M. and Taylor, A.J. (2000) 'Lack of correlation between psychological factors and sub-clinical coronary artery disease', *New England Journal of Medicine*, vol. 343, pp. 1298–304.

Pagel, M.D., Erdly, W.W. and Becker, J. (1987) 'Social networks: we get by with (and in spite of) a little help from our friends', *Journal of Personality and Social Psychology*, vol. 53, pp. 793–804.

Payne, R.L. (1999) 'Stress at work: a conceptual framework' in Firth-Cozens, J. and Payne, R.L. (eds).

Ragland, D.R. and Brand, R.J. (1988) 'Type A behaviour and mortality from coronary heart disease', *New England Journal of Medicine*, vol. 318, pp. 65–9.

Rahe, R.H. (1974) 'The pathway between subjects' recent life changes and their near-future illness reports: representative results and methodological issues' in Dohrenwend, B.S. and Dohrewend, B.P. (eds) *Stressful Life Events: Their Nature and Effects*, New York, Wiley.

Raymond, J.S., Wood, D.W. and Patrick, W.D. (1990) 'Psychology training in work and health', *American Psychologist*, vol. 45, pp. 1159–61.

Regehr, C., Hill, C. and Clancy, G.D. (2000) 'Individual predictors of traumatic reactions in firefighters', *Journal of Nervous and Mental Disease*, vol. 188, pp. 333–9.

Review Panel on Coronary-Prone Behaviour and Coronary Heart Disease (1981) 'Coronary-prone behaviour and coronary heart disease: a critical review', *Circulation*, vol. 63, pp. 1199–215.

Rosengren, A., Tibblin, G. and Wilhelmsen, L. (1991) 'Self-perceived psychological stress and incidence of coronary artery disease in middle-aged men', *American Journal of Cardiology*, vol. 68, pp. 1171–5.

Rosenman, R.H., Brand, R.J., Jenkins, C.D., Friedman, M., Straus, R. and Wurm, M. (1975) 'Coronary heart disease in the Western Collaborative Group Study: final follow-up experience of 8½ years', *Journal of the American Medical Association*, vol. 22, pp. 872–7.

Rotter, J.B. (1966) 'Generalised expectancies for internal versus external control of reinforcement', *Psychological Monographs*, vol. 80, no. 1, pp. 1–28.

Sanders, C. M. (1999) *Grief: The Mourning After. Dealing with Adult Bereavement* (2nd edn), New York, Wiley.

Sapolsky, R.M. (1998) *Why Zebras Don't Get Ulcers: An Updated Guide to Stress, Stress-Related Diseases and Coping*, New York, W.H. Freeman & Co.

Sarafino, E.P. (1994) *Health Psychology: Biopsychosocial Interactions* (2nd edn), New York, Wiley.

Schaufeli, W.B. (1999) 'Burnout', in Firth-Cozens, J. and Payne, R.L. (eds).

Schaufeli, W.B. and Enzmann, D. (1998) *The Burnout Companion to Study and Practice: A Critical Analysis*, London, Taylor and Francis.

Selye, H. (1956) *The Stress of Life*, New York, McGraw-Hill.

Shekelle, R.B., Hulley S.B., Neaton, J.D., Billings, J.H., Borhani, N.O., Gerace, T.A., Jacobs, D.R., Lasser, N.L., Mittlemark, M.B. and Stamler, J. (1985) 'The MRFIT behaviour pattern study: II. Type A behavior and incidence of coronary heart disease', *American Journal of Epidemiology*, vol. 122, no. 4, pp. 559–70.

Sheridan, C.L. and Radmacher, S.A. (1992) *Health Psychology: Challenging the Biomedical Model*, New York, Wiley.

Shumaker, S.A. and Hill, D.R. (1991) 'Gender differences in social support and physical health', *Health Psychology*, vol. 10, pp. 102–11.

Smith, T.W. (1992) 'Hostility and health: current status of a psychosomatic hypothesis', *Health Psychology*, vol. 11, pp. 139–50.

Steptoe, A. (1989) 'The significance of personal control in health and disease' in Steptoe, A. and Appels, A. (eds) *Stress, Personal Control and Health*, Chichester, Wiley.

Stone, G.L. and Archer, J. (1990) 'College and university counseling centres in the 1990s: challenges and limits', *The Counseling Psychologist*, vol. 18, pp. 539–607.

Stroebe, M.S. and Stroebe, W. (1983) 'Who suffers more? Sex differences in health risks of the widowed', *Psychological Bulletin*, vol. 93, pp. 279–301.

Stroebe, M.S., Stroebe, W. and Hansson, R. (eds) (1993) *Handbook of Bereavement*, New York, Cambridge University Press.

Summers, T.P., DeCotiis, T.A. and DeNisi, A.S. (1995) 'A field study of some antecedents and consequences of felt job stress', in Crandall, R. and Perrewé, P.L. (eds) *Occupational Stress: A Handbook*, London, Taylor & Francis.

Sutherland, V.J. and Cooper, C.L. (1990) *Understanding Stress: A Psychological Perspective for Health Professionals*, London, Chapman & Hall.

Tingey, H., Kiger, G. and Riley, P.J. (1996) 'Juggling multiple roles: perceptions of working mothers', *Social Science Journal*, vol. 3, pp. 183–91.

Toates, F. (2001) *Biological Psychology*, Harlow, Prentice Hall.

University College, Northampton (2000) *Stress* (Unpublished student information leaflet).

Violanti, J.M. and Aron, F. (1994) 'Ranking police stressors', *Psychological Reports*, vol. 75, pp. 824–6.

Wallston, B.S., Alagna, S.W., DeVellis, B.M. and DeVellis, R.F. (1983) 'Social support and physical illness', *Health Psychology*, vol. 2, pp. 367–91.

Weiss, R.S. (1986) 'Continuities and transformations in social relationships from childhood to adulthood', in Hartup, W.W. and Rubin, Z. (eds) *Relationships and Development*, Hillsdale, NJ, Lawrence Erlbaum Assoc. Inc.

Werner, E.E. (1987) 'Resilient children' in Fitzgerald, H.E. and Walraven, M.G. (eds) *Annual Editions: Human Development 87/88*, Guilford, CT, Dushkin.

Zitzow, D. (1984) 'The College Adjustment Rating Scale', *Journal of College Student Personnel*, vol. 25, pp. 160–4.

Post-traumatic stress disorder (PTSD)

Tim Dalgleish

Contents

This chapter offers a review of issues relating to the experience of post-traumatic stress disorder (PTSD). You may find some personal resonance with traumatic events discussed in the chapter, such as road traffic accidents, sexual violence, shipping disasters and war. You may also have experienced some of the responses to trauma outlined, and/or the associated therapeutic interventions described (behavioural, cognitive and pharmacological).

Aims

This chapter aims to:

- explain what we mean by trauma and the different ways that people react to it
- introduce the concept of post-traumatic stress disorder (PTSD): what it is, what different forms it takes, and what factors are associated with its development
- discuss the assessment and treatment of PTSD
- explore the main theories of PTSD
- consider the nature of psychiatric diagnosis and its pros and cons, using PTSD as an example
- examine the relationship between emotional disorders and their broader socio-historical context, using PTSD as an example
- discuss the medico-legal issues surrounding emotional disorders, using PTSD as an example.

1 Introduction

We begin our exploration of PTSD by looking at the hypothetical case of 'Jane'.

Case study: Jane

As Jane walked down the driveway to get into her car to make her usual journey to work, the sun was shining down on a beautiful spring morning. Jane drove down to the end of her road, through the village and eased onto the dual carriageway for the short 15-minute journey to her office. Jane was content to motor along in the slow lane until she came up behind a white van that was making such relaxed progress that she decided to overtake. It was as she pushed down on the accelerator to go past the van that everything started to go wrong. The van suddenly pulled out into the side of Jane's car. To Jane, it seemed that everything was happening in slow-motion. After what seemed like an age, there was a sickening crunch as the van collided with Jane's passenger door sending her car into an uncontrollable spin across the carriageway towards the central reservation barrier. In the collision, Jane's head had smashed against the driver's window and she could feel blood running down her face. The second collision with the barrier was even louder than the first with the van, and the car left the ground and started to cartwheel along the central reservation before coming to a crunching halt on its roof. By this time Jane was unconscious. The next thing Jane remembered was being cut out of the car by a fireman. There were the flashing lights of ambulances and a horde of concerned-looking people. The carriageway was blocked off and the van driver was standing by

Case study
An in-depth study of a single individual, often focusing on atypical psychological functioning, aimed at giving a detailed and comprehensive understanding of their experiences.

anxiously, surrounded by police. Jane lapsed into unconsciousness again and next woke in the ambulance on the way to hospital. Jane had broken one of her hips and suffered a crushed sternum and had to stay in hospital for several weeks. However, she made a good recovery from these injuries within a few months. It was the psychological problems that began to develop while she was in hospital that wouldn't go away. The first night in hospital, Jane had a nightmare about the accident happening all over again. She felt herself back in the car and somehow she just knew that the van was going to turn into her again and it was all going to recur. She awoke screaming in the ward and had to be sedated by the night staff. These nightmares continued, several times a week, for 18 months. During the day, Jane was plagued by intrusive images of the van veering across her vision and the crash barrier coming towards her. She couldn't stop thinking about the accident. Even when she was engaged with something else, such as shopping or watching a television programme, thoughts about the van, the road and the carnage used to pop into her mind. The slightest reminder would set her mind going, thinking about or seeing the accident all over again. She even started to 'see' the van driver's face as he swerved towards her, even though she hadn't seen him at the time.

To remedy this, Jane stopped thinking about the accident as much as she could by distracting herself and trying to 'keep busy'. She never talked about the accident with anybody, in the hope that this would make it go away. She also tried to keep any reminders of the accident out of her life. She never read newspaper articles about cars or motorways or road accidents and avoided television programmes. Indeed, she had not been in a car for six months after the accident and when she did venture to travel by car, she could only bear to be driven by members of her family as she didn't trust anybody else to drive her safely. These car journeys, though, were far from relaxed affairs. Jane was continually vigilant for possible dangers and steadfastly refused to be in the car if the driver intended to make any attempts at overtaking. She was petrified of driving herself and 'knew' she would never drive again. The worst situations involved busy roads and white vans. On several occasions Jane had full-blown panic attacks when white vans appeared behind the car in which she was travelling. Before the accident, Jane had been a fairly relaxed person, but now she was continually on edge. She was very, very irritable and this caused problems in her relationships with family, friends and her partner. It seemed they could do nothing right and, what's more, Jane felt they didn't really understand what she was going through. They mostly seemed to think that she should have got over it by now and should 'pull herself together'. She became more socially withdrawn and slightly depressed and began to lose interest in the things that she had previously enjoyed. Being on edge meant that her concentration wasn't what it used to be and this caused some problems at work as she kept making mistakes in her job. It also led to poor sleep and she was continually tired and exhausted by the slightest disruption to her daily routine. For the first few months after the accident, Jane convinced herself that these problems would only last for a while. They would then go away and she would be back to 'normal'. However, after six months when nothing had changed, she began to get quite badly depressed about the profound effect the accident had had on her life. After all, her physical injuries had now healed up and there was no reason for her to feel so disabled. After a year, when nothing substantive had changed, Jane became increasingly depressed and her GP prescribed her anti-depressants. She started to have quite long periods off work and her relationship with her partner broke up. Eighteen months after the accident Jane finally entered into psychological treatment and spoke to a mental health professional who talked her through the symptoms of something called '**post-traumatic stress disorder**' or PTSD.

Jane's experience is commonly referred to as a psychological 'trauma'. Her reaction to the trauma is by no means unusual – some 30 to 40 per cent of road traffic accident victims such as Jane go on to develop what is called post-traumatic stress disorder (PTSD) (American Psychiatric Association, 1994). It is not only after road traffic accidents that such reactions occur. Violent assaults, civilian disasters, accidents at work, domestic accidents, sexual violence, combat and warfare, and many other traumas lead some individuals to develop profound and debilitating levels of psychological stress. Perplexingly, however, other people who have experienced the same events, or at least similar ones, seem almost unaffected by them and can carry on with their lives as they had done before. By the end of the first part of this chapter, you will have an understanding of what we mean by 'psychological trauma' and why some people do go on to develop severe post-traumatic stress reactions, such as PTSD, while other people seem relatively unharmed. Various theories pertaining to this thorny question will be reviewed. Also, the assessment of PTSD and the different treatments available for those who have been involved in traumas will be discussed and their strengths and weaknesses debated.

In the second part of the chapter (Sections 8–10), PTSD will be used as a vehicle to introduce some more general topics surrounding the notion of emotional disorder. These topics comprise the status of PTSD as a psychiatric diagnosis, the socio-cultural context and history of PTSD, and medico-legal and forensic issues involving PTSD.

2   What is trauma and how do people react to it?

2.1 Defining trauma

What do we mean when we say that an event such as Jane's accident is 'traumatic'? There seem to be two clear ways to approach this question. First, we could try to develop some kind of consensus about certain events being traumatic because of their very nature. In other words, we could try to develop some objective criteria for a trauma. Alternatively, one could argue that any event could be traumatic if somebody reacts in an extremely distressed and disabling manner to that event (see also Chapter 1, where we introduced you to a transactional model of stress); in other words, trauma is a subjective phenomenon. The academic clinical literature on this topic tends to oscillate between these two rather extreme approaches to the definition of trauma. Initially, when the concept of PTSD was first introduced as a formal psychiatric **diagnosis** in *The Diagnostic and Statistical Manual for Mental Disorders* DSM–III (3rd edn) (American Psychiatric Association, 1980) there was a clear view that traumatic events had to be those 'outside the range of usual human experience' (p. 236) and ones that would be noticeably distressing to almost anyone. Guidelines were given as follows:

> *The trauma may be experienced alone (rape or assault) or in the company of groups of people (military combat). Stressors producing this disorder include natural disasters (floods, earthquakes), accidental man-made disasters (car accidents with serious physical injury, airplane crashes, large fires), or deliberate man-made disasters (bombing, torture, death camps). Some stressors frequently produce the disorder (e.g. torture) and others produce it only occasionally (e.g. car accidents). Frequently there is a concomitant physical component to the trauma which may even involve direct damage to the central nervous system (e.g. malnutrition, head trauma). The disorder is apparently more severe and longer lasting when the stressor is of human design.*

> *(American Psychiatric Association, 1980, p. 236)*

The response from the clinical and research community to these dictats was somewhat mixed. It seemed clear from the proposed definition of trauma that certain events, such as earthquakes, aeroplane crashes, combat, and so on, fulfilled the new criteria and could safely be labelled as 'traumas'. However, what about, for example, the death of a loved one through cancer (Joseph *et al.*, 1997)? People develop extreme psychological distress faced with such an experience but it cannot really be classified as an event 'outside the range of usual human experience'. However, thinking of this kind of event as non-traumatic does not seem right either.

Such arguments were persuasive and so, more recently, the definition of what constitutes a trauma has been refined to include more subjective factors. In the later edition of *The Diagnostic and Statistical Manual* DSM–IV (4th edn) (American Psychiatric Association, 1994), trauma is defined thus:

> *The person has been exposed to a traumatic event in which both of the following were present: 1. The person experienced, witnessed, or was confronted with an event or events that involved actual or threatened death or serious injury, or a threat to the physical integrity of self or others. 2. The person's response involved fear, helplessness, or horror.*

> *(American Psychiatric Association, 1994, pp. 427–8)*

Diagnosis
The process of placing an individual's pattern of symptoms as reliably as possible within a recognised category, for purposes of identification, research and treatment.

Even this broader, more inclusive definition leads to problems. In the case of Jane's accident, what if Jane had not seen the van coming and had been knocked unconscious on impact? It is still possible that she could have gone on to develop all of the symptoms of post-traumatic stress and she may even have tried to imagine what had happened and tried to piece together how the accident must have unfolded over time. However, with the current definition of trauma in the DSM–IV requiring the person to experience either intense fear, helplessness or horror at the time of the event, Jane's experience not be labelled as traumatic as she would have been unconscious at the time of the event.

Given these pitfalls, why do we need to have an agreed definition of a 'trauma' at all? Is it not reasonable to suggest that people who are in distress, regardless of the events that they have experienced, require help, support and understanding? What's more, as psychologists, should we not be interested in understanding the nature of any form of psychological distress, not just forms of distress that follow a particular, delineated type of event? The principal reason for such a strong emphasis in the clinical and research literature on an exact definition of a 'traumatic event' is that, having experienced adverse reactions to particular events, many people will pursue litigation through the courts to obtain some form of compensation for their 'loss'. At this point, the world of psychology and psychiatry collides with the world of legislation and lawyers. The law argues that an entirely subjective definition of trauma would open the floodgates to thousands of people seeking compensation for any experience they didn't like. As things stand, therefore, the legal systems in the UK, Europe, and the rest of the world require tight definitions of the types of events (namely, traumatic events) that individuals can pursue compensation for. Hence the somewhat unhealthy emphasis on exact definitions of what constitutes a trauma in the existing literature.

2.2 Different levels of trauma exposure

This 'objective' approach to defining traumatic events was continued by McFarlane and De Girolamo (1996) who tried to systematically map a hypothetical hierarchy of potential elements of a traumatic experience based on various research studies, such as Pynoos and Nader's study (1990) concerning a school-yard sniper attack (described later in Section 3.4) and other studies. Their hierarchy is shown in Figure 2.1. The hierarchy tries to span situations that involved actual impact of a given event on an individual as well as events that the person merely witnessed. However, it is important to bear in mind that this is an attempt to objectify aspects of traumatic exposure and that any thorough assessment of the effect of a given event on somebody's psyche must also take into account the person's mental state at the time and his/her perceptions of risk and capacity to act adaptively at the time of the trauma – in other words, their subjective experience of what happened (refer back to Chapter 1 for a similar analysis with respect to stress).

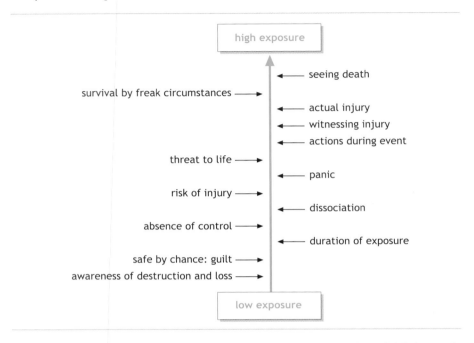

Figure 2.1   A hypothetical hierarchy of elements of a traumatic experience (McFarlane and De Girolamo, 1996)

2.3 Different reactions to trauma

Having at least arrived at a working definition of what constitutes a traumatic event (from the DSM–IV), we can now turn to the more important issue of the various types of psychological reactions that people experience to such events. Following exposure to trauma, people frequently experience a range of cognitive, emotional, behavioural and physical problems. Often these problems constellate into discrete psychiatric disorders such as anxiety disorders, depression, PTSD and/or profound changes in personality. Similarly, traumatised individuals experience a range of problems that fall outside these rather delimited, psychiatric categories. Emotions such as guilt, shame, rage, anger and disgust are often highly prevalent and extreme. Behavioural problems such as anger outbursts, sleep disturbance, social avoidance and obsessive checking and cleaning are also frequent. Not everybody's reaction to trauma is highly negative in this way, however: for every Jane, there are others for whom traumatic events seem to be little more than minor disruptions in the passage of life and these individuals remain remarkably unscarred by their experiences. Indeed, for some, there are often positive psychological reactions to trauma, such as an increased ability to appreciate the fragile nature of life and the problems that other people might be suffering (Taylor *et al.*, 1984). In Chapter 1 on stress, it was also noted that people's reactions to stressors will vary along these lines, with some responding positively and some responding negatively. In this chapter we focus on one of the major categories of negative response to trauma, namely PTSD, and use it as an example to look at a number of issues concerning the clinical and research approach to mental health problems. Some other responses to trauma are, however, briefly reviewed in Section 4.

Summary Section 2

- Traumatic events are defined as those events in which people witness or risk death or injury and during which they experience intense fear, helplessness or horror.
- People are likely to become more distressed following such events the closer they are to the event. So, on average, bystanders will be less distressed than actual victims.
- There is a range of positive and negative reactions to traumas and one of those negative reactions is post-traumatic stress disorder (PTSD).

3   Post-traumatic stress disorder (PTSD)

3.1 PTSD — the psychiatric diagnostic criteria

PTSD is a psychiatric label applied to a constellation of psychological problems that co-occur in individuals who have experienced trauma. The exact symptoms that make up what is called PTSD vary as a function of the different diagnostic systems that are used in Europe and the US (see Box 2.1 on diagnosis). However, there are more commonalities than differences in the two symptom lists for PTSD. The groups of symptoms according to the American Psychiatric Association's *Diagnostic and Statistical Manual for Mental Disorders* DSM–IV (4th edn) (American Psychiatric Association, 1994) are reproduced in Table 2.1, which we shall use as the definition of PTSD throughout the chapter. We have already looked at the DSM–IV's definition of a traumatic event in Section 2.1.

There are many different types of psychiatric disorder – obsessive compulsive disorder, PTSD, schizophrenia, borderline personality disorder, autism, and so on – and their diagnosis is based on patients meeting a set of symptom criteria laid down in two principal publications. In Europe there is the manual for the *International Classification of Diseases* (ICD), published by the World Health Organisation, and in the US there is the *Diagnostic and Statistical Manual for Mental Disorders* (DSM), published by the American Psychiatric Association. The symptom criteria and indeed the names for the various psychiatric disorders differ between the two systems and across different editions within the same system. So, for example, the label of PTSD did not exist until 1980. This is because of the way in which the classification of psychiatric disorders comes about. Essentially, clusters of symptoms that emerge into the academic and clinical community's consciousness are reviewed by a series of committees and potentially given a label if the clustering is felt to be reliable and consistent. Field trials are then conducted (though this is not always the case) to try and verify more carefully the usefulness of a particular label to identify a particular cluster of symptoms. The various disorders are then organised into different categories within the respective psychiatric manuals, the idea being that disorders in the same category have features in common. For example, the anxiety disorders include PTSD and also other clinical problems that have anxiety as a central feature, such as panic disorder. The categories are then further organised into larger groupings.

Table 2.1   **DSM–IV criteria for PTSD**

A   The person has been exposed to a traumatic event in which both the following were present:

    1   The person experienced, witnessed, or was confronted with an event or events that involved actual or threatened death or serious injury, or a threat to the physical integrity of self or others.

    2   The person's response involved fear, helplessness, or horror. *Note*: in children, this may be expressed instead by disorganised or agitated behaviour.

B   The traumatic event is persistently re-experienced in one (or more) of the following ways:

    1   Recurrent and intrusive distressing recollections of the event, including images, thoughts, or perceptions. *Note*: in young children, repetitive play may occur in which themes or aspects of the trauma are expressed.

    2   Recurrent distressing dreams of the event. *Note*: in children, there may be frightening dreams without recognisable content.

    3   Acting or feeling as if the traumatic event were recurring (includes a sense of reliving the experience, illusions, hallucinations, and dissociative flashback episodes, including those that occur on awakening or when intoxicated). *Note*: in young children, trauma-specific re-enactment may occur.

4   Intense psychological distress at exposure to internal or external cues that symbolise or resemble an aspect of the traumatic event.

5   Physiological reactivity on exposure to internal or external cues that symbolise or resemble an aspect of the traumatic event.

C   Persistent avoidance of stimuli associated with the trauma and numbing of general responsiveness (not present before the trauma), as indicated by three (or more) of the following:

1   Efforts to avoid thoughts, feelings, or conversations associated with the trauma.

2   Efforts to avoid activities, places, or people that arouse recollections of the trauma.

3   Inability to recall an important aspect of the trauma.

4   Markedly diminished interest or participation in significant activities.

5   Feeling of detachment or estrangement from others.

6   Restricted range of affect (e.g. unable to have loving feelings).

7   Sense of foreshortened future (e.g. does not expect to have a career, marriage, children, or a normal life span).

D   Persistent symptoms of increased arousal (not present before the trauma) as indicated by two (or more) of the following:

1   Difficulty falling or staying asleep.

2   Irritability or outbursts of anger.

3   Difficulty concentrating.

4   Hypervigilance.

5   Exaggerated startle response.

E   Duration of the disturbance (symptoms in criteria B, C, and D) is more than one month.

F   The disturbance causes clinically significant distress or impairment in social, occupational, or other important areas of functioning.

Specify if: *Acute*: if duration of symptoms is less than three months.
               Chronic: if duration of symptoms is three months or more.

Specify if: *With delayed onset*: if onset of symptoms is at least six months after the stressor.

(American Psychiatric Association, 1994, pp. 427–9)

As can be seen, there are three broad clusters of symptoms that are important in making a diagnosis of PTSD: the individual must re-experience the event in various intrusive and distressing ways, as Jane did with her nightmares and intrusive thoughts and images; the traumatised individual must also attempt to avoid such distress caused by the event, again in a number of different ways, such as Jane's 'keeping busy'; and, finally, the individual must describe ongoing hyperarousal following the event, again in various different manifestations, such as Jane's poor sleep, irritability, and so on. Overall, we can see that Jane's experiences following the road accident fit into these various different symptom categories. Indeed, Jane was given a diagnosis of PTSD when she finally made contact with a mental health professional. As well as this cluster of 'core' symptoms, the duration of psychological disturbance must also last for more than one month and most importantly, in thinking of PTSD as a disorder, the disturbance must cause clinically significant distress or impairment.

Activity 2.1   Avoiding unwanted thoughts

Avoiding unwanted thoughts is a core feature of PTSD but it is not a particularly easy mental manoeuvre to carry out. To find this out, stop reading and try not to think about pink elephants for the next 30 seconds.

Comment

You probably had one or more pink elephant thoughts even though you were trying not to. This is called ironic mental processing (Wegner, 1994) and is thought to be due to the fact that in order to not think about something you have to activate it in your mind as the thing to be avoided. Ironically, this means that it is more likely to pop up as an unwanted thought.

3.2 Subtypes of PTSD

Within the DSM–IV, PTSD is not considered to be a *uniform diagnostic category*; rather, it is thought to involve several sub-types (see Chapter 5 for similar discussions of sub-types in autism). These are PTSD-*Acute*, PTSD-*Chronic*, and PTSD-*Delayed*.

Acute PTSD involves symptoms that begin within one month of the trauma but do not last for more than three months. Chronic PTSD, on the other hand, is indicated when the duration of symptoms has exceeded three months. The choice of three months as the demarcation point is essentially an arbitrary one. Delayed PTSD refers to symptoms that appear for the first time six months or more *after* the stressful event. The research evidence seems to indicate that some types of event are more likely than others to lead to chronic PTSD, sometimes many years or even decades after the occurrence of the event. For example, Kilpatrick *et al.* (1987) reported that almost 17 per cent of the women whom they had assessed following a sexual assault still met full PTSD criteria *17 years later.* Similarly, studies have revealed PTSD 40 years post-event in Second World War combat veterans and prisoners of war (Davidson *et al.*, 1990) and in Jewish survivors of the Holocaust (Kuch and Cox, 1992). In such cases, it is not always true that PTSD has been a continuous problem (see the hypothetical case study of 'Arnold' below). Survivors may only be intermittently troubled by the symptoms, and PTSD can have a varied course. The principal evidence for this has emerged from a study by Sandy McFarlane in Australia (McFarlane, 1988). McFarlane assessed over 300 firefighters, using a popular self-report psychiatric questionnaire (the General Health Questionnaire) which was filled in by the firefighters 4, 11, and 29 months after a traumatic fire-fighting event. McFarlane identified eight different patterns of response (see Table 2.2).

Table 2.2   The eight categories of response to trauma identified by McFarlane (1988) in his study of firefighters at three time points (4, 11 and 29 months)

Category	Responses
1	50 per cent fell into the *no disorder* group.
2	9 per cent fell into the *acute* group (PTSD at 4 months but not later).
3	10 per cent fell into the *persistent and chronic* group (PTSD at all 3 time points).
4	6 per cent fell into the *resolved chronic* group (PTSD at 4 and 11 months only).
5	5 per cent fell into the *recurrent group* (PTSD at 4 and 29 months but not at 11 months).
6	3 per cent fell into the *persistent delayed onset* group (PTSD at 11 and 29 months only).
7	5 per cent fell into the *11-month delayed-onset* group (PTSD at 11 months only).
8	11 per cent fell into the *29-month delayed-onset* group (PTSD at 29 months only).

PTSD, then, comes in numerous guises and it is important to bear this in mind when considering the issues discussed in the rest of the chapter.

Case study: Arnold

Arnold was a 74-year-old successful, self-made businessman who, at long last, was due to retire. The business was passed on to his daughter, the speeches had been made, the champagne drunk and finally Arnold's 14 hours-a-day, 6 days-a-week routine had been wound up. The first few months were idyllic. Arnold recharged his batteries, joined the gym (mostly for the jacuzzi) and realised how little he knew about gardening. He and his wife took a few long-awaited holidays and generally settled effortlessly into a life of richly deserved leisure. Arnold's last holiday, however, was shattered somewhat when he received news that one of his oldest friends, John, had died. John and Arnold went way back. They had been drafted into the army on the same day in 1938 and had fought side by side in Burma during the Second World War. Not that Arnold and John ever talked about those days, however. It was an unwritten understanding between them that the past was the past and best left alone.

Arnold was devastated by John's death and soon afterwards he began to wake in the night covered in sweat following horrible dreams about the war and the jungles of south-east Asia. Arnold remembered things in his dreams that he didn't even realise that he knew. The dreams were vivid to the point that Arnold sometimes believed he was back in the jungle for real. Soon, these experiences began to intrude into his waking life. He found himself thinking increasingly about the war and the horrible things that he had seen and in some cases done. He saw images flash before his eyes and he became anxious and irritable with those around him. Arnold kept these things to himself as he was very embarrassed by them. He felt ashamed that he was not coping and couldn't help wondering if he was going mad. In his view, all of these memories should have remained in the past and he found it very distressing that they had come back to haunt him after all this time.

During the autumn, Arnold received the annual invitation to his regiment's Christmas reunion. Neither Arnold nor John had ever been to one of these and, to be honest, had looked down their noses to some extent at those who did. This year, however, Arnold felt compelled to go and made the journey north in the cold week before Christmas. At the reunion, after loosening his tongue with wine and spirits, Arnold found himself talking about the dreams and the memories from 50 years before. Instead of being met with incredulous looks, Arnold found that many of the others there had been through the same experiences and come out the other side. They said that working hard and keeping busy for many years had kept these things at bay, but once the pressure was off and the mind was less occupied then something could come along and lift the lid off the mental box in which all the memories of the war had been locked away. Arnold's regimental colleagues put him in touch with an organisation that helped ex-soldiers to deal with these experiences and the psychologist there diagnosed him with delayed-onset PTSD. Arnold gradually overcame the difficulties that he had been having and never missed a regimental reunion after that.

Dissociation
A lack of integration between aspects of memory and conscious awareness observed during and after extremely stressful experiences.

A slightly confusing thing about the diagnosis of PTSD is that it can only be assigned to a trauma victim once the required symptom constellation has persisted for at least one month (see Table 2.1). As might be imagined, this presents some problems in diagnosing and evaluating the treatment needs for an individual in the first days and weeks following a trauma. The category of acute stress disorder (ASD) for stress reactions in the first month following trauma was therefore introduced. There is considerable overlap in symptom profile between PTSD and ASD. The main difference is that ASD emphasises symptoms of dissociation more than does PTSD. Pierre Janet in the late nineteenth century coined the word **'dissociation'** *to describe a lack of integration between aspects of memory and conscious awareness observed during and after extremely stressful experiences. Such symptoms seem relatively frequent in trauma survivors, especially those who have been involved in severe traumas such as crime, sexual assault and combat (Foa and Rothbaum, 1998).*

3.3 PTSD in children and adolescents

Although there is now a host of studies looking at PTSD in adult victims of trauma, until recently far less was known about the manifestations of post-traumatic stress reactions in children and adolescents. Until the mid-1980s, received wisdom regarding stress reactions in younger people was that, although a few individuals may develop emotionally disabling disorders, the majority would only experience minor symptoms. Furthermore, those who did develop emotional disorders would be likely to recover within a relatively short time. More recently, however, a number of key studies have indicated just how serious and common PTSD is in children and adolescents (see the description of the 'sniper' study by Pynoos and Nader in Section 3.4. below). Within the DSM–IV there are remarkably few differences in the description of PTSD for adults and for children. In fact, the only real difference is that the DSM–IV emphasises repetitive play and trauma-specific re-enactment as well as distressing dreams in children (see Table 2.1).

3.4 How common is PTSD?

Before we can answer this question, it is important to clarify some of the terms that are used in epidemiological studies that look at questions like these. The two commonest terms are **current prevalence** and **lifetime prevalence**.

    If we were to take a large community sample of members of the public and assess them all for whether or not they have PTSD at the moment of sampling, this would lead to a good estimate of the current prevalence of PTSD. If we then asked if they had ever had PTSD, this would give a good estimate of the lifetime prevalence.

    A good example of a prevalence study was carried out by Resnick *et al.* (1993). In their study 4008 women across the US were sampled via random dialling of telephone numbers and asked about their experiences of trauma. The authors used the results of this survey to estimate the number of women in the US who had experienced different types of trauma. They assumed that the sample of 4008 women was *representative* of the US Bureau of Census estimate of the population of US adult women (aged 18 or over) of 96,056,000. So, for example, in the telephoned sample, about 13 per cent of the women reported experiencing rape. Therefore, the authors estimated that this had occurred in approximately 12,151,084 American women – a shockingly high number. Of those women in the telephone sample who had reported experiencing completed rape, 32 per cent reported a history of PTSD in their lifetime (lifetime prevalence) and 12.4 per cent indicated current PTSD at the time of the telephone interview (current prevalence). Overall, across a range of traumatic events including what is termed 'completed rape', 12.3 per cent

Current prevalence
Refers to how many people meet the criteria for a particular event, e.g. disorders such as PTSD, at any given time.

Lifetime prevalence
Refers to how many people at a given time have *ever* met the criteria for a particular event, e.g. disorders such as PTSD.

of women who participated in the study reported having experienced PTSD at some point in their lifetime and 4.6 per cent were currently experiencing PTSD at the time of the study.

Phone surveys of community populations to examine the prevalence of psychiatric disorders clearly generate important data that can be used in planning healthcare and policy. However, there are ethical issues involved, especially in the case of PTSD where the respondent is required to revisit a traumatic event. Pause for a minute and think what these ethical issues might be. One main issue is that the respondent may be re-traumatised by the phone call and develop new symptoms or experience the exacerbation of existing problems.

Studies such as the Resnick *et al.* (1993) survey are extremely important. A figure of between 4 and 5 per cent, when dealing with a population of almost one hundred million women in the US, suggests that some 4 million – 5 million women in the US at any one time meet the criteria for PTSD. If we were then to include the numbers of men and children who may also meet the criteria for the disorder, it is clear that PTSD potentially poses a serious health problem for the US population. On the basis of such studies, health service provision can therefore be planned and organised.

Another good example of a study that has examined the prevalence of PTSD, this time following a particular trauma, is the National Vietnam Veteran Re-adjustment Study, again in the US. This study set out to assess as many of the individuals who were either active-combat or non-active-combat veterans from the Vietnam conflict as could be contacted. The prevalence of current PTSD, more than 15 years post-service at the time of assessment, was about 15 per cent for the men and 8.5 per cent for the women (nearly 500,000 people) among the active combat veterans. Lifetime prevalence rates were therefore unsurprisingly very high. Among active combat veterans, 31 per cent reported experiencing PTSD at some point following their service. Perhaps the most alarming statistic was reported by the principal investigators of the study who noted that of the 1.7 million veterans who ever experienced significant symptoms of PTSD after the Vietnam War, approximately 830,000 (49 per cent) still experienced PTSD symptoms (Weiss *et al.*, 1992) almost 20 years later. This is a massive mental health legacy from one conflict and, as we shall see later, this helped to fundamentally shape society's response to post-traumatic stress.

There are fewer studies looking at the prevalence of PTSD in children. One of the better ones was carried out by Pynoos and Nader (1990), who examined 159 children aged 5 to 13 after a fatal sniper attack in their school playground. Researchers found that the rates of PTSD in the children varied with the degree of exposure to the sniper. At the first interview, 77 per cent of the children who were actually in the playground during the attack were classified as having PTSD, whereas 67 per cent who were inside the school building had PTSD. One hundred of the children were also followed up 14 months later. At this point 74 per cent of the children who were in the playground still manifested PTSD, compared to fewer than 19 per cent of those who were in the school building. In fact, this latter group did not differ in terms of PTSD levels from those children who were not at school during the attack but had heard about it.

A common pattern emerges from the various studies on the prevalence of PTSD (Foa and Rothbaum, 1998). Following sexual assault, rape and other serious crime, a high incidence of PTSD is the norm. This decreases gradually over time but a certain proportion of victims will develop chronic PTSD that can last for many years. Similarly, a significant number of combat veterans continue to suffer from PTSD even decades or more after their service (see Arnold's case study in Section 3.2). In contrast, civilian victims who have not experienced sexual assault or crime may also respond with a high rate of PTSD initially, but will mostly recover relatively quickly. Our first case study, Jane, is an exception to this. Finally, from what we know of children in the limited studies that have been carried out, reactions appear to vary with their proximity to the original trauma but more research is needed.

Summary Section 3

- PTSD following a trauma consists of three symptom clusters – re-experiencing the traumatic event (e.g. nightmares), avoiding reminders of the event (e.g. refusing to talk about it), and hyperarousal (e.g. poor sleep) – that have a clinically significant effect on normal functioning.
- There are different sub-types of PTSD: acute (lasting up to three months), chronic (lasting longer than three months) and delayed (beginning six months or more after the trauma).
- PTSD is a fairly common disorder (e.g. compared to autism – see Chapter 5) with between 2 and 5 per cent of adults thought to be suffering from it at any one time in Western countries.

4   Symptoms and problems commonly associated with PTSD

A diagnosis of PTSD represents a particular circumscribed constellation of symptoms commonly experienced by survivors of traumatic events, that the working parties who established the diagnostic guidelines have decreed co-occur with sufficient frequency to be given a diagnostic label (see Box 2.1). However, as well as the core symptoms of PTSD (see Table 2.1), a number of other associated symptoms and problems are highly prevalent in trauma survivors.

A number of factors appear to determine the course, severity and nature of post-trauma psychological reactions. Brewin *et al.* (2000) carried out a **meta-analysis** of 14 such factors in which they reviewed 85 separate data sets from different studies. Only three factors consistently predicted PTSD – a pre-trauma psychiatric history, reported childhood abuse, and a family psychiatric history. Other factors were less consistent but still marked and these included relatively poor education, previous trauma, and general childhood adversity.

Meta-analysis
A statistical technique for combining the results of many different studies into one large analysis.

4.1 Psychiatric and psychological problems

Trauma survivors with PTSD may also meet criteria for other psychiatric diagnoses. For example, McFarlane and Papay (1992) investigated over 450 firefighters who had been exposed to a bushfire that devastated much of south-eastern Australia in the early 1980s. Of the 450 firefighters included in the study, a high-risk group of 147 was identified using a screening questionnaire that assessed PTSD symptoms. This subgroup of firefighters then took part in a formal psychiatric interview. Although PTSD was the most common psychiatric disorder present (18 per cent), there were also significant levels of depression (10 per cent). Indeed, only 23 per cent of those participants who had developed PTSD did not attract a further psychiatric diagnosis.

Another common problem in trauma survivors is increased substance abuse, particularly in combat veterans. In fact, substance abuse is a common co-diagnosis along with depression and anxiety. In a key study of 40 Vietnam veterans with PTSD it was found that 63 per cent reported heavy and often abusive alcohol consumption (Keane *et al.*, 1983). Similar findings have been found in survivors of sexual assault, child sexual abuse and disaster (Joseph *et al.*, 1993). Impairments in cognitive processing are also a common accompaniment of PTSD. Wilkinson (1983) in his study of survivors of the Hyatt Regency Hotel skywalk collapse, found that over 40 per cent of his participants had problems with concentration and memory.

As noted already, PTSD is predominantly characterised by an intense experience of fear and anxiety. However, these are not the only emotions that are prevalent in survivors of trauma. Anger has been repeatedly observed in rape victims, combat veterans, and victims of interpersonal crime. For example, Riggs *et al.* (1992) in a **prospective study** of rape and crime victims found that these traumatised individuals experienced and expressed far more anger than a non-victim control group. Certain variables associated with the crimes, such as the use of a weapon and the victim's response to the attack were significantly related to the anger response. Furthermore, it was found that elevated anger around the time of the rape predicted the development of PTSD at a later date. Other emotions such as shame, guilt, and disgust are also frequently associated with PTSD.

Prospective study
A study that selects people immediately following an event such as a traumatic event and follows them up over time.

Sexual difficulties associated with post-traumatic stress in victims following rape or sexual assault are also common. In a study by Ellis *et al.* (1981) it was found that, two weeks post-assault, 61 per cent of victims reported less frequent sexual activities since the assault. By four weeks post-assault, 43 per cent reported total avoidance of sexual activity. Finally, one year post-assault, 12 per cent of the victims still reported sexually induced flashbacks.

4.2 Physical health and social problems

As well as the frequent psychological problems associated with PTSD, there is a growing body of evidence that physical health consequences follow on from exposure to trauma. Various studies have shown that trauma is associated with: lower scores on subjective physical health ratings; increased use of medical services; the development of a wide range of physical health conditions including fatigue, headaches, chest pain, gastro-intestinal problems, cardio-vascular problems, renal problems, coronary respiratory diseases and infectious diseases; as well as a decline in immune system efficiency (Joseph *et al.*, 1997). (See also Chapter 1 for a discussion of physical health and stress.)

Finally a number of problems that affect the individual's functioning in relation to others are also common in victims of trauma with PTSD. For example, McFarlane (1987) followed up disaster-affected families following an Australian bushfire. Compared to non-affected families, at 8 and 26 months post-trauma, interactions in the disaster-affected families were characterised by increased irritability and anger, in-fighting, withdrawal and decreased pleasure from shared activities. Finally, there is considerable evidence of social and adjustment problems in combat veterans especially those, again, from the Vietnam War (Joseph *et al.*, 1997).

Summary Section 4

- PTSD is commonly associated with a number of other intra- and inter-individual problems in sufferers.
- These problems include other psychiatric diagnoses such as depression and substance abuse.
- Other problems include physical problems and social problems such as damaged relationships.

5 Assessment of PTSD

So far we have concentrated very much on discussing the nature of PTSD and issues related to this. However, how do we know whether somebody is suffering from PTSD? What are the various methods that we can use to assess the existence of PTSD in trauma survivors? There are a number of reasons why such assessment is important. Clinicians, for example, need to carry out detailed assessments of their clients who have survived traumas in order to understand what the key problem areas are. Then, they can formulate a case and decide upon and implement some kind of treatment regime. Clinicians will also want to reassess clients during and after treatment to gauge how much improvement they have made as a function of the particular treatments. On the other hand, researchers interested in understanding the underlying mechanisms of PTSD may want to pool assessment information collected by many clinicians to find out more systematically which treatments work and which do not. Researchers will also work independently from the clinic by conducting surveys of groups of trauma survivors to investigate the effects of particular types of trauma (prevalence studies), or by running more basic research studies to look at the psychological processes associated with PTSD. Between them, then, researchers and clinicians in the field of PTSD have settled upon a number of standardised assessment techniques. The principal ones that are used, both in the clinic and in the laboratory, are structured clinical interviews and self-report questionnaires. However, increasingly, techniques such as psychophysiological measurement and brain imaging are being employed.

5.1 Interview measures of PTSD

There are two broad ways in which PTSD is assessed using clinical interviews. Firstly, trauma survivors take part in a general, standardised, structured psychiatric interview that asks questions not only about PTSD but also about a whole range of other psychiatric disorders. One of the more common schedules is the Structured Clinical Interview for the Diagnostic and Statistical Manual or SCID (First *et al.*, 1997). A sample extract from the SCID is reproduced in Table 2.3. These interview schedules have the considerable advantage of being able to provide a diagnosis of PTSD as well as any other **co-morbid diagnoses** that the individual may present with. As we have already seen, co-morbid diagnoses, especially depression, are extremely common in trauma survivors, and it is important for the purposes of research and for the development of clinical treatments that the entire symptom picture is captured in those who have experienced trauma.

Co-morbid diagnoses
A term that applies when an individual meets the criteria for more than one medical diagnosis, e.g. an individual may have co-morbid diagnoses of PTSD and depression.

Table 2.3   **Some interview questions from the SCID**

	Interview question	DSM–IV symptom	
	Now I would like to ask a few questions about specific ways that it may have affected you. For example:	B. The traumatic event is persistently re-experienced in one (or more) of the following ways:	
F42	did you think about (TRAUMA) when you did not want to or did thoughts about (TRAUMA) come to you suddenly when you didn't want them to?	1 recurrent and intrusive distressing recollections of the event, including images, thoughts or perceptions. *Note*: in young children, repetitive play may occur in which themes or aspects of the trauma are expressed.	F42
F43	what about having dreams about (TRAUMA)?	2 recurrent distressing dreams of the event. *Note*: in children, there may be frightening dreams without recognisable content.	F43
F44	what about finding yourself acting or feeling as if you were back in the situation?	3 acting or feeling as if the traumatic event were recurring (includes a sense of reliving the experience, illusions, hallucinations, and dissociative flashback episodes, including those that occur on awakening or when intoxicated). *Note*: in young children, trauma-specific re-enactment may occur.	F44
F45	what about getting very upset when something reminded you of (TRAUMA)?	4 intense psychological distress at exposure to internal or external cues that symbolise or resemble an aspect of the traumatic event.	F45
F46	what about having physical symptoms – such as breaking out in a sweat, breathing heavily or irregularly, or your heart pounding or racing?	5 physiological reactivity on exposure to internal or external cues that symbolise or resemble an aspect of the traumatic event.	F46

(Source: taken from First et al., 1997, p.74)

However, for many clinicians and researchers, such general psychiatric interviews are too unwieldy and, consequently, several structured interviews that focus specifically on the symptoms of PTSD have also been developed. Perhaps the most widely used of these is the Clinician Administered PTSD Scale or CAPS (Blake *et al.*, 1990). This consists of a number of questions based on the diagnostic criteria for PTSD outlined in Table 2.1. The interview assesses both lifetime and current presence of PTSD in the trauma survivor and focuses on both the frequency and the intensity of the PTSD symptoms. In statistical terms, the CAPS has been found to have good agreement with the opinions of clinicians about diagnosis, and also good agreement with self-report questionnaires of PTSD symptoms and thus has strong **convergent validity**. There is also now a version of the CAPS developed for children (CAPS-C).

Convergent validity
The extent to which different methods that attempt to measure the same phenomenon produce results that are in agreement with each other.

5.2 Self-report measures of PTSD

For many clinical and research purposes, even the specialist PTSD clinical interviews are sometimes too lengthy. For this reason, a number of self-report questionnaires that the trauma survivor can complete in a few minutes have been developed. Some of these focus on a specific trauma. For example, the Mississippi Scale for Combat-Related PTSD (M-PTSD) is a 35-item, self-report questionnaire (Keane *et al.*, 1988) and is one of the most widely used measures for combat veterans seeking treatment. The M-PTSD assesses both standard PTSD symptoms and features of depression, substance abuse and suicidal intent. A key aspect of questionnaire measures of PTSD is how well they simulate the results of a full, structured diagnostic interview such as the SCID or the CAPS. The developers of questionnaires normally recommend a cut-off score, above which one can have a degree of certainty that individuals in question would meet the full criteria for a diagnosis of PTSD if they were to be formally assessed using a more rigorous interview technique. Two terms are used to assess these aspects of a questionnaire. *Sensitivity* is a measure of how good the questionnaire is at differentiating PTSD from non-PTSD patients. *Specificity* is the term used to see how well the questionnaire discriminates PTSD patients from patients with other similar disorders.

One of the most widely used self-report instruments for the assessment of post-traumatic symptomatology has been the Impact of Event Scale or IES (Horowitz *et al.*, 1979). The IES can be anchored to any specific life event, including traumatic events, and taps the three symptom clusters that are central to the diagnosis of PTSD: re-experiencing, avoidance and hyperarousal.

The items on the IES were chosen from a long list of statements that had been most frequently used to describe episodes of distress by people attending a stress clinic. The participants in the initial study had either suffered various forms of bereavement or received personal injuries resulting from road traffic accidents, violence, illness, or surgery. An extract from the IES is shown in Table 2.4.

Table 2.4   **Extract from the Impact of Event Scale**

On .... (date)   you experienced .... (life event)

Below is a list of comments made by people after stressful life events. Please check each item indicating how frequently these comments were true for you DURING THE PAST SEVEN DAYS. If they did not occur during that time, please mark the 'not at all' column.

Comment	Frequency			
	Not at all	Rarely	Sometimes	Often
1 I thought about it when I didn't mean to.				
2 I avoided letting myself get upset when I thought about it or was reminded of it.				
3 I tried to remove it from memory.				
4 I had trouble falling or staying asleep because of pictures or thoughts about it that came into my mind.				
5 I had waves of strong feelings about it.				
6 I had dreams about it.				
7 I stayed away from reminders about it.				
8 I felt as if it hadn't happened or it wasn't real.				
9 I tried not to talk about it.				
10 Pictures about it popped into my mind.				

(Source: adapted from Horowitz et al., 1979, p.214)

2.2 Questionnaire measures and reliability

When analysing how effective a questionnaire is as a measure of PTSD there are a number of other indices that are important, as well as the constructs of sensitivity and specificity that have been discussed above. The first of these is the internal reliability of the questionnaire. Internal reliability allows one to quantify the extent to which all of the questions on the instrument measure the same thing. So, for example, do the questions on the IES that concern re-experiencing all measure re-experiencing symptoms to more or less the same degree, or are some of the questions assessing something different to others? The usual measure of internal reliability for a questionnaire is a statistic called Cronbach's Alpha and the higher the Cronbach's Alpha, the more internally reliable the questionnaire is. Cronbach's Alpha ranges from 0 (no internal reliability) to 1 (perfect internal reliability). A questionnaire measure should have a Cronbach's Alpha of more than 0.7 to be considered to have sufficient internal reliability.

The second construct that is important in assessing the value of a questionnaire is test–retest reliability. Test–retest reliability refers to the extent to which the scores on the questionnaire at one point in time are the same as scores on the questionnaire at a second point in time, if the circumstances for the person who is completing the questionnaire have not changed. So, for people with stable PTSD symptoms, their scores on a PTSD questionnaire one week should be fairly similar to their scores on the same questionnaire a week or two weeks later, as there have been no major symptom changes. If this is the case then the questionnaire is deemed to have good test–retest reliability. Alternatively, if one finds that, even though there has been little change in the person's circumstances, the scores on the questionnaire with a time gap are markedly different, then the questionnaire is deemed to have poor test–retest reliability. This means that the questionnaire is obviously a poor measure of post-traumatic distress as it produces different scores under the same circumstances at different time points. Test–retest reliability, as with internal reliability, is measured on a 0–1 scale, and again a score of 0.7 or more is usually taken as the benchmark for a good self-report instrument.

The internal reliability for the IES (see Box 2.2) – the most widely used measure of PTSD – is satisfactory, with a Cronbach's Alpha of 0.78 for the re-experiencing symptoms and 0.82 for the avoidance symptoms, and a test–retest reliability of 0.89 for the re-experiencing symptoms and 0.79 for the avoidance symptoms (Horowitz *et al.*, 1979). These figures, or figures very similar to them, have been replicated in a number of separate research studies. Furthermore, the IES correlates very well with other PTSD measures across a range of traumas including sexual abuse, civilian accidents and natural disasters. The IES has been translated into many languages, for example Hebrew and Dutch.

The IES has also been successfully adapted for use with children. Indeed, it has been described as probably the best questionnaire available for evaluating a child with PTSD (McNally, 1991). The IES was pioneered with children who had survived the *Herald of Free Enterprise* ferry sinking in 1987 (Yule and Williams, 1990). Following this disaster, Yule and Williams reported that children as young as eight years old found the IES to be generally meaningful and relevant to their experiences. More recently, a short version of the scale for children has been developed.

The sinking of *The Herald of Free Enterprise* ferry

5.3 Psychophysiological assessment

One problem with self-report and clinical interview assessments of PTSD is that should individuals wish to misrepresent their symptoms, perhaps for personal gain (e.g. claiming damages), then it is relatively straightforward for them to do so (this issue is discussed further in Section 10.3). Therefore, one advantage of **psychophysiological assessment,** or biological tests on individuals who have survived trauma, is that they side-step this issue of potentially biased self-report. Psychophysiological measures used with trauma survivors typically include assessments of heart rate, blood pressure, muscle tension, **skin conductance** level, and peripheral body temperature. In the case of PTSD, psychophysiological assessment has most usually assumed the form of 'challenge tests'.

In challenge tests, individuals who have experienced a trauma are presented with either standardised or personalised reminders of their trauma, such as

Psychophysiological assessment
A term that refers to the measurement of changes in a person's physiology which reflect psychological events such as anxiety.

Skin conductance
The amount of electricity that the skin conducts, which varies as a function of how much sweat is being secreted by the pores.

pictures. These reminders, or cues, are either presented visually or aurally and physiological measures are simultaneously taken. So, for example, someone who has been in a road traffic accident (such as Jane in our first case study) may be wired up to various psychophysiological instruments while being shown pictures of road traffic accidents on a screen. Such analysis of an individual's reaction to trauma cues allows at least three types of data to be gathered simultaneously: first, the physiological activity measures themselves; second, the individual's subjective ratings about how distressing the pictures are; and, third, the clinician's or researcher's observations of the individual's behaviour while the pictures are being presented. Both subjective and physiological measures in such situations have been found to reliably distinguish the trauma survivors who have PTSD from those who have experienced the same trauma but do not have PTSD. In technical terms, however, as discussed above, it seems at the moment that physiological measures provide good specificity following a trauma but that estimates of sensitivity are much more variable. To this extent, the jury is still out on how useful physiological measures will be in the clinic and at the moment they can only really be regarded as an interesting and pioneering supplement to the more usual clinical interview and questionnaire measures.

You may also have thought of some ethical issues associated with such measures. We will consider the issue of revisiting traumatic events in more depth later on.

Summary Section 5

- There are various subjective and objective ways of assessing the presence of PTSD in a trauma survivor.
- More subjective methods include structured clinical interviews such as the SCID or the CAPS, and self-report questionnaires such as the IES.
- More objective measures include monitoring heart rate, skin conductance and muscle activity.

6 Theoretical approaches to PTSD

There are numerous theories of PTSD that hold more or less sway with members of the research and clinical communities. Some of these theories concentrate on imbalances of neurotransmitters in the brain, some look at changes in brain structure following trauma, some look on PTSD as a problem involving specific behaviours following a trauma, other theories see PTSD as a problem of the cognitive processing of traumatic information, and yet other theories think of the disorder as a problem of conditioned fear responses. Finally, PTSD is conceptualised by some as a social or interpersonal disorder. Any theory that argues that PTSD is solely a function of any one of these problems, for example chemical imbalance or conditioning, is more or less discredited within contemporary psychology and psychiatry, and it is more normal for people to view complex disorders such as PTSD as comprising problems in all of the domains of behaviour: emotion, cognition, neurochemistry, neurobiology, and the psychosocial.

It is beyond the scope of this chapter to consider all of the theories on PTSD. Instead, we will focus on a number of key theories to illustrate the types of ideas that clinicians and researchers working with trauma victims have used to guide their thinking and treatment. Three types of theory will be considered: a behavioural learning theory, a cognitive theory and a neurobiological theory.

Most researchers and clinicians acknowledge that any theory of PTSD that concentrates on one type of explanation such as neurobiology, conditioning, cognitions, and so on is bound to be incomplete. However, there is much less acknowledgement that theories should have a broader focus than a specific disorder such as PTSD. Perhaps a comprehensive theory should be able to account for all types of emotional disorder and even normal emotion processing. However, such macro-theories are rare in the literature and a truly global theoretical approach to mental health is a long way off.

6.1 Behavioural learning theory

Perhaps the most influential learning theory of PTSD derives from Mowrer's two-factor theory (1960) which was influential in the development of exposure therapy for a range of anxiety disorders (see Section 7.1 on treatment). According to Mowrer, the development of fear reactions occurs

Classical conditioning
Learning arising from a pairing of two events outside the control of the learner.

Unconditional stimulus
A stimulus, such as food or pain, which evokes a response without the necessity for a history of conditioning.

Conditional stimulus
A stimulus which does not naturally evoke a response, but can do so if paired with an unconditional stimulus.

Unconditional response
A response which does not require learning, such as salivating in the presence of food or avoiding something painful.

Conditional response
A response which is triggered by a conditional stimulus, such as salivating when a bell sounds.

Operant conditioning
A form of conditioning which depends on the individual performing behaviours that are reinforced by the outcome of those behaviours.

through a process of classical conditioning (see Chapter 3, Book 1). The prototypical example of **classical conditioning** is Pavlov's experiment with his dogs (Pavlov, 1928). In Pavlov's landmark experiment, a bell was rung every time the dogs were fed. In the language of learning theory, the food was an **unconditional stimulus** (UCS) and the bell was a **conditional stimulus** (CS). Whenever the food was presented, not surprisingly, the dogs began to salivate. This is an **unconditional response** (UCR) to the unconditional stimulus (UCS) of food. After a while, the bell was rung without the food being presented. What Pavlov found, famously, was that even though the food (UCS) was no longer present, the dogs still salivated to the sound of the bell. In learning terms, they provided a **conditional response** (CR) of salivation to the conditional stimulus (CS) of the bell. Similar experiments have been carried out where the bell (CS) was rung at the same time as an electric shock was administered (UCS). The UCR to the shock was to avoid it and, in time, this can to be elicited as a response (CR) to the CS of the bell alone (with no shock).

The concept of classical conditioning has been applied to PTSD in the following way. Emotionally neutral stimuli (conditional stimuli) such as the white van in the case of Jane are present during the trauma when the individual is experiencing fear (unconditional response) because of core aspects of the traumatic situation such as the threat of death (unconditional stimulus). The neutral (conditional) stimuli then come to elicit the (conditional) response of fear at a later date, even when the threat of death (unconditional stimulus) is no longer present. So, in Jane's case, whenever she later saw a white van she experienced an automatic, conditioned fear response. Classical conditioning then, is the first factor in Mowrer's two-factor theory.

The second factor in Mowrer's model involves **operant conditioning**. Operant conditioning refers to a process whereby a particular behaviour is *reinforced* such that it increases in the future; so, for example, dogs may learn to stand by the front door if they want a walk because, previously, the behaviour of standing by the front door has been reinforced by their owners taking them for a walk shortly afterwards. Applying this idea to PTSD, the suggestion is that the traumatised individual learns to reduce trauma-related fear or anxiety by avoiding or escaping from cues or reminders of the trauma. Escape and avoidance behaviours become reinforced as a function of their predicted ability to end the aversive fear state. A problem with such persistent avoidance, however, is that the trauma survivor never learns that the conditional stimulus is no longer occurring in the presence of the unconditional stimulus, namely the original trauma, and so conditioned fear to the conditional stimulus is maintained. In the case of Jane, she controls her conditioned fear to white vans by avoiding them. Her avoidance is reinforced because it leads to her feeling less fear. However, because she avoids white vans she never gets to learn that they are actually generally harmless. In her mind they are always associated with the accident (the unconditional stimulus) and this relationship never becomes unlearned.

The treatment approach of exposure therapy (see Section 7.1, later in the chapter) was developed from this two-factor theory. It follows logically from the theory that successful treatment should include confrontation with the CS (reminders of the trauma) in the absence of the UCS (the original trauma) until the CR (fear to the CS) diminishes or is 'extinguished'. In other words, by encouraging Jane to spend time with white vans so that she learns that nothing bad usually happens, her fear of white vans will gradually go away.

The main problem with the behavioural model of PTSD is that there is too little attention paid to 'higher-order' psychological constructs such as attribution, motivation, thoughts, interpretations, beliefs, and so on. This has led clinicians and researchers to develop cognitive theories of PTSD to complement this purely behavioural account.

6.2 A cognitive theory of PTSD

A good example of a cognitive theory of PTSD was proposed by Power and Dalgleish (1997). The suggestion was that, as well as the *conditioned* fear reactions that develop following trauma (as discussed in the previous section), traumatised individuals also experience fear because they cognitively evaluate the trauma and the effect of it on their lives as currently threatening. This cognitive evaluation of the current impact of something is called a cognitive appraisal (see also Chapter 1, which discussed the role of cognitive appraisal in stress).

Cognitive theories propose that traumatised individuals suffer from *appraisal-driven fear* in this way, as well as *conditioned fear* to stimuli that remind them of the original trauma. They also suggest that these two types of fear reaction occur through different routes in the mind (see Figure 2.2). In the Power and Dalgleish model (1997), conditional fear responses occur via what they call **associative representations** in the mind and appraisal-driven fear responses occur via **schematic model representations** in the mind. The treatment approach of cognitive therapy has arisen out of cognitive models of emotional disorder. This approach examines the types of appraisals that people make following trauma and encourages them to change them (cognitive therapy is discussed below in Section 7.2).

Associative representations Mental representations that link different pieces of information in the mind.

Schematic model representations Mental representations that code generalities across lots of different experiences.

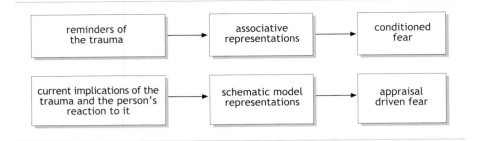

Figure 2.2   A diagram illustrating two routes to fear in PTSD (based on Power and Dalgleish, 1997)

6.3 A neurobiological theory of PTSD

The most influential neurobiological theory relating to understanding PTSD is LeDoux's model of conditioned fear reactions (LeDoux, 1995). LeDoux's work centres on a part of the brain called the amygdala. The earliest indications of the importance of the amygdala came from the famous but controversial work of Kluver and Bucy (1937). They found that following surgical removal of large parts of the brain including the amygdala, monkeys lost their usual fear of humans and normal aggressiveness, and instead became docile and lacking in facial expression. These effects (along with some others) were labelled the Kluver–Bucy Syndrome and it is now known that the Kluver–Bucy Syndrome is a result of removal or damage specifically to the amygdala.

LeDoux has argued that the amygdala is the central 'emotional computer' for the brain, analysing sensory input for any emotional significance it might have and performing more sophisticated cognitive functions to evaluate emotional information. Certainly the amygdala has all the right brain connections to perform this role. It receives inputs from the regions of the brain concerned with visual recognition and auditory recognition, and it also has close connections with the parts of the brain known to be concerned with emotional behaviour. Perhaps the most distinctive aspect of LeDoux's theory is his suggestion that the amygdala can compute the emotional consequences of sensory information from two sources: detailed sensory information from the visual and auditory brain regions and crude sensory information directly via a more primitive route (a part of the brain known as the thalamus). In this way, the amygdala can generate conditioned fear reactions in sufferers of PTSD as a result of processing very basic attributes of a stimulus (for Jane in our first case study this might be a big, fast moving shape) via the thalamus, or more sophisticated representations (in the case of Jane, any type of large vehicle) via the sensory cortex, right up to very specific representations similar to the original trauma (in the case of Jane, white vans) via the rhinal cortex and hippocampus. These different routes to conditioned fear are represented in Figure 2.3.

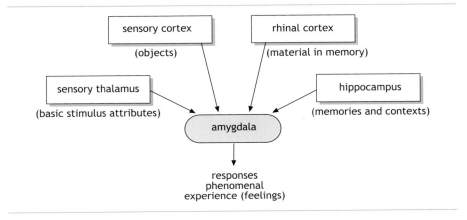

Figure 2.3   Schematic illustration of LeDoux's model

Summary Section 6

- There are numerous theories of PTSD at different levels of explanation such as the behavioural, the cognitive and the biological. Some of these have been considered here.
- Behavioural learning theories conceptualise PTSD as a combination of classically and operantly conditioned responses. Classical conditioning means that many cues set off a fear reaction in the PTSD sufferer and operant conditioning ensures that avoidance of these cues is reinforced because it leads to the avoidance of fear.
- Cognitive theories build on these arguments by adding that some fear reactions in PTSD are about evaluating the sufferer's current situation as threatening and dangerous.
- Neurobiological theories attempt to provide a biological basis for the psychological explanation contained in learning and cognitive accounts.

7 The treatment of PTSD

In considering treatment intervention in cases of PTSD, it is wise to step back and take a somewhat broader view of the area of trauma response in general. Essentially, dealing with psychological distress following trauma falls into three phases. First, there is the immediate aftermath of the trauma when psychosocial aspects of individual care can be arranged, debriefing and education about the possible consequences of trauma can be provided, and screening of potential long-term problems can take place. Second, there is ongoing specific help involving treatment of specific disorders such as PTSD with psychological therapies or medication. Finally, there are also the longer-term aspects of psychosocial care, such as the setting up of survivor groups and other such out-reach services. Here we focus on the second phase – specific treatments of PTSD.

7.1 Exposure therapy for PTSD

A variety of terms have been used in the psychological and psychiatric literature to describe the idea that prolonged exposure to any stimulus that a patient finds anxiety-provoking, in the absence of relaxation or other anxiety-reducing methods, may lead to eventual diminution in the anxiety response. These terms include flooding, imaginal exposure, in-vivo exposure, prolonged exposure and directed exposure. We shall refer to all of these collectively as 'exposure therapy' (Foa and Rothbaum, 1998). Exposure therapy typically begins with development of what is called an 'anxiety hierarchy'. This is an individual list prepared *by the client* of the aspects of a stimulus that produce fear and distress (in the case of PTSD this is the traumatic event). At the bottom of the hierarchy would be those aspects that only elicit mild fear. As one goes up the hierarchy, the elements should have the potential to elicit progressively more and more fear until the top of the hierarchy which represents the most feared aspect of the trauma. In some forms of exposure therapy, such as flooding, treatment sessions begin with exposure to the top item on the hierarchy. In other forms of exposure therapy, items rated as moderately anxiety-provoking are the starting point. All exposure therapy methods share the common feature that the person confronts the fear-inducing stimulus until the anxiety is reduced. See Figure 2.4 for an example of an exposure hierarchy for someone who has been involved in a shipping disaster.

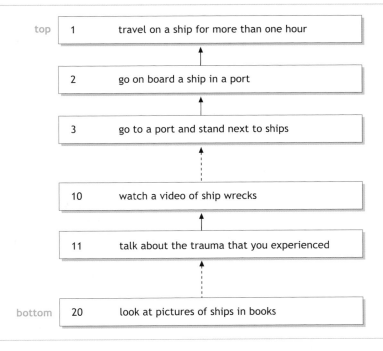

top   1   travel on a ship for more than one hour

        2   go on board a ship in a port

        3   go to a port and stand next to ships

        10   watch a video of ship wrecks

        11   talk about the trauma that you experienced

bottom 20   look at pictures of ships in books

Figure 2.4   Exposure hierarchy for someone involved in a shipping disaster

Activity 2.2   An exposure hierarchy for Jane

Imagine that you are the psychologist working with Jane following her accident (see the case study at the beginning of this chapter) and that you had to help Jane generate an exposure hierarchy as part of her treatment. Jane states that at the bottom of the hierarchy she would place being a passenger in a car driven by someone she trusts. Have a go at drawing up the rest of the hierarchy. It is useful to start at the top and then work from both ends. Remember, there are no right or wrong answers (the client, in this case Jane, would usually do this him/herself) and the main thing is to have a go.

There are several variants of exposure therapy in the PTSD domain. In imaginal exposure therapy, patients confront their memories of the traumatic event in imagination. Some imaginal methods involve clients providing their own autobiographical narrative of the trauma in detail in the present tense, for a prolonged period of time (for example, 45 to 60 minutes), with prompting by the therapist for any details that may be omitted. This narrative is then taped and the person takes it away and listens to it in between therapy sessions. Other forms of imaginal exposure involve the therapist presenting a scene to the client, based on information gathered prior to the exposure exercise. The duration and number of exposure therapy sessions also varies across different conceptualisations of the treatment. However, in general, exposure sessions are between one and two hours in length and a course of at least ten sessions of therapy is usual. Finally, it is important to note that exposure therapy is rarely used alone as a treatment but it is often combined with other treatment components such as education about the course and symptoms of PTSD, relaxation training and cognitive therapy.

Systematic desensitisation (SD) is a specific form of exposure therapy that is paired with relaxation training and was first put forward by Wolpe (1958). The central thesis is that relaxation is thought to be fundamentally incompatible with an anxiety response. Therefore by exposing the person to the traumatic event, thus eliciting anxiety, and following this immediately with relaxation procedures, it is thought that the anxiety will be reduced. As with other forms of exposure therapy, the first step in SD is typically to develop an anxiety hierarchy. Relaxation training is then taught until clients become proficient in being able to relax their body in a few minutes. Upon gaining this skill, the exposure session begins, pausing for the initiation of relaxation when the anxiety begins to mount. The therapist oscillates between relaxation and exposure until the client is able to tolerate all the stimuli on the hierarchy without any anxiety.

As already mentioned in Section 6.1, exposure therapy for PTSD has its origins in behavioural-learning theories of the disorder. The idea is that exposing the individual to various conditioned stimuli that elicit fear (see Figure 2.4) will demonstrate that these stimuli are not threatening, provided the individual can remain in the exposure situation until the fear subsides.

7.2 Cognitive therapy

Cognitive therapy (CT) is a widely used clinical technique that was initially developed by Beck (e.g. Beck *et al.*, 1979) for the treatment of depression. It was then developed further as a treatment for anxiety disorders, substance abuse and personality disorders. CT is based on Beck's early theory that the *interpretation* of an event, in this case a trauma, rather than the event itself is what determines mood states. The example often used in CT is where clients are asked to imagine lying in bed at night and hearing a loud noise downstairs in their house. The interpretation that the noise has been produced by the cat leads to benign feelings such as relief. Alternatively, the interpretation that the noise was produced by a burglar leads to negative feelings of fear and distress. Beck argues that certain individuals are prone to interpret such ambiguous situations in a negative manner and that this may lead to chronic negative mood states. These erroneous and dysfunctional interpretations, generally referred to by Beck and allied theorists as *negative automatic thoughts*, are conceptualised as either inaccurate or too extreme for the situation that elicited them. The aim of CT is to assess systematically the patterns of these automatic thoughts that individuals present with and teach clients skills that might help to modify them. This process occurs in stages whereby clients are taught to identify negative automatic thoughts, then to challenge those evaluated as inaccurate or biased, and, finally, to replace them with more 'rational' thoughts. In the domain of trauma, much of this work revolves around issues such as safety, danger, trust, responsibility, shame and guilt.

Let us consider Arnold in the second case study: he had lots of thoughts to the effect that he should not be troubled by the war any more as it was 50 years ago, and that therefore the fact that he was so distressed might mean that he is going mad, that he is weak, or that he should be feeling ashamed and guilty, and so on. Within cognitive therapy, these thoughts would be challenged by the evidence that the sort of reaction that Arnold was having was normal, was not a sign of going mad, and was not something to be embarrassed about. This would help Arnold to come to terms with his feelings and perhaps to embark on some exposure therapy to reduce some of the conditioned fear reactions that he was suffering from.

7.3 Pharmacotherapy for PTSD

As with any psychological condition, there are neurobiological changes that are associated with the symptoms of PTSD (see LeDoux's theory in Section 6.3). Table 2.5 indicates the symptoms of PTSD allied to the possible psychobiological abnormalities that underlie them.

Table 2.5   **Psychobiological abnormalities possibly associated with PTSD**

Proposed psychobiological abnormality	Possible clinical effect
Adrenergic hyperactivity	Hyperarousal, re-experiencing, dissociation, rage/aggression, abnormal information/ memory processes, panic/anxiety
Hypothalamic-pituitary-adrenocortical enhanced negative feedback	Stress intolerance
Opioid dysregulation	Numbing
Elevated corticotropin-releasing factor levels	Hyperarousal, re-experiencing, panic/anxiety
Sensitisation/kindling	Hyperarousal, re-experiencing
Glutametergic dysregulation	Dissociation, impaired information and memory processing
Serotonergic dysregulation	Numbing, re-experiencing, hyperarousal, poorly modulated stress responses, associated symptoms*
Increased thyroid activity	Hyperarousal

* Associated symptoms: rage, aggression, impulsivity, depression, panic/anxiety, obsessional thoughts, chemical abuse/dependency

(Source: taken from Friedman et al., 2000, p.85)

Various types of medication have been used to treat the symptoms of PTSD and a large number of treatment trials have been carried out to investigate the effectiveness of these drugs (Friedman *et al.*, 2000). Summarising across this wealth of data, it seems that there is a limited number of things that we can state for certain: first, many people are indeed already receiving medication following trauma; second, clinical trials usually show that at least some patients benefit tremendously from pharmacotherapy while others seem to receive very little or no benefit; third, one particular class of drugs, namely selective serotonin re-uptake inhibitors (SSRIs), a type of anti-depressant, seems particularly effective for PTSD and is currently the best established drug treatment in existence. SSRIs are also an attractive choice because they may improve associated problems in PTSD cases such as depression, panic and obsessive compulsive disorder, as well as reducing alcohol consumption (Brady *et al.*, 2000).

7.4 How effective are treatments for PTSD?

Box 2.3 considers the ways in which studies that evaluate the effectiveness of PTSD treatments should be set up. Clearly, any treatment that is targeted towards serious disorders such as PTSD has to be something that patients and clinicians have faith in. The treatments that we have described above are supported by several well-controlled studies (of the sort described in Box 2.3).

2.3 *Guidelines for well-controlled treatment studies in PTSD*

The International Society for Traumatic Stress Studies (ISTSS) has published practice guidelines for the treatment of PTSD (Foa *et al.*, 2000). These guidelines are derived from a number of carefully controlled treatment outcome trials that were carried out at great expense by researchers and clinicians throughout the world. A number of guidelines regarding what constitutes a well-controlled research study (to establish whether or not a treatment is helpful in reducing PTSD symptoms) have been developed. According to the ISTSS well-controlled studies should possess the following features:

1 *Clearly defined and evaluated target problems*

Treatment trials which are aimed at PTSD must be sure to include only those individuals who meet the criteria for PTSD. To this end, it is important that measures with good statistical properties (such as valid and reliable structured clinical interviews) are used in diagnosing individuals who will be included in any treatment-based research.

2 *Assessor training*

As well as using very good assessment measures such as structured clinical interviews, it is imperative that the assessors who are using those interviews are well trained.

3 *Manualised, replicable, specific treatment programmes*

Detailed treatment manuals help to ensure consistent treatment delivery across patients by the same therapist, and across different therapists. They also allow the same treatment regime to be taken on by clinicians after the trial has finished and employed in a more day-to-day healthcare setting.

4 *Unbiased treatment assignment*

In order to get round one potentially large source of bias in treatment trials, it is important that patients should be assigned randomly to treatment conditions or assigned using some form of sampling approach devised by a statistician. This is necessary so that we can make sure that any differences or similarities among different types of treatment are a function of the treatment technique, rather than any biasing in terms of putting some patients in one treatment group and other patients in another for extraneous reasons. Similarly, to separate the effects of a given treatment from the effects of a particular therapist, each treatment should be delivered by at least two therapists and, again, patients should randomly be assigned to therapists within each treatment condition.

5   *Treatment adherence*

Treatment adherence ratings allow us to understand whether treatments are really carried out as planned and where the components of one treatment condition drift into being very similar to components of another treatment condition. Monitoring of treatment adherence should be carried out by trained evaluators listening to tapes of the treatment sessions and rating those tapes as to how close they are to the treatment manual.

6   *The use of blind evaluators*

Many of the early studies of the treatment of PTSD relied primarily on asking the treating therapist and/or the patient to report how well they thought the treatment had gone. Clearly, such views may not be unbiased and expectancy and demand effects may come into the evaluation. Therefore, for any credible treatment outcome study, it is essential that **blind evaluators** are used.

(Source: based on Foa et al., 2000)

Blind evaluators
Evaluators who do not know what type of treatment or condition the patient or research participant they are assessing has received.

Any study adhering to the above criteria will provide extremely important data in developing treatments for PTSD. However, it is important to be aware that even when following these guidelines, studies can have limitations. For example, the strict requirements for entry into PTSD studies can mean that the samples that are included are not really representative of trauma survivors in general. This may mean that the effects of the treatment in these studies may not be generalisable to the everyday clinic. Similarly, in most treatment trials it is necessary to follow up the treatments for one or two years to see that they are effective in the long term as well as the short term. With such stringent research practices, it is not uncommon for lots of people to drop out of the trials and for others to be difficult to find or contact in the follow-up period. Therefore, it may be that the people who have dropped out of the study could be more informative than the people who stayed in but that we do not have access to that information and therefore the information that is reported is incomplete.

Generally speaking, exposure therapy (ET) and cognitive therapy (CT) are the psychological treatments of choice for PTSD. A number of recent large scale, randomised, controlled studies (Foa *et al.*, 1991; Foa *et al.*, 1999; Marks *et al.*, 1998; Tarrier *et al.*, 1999) have all compared ET and/or CT with more than one other therapy and found them both to be effective treatments. There have also been a number of other studies examining the efficacy of ET and/or CT that are less well controlled but that report broadly similar findings.

For example, in the Foa *et al.* study (1991), ET was compared with a **wait list control**, and two other active treatments – supportive counselling and stress inoculation training (a form of anxiety management technique involving, among other things, deep muscle relaxation, breathing control and role playing). There were nine treatment sessions over five weeks and the clients were rape victims. At the three-month follow-up there were no significant differences between the three active treatments (although all three were significantly different from the control), with all three groups showing approximately 50 per cent remission rates of PTSD. In a follow-up study Foa *et al.* (1999) replaced supportive counselling with ET combined with stress inoculation training. Again there were no statistically significant differences between the three active treatment conditions at follow-up points up to one year post-treatment.

In the Marks *et al.* (1998) study, the client group was a sample with chronic PTSD following a variety of traumas. The treatments were ET, CT, ET and CT combined, and a relaxation control. Again, there were no significant differences at three-month follow-up between the three active treatments, and again all were significantly different from control, with approximately 70 per cent showing remission from PTSD. Finally, in the Tarrier *et al.* study (1999) ET and CT were compared in a chronic PTSD sample. Both treatments were effective; again there was no difference between treatments.

Wait list control
A comparison group who receive no treatment and therefore remain on the waiting list for treatment, to provide an estimate of the natural improvement of symptoms over time.

Summary Section 7

- A number of different treatments for PTSD exist.
- Exposure therapy is based on behavioural learning theory and principally involves encouraging trauma survivors to go over the details of their trauma systematically and repeatedly until the resulting distress subsides.
- Cognitive therapy involves helping trauma systematically and repeatedly survivors to challenge their thoughts and interpretations about the trauma and their reactions to it.
- Pharmacotherapy is used mainly in conjunction with the psychological therapies; the drugs of choice for the treatment of PTSD are SSRIs.

8 The status of the classification and the psychiatric diagnosis of PTSD

In the remainder of the chapter we consider three broader issues in mental health using PTSD as one example of an emotional disorder.

8.1 Psychiatric labels in general

Earlier in the chapter we looked at two individual case studies illustrating aspects of post-traumatic distress. In doing so, it has been possible to determine aspects of what is unique about each individual case. However, it is also extremely important to learn how the different cases may be similar to each other in terms of the types of symptoms and problems that are involved. Barlow and Durand (1995) give several reasons for making such a comparison. In the first place, if there are other people in the past who have had the same sorts of problems or difficulties, we can use this historical knowledge to find a lot of information that might be applicable to the cases we are currently thinking about. For example, we can see how the problems started for those other individuals, what things seemed to be around at the same time that the problem started and how they contributed to the problem, how long the problem lasted, whether the problem just went away or needed treatment, what sort of factors were around that helped the person recover from the problem, and so on. Most importantly, we can potentially understand exactly what treatments might have helped that person and what treatments may have had no effect. By making these kinds of general conclusions based on similarities across different cases we do not have to start from the beginning with each new case that comes into the clinic. This is not to disregard the individual aspects of each case but just to take care not to assume that every case is entirely unique.

Consequently, what the clinical and research communities have done in the area of mental health is to try to systematise the similarities in psychological problems that exist across groups of individuals or cases. One aspect of this is trying to name or classify a particular problem and make a diagnosis. The diagnosis of PTSD, as exemplified in Table 2.1, is a classic example of such an approach. Diagnosis is not only useful in the clinic but also helpful for research, in that groups of individuals with the same diagnosis – that is, those individuals who have similarities across a range of symptoms – can be included in research studies to understand more about the particular problems that they suffer from. Furthermore, some people find it very helpful to be given a diagnosis as this gives them a conceptual framework within which they can understand the sorts of things that have happened to them (see also Chapter 5 on autism).

Exactly what does and does not constitute a disorder is, however, a difficult question to answer. A reasonable definition of disorder is: *some form of psychological dysfunction associated with distress or impairment in day-to-day functioning, which is not a typical or culturally normal response.* However, even with this definition to guide us, all is not clear-cut. For example, imagine the hypothetical case of John. John has lots of friends, a good marriage, and a healthy and active social life. He has a good job, working in an open-plan office as an accountant. John has one peculiarity, however. Once or twice a day, he lets out a loud yelp which he is unable to control. He then goes into a strange hypnotic-like state and stares into the distance for about five or six minutes. No organic or physical cause has ever been found for John's condition and it is generally assumed that it is 'psychological in nature'. However, the problem has been around for so long that John's friends, family and colleagues hardly notice when it happens anymore and certainly aren't bothered by it. Furthermore, John himself is almost completely untroubled by this, having come to terms with it a long time ago. His work is exemplary, his friends enjoy his company, and he otherwise has a very successful and enjoyable life. Nevertheless, strangers notice John's behaviour. They can act in a very disturbed and distressed way, often thinking that perhaps they should call a doctor or try to revive John and get him to respond to communication. So, would we diagnose John as having a psychological disorder? He does have what has been diagnosed as a psychological dysfunction and there is distress in other people at its manifestation and, for short periods at least, some impairment in his functioning. Furthermore it is not a typical or culturally expected behaviour. However, it has barely any effect on John's day-to-day life and he seems perfectly happy, as do the people around him.

However, once a disorder has been diagnosed there is then the problem of **labelling**. Labelling is essentially the inappropriate application of a formal (often diagnostic) term given to a phenomenon or pattern of behaviour, as if it were a definition of the individual. For example, as described in Section 3, PTSD is a term (or label) used to denote the presence of a pattern of symptoms. However, something about the way human beings conceptualise the world means that any label, even one as superficial as someone's nationality, can be taken to symbolise the totality of the person to whom the label is applied. This can lead to unintended negative consequences if the label applied to, for example, a set of psychological or psychiatric symptoms is used as the defining characteristic of the person exhibiting those symptoms.

Labelling
Applying a formal term to a phenomenon or pattern of behaviour, which may give rise to unintended negative consequences if it is taken as a definition of the person.

This problem is rife in the area of psychiatric disorders – psychiatric labels are extremely prone to picking up negative connotations. Labelling people as schizophrenic, depressed or traumatised builds stigma for them, may result in them being treated in a discriminatory way by others, and may interfere with their social and occupational functioning. Furthermore, once labelled, individuals with a disorder may identify with the negative connotations that the label carries. This may affect their self-esteem and self-concept and exacerbate the symptoms associated with their disorder, or even lead to co-morbid disorders such as depression.

One might think that in forward-looking, educated societies, the stigma associated with labelling should be on the decrease. However, pause for a moment and think about your own reactions to people who are described as mentally ill and ask yourself whether you sometimes expand your view of that person beyond a label describing a few specific behaviours to a concept of them as a complete individual.

8.2 PTSD as a diagnosis – some problems

In Section 8.1 we discussed some of the pros and cons of using a concept such as mental disorder and of applying psychiatric labels. At a more specific level, there are a number of problems in particular with using the label of PTSD. For example, the focus on one post-traumatic syndrome can hinder exploration of alternative forms or variations of the disorder, and can also lead to discrepancies in definitions between different classification manuals. During the production of the DSM–IV, for example, there was discussion about the inclusion of 'Disorders of Extreme Stress Not Otherwise Specified' (DESNOS), sometimes also called 'complex PTSD'. DESNOS involve very similar symptoms to PTSD along with profound changes of personality. During the publication of DSM–IV a decision was made, finally, not to include DESNOS in the manual. However, the corresponding publication by the World Heath Organisation, the ICD–10 (World Health Organisation, 1992), does include personality changes following a traumatic experience.

A second problem with the diagnosis of PTSD is the restriction of the diagnostic criteria to essential features (that is, only those symptoms necessary and sufficient for making the diagnosis). This leaves out many characteristics of post-traumatic stress which have extreme clinical relevance and which occur more often than they do not occur. The problem here is that the criteria as laid down in the DSM–IV, for example, are often employed by clinicians as if they were a complete description of the problem. Consequently, associated symptoms and features are often ignored and missed in treatment formulations. The reverse problem also occurs in that because someone has a diagnosis of PTSD, the naive clinician might assume that all of the symptoms of PTSD are present and organise the treatment accordingly. Alternatively, a PTSD diagnosis might be missed altogether because of the overbearing nature of associated features which, if they are not described in the diagnostic manual, may mislead the assessor. Finally, the diagnosis of PTSD at one point in time compromises efforts to conceptualise the course of stress disorders as they evolve over months, years and even decades after the original trauma. It has been clear since original work by Kardiner (1941) that the first stage of traumatic response very much resembles what we now call PTSD but the second stage, which can occur after several years and last a lifetime, can have almost any diagnostic manifestation and can be particularly exemplified by profound changes in the individual's personality.

Summary Section 8

- There are possible benefits and problems of psychiatric diagnoses in general and with PTSD specifically.
- Diagnosis can provide people with a framework within which to understand their problems, although labelling can have negative consequences such as stigmatisation.

9 The social-historical context of PTSD

9.1 Freud, Janet and their legacy

So far we have talked about PTSD as if it has always been with us. However, remember that PTSD has only been a formal psychiatric diagnosis since 1980. In this section, we briefly examine approaches to trauma and its psychological effects before 1980. In particular, we address the issue of why it has been so difficult to establish the diagnostic entity of PTSD and consider the proposal that social denial of the reality of trauma has a part to play.

The fact that exposure to overwhelmingly terrifying events can lead to psychological distress has been around in the 'common-sense' database of

Pierre Janet (1859–1947)

human knowledge for thousands of years. In contrast, psychiatry and psychology as professions have been far more ambivalent about the reality of whether the experience of particular events can permanently and significantly alter someone's mental health. Thorny questions such as whether post-traumatic stress is physical or psychological, whether the trauma causes the problems or the problems are a function of pre-trauma vulnerabilities, or whether post-traumatic stress patients are malingering or somehow deficient in character, and so on, have never really gone away. A watershed in our understanding of the relationship of trauma to the psyche occurred around the end of the nineteenth century and the beginning of the twentieth century. At this time, two patriarchs of the psychotherapy world, Pierre Janet and Sigmund Freud, both formulated ideas about the relationship between trauma and the mind.

In his first four books, Pierre Janet described a total of 591 patients and reported a traumatic cause of their problems in 257 of them. Janet argued that when people experienced overwhelming emotions, their minds may be unable to fit this frightening traumatic experience into their existing mental representation of the world. As a result, the memories of the experience will not be integrated into the person's own awareness and, instead, these memories will be split off or dissociated from consciousness and, hence, from any voluntary control. Trauma, then, lingers in memory within the unconscious and intrudes when the person's psychological defences are weak or compromised (Janet, 1925 [1919]).

Breuer and Freud drew on this work of Janet in their famous book *Studies on Hysteria*. They argued that 'Hysterics suffer mainly from reminiscences' (Freud and Breuer, 1986 [1895], p. 58). The traumatic experience continues to impact on the patient. Through these intrusive memories the patient becomes fixated on the trauma. Later, Freud was to concentrate more specifically on cases of so-called hysteria (now generally agreed to be a form of post-traumatic stress reaction) where he famously and controversially argued that 'A precocious experience of sexual relations ... resulting from sexual abuse committed by another person ... is the specific cause of hysteria' (Freud, 1962 [1896], p. 152).

This seemingly great advance in our understanding of the nature of the mind, pioneered by Freud, was, however, turned on its head within a few years when Freud abandoned what had come to be known as the 'seduction hypothesis' and stated, in contrast, that hysteria in adults was a function of *fantasies* about early sexual experiences, rather than a result of *real* sexual experiences. Later in his life, in *An Autobiographical Study*, he wrote:

> *I believed these stories [of childhood sexual trauma] and consequently supposed that I had discovered the roots of the subsequent neurosis in these experiences of sexual seduction in childhood … If the reader feels inclined to shake his head at my credulity, I cannot altogether blame him … I was at last obliged to recognise that these scenes of seduction had never taken place, and that they were only phantasies which my patients had made up.*
>
> *(Freud, 1959 [1925], pp. 60–1)*

It is important to remember that although Freud's idea of fantasy is controversial in the case of alleged sexual abuse, it is nevertheless an important concept in psychoanalysis more generally.

Freud's about-turn set back our understanding of the relationship between trauma and the psyche considerably. Following the two world wars in the twentieth century there were brief revivals of the view that there is a relationship between *genuine* trauma and psychological distress. However, even when he was faced with incontrovertible evidence that the experiences of psychologically distressed soldiers returning from the front with shell shock had their origins in *genuine* trauma, rather than in some form of fantasy, Freud remained unconvinced and ended up proposing two theories of post-traumatic stress. One was based on what he called 'unbearable situations' such as combat, and the other on what he called 'unacceptable impulses', which does not need to have its origins in genuine trauma. This distinction was helped by the view that hysteria was mainly a problem suffered by women whereas combat stress was suffered principally by men.

From the beginning of the twentieth century until the 1970s, the proposal that post-traumatic stress was a genuine psychological reaction to external events was promoted by only a few lone voices such as Kardiner (e.g. Kardiner, 1941). Indeed, it was not until the emergence of the women's movement, combined with swathes of traumatised soldiers returning from the Vietnam War, that a resurgence in commitment to the idea that psychological distress can have its origin in external traumatic events came about. We look next at a number of key events which stand out in this resurgence.

9.2 The 1970s and beyond

In 1974, Anne Burgess and Linda Holstrom at the Boston City Hospital in the US first described what they called 'rape trauma syndrome', noting that the experiences of flashbacks, nightmares, and intrusive thoughts and images resembled the traumatic neuroses of war that had been described by Kardiner and his colleagues. At around the same time, systematic work on battered children and family violence began to be carried out. Gradually, the widespread sexual abuse of children and the devastation that it caused came to be documented (Herman, 1992). Despite this, a leading US textbook of psychiatry in 1980 still claimed that incest happened to fewer than one in a million women and that its impact was not particularly damaging (Kaplan *et al.*, 1980).

Advances in our understanding of trauma and a greater focus on the toxic effects of childhood sexual abuse as a function of the women's movement were paralleled in another domain by the development of RAP groups (small discussion groups for combat veterans) consisting of recently returned Vietnam veterans. In these RAP groups, veterans talked about their war experiences and began to delve into the literature of Kardiner and other psychiatrists who had worked with trauma victims from the First and Second World Wars. Based on these experiences, the RAP groups made a list of the 27 most common symptoms of traumatic stress that were reported in the literature and compared these with over 700 clinical records of Vietnam veterans. Through this process they were able to whittle down the symptom list to what they regarded as the most critical elements. The final list, unsurprisingly, was very close to the one that Kardiner had described in 1941.

Various events such as these in the 1970s culminated in the inclusion of PTSD for the first time in the DSM, in DSM–III (American Psychiatric Association, 1980). The various different syndromes that had been formulated – rape trauma syndrome, battered woman syndrome, Vietnam veterans' syndrome, and abused child's syndrome – came under the umbrella of the new diagnosis. However, PTSD as a formal diagnostic entity did not come out of the blue and Table 2.6 illustrates the evolution of international and US diagnoses for stress reactions from 1948 to 2001.

Table 2.6 Comparison of international and US diagnoses for traumatic stress

International	US

ICD–6 (1948)
 	
Acute situational maladjustment
	DSM–1 (1952)
	
	Transient situational personality disturbance
	
	Gross stress reaction
	
	Adult situational reaction
	
	Adjustment reaction of:
	
	    Infancy
	    Childhood
	    Adolescence
	    Late life

ICD–8 (1968)
 	
Transient situational disturbance
	DSM–11 (1968)
	
	Adjustment reaction of:
	
	    Infancy
	    Childhood
	    Adolescence
	    Adult life
	    Late life

ICD–9 (1977)
 	
  Acute reaction to stress:
 	
    With predominant disturbance of emotions
    With predominant disturbance of consciousness
    With predominant psychomotor disturbance
 	
  Other mixed	

ICD–10 (1992) Acute stress reaction Post-traumatic stress disorder Enduring personality changes after catastrophic experience	DSM–111, DSM–111–R (1980, 1987) Post-traumatic stress disorder
	DSM–IV (1994) Acute stress disorder Post-traumatic stress disorder

(Source: taken from Brett, 1996)

Despite this progress culminating in the diagnostic category of PTSD, question marks about the validity of traumatic experiences (especially childhood sexual abuse) have again been raised since the late 1980s in the form of the recovered memory debate. This debate centres on claims by individuals that they have recalled memories of childhood trauma (normally sexual abuse), having previously had no recollection of such experiences. Often such memories are 'recovered' in psychological therapy. Proponents of recovered memories argue that it is perfectly possible for someone to experience an event that is so disturbing that they do not remember it for a period of years or even decades, until circumstances change (for example, by entering therapy) and the memory is then recovered. Opponents of recovered memories, however, suggest that it is inconceivable that such salient events could be totally forgotten. They propose that recovered memories are in fact 'planted' by inexperienced therapists who 'persuade' patients to fabricate experiences of childhood sexual abuse. The reality seems to be that there are indeed clear cases of genuine recovered memories of abuse but that there are also clear cases of implanted or fabricated memories of abuse. It seems that the task for the clinical and research community is to try and establish some guidelines and some techniques to reliably distinguish those memories that are genuine from those memories that are 'false'.

It is interesting to think about whether any memories are really 'true' in the sense that they are exact 'photographic records' of events. Memories are always encoded in the mind in the context of what is already there. New memories are always linked to existing memories and become influenced by them. How many times have you found that your memory for a situation is different to that of somebody else who was also there?

9.3   Relating the social and the individual in the history of post-traumatic stress

Reviewing the history of social, academic and clinical approaches to post-traumatic stress, it becomes clear that there are a number of striking parallels between society's 'experience' of trauma, and its sequelae, and the experiences of the individual trauma survivor (Dalgleish and Morant, 2001). Individuals who experience trauma, as can be seen from the symptom profile of PTSD, often undergo oscillating cycles of intrusion and avoidance concerning the traumatic event. As we have seen, attempts to forget, suppress and repress the trauma are interspersed with resurgences of the trauma in the form of nightmares, flashbacks, and intrusive thoughts and images. Similarly, society has also tried relatively to 'repress' the reality of trauma and its effects on the traumatised. In the arena of combat, despite a sharp focus on the effects of post-traumatic distress following the First and Second World Wars, it was a matter of only a few years following each of these international conflicts that social, academic and clinical interests had largely moved on and the reality of combat distress had little contemporary currency. This led, essentially, to the same ideas being revisited following the First World War, the Second World War and more recent conflicts such as Vietnam.

Similarly, in the arena of child sexual abuse, the original conceptualisation of the great neurologist Charcot and colleagues in the late nineteenth century was that hysteria and other post-traumatic stress presentations were entirely physical or organic in origin. As discussed above, these ideas were turned on their head by the work of Janet and Freud who, for really the first time in the history of clinical thought, conceptualised post-traumatic stress reactions such as hysteria as having their origins in genuine traumatic experiences, such as childhood sexual abuse. However, as noted in Section 9.1 it is well documented that, within a few years, Freud was to renege on his controversial claims and suggest that, in fact, hysteria was a function of fantasies about early trauma, rather than genuine experiences.

Although in the present analysis we are focusing on possible problems associated with Freud's emphasis on sexual fantasy rather than sexual trauma as the source of adult hysteria, it is important not to forget that his overall analysis of the hysterical presentation was incredibly pioneering. For example, by introducing the idea of psychological defence mechanisms as a way of dealing with unbearable psychic pain, he revolutionised the way in which therapists thought about emotional disorders.

The oscillation, therefore, between intrusion and avoidance that the individual trauma survivor experiences seems to be mirrored by similar intrusion and avoidance of the reality of trauma and its consequences in society. Herman (1992) has called this social process 'intermittent amnesia'. It seems that for both the individual trauma survivor and for society as a whole, the reality of certain types of trauma such as combat or sexual abuse is so emotionally disturbing that it can only be acknowledged for short periods of time before defensive processes of avoidance and repression begin to take hold. One could argue, perhaps, that this picture has now changed in that Western society at least seems relatively enlightened regarding the effects of trauma on individuals. However, it is important to note that a similar view held sway at the end of the nineteenth century amongst academics and clinicians and yet this was followed swiftly by 70 years of relative neglect of the reality of the effects of trauma on the individual.

Summary Section 9

- The social history of trauma started with Freud's and Janet's early views on hysteria.
- The revolution in views on trauma was precipitated by the women's movement in the 1970s and by the Vietnam veterans.
- Social oscillation in the acceptability of the reality of trauma mirrors the oscillation that the individual with PTSD experiences.

10 Medico-legal and forensic issues associated with PTSD

PTSD has influenced and been influenced by the legal profession more than any other psychiatric or, indeed, medical disorder. PTSD diagnosis and its implementation in the judicial system has been a source of considerable controversy. In terms of civil law, a diagnosis of PTSD is recognition that an external event can be the *direct cause* of a mental disorder. In the criminal law system, PTSD is perhaps unique among psychiatric problems in that it is invoked by both the prosecution and the defence. This section examines some of these complex legal issues surrounding the diagnosis of PTSD while also commenting more generally on the place of psychiatric diagnoses within the legal system.

10.1 Civil law issues with respect to PTSD

The most common use of a PTSD diagnosis in civil law is to obtain some form of personal injury compensation. The rationale is that the development of PTSD following an event that was not the person's fault is a just reason for that individual to be compensated for their psychological suffering by whoever is responsible for the event's occurrence. The diagnosis of PTSD represents the culmination in a lengthy history of the concept of mental injury as a compensatable category within the legal system. Conditions that today would be regarded as psychiatric problems appeared in the late nineteenth and early twentieth centuries as physical disorders such as 'railway spine', 'irritable heart', and 'shell shock' (see also Table 2.6). However, as the availability of compensation for mental disorders (as opposed to physical problems) has become more widespread, there has been a concomitant increase in levels of suspicion about the validity of symptoms reported by traumatised individuals. This is because of the perceived possibility that the PTSD that they present with is motivated by material gain. Indeed, the phrase 'compensation neurosis' was coined at the beginning of the twentieth century to describe complaints of railway accident victims that could not be explained on the basis of organic bodily problems. Similarly, after the First World War, the availability of pensions for shell shock was blamed for the severity of the persisting symptoms. Indeed, after the Second World War, a number of countries (including Germany) did not compensate shell shock victims for this reason.

A clear prediction for those who claim that PTSD is usually nothing more than a form of compensation neurosis would be that, once litigation has been completed, the symptoms would quickly disappear. However, the available evidence seems to indicate that this is not the case. For example, Mayou *et al.* (1993) looked at the psychological effects of road traffic accidents in cases where only a proportion of the victims were able to pursue compensation. The results showed that litigation status did not influence the level or severity of psychiatric symptoms, the course of psychiatric symptoms, or the chronicity of associated disabilities. These problems were the same in the litigating and the non-litigating groups.

One could even turn such arguments about compensation neurosis on their head by suggesting that the effects of the litigation process on trauma survivors are so sufficiently distressing as to turn a number of people away from litigation, even in situations where they have a perfectly justified case. The idea that litigation may influence core PTSD symptoms through a process of traumatisation in this way is gathering considerable currency in contemporary psychological literature. PTSD patients pursuing litigation are required to confront their traumatic history during interviews with lawyers and consultants, in the making of statements, and in courtroom testimony. This compromises their characteristic efforts at avoidance of trauma-related information and predictably can result in the resurgence of intrusive thoughts, images and dreams, as well as increased hyperarousal. Furthermore, the adversarial system of justice will pit the plaintiff once again against the defendant who may have been perceived by the victim as the cause of the trauma. This may exacerbate any sense that a PTSD patient has of vulnerability and victimisation. Finally, a trauma victim, who invariably has already sustained major loss as a result of the original traumatic event, will also be taking a financial and personal risk when pursuing litigation because a positive outcome is not always guaranteed. The situation has been summed up by Napier:

> *The legal system ... is poorly designed to cope with disaster aftermath ... the victims frequently feel that in the legal process their interests come well down in the list of considerations ... The result is that the medical trauma of the disaster is worsened by further trauma to the victims as they battle with a confusing system that is often slow and ineffective in providing the answers that they and the public reasonably seek.*

(1991, p. 158)

10.2 Criminal law issues associated with PTSD

Controversy concerning the diagnosis of PTSD is not only a function of civil law. Increasingly, the dissociative states that are associated with PTSD have been used as part of criminal defences against a number of offences. Almost the only way that PTSD can qualify a defendant for any such kind of defence is for the disorder to have manifested itself at the time of the crime in a full-blown dissociative state or flashback. The defendant would then have the burden of proving that he or she lost contact with reality for a short period whilst the crime was committed. Despite the appeal of PTSD to criminal defence lawyers, an **insanity defence** has historically been mostly unsuccessful. A recent study of 967,209 indictments revealed insanity pleas in only 8953 cases (0.93 per cent) with an acquittal rate of only 26 per cent (Callahan *et al.*, 1991). Of these insanity pleas, only 28 (0.3 per cent of the original 0.93 per cent) were based on a PTSD diagnosis, with a comparable acquittal rate of 29 per cent (Appelbaum *et al.*, 1993). PTSD is therefore a better candidate for a diminished capacity defence (rather than an insanity defence), in which the distress at the time of the trauma, it is argued, has compromised the individual's ability for rational thought and behaviour. Several aspects of PTSD have regularly been implicated in such incapacity defences (Pitman *et al.*, 1996). These include: 'addiction to trauma' or 'sensation-seeking'; various forms of substance or alcohol abuse in an attempt to self-medicate against post-traumatic symptoms, with resultant disinhibition of behaviour; and some need for 'punishment' to help deal with the sense of guilt connected with surviving the trauma.

In addition to being used by the defence in this way within criminal law, PTSD has been called upon by the prosecution in a number of cases as evidence that a crime of some sort must have been committed. The argument goes that the existence of PTSD is evidence for the existence of the trauma and that is evidence, in some cases, for the existence of a crime. This is known as **syndrome evidence** and has been most commonly used in cases of rape and/ or sexual assault.

Insanity defence
A legal plea that a defendant should not be found guilty for a crime because s/he was mentally ill at the time it was committed.

Syndrome evidence
A legal definition whereby the existence of a medical syndrome is used as evidence that something else must have occurred.

10.3 The assessment of PTSD in forensic cases

Assessing PTSD is an extremely sensitive issue when criminal or civil legal outcomes are riding on the diagnosis and there are two major and somewhat contradictory problems facing the assessor in a potential PTSD case in the forensic arena. The first is the fact that the genuine trauma survivor is likely to under-report symptoms and distress as a function of efforts to avoid recollections of the trauma and discussion of the problems that have ensued as a result of it. On the other hand, the spectre of possible faked PTSD cases means that some individuals may present with PTSD symptoms that are over-statements or complete fabrications in relation to how they actually feel.

The best tool that the assessor can use to combat both of these problems is to begin with non-directive interviewing followed up by questions closely tied to what the person has originally stated. The reason for this is that the diagnostic criteria for PTSD are widely available through publication in books and the internet and so there is little to stop a motivated claimant from learning what symptoms must be reported in an attempt to qualify for the diagnosis. This is made even easier if the trauma victim is provided with closed questions such as 'Have you got symptom X?' or 'Do you suffer from problem Y?' Consequently, the interviewer should begin by asking the trauma survivor to describe the problems that he or she has been having and just allow the survivor to talk and discuss these problems with as little interruption as possible. A trauma survivor who talks for half an hour and hardly mentions a symptom consistent with PTSD but then goes on to answer affirmatively to all the PTSD symptoms during subsequent closed questions in a formal psychiatric interview should, of course, be regarded with deep suspicion.

However, even the use of open-ended initial questions is not proof against falsification of symptoms. As noted above, the symptoms for PTSD are widely available and somebody could just trot them out in their own words upon the appropriate cue. Another tool, therefore, that a good assessor might use is to insist on clear and detailed illustrations of each symptom. Knowing what the symptoms of PTSD are is one thing, but being able to illustrate each symptom with details from one's own autobiography is an altogether more complicated issue. A good interviewer should therefore pick up on the fact that spontaneous illustrations of symptoms that the claimant has made up will have a vague, undetailed and stilted quality. As Pitman *et al.* (1996) note: 'The interviewer must determine whether the history being presented has the quality of a personal autobiography or merely a textbook recitation' (p.389). For example, if trauma survivors claim that they have flashbacks to the original event, the assessor can ask when the last flashback was, what the precipitating circumstances were, where the individual was at the time, how long it lasted, and how it manifested itself.

Despite the obvious problems with the use of structured interview instruments (such as the SCID and the CAPS described earlier) to diagnose PTSD and related psychiatric problems in a forensic setting, it is still important that these instruments are included as part of a complete assessment package in order that a formal psychiatric diagnosis can be made should the assessor be confident that the information given is genuine and reliable.

Lastly, in Box 2.5 we look at one other aspect of the application of psychology to law in relation to PTSD – the use of psychologists as expert witnesses.

2.5 Expert testimony

The use of psychologists as expert witnesses in medico-legal cases is increasing in the contemporary judicial climate across the world (see also Chapter 7, 'Psychological factors in witness evidence and identification'). Such a state of affairs underlines the need for some form of quality assurance both in the assessment process and in the training of such experts. We have already discussed how, in assessing possible PTSD, we can take reasonable precautions to avoid problems of unreliability in the accounts that are elicited. However, it is also essential that any mental health professional entering into the dock in order to give expert testimony sticks closely to describing the evaluee's history, signs and symptoms, diagnosis, and any cognitive or psychological disabilities outside of the PTSD spectrum that have been reported. Expert witnesses should not, under any circumstances, try to comment on matters outside their range of expertise. This includes matters to do with any legal minutiae that may be associated with such cases.

There are a number of potential traps that the psychologist might fall into in the 'expert witness' role. The first of these is paying insufficient attention to educating the judge and jury about the nature of the condition. Jurors, in particular, may find it very difficult to understand how, in a given situation, individuals would have acted any differently to themselves. They may intuitively feel that following, for example, a road traffic accident, they would be shaken up for a few days but would then get back to normal. It is therefore important for the expert witness to try to overturn some of these prejudices and describe how trauma can affect even the most 'mentally healthy' individual. A second possible pitfall for the naïve expert witness is to regard virtually any emotional problems following a traumatic event as synonymous with PTSD and thereby fail to apply the diagnostic criteria with sufficient rigour.

On the other side of the coin, of course, there are those experts who never seem to find PTSD, even where it genuinely exists. Perhaps they do not know how to recognise it, or perhaps they are just cynical about the existence of the disorder. Finally, it is important that experts beware the skill and persistence of the counsel who may cross-examine them. However much experts know about their subject, a sophisticated barrister might still be able to catch them out. It is always important, therefore, that the expert doesn't get caught up in a war of words with the counsel: if in doubt about any of the questions, or any of the answers, the expert should ask for the judge's assistance in order to get out of a potentially difficult situation.

Summary Section 10

- There are medico-legal and forensic issues surrounding the diagnosis of PTSD.
- There is controversy surrounding the diagnosis of PTSD in civil law, with a tension between the possibility that trauma survivors are exaggerating their problems to secure compensation and the idea that PTSD is very real and that pursuing litigation can actually exacerbate it.
- There is the more minor role of PTSD within criminal law where it is used as part of either an insanity or an incapacity defence or by the prosecution as syndrome evidence that a crime may have taken place.

11 Summary

This chapter has principally been about understanding the psychiatric condition of post-traumatic stress disorder (PTSD). In the first part of the chapter we covered the basic facts about PTSD. We learned about what a trauma is and how the concept of PTSD as a reaction to trauma is defined. We also examined the assessment, treatment and theoretical basis of PTSD. In the second part of the chapter we broadened our horizons and looked at three issues in the psychology of mental health problems using PTSD as an example. The first of these was the nature of psychiatric diagnosis, where we looked at the advantages and disadvantages of psychiatric labels such as PTSD. The second issue was the status of psychiatric diagnoses in their historical and social context where we saw that individual psychology must always be considered in terms of the social climate in which it exists. The last issue focused on the medico-legal and forensic issues surrounding emotional disorders.

This chapter has focused on a single so-called psychiatric diagnosis and it is hoped that the reader has a clear idea now about what the label PTSD refers to and the complex issues that are associated with it. However, the chapter has also been a vehicle to explore more general issues relating to the nature of psychological/psychiatric 'abnormality': how to define it, research it, assess and 'treat' it. As with many areas of psychology, there are no right or wrong answers about some of these issues, just ideas, opinions and, of course, research data. The aim of the chapter has been to give a flavour of the interesting questions rather than to provide simple answers to them.

 ## Further reading

Joseph, S., Williams, R. and Yule, W. (1997) *Understanding Post-Traumatic Stress: A Psychosocial Perspective on PTSD and Treatment*, Chichester, Wiley.

This book provides more general information on PTSD and is very readable. It is illustrated throughout with detailed case examples.

Herman, J.L. (1992) *Trauma and Recovery: From Domestic Abuse to Political Terror*, London, Pandora.

This book is excellently written by one of the leading feminist trauma writers and provides a good introduction to the social, gender and historical issues surrounding trauma.

 ## References

American Psychiatric Association (1980) *Diagnostic and Statistical Manual of Mental Disorders* DSM–III (3rd edn) Washington, DC, American Psychiatric Association.

American Psychiatric Association (1994) *Diagnostic and Statistical Manual of Mental Disorders* DSM–IV (4th edn) Washington, DC, American Psychiatric Association.

Appelbaum, P.S., Jick, R.Z., Grisso, T., Givelber, D., Silver, E. and Steadman, H.J. (1993) 'Use of post-traumatic stress disorder to support an insanity defence', *American Journal of Psychiatry*, vol. 150, pp. 229–34.

Barlow, D.H. and Durand, V.M. (1995) *Abnormal Psychology: An Integrative Approach*, Pacific Grove, CA, Brooks/Cole Publishing Co.

Beck, A.T., Rush, A.J., Shaw, B.F. and Emery, G. (1979) *Cognitive Therapy of Depression: A Treatment Manual*, New York, Guilford Press.

Blake, D.D., Weathers, F.W., Nagy, L.M., Kaloupek, D.G., Klauminzer, G., Charney, D.S. and Keane, T.M. (1990) 'A clinician rating scale for assessing current and lifetime PTSD: the CAPS-1', *The Behavior Therapist*, vol. 18, pp. 187–8.

Brady, K., Pearlstein, T., Asnis, G.M., Baker, D., Rothbaum, B., Sikes, C.R. and Farfel, G.M. (2000) 'Double-blind placebo-controlled study of the efficacy and safety of sertraline treatment of post-traumatic stress disorder', *Journal of the American Medical Association*, vol. 283, pp. 1837–44.

Brett, E.A. (1996) 'The classification of post-traumatic stress disorder' in van der Kolk, B.A., McFarlane, A.C. and Weisaeth, L. (eds) *Traumatic Stress: The Effects of Overwhelming Experiences on Mind, Body and Society*, New York, Guilford Press.

Brewin, C.R., Andrews, B. and Valentine, J.D. (2000) 'Meta-analysis of risk factors for post-traumatic stress disorder in trauma-exposed adults', *Journal of Consulting and Clinical Psychology*, vol. 68, pp. 748–66.

Burgess, A.W. and Holmstrom, L.L. (1974) 'Rape trauma syndrome', *American Journal of Psychiatry*, vol. 131, pp. 981–6.

Callahan, L.A., Steadman, H.J., McGreevy, M.A. and Robbins, P.C. (1991) 'The volume and characteristics of insanity defence pleas: an eight-state study', *Bulletin of the American Academy of Psychiatry and the Law*, vol. 19, pp. 331–8.

Dalgleish, T. and Morant, N. (2001) 'Representations of child sexual abuse: a brief psychosocial history and commentary' in Davies, G. and Dalgleish, T. (eds) *Recovered Memories: Seeking the Middle Ground*, Chichester, Wiley.

Davidson, J.R.T., Kudler, H.S., Saunders, W.B. and Smith, R.D. (1990) 'Symptom and comorbidity patterns in World War II and Vietnam veterans with post-traumatic stress disorder', *Comprehensive Psychiatry*, vol. 31, pp. 162–70.

Ellis, E.M., Atkeson, B.M. and Calhoun, K.S. (1981) 'An assessment of long-term reaction to rape', *Journal of Abnormal Psychology*, vol. 90, pp. 262–6.

First, M.B., Spitzer, R.L., Gibbon, M. and Williams, J.B.W. (1997) *Structured Clinical Interview for DSM–IV*, Washington, DC, American Psychiatric Press.

Foa, E.B., Dancu, C.V., Hembree, E.A., Jaycox, L.H., Meadows, E.A. and Street, G.P. (1999) 'A comparison of exposure therapy, stress inoculation training and their combination for reducing post-traumatic stress disorder in female assault victims', *Journal of Consulting and Clinical Psychology*, vol. 67, no. 2, pp. 194–200.

Foa, E.B., Keane, T.M. and Friedman, M.J. (eds) (2000) *Effective Treatments for PTSD*, New York, Guilford Press.

Foa, E.B. and Rothbaum, B.O. (1998) *Treating the Trauma of Rape: Cognitive Behavioural Therapy for PTSD*, New York, Guilford Press.

Foa, E.B., Rothbaum, B.O., Riggs, D. and Murdock, T. (1991) 'Treatment of post-traumatic stress disorder in rape victims: a comparison between cognitive behavioural procedures and counselling', *Journal of Consulting and Clinical Psychology*, vol. 59, pp. 715–23.

Freud, S. (1959 [1925]) *An Autobiographical Study, vol. 20*, London, Hogarth Press.

Freud, S. (1962 [1896]) *Heredity and the Aetiology of the Neuroses, vol. 3*, London, Hogarth Press.

Freud, S. and Breuer, J. (1986 [1895]) *Studies on Hysteria*, Harmondsworth, Penguin Books.

Friedman, M.J., Davidson, J.R.T., Mellman, T.A. and Southwick, S.M. (2000) 'Pharmacotherapy', in Foa, E.B., Keane, T.M. and Friedman, M.J. (eds).

Herman, J.L. (1992) *Trauma and Recovery: From Domestic Abuse to Political Terror*, London, Pandora.

Horowitz, M.J., Wilner, N. and Alvarez, W. (1979) 'Impact of event scale: a measure of subjective stress', *Psychosomatic Medicine*, vol. 41, pp. 209–18.

Janet, P. (1925 [1919]) *Psychological Healing: A Historical and Clinical Study*, (Eden and Cedar Paul, Trans.), London, George Allen & Unwin Ltd.

Joseph, S., Williams, R. and Yule, W. (1997) *Understanding Post-Traumatic Stress: A Psychosocial Perspective on PTSD and Treatment*, Chichester, Wiley.

Joseph, S., Yule, W., Williams, R. and Hodgkinson, P. (1993) 'Increased substance use in survivors of the Herald of Free Enterprise disaster', *British Journal of Medical Psychology*, vol. 66, pp. 185–91.

Kaplan, H.I., Freedman, A.M. and Sadock, B.J. (eds) (1980) *Comprehensive Textbook of Psychiatry*, Baltimore, MD,Williams & Wilkins.

Kardiner, A. (1941) *The Traumatic Neurosis of War* (vol. II–III), New York, Paul B. Hoeber.

Keane, T.M., Caddell, J.M., Martin, B., Zimering, R.T. and Fairbank, J.A. (1983) 'Substance abuse among Vietnam veterans with post-traumatic stress disorder', *Bulletin of Psychologists and Addictive Behaviour*, vol. 2, pp. 117–22.

Keane, T.M., Caddell, J.M. and Taylor, K.L. (1988) 'Mississippi scale for combat-related post-traumatic stress disorder: three studies in reliability and validity', *Journal of Consulting and Clinical Psychology*, vol. 56, pp. 85–90.

Kilpatrick, D.G., Saunders, B.E., Veronen, L.J., Best, C.L. and Von, J.M. (1987) 'Criminal victimization: lifetime prevalence, reporting to police, and psychological impact', *Crime and Delinquency*, vol. 33, pp. 479–89.

Kluver, H. and Bucy, P.C. (1937) '"Psychic blindness" and other symptoms following bilateral temporal lobectomy', *American Journal of Physiology*, vol. 119, pp. 254–84.

Kuch, K. and Cox, B.J. (1992) 'Symptoms of PTSD in 124 survivors of the Holocaust', *American Journal of Psychiatry*, vol. 149, pp. 337–40.

LeDoux, J.E. (1995) 'Emotion: clues from the brain', *Annual Review of Psychology*, vol. 46, pp. 209–35.

McFarlane, A.C. (1987) 'Family functioning and overprotection following a natural disaster: the longitudinal effects of post-traumatic morbidity', *Australian and New Zealand Journal of Psychiatry*, vol. 21, pp. 210–18.

McFarlane, A.C. (1988) 'The longitudinal course of post-traumatic morbidity: the range of outcomes and their predictors', *Journal of Nervous and Mental Disease*, vol. 176, pp. 30–9.

McFarlane, A.C. and De Girolamo, G. (1996) 'The nature of traumatic stressors and the epidemiology of post-traumatic reactions' in van der Kolk, B.A., McFarlane, A.C. and Weisaeth, L. (eds), *Traumatic Stress: The Effects of Overwhelming Experience on Mind, Body and Society*, New York, Guilford Press.

McFarlane, A.C. and Papay, P. (1992) 'Multiple diagnoses in post-traumatic stress disorder in the victims of a natural disaster', *The Journal of Nervous and Mental Disease*, vol. 180, pp. 498–504.

McNally, R.J. (1991) 'Assessment of post-traumatic stress disorder in children', *Psychological Assessment: A Journal of Consulting and Clinical Psychology*, vol. 3, no. 4, pp. 531–7.

Marks, I., Lovell, K., Noshirvani, H., Livanou, M. and Thrasher, S. (1998) 'Treatment of post-traumatic stress disorder by exposure and/or cognitive restructuring: a controlled study', *Archives of General Psychiatry*, vol. 55, no. 4, pp. 317–25.

Mayou, R., Bryant, B. and Duthie, R. (1993) 'Psychiatric consequences of road traffic accidents', *British Medical Journal*, vol. 307, pp. 647–51.

Mowrer, O.H. (1960) *Learning Theory and Behavior*, New York, Wiley.

Napier, M. (1991) 'The medical and legal trauma of disasters', *Medico-Legal Journal*, vol. 59, pp. 157–79.

Pavlov, I.P. (1928) *Conditioned Reflexes*, London, Oxford University Press.

Pitman, R.K., Sparr, L.F., Saunders, L.S. and McFarlane, A.C. (1996) 'Legal issues in PTSD' in van der Kolk, B.A., McFarlane, A.C. and Weisaeth, L. (eds) *Traumatic Stress: The Effects of Overwhelming Experience on Mind, Body and Society*, New York, Guilford Press.

Power, M.J. and Dalgleish, T. (1997) *Cognition and Emotion: From Order to Disorder*, Hove, Psychology Press.

Pynoos, R.S. and Nader, K. (1990) 'Children's exposure to violence and traumatic death', *Psychiatric Annals*, vol. 20, pp. 334–44.

Resnick, H.S., Kilpatrick, D.G., Danski, B.S., Saunders, B.E. and Best, C.L. (1993) 'Prevalence of civilian trauma and post-traumatic stress disorder in a representative national sample of women', *Journal of Consulting and Clinical Psychology*, vol. 61, pp. 984–91.

Riggs, D.S., Dancu, C.V., Gershuny, B.S., Greenberg, D. and Foa, E.B. (1992) 'Anger and post-traumatic stress disorder in female crime victims', *Journal of Traumatic Stress*, vol. 5, pp. 613–25.

Tarrier, N., Pilgrim, H., Sommerfield, C., Faragher, B., Reynolds, M., Graham, E. and Barrowclough, C. (1999) 'A randomized trial of cognitive therapy and imaginal exposure in the treatment of chronic post-traumatic stress disorder', *Journal of Consulting and Clinical Psychology*, vol. 67, no. 1, pp. 13–18.

Taylor, S.E., Lichtman, R.R. and Wood, J.V. (1984) 'Attributions, beliefs about control, and adjustment to breast cancer', *Journal of Personality and Social Psychology*, vol. 46, 489–502.

Wegner, D.M. (1994) 'Ironic processes of mental control', *Psychological Review*, vol. 101, pp. 34–52.

Weiss, D.S., Marmar, C.R., Schlenger, W.E., Fairbank, J.A., Jordan, B.K., Hough, R.L. and Kulka, R.A. (1992) 'The prevalence of lifetime and partial post-traumatic stress disorder in Vietnam theatre veterans', *Journal of Traumatic Stress*, vol. 5, pp. 365–76.

Wilkinson, C.B. (1983) 'Aftermath of a disaster: the collapse of the Hyatt Regency Hotel skywalk', *American Journal of Psychiatry*, vol. 140, pp. 1134–9.

Wolpe, J. (1958) *Psychotherapy by Reciprocal Inhibition*, Stanford, CA, Stanford University Press.

World Health Organisation (1992) *The ICD-10 Classification of Mental and Behavioural Disorders: Clinical Descriptors and Guidelines*, Geneva, WHO.

Yule, W. and Williams, R.A. (1990) 'Post-traumatic stress reactions in children', *Journal of Traumatic Stress*, vol. 3, pp. 279–95.

Computer-mediated communication: living, learning and working with computers

Adam Joinson and Karen Littleton

Contents

This chapter offers a review of issues relating to communication via the computer and the internet in our homes, the workplace and in education. You may find a degree of personal resonance with some of the issues raised here, such as unpleasant emails, negative experiences in 'chat-rooms' and relationships formed over the internet.

Aims

This chapter aims to:

- identify the key components that determine how we interact with new technology, specifically computers
- describe and evaluate early approaches to telephone and computer communication that focused on the loss of cues during interaction
- describe and evaluate theories that have suggested we communicate differently online compared with face-to-face, and also the application of social identity theory to computer-mediated communication
- consider how computers in the workplace have affected both the speed and the quality of communication
- outline how computers have been used in education, and how they influence our learning
- examine the impact of computer-mediated communication on group dynamics, communities and identity.

1   Introduction

'Computers in the future may weigh no more than 15 tons.'
(Popular Mechanics, *1949)*

In 1943, Thomas Watson, then chairman of computer company IBM, stated that 'I think there is a world market for maybe five computers.' Sixty years later, in the early years of the twenty-first century, it is difficult to imagine many aspects of work, learning or indeed leisure without the involvement of information communication technology (ICT) in some form. Traditionally non-computerised activities (e.g. television, radio, cooking dinner) now have digital technology embedded in their very functioning. Within the space of a decade, mobile telephones and, latterly, wireless internet devices have moved from being status symbols to virtual saturation of the marketplace.

The growth of mobile phone text messaging at the turn of the century illustrates the speed of growth of ICT: in August 2000, 560 million text messages were sent in the UK, according to the Global System for Mobile Communications, more than 10 times the 50 million recorded in May, 1999. Worldwide, the number of short text messages sent to mobile phones in October 2000 reached 10 billion, compared with 1 billion in early 1999. Meanwhile, email traffic exceeded 31 billion a day in 2003, compared with 1.4 billion a day in 2000.

Unlike other 'not so new' technologies, psychologists have not only tracked and researched the development and impact of computers, but they have also been instrumental in their design and evolution. In this chapter we consider both the ways in which humans interact with computers, and the ways in which humans interact with each other using computers.

It is important to recognise that, at the time of writing this chapter, information technology is used predominantly in developed countries. Even in the UK, the percentage of the population with access to (and the skills to use) a computer and internet connection is low compared to the USA. However, like in the UK where most people are usually a few steps removed from the internet (e.g. when using a cash machine or phoning a call centre), so developing countries with little or no internet infrastructure have found that the internet still impacts upon their lives. This may be in the dissemination of information outside official sources, global economics or the provision of services using the internet.

Psychologists have tended to apply pre-existing theories to internet behaviour, rather than consider wider questions about the societal, economic and cultural impact of the internet. However, this does not mean that they are not aware of the wider context in which the behaviour they are studying is conducted. You will notice as you read this chapter that the vast majority of research has investigated social interaction – this is primarily because many of the features of communication using computers (e.g. not being able to see the other person) have previously been implicated in social psychological models of behaviour that suggest certain patterns of interaction. As a body of research, this area is called **computer-mediated communication** (or CMC). Whether or not psychologists will continue examining the minutiae of human communication on the internet, or move to wider questions, remains to be seen. Of course, the research discussed in this chapter also mirrors the technology available for people to communicate on the internet in the early years of the twenty-first century – primarily text-based electronic mail. It is hoped that the ideas outlined here may help us to understand people's behaviour using future technologies, whatever they might be.

Computer-mediated communication
Any communication between people via computers.

2   Interacting with technology

You are probably reading this text in the printed course book. The design of the book – its typeface, the length of the lines and the space between them, the organisation of the text into sections, and so on – will have an effect on things like how easy it is to read, and possibly how readily you understand the content. Similarly, this chapter was generated on a word-processing package, which again has implications for how it is constructed – as authors we can afford to write speculatively and edit later, but we can only work on a small area of the chapter at one time because most PC screens display only around 20 double spaced lines at any one time. The journalist Steven Johnson (1997) discusses how his use of a word-processing package changed his whole process of writing:

> In the years when I still wrote using pen and paper or a typewriter, I almost invariably worked out each sentence in my head before I began transcribing it on to the page … . All this changed when the siren song of the Mac's interface lured me into writing directly at the computer. I began with my familiar start-and-stop routine, dutifully thinking up the sentences before typing it out, but it soon became clear that the word-processor eliminated the penalty that revisions normally exact … . I noticed a qualitative shift in the way I worked with sentences: the thinking and typing processes began to overlap.

(Johnson, 1997, pp. 143–4)

Activity 3.1

Steve Johnson's word processor clearly had a fundamental effect on how he worked. Write down the names of any tools or objects that have had a similar effect on your life, and note the ways in which they influenced your behaviour.

When we think about technology generally, and new technology more specifically, the environment it provides (usually in the form of its design) influences how people interact with it. As an example, the telephones on the office desks of the authors of this chapter have 12 basic buttons (bearing the numbers 0–9, plus # and *). They have two further buttons labelled R and S, but we are not quite sure of their function. They also have voicemail (with a 26-page printed manual) and 30 different 'facility codes' (described on a label stuck on the base of the phone). This label tells us that, for example, the telephone can 'Call hold – remote retrieve' using the keys * * 1 X (where the X is to be replaced with an internal telephone extension number). The telephone also allows us to conference (R X R * 4), and use call forwarding to indicate 'We are here' (* * 8 X). Now, although it's easy for us to press the phone buttons in the order indicated, there is little evidence of what the sequence will actually achieve. It is also impossible to know whether our actions have achieved what was intended because most of the time the telephone doesn't give direct feedback (unlike that provided by the 'hold' light on older style phones).

Affordances
The fundamental
properties of an object
that determine how it can
be used – that is, what
behaviour it allows.

Usability
The ease of use of an
object or tool.

Two key aspects of an object's design mediate its impact on our behaviour: its **affordances** and its **usability**. The term affordance refers to the 'perceived and actual properties of the thing, primarily those fundamental properties that determine just how the thing could possibly be used' (Norman, 1988, p.9). For instance, our office telephones allow us to do lots of different things as well as to speak to other people. Usability, on the other hand, determines how easy (or usable) these fundamental properties are. In the case of our office telephones, usability is sadly lacking.

A similar example found in the home is the video recorder. The features seem easy enough to follow, yet they rarely are. Programming the video to record, say during the night, again often lacks feedback – how often have you set the video to record and then had doubts that it would actually work or later found that it had not? If you have, did you wonder what you had done wrong when setting it? In fact, the timed recording function of many home video recorders has never been used. Too often we seem happy to blame ourselves for these problems, when usually it's bad design that is at fault.

In his book The Psychology of Everyday Things *(1988), Don Norman discusses the design of a number of everyday objects, and how design can lead to certain types of behaviour. One example he uses is doors. The design of a door needs to fulfil the requirements of the technology – that is, it needs to shut and open. It also needs to be designed to allow ease of use. This means that anyone using the door needs to be able to tell which side opens and which side has the hinges, and whether the door is a 'push' or 'pull' design. Some design features (e.g. handles) suggest a pulling action, while others (e.g. flat areas) suggest a pushing one. According to Norman, if a door has instructions (e.g. a handle that says 'push' on it), it's probably a case of bad design.*

Computers and the software they run can also be understood in terms of affordances and usability. The number of possible things that a computer can do is virtually limitless, dependent only on the imagination of the computer programmers and the development of suitable enabling technology (e.g. wings if it is to fly). The word-processing package used to write this chapter also has a large number of properties. It provides pretty good feedback to the user because it has a technology known as WYSIWYG (What You See Is What You Get, usually pronounced 'wizzy wigg') – so if we want to make a word stand out in bold, we can see on the screen whether or not we've succeeded. However, computers suffer quite badly from **feature creep** (Norman, 1988). A quick check on a typical PC reveals options like the visual basic toolbar; the field command; the built-in style gallery; or macros – all gobbledegook

Feature creep
The tendency for more
and more features to be
added to a tool.

to the average user (the authors included) – which seem to do nothing to make the word-processing task more efficient. Feature creep suggests that increasing the affordances of a new technology may often be to the detriment of usability.

A case of bad design

Activity 3.2

List three objects or tools that you use that seem to have too many options or additional features. Do these added features enhance or detract from their ease of use?

Feature creep seems to follow a pattern of increasing when a technology has begun to be widely adopted, and then reducing once it's clear that few consumers use these new features. Sometimes the extra features can actually get in the way of ease of use (e.g. a remote control or a microwave oven with lots of buttons). It is also worth noting how many consumer goods that seem to have good design (e.g. Bang & Olufsen hi-fi equipment) have very few controls (with the more 'optional' controls hidden away).

2.1 Psychology and human–computer interaction

Human–computer interaction (HCI – also called computer–human interaction, or CHI) is the area of study that addresses fundamental questions about the design of computers and its impact on usability. The importance of design on human–computer interaction was not missed on the designers of the first **graphical user interface (GUI)**. The Xerox Star personal computer was developed by researchers at Rank Xerox's Palo Alto Research Centre during the late 1970s. Released in 1981, the Xerox Star was a direct precursor to both the Apple Macintosh computer in 1984 and Microsoft's Windows software much later. The Xerox Star used a 'desktop metaphor' common to most late twentieth- and early twenty-first-century computers. The desktop metaphor means that files and applications are graphically represented on the screen by icons that look like pieces of paper, or a cardboard folder, or other everyday objects (e.g. a bin, calendar, clock, etc.), and these icons are selected using a mouse. Deleting a file is done in a way equivalent to what we would do without a computer – it's thrown in the bin. Also of interest to psychologists is the care taken in the design of the system – the colours for the desktop are carefully chosen to provide very little contrast outside the area of focus (e.g. the document you are typing), while the black type on white background replicates print on paper.

> **Graphical user interface (GUI)** Software that allows users to interact with a computer by means of a visual interface, rather than by learning and using computer code. For example, Microsoft Windows is a GUI, whereas DOS (the hidden operating software) is a command line interface where the computer is controlled using typed commands.

As a discipline, HCI draws on a number of areas, including design, art and linguistics, as well as psychology. The primary input of psychology is to try to understand the user of the computer, to model their behaviour, and to understand how the design of the system influences this behaviour (Faulkner, 1998). The most obvious starting point is to look at how a person's sensory and cognitive abilities lead to different ways of interacting with computers. Take, for instance, the role of colour in designing computer interfaces. Although humans with unimpaired colour vision can typically perceive and distinguish more than 7 million colours, this sensitivity is not uniform across the field of vision. At the periphery of the visual field (around 90 degrees from the straight-ahead position), people are less able to distinguish red, green and yellow light, and are most sensitive to blue light. Similarly, the combination of colours can influence, for instance, the ability of users to distinguish the object (e.g. text) from the field (e.g. the background colour). Although it might seem obvious that black on white is the most suitable combination, this depends on factors like the brightness of the screen and the other surrounding colours. Too much brightness can lead to increased screen 'flicker', which can induce feelings of nausea and headaches. The other senses also have an impact on HCI – for instance, in determining the best type of alert sounds (those beep noises that tell us we've done something wrong), and the best combination of sound and visual alerts to gain the user's attention (not so important for the home user, but critical for air-traffic controllers).

Activity 3.3

Write down the names of some of the objects in your own environment (a maximum of five) that you have difficulty operating either effectively or quickly, where the difficulty does not arise from the object having too many features. Try to think beyond 'hi-tech' objects to supposedly simple things like doors, cookers, and so on. For instance, one of us recently bought some venetian blinds that are almost impossible to operate. Next to each object, write why you find it difficult to operate – but you are not allowed to blame yourself!

Comment

Norman (1988) argued that a well-designed system should have good **mapping** and provide immediate feedback. Mapping refers to the relationship between a control device (for example, a keyboard or mouse action) and an intended outcome (for example, to open a file). A high level of mapping is when the control device is linked in action to the intended outcome. Norman gives the example of a steering wheel on a car – turning the wheel to the left is closely mapped to the car turning left. Try to imagine driving if an anticlockwise turn sent the car to the right. Norman also gives the example of cooker hobs: if the control dials map naturally on to the layout of the rings, the cooker is easier to use than when the dials rely on labels for guidance. In Figure 3.1, the cooker on the left has a high level of mapping between the controls and the rings; the cooker on the right has a low level of mapping. Were any of your difficult-to-use objects chosen because of poor mapping? An alternative reason for your selection could be that quite a few objects do not provide feedback that your action has achieved the desired outcome – like setting a video without being sure you were successful. Finally, like door handles that say 'push', perhaps your objects just suffer from counterintuitive design?

Mapping
The link between a control and the intended outcome of that control.

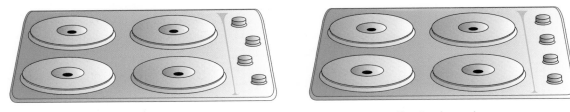

Natural mapping   Unnatural mapping

Figure 3.1   Examples of natural and unnatural mapping

Computer systems should be designed to provide a close link between the action undertaken and the outcome. The development of GUIs like Microsoft Windows has arguably made computers much more usable, in part because they do provide mapping between an intention (e.g. to delete a file) and an action (e.g. dragging a file icon across the screen and 'dropping' it in the bin). Before the development of the graphical user interface, mapping was low – for example, to copy a file to a floppy disk on a DOS PC you would have to type 'c: copy c:/files/filename.txt a:/myfiles/'. On more recent machines, the mapping between the action (drag and drop) and the outcome (copying) is closer, enhancing usability. Importantly, modern systems also provide feedback on the progress of the action. In the past, users would invariably type in 'a:/myfiles dir' to check that they had succeeded.

An early computer

Box 3.1 highlights the importance of considering HCI in the workplace.

3.1 Human–computer interaction in the workplace

In the past, HCI within an organisation was primarily focused on how workers used the technology supplied to them, and its effects on working conditions and output. However, as more and more companies have moved to the World Wide Web for both customer information and trading, so the focus on the importance of usability in human–computer interaction has shifted from how staff interact with computers to how customers and staff interact with companies' internet and intranet ('within-organisation' networks using internet technology) systems. Jacob Neilson, a usability 'guru', advises organisations on designing usable websites for their customers. He identifies a series of key problems with most websites, including too many pictures (increasing time to load), too complex structures and too many steps between deciding to purchase and actually being able to buy. A similar rethink is also needed for intranets within an organisation. It is common for organisations to install and develop a complex knowledge-management system, only to find that no one uses it. For instance, the Ford Motor Company in the USA found that between 750 and 1000 members of staff were regular users of their new intranet system, while 100,000 used the system infrequently or never. There is a whole series of reasons why this might have happened – the content might not have been right, perhaps the system had too much information, or the information may have been difficult to find.

The introduction of computer–mediated communication systems can impact on people's work in a variety of ways. CMC, whether in the form of email, bulletin boards or conferencing, is becoming commonplace in the workplace. There is some evidence that the use of CMC in the workplace can be beneficial not just in speeding communication, but in increasing the quality of that communication. For instance, Shirani *et al.* (1999) compared email and group support system (a bulletin board system with editing tools) teams on a decision-making task that was either structured or unstructured. The group support system participants came up with more ideas, but 'groups using e-mail performed a deeper problem analysis' as indicated by 'a higher proportion of inferential ideas generated by these groups' (1999, p. 139). Moreover, the number of inferential ideas was significantly higher when the task was unstructured. Similarly, Adrianson and Hjelmquist (1999) found that CMC decision making (compared with face-to-face) leads to more ideas being generated. Furnham (2000) reviewed evidence to suggest that brainstorming face-to-face inhibits creativity. He concluded that computer-based brainstorming might address the problem observed in the lack of creativity of face-to-face groups, because it reduces concerns about being judged and makes conspicuous anyone not contributing.

Users' interaction *with* a computer is quite different from the interactions they have with other people via the computer. However, these two processes are not exclusive – indeed, the design and capabilities of a piece of new technology will influence the type of interpersonal behaviour conducted through the technology. According to Donald Norman, 'Tools affect more than the ease with which we do things; they can dramatically affect our view of ourselves, society, and the world ... Even apparently simple innovations can bring about dramatic changes, most of which cannot be predicted' (Norman, 1988, p. 209). Looking back to the start of this chapter, who would have predicted that the main use of the mobile telephone amongst young people in the early part of the twenty-first century would be for text messaging? In the following section we move away from considering how humans and computers interact, and move to how humans interact with each other using CMC.

Summary Section 2

- How people interact with technology is influenced by two key design factors:
  - the affordances of the technology
  - the usability of the technology.
- Other factors that determine how we interact with technology include the choice of features, the graphical user interface, the level of mapping between control device and outcome, and feedback to the user.
- Usability may be associated with staff efficiency in the workplace and with frequency of use of websites.

3   Interacting using new technology

3.1   A case study of the telephone

On 10 March 1876, Alexander Graham Bell became the first person ever to communicate electrically using what became known as the telephone. Like many new technologies, the potential of the telephone was missed by many – when turning down the offer to purchase the patent for the telephone (and so monopolise the market), the President of the Western Union Telegraph Company asked, 'What use could this company make of an electrical toy?' Indeed, the early years of the telephone were beset by notions of the telephone as a device for broadcasting rather than for one-to-one communication. For instance, visions of future telephone use involved the broadcasting of speeches by 'distinguished men' to remote audiences in various music halls (*Boston Transcript*, 18 July 1876) or even a 'dancing party [with] ... no need for a musician' (*Nature*, 24 August 1876). Although the early uses of the telephone tended to be in business (and especially hotels), it wasn't until the middle of the twentieth century that the use of the telephone for socialising became relatively commonplace.

The eventual popularity of the telephone for social uses should have been easy to predict. Even the telegraph, which required conversational partners to use Morse code, was employed extensively by telegraph operators for social interaction during quiet spells (Standage, 1998). A novel, *Wired Love*, was published in 1879 to document the use of the telegraph to 'keep up flirtations', while the *Boston Globe* published an article in 1886 warning of the 'dangers of wired love'. The potential use of the telephone for romantic liaisons was also a cause for some concern. In 1884, *Electrical World* magazine warned that: 'The serenading troubadour can now thrum his guitar before the telephone, undisturbed by apprehension of shotguns and bull dogs. Romeo need no longer catch a cold waiting at Juliet's balcony.'

In the late 1960s and early 1970s, the psychology of telecommunication use became a topic of interest to a group of researchers based at University College London. Called the Communication Studies Group, these researchers were interested in the psychological processes involved in technological communication (primarily the telephone). Their research culminated in a book, *The Social Psychology of Telecommunications* (Short *et al.*, 1976).

The Communication Studies Group focused on two key questions: what factors determine use of the telephone and what social psychological processes are invoked by telephone communication? In common with many later theories of CMC, the starting point of their research was what people lost when they communicated by telephone rather than face-to-face. Much of this effort was directed at the 'most obvious defect of the simple telephone – the fact that one cannot see the other person or group' (Short *et al.*, 1976, p. 43). Traditional social psychological literature tends to stress the importance of visual cues in communication: for instance, in showing mutual attention, controlling who speaks when, providing feedback and conveying liking and agreement during an interaction in the form of gestures, facial expressions, emblems (e.g. a nod of the head), and other social information like physical appearance, nonverbal communication using body posture and movement, and the proximity between speakers (Short *et al.*, 1976). Although some of these nonverbal cues might be transferable to the telephone, the majority are not (e.g. gesture, body posture, facial expressions).

The Communication Studies Group conducted a series of experiments to test whether the lack of visual cues had an impact on people's behaviour (Reid, 1981). Of most interest here are the studies they conducted into group discussions and the resolution of conflict and person perception. John Short and colleagues asked participants to argue a case, from a viewpoint provided by the experimenter (e.g. as a union representative or an employer), using either just an audio channel of communication or face-to-face (Short *et al.*, 1976). In the first study, Short *et al.* found that strong arguments were more persuasive in audio-only communication compared with face-to-face discussions. In a second experiment, Short *et al.* manipulated whether the disagreement between participants was due to a difference of opinion or objective. A difference of opinion occurred when the two participants held different attitudes to a topic, while a difference of objective resulted when they were aiming for different, often contradictory, outcomes to the discussions (e.g. a pay rise vs. a pay cut). He found that the stronger argument had more influence face-to-face when it was a difference of opinion, and more influence during audio-only communication when it was a difference of objective. A third condition, with two-way television screens (so the participants could see each other), showed no difference from the face-to-face condition. However, in a series of follow-up studies, Short *et al.* found that, when discussing differences of opinion, their participants *were* persuaded more by strong arguments over the audio channel than face-to-face. These findings led Reid (1981) to conclude that, 'the clearest and most consistent finding in this series of ... experiments using conflict tasks is the unexpected result that audio discussions produce more opinion change than do face-to-face discussions' (pp. 404–5).

A second series of experiments addressed the accuracy and confidence of face-to-face and telephone judgements. For example, in general there is little difference in the accuracy of people's judgements of others' personalities and attitudes across media, but face-to-face participants tend to express greater confidence in their own judgements (Reid, 1981).

It is perhaps not surprising that we think we can judge people better face-to-face than over the telephone (or indeed the internet). What might strike you as surprising is that the accuracy of our impressions is about the same whether we can see the other person or not. In Chapter 4 of this book, Aldert Vrij discusses the example of detecting deception. Nonverbal cues are relatively easy to control when we are lying – in fact, we tend to over-compensate. However, people still tend to believe that to spot a liar you need to 'look them in the eye'.

Williams (1972) found that participants evaluated their communication partner more favourably if they could see and hear them using a videophone rather than just hear them. In a follow-up study, Williams (1975) set teams of four participants the task of brainstorming topics selected by the experimenter, either face-to-face, by video link, or by audio link. In the two telecommunication conditions, the groups consisted of two people at each end of the line (giving groups of four in total). Williams found that the two people stationed together tended to agree more with each other than with the distant members of their group, and that any dissent to an idea raised was significantly more likely to emanate from the other end of the line, not from the person next to them. Moreover, participants in the audio condition were significantly more likely to rate their fellow group members on the other 'node' as lower in both sincerity and intelligence. Such findings were not observed in the face-to-face or video link conditions, where such ratings were more evenly distributed.

Short *et al.* (1976) developed the social presence theory to explain these findings. They began by arguing that interpersonal attitudes are primarily conveyed using visual cues, while the verbal channel contains only interparty, task-oriented, cognitive material. So, if the visual channel is removed (as in the case of the telephone), what remains is simply the capacity to transmit the task-oriented material, not the social, interpersonal information.

Short *et al.* went on to argue that the salience of the other person in the interaction and the consequent salience of the interpersonal relationships is an objective quality of the medium of communication. They termed this quality **social presence**. What is meant by 'objective quality' is that social presence is a property of the medium (like its affordances), rather than just arising from users' reactions to the medium. According to Short *et al.*, the 'capacity to transmit information about facial expression, direction of looking, posture, dress and non-verbal cues, all contribute to the social presence of a communications medium' (1976, p. 65).

However, social presence also seems to have a phenomenological aspect, in that it relates to people's subjective responses to a medium. The social presence of different media like the telephone, email and so on was measured by Short *et al.* by asking users to score them on a series of scales labelled, for instance, personal–impersonal, sociable–unsociable and cold–warm. A medium with high social presence would tend to be rated as more warm, personal and sociable than a medium with low social presence. Short *et al.* (1976) report that, using these types of measure, people rate non-visual communication (e.g. by telephone) as low in social presence, with face-to-face communication rated highest in social presence. Communication over a video link is reported by Short *et al.* as having relatively high social presence, but still less social presence than face-to-face communication. Indeed, the only communication medium rated as having less social presence than the telephone was the business letter.

The social presence of a medium will, according to Short *et al.*, have implications for the intimacy of a communication. They predicted that the higher the social presence of a medium, so the greater the intimacy between users, all other things being equal. This prediction is based on Argyle and Dean's intimacy-equilibrium theory (1965), which argues that people have an optimum level of intimacy during an interaction. Because intimacy can be communicated in many different ways (e.g. eye-contact, proximity, self-disclosure), an increase in one form of intimacy will lead to a reduction in another to redress the balance. Thus, for instance, people reduce eye-contact when they are about to discuss personal intimacies (Exline *et al.*, 1965). However, instead of arguing that the reduction in intimacy caused by the removal of many visual cues will lead to a compensatory increase in intimacy via verbal behaviour, Short *et al.* argue the opposite – that because eye-contact is so important in intimacy, its removal may well lead to conflict rather than greater intimacy. So, in the case of the telephone, because visual cues are absent, we should, according to Short *et al.*, be less intimate on the telephone than face-to-face. Media with low social presence are, according to Short *et al.*, best suited for tasks such as information transmission and simple problem

Social presence
Social presence is a quality of the communications medium that relates to the capacity of that medium to transmit social information.

solving. Indeed, Short *et al.* argue 'telephone communication is intrinsically less sociable, more impersonal, and that, unless the task requires such psychological "distance", the mismatch is felt to be unpleasant' (1976, p.81). In Section 4 of this chapter, we will consider alternative evidence that the removal of visual cues in CMC has in fact led to *greater* intimacy rather than *lower* levels of intimacy as might be predicted by the original social presence theory.

Activity 3.4

Do you think that visual cues are crucial to social interaction? Or could they be a hindrance to communication? Write down who you have called in the last few weeks and the main purpose(s) of the communication.

Comment

Looking at your list, how many of the uses are purely task-oriented information transmission without any social component? Very few, we would imagine. Bell predicted over one hundred years ago that talking on the telephone would be predominately a social activity. Even conversations we might expect to be task oriented (e.g. phoning for an insurance quotation) have a social element. Looking again at your list, are there any occasions when you think it might be easier to communicate by telephone than face-to-face (or vice versa)? Are these due to the affordances of the telephone (e.g. distance) or because you feel more comfortable (i.e. less anxious) on the telephone?

There have been various attempts to extend the general theme of social presence (Rutter, 1987; Rutter and Stephenson, 1979). The general tendency of these approaches is to argue that the reduced social cues transmitted during communication across new media (including the telephone) will lead to task-oriented and depersonalised communication. Early studies of CMC attempted to use the social presence/cuelessness models to predict that CMC will be 'less friendly, emotional, or personal and more serious, business-like, or task oriented' (Rice and Love, 1987, p. 88). Whether CMC is indeed task oriented is discussed later, in Section 4.1.

3.2 Reduced social presence and computer-mediated communication

Psychological processes during CMC were researched extensively by Sara Kiesler and her colleagues at Carnegie Mellon University during the 1980s. Although the general theme of this approach was once again on the effects of 'loss' of visual cues on non-face-to-face communication, the specific focus was on the loss of 'social cues' or social context cues when people communicate using computers. According to Kiesler *et al.* (1984), social context cues take two main forms: static (e.g. physical appearance, location, etc.) and active (e.g. nonverbal behaviour). Box 3.2 describes the different types of CMC that can be investigated.

3.2   *Types of computer-mediated communication (CMC)*

Computer-mediated communication refers to any communication between people that is conducted via computer. However, there are a number of different types of CMC:

- **Asynchronous:** CMC that occurs when people are communicating across time rather than instantaneously. Email is an asynchronous CMC – the conversation can take place over days or months, with each person having time to read the message, compose a reply and send it when ready.
- **Synchronous:** CMC that occurs in 'real time' so the participants (any number) have to be at a computer terminal at the same time. 'Chat' or 'IRC' (internet relay chat) is synchronous CMC – it progresses more like a normal conversation, rather than an exchange of letters.
- **One-to-one:** CMC that only involves two people communicating directly with each other: usually email, but can be 'chat' as well if just two people are talking privately.
- **Many-to-many:** CMC that usually occurs by sending messages to a central place to be read by as many people as access it. An example is Usenet, where messages are 'posted' to a newsgroup and can be read by everyone with access to that group.

The model Kiesler *et al.* developed was based on a large number of experimental studies that looked directly at CMC. This approach has been termed the reduced social cues model, although the work of Kiesler *et al.* encompasses many other effects of CMC. Kiesler and her colleagues (e.g. Kiesler *et al.*, 1984), like the social presence researchers before them, argue for the importance of social context cues to provide conversational regulation and feedback, to give obvious status/position cues and to provide accountability. When these cues are removed during CMC, they predict that: 'Social standards will be less important and communication will be more impersonal and more free because the rapid exchange of text, the lack of social feedback, and the absence of norms governing the social interaction redirect attention away from others and toward the message itself' (Kiesler *et al.*, 1984, p. 1126).

So, just like social presence theorists before them, Kiesler *et al.* effectively argue that the social aspects of communication are downgraded during CMC and the focus becomes the message itself. Indeed, Kiesler *et al.* go further and argue that the nature of electronic communication (the lack of social cues, a

De-individuation
De-individuation is a
psychological state where
people essentially lose
their individuality, and
behave in an anti-
normative way.

possible reduction in self-awareness) seems to be similar to **de-individuation**. De-individuation theory was developed, amongst others, by Zimbardo (1969) to explain antisocial behaviour in crowds. He argued that a series of factors, including reduced focus on the self, anonymity and high arousal levels, would lead to a state of de-individuation, where people were not behaving in accordance with their normal morals and attitudes but rather were pushed toward antisocial, aggressive behaviour.

The idea that communicating using computers leads to de-individuation is an intriguing one. It relies on the anonymity of users to create a 'state of mind' where their inhibitions are loosened. When psychologists talk about anonymity they usually mean 'lack of identifiability' (for instance, when you are a member of a large crowd). However, computer-mediated communication is usually conducted in a state of visual anonymity (you can't see the person you're talking to), but without lack of identifiability (you know their name from their email address, unless the person is using a pseudonym to identify themselves). The reduced social cues approach combines the effects of visual anonymity (lack of social cues) with lack of identifiability (reduced accountability) under one term: anonymity. Other later work tried to separate the effects of these two different types of anonymity.

The research of Kiesler *et al.* on the effects of reduced social cues during CMC was focused on two main outcomes: uninhibited hostile behaviour (also called 'flaming') and social influence.

Reduced social cues and 'flaming'

Flaming
Flaming is the term used
to describe antisocial,
negative behaviour
during CMC like
swearing, hostility and
aggressiveness.

Originally, the term **flaming** was used within the hacker community to indicate continual chattering without thought for others. More recently, flaming has come to mean the usually anonymous venting of anger or hostility using CMC. Kiesler *et al.* (1984) maintained that people using computers to communicate 'overstep conventional time boundaries dividing office and home; they mix work and personal communications; they use language appropriate for boardroom and ballfield interchangeably; and they disregard normal conventions for privacy' (1984, p. 1126). Furthermore, Kiesler *et al.* predicted that CMC will 'be more impersonal and more free' (p. 1126). Thus, according to Kiesler *et al.*, uninhibited communication is caused by a combination of factors, including reduced social cues, de-individuation and the pervading 'hacker' culture on the internet (the assumption that the internet is akin to the Wild West as far as lawlessness is concerned).

In three early studies, Siegal *et al.* (1983) compared levels of uninhibited verbal behaviour in four conditions: face-to-face communication, anonymous computer conferencing (many-to-many), non-anonymous computer conferencing (many-to-many), and email (one-to-one). In the experiments, groups of three people were asked to reach a consensus using a choice-dilemma task (a dilemma where groups weigh up two possible choices, often a risky and cautious option, and come to a joint decision). When Siegal and her colleagues looked at the level of uninhibited communication (which they defined as hostile comments such as swearing, name-calling and insults), they found higher levels of uninhibited verbal behaviour, in each experiment, when people used computers to communicate. The highest levels of uninhibited behaviour were recorded when people discussed anonymously using the computer-conferencing system.

In a later study, Sproull and Kiesler (1986) studied the email system of a large organisation in the USA. They studied the email communication of 96 staff members, as well as collecting questionnaire responses. In accordance with their model, Sproull and Kiesler predicted that:

- There would be fewer social context cues communicated by email (e.g. geographic location, job category, age or sex).
- Email users would be self-absorbed rather than focused on the 'other' during communication because of the lack of social cues about the other person.
- Email messages would look similar regardless of the status of the sender or recipient (e.g. managers or subordinates).
- Email would be uninhibited and non-conforming compared with face-to-face communication (e.g. with regard to flaming).

In accordance with their predictions, Sproull and Kiesler found that social cues were typically low for communication from an unknown (to the recipient) source. That is, relatively little information about the person (e.g. their gender, age, race, and so on) was communicated. They also found that the typical email salutation ('Hi') was only a third as long as the typical closing ('Bye for now'). Because salutations tend to be focused on the other person (e.g. 'How are you?'), while closings are indicative of a focus on the self, they argued that email users are self-absorbed. Email users also reported seeing 33 flames (antisocial messages) on email in a month, and just 4 in face-to-face interaction. Sproull and Kiesler concluded that reduced social cues in email are potentially beneficial within an organisation (because of the speed of communication), but that they could also lead to problems through their encouragement of uninhibited behaviour.

However, closer examination of empirical work on CMC has tended to find that flaming is hardly characteristic of CMC. For instance, Lea *et al.* (1992) argued that flaming accounts for less than 5 per cent of communication in CMC. They concluded that, like many negative events, flaming tends to be remembered more often than benign CMC, which has contributed to 'the illusion of universality' (1992, p. 108).

Similarly, Walther *et al.* (1994) argued that much of the acceptance of flaming as a widespread phenomenon during CMC is based on 'erroneous analysis and reporting practices' (p. 463). For instance, there is little agreement across different studies as to what exactly constitutes 'flaming'. In some studies, blasphemy and excessive praise are included. In others, only negative comments are recorded. What is certain is that negative behaviour forms only a small part of CMC.

Reduced social cues and social influence

The second focus of work from a reduced social cues perspective was on social influence in CMC. This work specifically focused on a phenomenon in social psychology termed *group polarisation*. Group polarisation is the tendency for a group's consensus to become more extreme following discussion (e.g. the group expresses *a more positive attitude* to, say, increased health service funding following group discussion) compared with the average pre-discussion opinions of the group's members. The general finding of CMC research was that group decisions became more extreme (i.e. polarised) when discussions were held over CMC systems compared with face-to-face.

Remember the studies on telephone use discussed earlier? One of the key findings was 'the unexpected result that audio discussions produce more opinion change than do face-to-face discussions' (Reid, 1981, pp. 404–5). Here we have a clear continuity between findings from telephone research and CMC research. This would suggest that there is a shared feature of the telephone and CMC (for instance, visual anonymity, reduced social presence/social cues or even de-individuation) that can explain these findings regardless of the medium.

Kiesler *et al.* (1984) explained these findings using reduced social context cues. Put simply, they maintained that the reduced cues inherent in CMC lead to more uninhibited, anti-normative behaviour, which leads to more extreme opinions being expressed, which in turn leads to the group decision becoming more extreme (see Figure 3.2). Thus, the basis for group polarisation during CMC is that participants voice more extreme opinions during CMC because of the reduced role of status and leadership in a cue-free environment, because they may be de-individuated and because they are focused on the message rather than the social context. Furthermore, not only are the opinions expressed more extreme, but because participation is more equal, so more of these extreme arguments are likely to be voiced. When these two factors (more extreme opinions and more people stating them) are added together, Kiesler *et al.* propose, social influence occurs based on the number and strength of the arguments made.

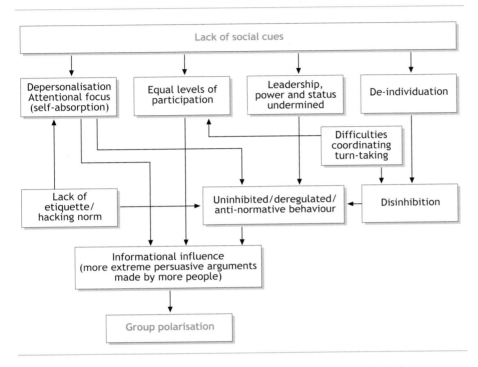

Figure 3.2   Reduced social cues approach to group polarisation during CMC (Source: adapted from Spears and Lea, 1992, Figure 2.1, p. 39)

The reduced social cues approach has been criticised by Spears and Lea (1992) for combining a number of contradictory ideas. For instance, Kiesler *et al.* use both de-individuation and self-absorption to explain uninhibited behaviour, yet de-individuation depends upon a reduction in self-awareness, so the two should be mutually exclusive. Similarly, Kiesler *et al.* argue for anti-normative behaviour during CMC (via the lack of social cues and de-individuation), and also argue that one norm – that of the computing subculture (e.g. hacking) – could lead to uninhibited behaviour. However, they don't explain how this one norm can infiltrate a 'normless' environment.

Models that see CMC, because of the loss of social cues, leading to a reduction in the level of sociability, flaming, and so on have been termed 'cool' models of CMC (Rice, 1984). Rice called models that focus on the potential benefits of CMC (e.g. through fast and efficient communication) 'warm'. Although some models (e.g. Kiesler *et al.*, 1984) combine warm and cool aspects of CMC, in the main they are 'cool' in that they focus on the negative impact of CMC. For this reason in this chapter we refer to them as loss models. The potential social benefits are considered further in the next section.

Summary   Section 3

- Early models of mediated communication, like social presence and reduced social cues, focused on the 'loss' of social cues.
- These models predicted both task-based discussions using computers and uninhibited antisocial behaviour.
- The reduced social cues approach has been criticised on two main grounds: first, that estimates of uninhibited communication are overstated; and, second, that the explanation of group polarisation is inadequate.
- This second point is important, because communication without visual cues is argued to be 'non-social' and conducive to anti-normative behaviour. Thus any explanation of social behaviour (e.g. group polarisation) is argued to rely on the information exchanged, not any other social processes within the group.
- Spears and Lea challenge the view that CMC is 'anti-normative'.

4   Computer-based behaviour and social communication

As we have discussed, one aspect of the design of a computer system is its affordances – the built-in mechanisms that allow users to engage in certain types of behaviour. It has been argued by a number of theorists, most notably Joseph Walther, that the unique characteristics of communication over the internet and other networks tend to lead to certain types of behaviour in both the workplace and at home. Walther began by considering why some studies of CMC seemed to confirm that, when people solve problems collaboratively over a computer system, the discussions tend to be 'task focused'. As we discussed earlier, one explanation for task-focused CMC was that CMC effectively 'de-socialises' communication.

Walther's argument was that the task focus found in many of these studies occurred because people had only a short amount of time to solve the problem, and they didn't expect to have to work together again. This argument was based on Walther's social information processing model (Walther, 1992). In this model, Walther proposed that users of CMC have the same interpersonal needs as face-to-face communicators, and that CMC is quite capable of transferring social information between people, such as status, affiliation and liking, and even attraction to the other person. However, because most CMC is typing-based, the rate of message exchange is lower than in face-to-face interaction (especially using asynchronous systems like email). If this is the case, then the transmission of social information will be considerably slower during CMC than face-to-face. Thus, 'given sufficient time and message exchanges for interpersonal impression formation and relational development to accrue, and all other things being equal, relational (communication) in later periods of CMC and face-to-face communication will be the same' (Walther, 1992, p. 69).

In keeping with earlier reduced social cues theories, Walther (1992) sees the loss of visual cues inherent in CMC as a disadvantage to be overcome over time, and through the development of 'various linguistic and typographic manipulations which may reveal social and relational information in CMC' (Walther, 1995, p. 190). Thus, the social information processing model offers a clear explanation in terms of time constraints of why early studies tend to find task focus in CMC. Many CMC studies only have people discussing a topic for 15 to 30 minutes – not enough time, according to Walther, for social and relational information to be passed across the 'limited' channel of CMC.

Walther *et al.* (1994) conducted a meta-analysis of 21 experiments on CMC. Remember from Chapter 2 that meta-analysis is a statistical technique for combining the results of many different studies into one large analysis. This technique allowed Walther *et al.* to use the findings from a large number of separate studies to test a specific hypothesis using the data reported in those experiments. In the case of Walther *et al.*, the variable under consideration was whether CMC in the 21 experiments they included in their meta-analysis was time-limited or not. One of the dependent variables was the proportion of socially oriented, rather than task-oriented, communication. Walther *et al.* found higher levels of socio-emotional communication in time-unrestricted CMC groups compared with time-restricted groups. They also found that there was less of a difference in the level of socio-emotional communication between CMC and face-to-face groups when there was no time restriction compared with those studies with a time restriction.

The meta-analysis therefore confirmed one of the key predictions of the social information processing model: that, over time, the amount of social information communicated using CMC converges with the amount sent verbally in face-to-face communication. The simple explanation for this finding is that typing is much slower than talking, so any social exchange will take place more slowly over CMC than face-to-face. Another key factor is that the communication of social information across a computer network requires the learning, and use, of linguistic and textual cues to convey relational information. Although there is plenty of evidence of 'users' developing such 'paralanguage' (Walther, 1992), it may take time for CMC users to develop adequate skills in paralanguage to convey social information competently. The most obvious examples are the use of **emoticons** or 'smileys', and acronyms (see Table 3.1). The use of some emoticons is such a widely accepted part of online communication that many email programs now convert them to images automatically. You will need to turn the page sideways to see the faces in Table 3.1.

Emoticons
Emoticons are symbols, formed from combinations of punctuation and other symbols, used to convey emotions during text-based communications.

Table 3.1   **Some common emoticons and social language acronyms**

Emoticon	Meaning	Acronym	Meaning
:-)	Smile	LOL	Laugh out loud
;-)	Wink	ROFL	Roll on floor laughing
:-P	Stick tongue out	LOL@	Laughs out loud at
:-(	Sad	A/S/L	What is your age/sex/location?
:-0	Shocked	TY	Thank you
		G (and BG)	Grin (Big grin)

Often these paralanguage cues are used to convey social information and help build relationships (e.g. by conveying a joke, or laughter). If it takes users time to pick up these skills, then it is reasonable to assume that the communication of social information will be impaired if subject to time restriction. Sonia Utz (2000) studied the impact of CMC experience (and therefore time spent developing paralanguage skills) on the development of relationships. She found that the longer people had spent using CMC on the internet, so the more paralanguage they used, and the more relationships they formed.

One criticism of the social information processing model is that it is still firmly located in the 'loss' camp of CMC – Walther argued that, given time, CMC might be able to match face-to-face communication in its 'socialness'. For instance, he conducted a study (Walther, 1995) in which it was predicted, based on the social information processing model, that social behaviour would be greater in face-to-face than CMC groups, but that the difference would subside over a large amount of time. Walther had coders rate each person discussing face-to-face or by CMC. The coders then blind-rated (i.e. were unaware of the experimental condition) the complete discussions using a 'relational communication' questionnaire (a way of organising their overall impressions of the 'socialness' of the discussions). The CMC and face-to-face groups discussed three separate issues on three different occasions, allowing a comparison of social communication across time.

Walther was surprised to find that the effect was the opposite of his prediction: CMC groups were rated higher in most aspects of relational communication than the face-to-face groups, regardless of timescale. For instance, the coders rated the CMC groups as higher than face-to-face groups on the level of affection seen in the group discussions, on how similar the group members seemed, and on how composed and relaxed during the discussion the participants seemed. Most importantly, the CMC groups were rated as significantly *less* task oriented, and *more* socially oriented, than the face-to-face groups during all the time slots. Thus, the key theoretical predictions of the social information processing model were refuted by Walther's 1995 study: CMC was significantly more social than face-to-face communication, and the developments over time were not in the predicted direction in most cases. Walther's explanation for these findings is discussed in Section 4.1.

Before we move on, it is worth noting that Walther's conclusion that 'social information processing underestimates the positive effect of computer-mediation on relational communication' (Walther, 1995, p. 198) is equally applicable to all 'loss' models of mediated communication. By focusing on the loss of social cues inherent in CMC (and the telephone), the potential increases in social behaviour, and plasticity of human behaviour when it comes to communicating social information, were ignored.

4.1 'Hyperpersonal' social interaction using computers

As we outlined above, Walther (1995) found that CMC groups were consistently rated as more affectionate than face-to-face groups. Indeed, there are numerous examples of relationships and romances occurring in many different areas of the internet, including chat groups (Reid, 1991), newsgroups (Parks and Floyd, 1996), role-playing environments, also known as MUDs (Multi-User Dungeons, Domains or Dimensions) (Utz, 2000), and within online communities (Rheingold, 1993). Some of these relationships are serious enough to culminate in cohabitation or marriage (Parks and Floyd, 1996). In fact, for a communication medium that, according to early theorists, should discourage it, social interaction is now the main use of the internet in the home (Kraut *et al.*, 2000). Both **anecdotal evidence** and experimental evidence have shown that people use computers to form or maintain social relationships. Two pertinent questions are: in what contexts is CMC highly social, and how can this be reconciled with early findings that CMC is task oriented?

To address these questions, Walther's (1995) finding that CMC groups are more socially orientated than face-to-face groups is consistent with other research. For instance, Chilcoat and DeWine (1985) found that participants who

Anecdotal evidence
Evidence based on informal reports, stories, personal accounts and related sources. Anecdotal evidence is not considered scientific, as it is not open to rigorous scrutiny.

could not see each other rated each other more highly on attitude similarity, and on social and physical attractiveness.

Walther (1994, 1995, 1996) argues that one possible explanation for this is that long-term CMC groups anticipate future interaction, and so have higher levels of social communication compared with one-off groups who do not expect to meet again in the future. This may explain why early studies using 'one-shot' experimental groups tended to find low levels of social communication. Moreover, the time limits imposed on most early studies would not have allowed the time for social information to be communicated due to the reduced rate of socio-emotional communication in CMC (Walther *et al.*, 1994).

So, according to Walther's explanation, for CMC groups to exhibit high levels of affiliation, they need to either anticipate future interaction (if they seem to be social from the word go), or meet over a length of time (if they are task oriented at the beginning). Walther distinguishes between CMC environments that seem to encourage *impersonal* interaction (e.g. time-limited, no anticipation of future interaction) and those that encourage *interpersonal* interaction (e.g. time-unlimited, anticipation of future interaction). Indeed, Walther argues that: 'There are several instances in which CMC has surpassed the level of affection and emotion of parallel FtF [face-to-face] interaction' (Walther, 1996, p. 17). He termed this phenomenon **hyperpersonal communication**.

Hyperpersonal communication
Communication which exceeds normal interaction in terms of pro-social behaviours, such as affection and emotional expression.

According to Walther's model (1996), hyperpersonal interaction is created by four main factors. First, because many online communicants share a social categorisation (e.g. Open University student), they will also tend to perceive greater similarity between themselves and their conversational partner. As we tend to like those whom we see as similar to ourselves, people communicating online will be predisposed toward liking their communication partners.

Second, the sender of a message can optimise their self-presentation – that is, they can present themselves in a more positive light than they might be able to face-to-face because they don't have to worry about their nonverbal behaviour. Being freed from having to allocate scarce mental resources to controlling our visual cues and appearance means that we can allocate more resources to message construction – again, leading to a more positive impression being conveyed to the recipient (see Figure 3.3). Recalling the phrase 'the waist is a terrible thing to mind', Walther also suggests that being freed from concerns about our appearance might be linked to a heightening of focus on our own inner self. This would mean that messages sent during CMC would include more content about personal feelings and thoughts, and that the senders might be more in touch with their self-ideals (again, helping with their self-presentation).

A third factor in hyperpersonal communication is the format of the CMC. Walther argues that asynchronous CMC (e.g. email) is more likely to lead to hyperpersonal interaction because the communicants: (a) can devote a special time slot to CMC, rather than being distracted by other goings on; (b) can spend more time composing/editing the message; (c) can mix social and task-oriented messages; and (d) do not need to use up cognitive resources answering immediately, so can pay more attention to the message.

The final factor Walther invokes is a feedback loop that causes these effects to be magnified through social interaction (see Figure 3.3). As the interaction progresses, so the inflated positive impressions will be magnified as the communicators seek to confirm their initial impressions, and in turn respond to the positive impressions conveyed by their partners (Walther, 1996).

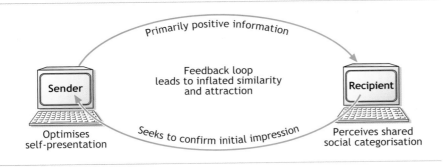

Figure 3.3   The feedback loop in hyperpersonal communication

Walther's model of hyperpersonal communication relies on visual anonymity and asynchronous communication. Indeed, Walther (1999) warns against the trend to plug video cameras into PCs, arguing that visual cues *detract* from social impressions during CMC. For instance, Walther *et al.* (1999) report that long-term CMC groups show lower attraction and affinity if they have seen a still picture of their fellow participants. One other factor that might be involved in hyperpersonal CMC is self-disclosure – the tendency to tell someone intimate facts about yourself.

Stafford and Reske (1990) looked at how couples who were geographically close felt about each other compared to couples who were geographically distant. Being geographically distant, and communicating by letter, was associated with feeling more in love. Could Walther's hyperpersonal approach to CMC explain this decidedly low technology effect of medium as well? One problem is that these couples have obviously met, so there might be little opportunity for optimising self-presentation. On the other hand, letter writing is asynchronous and visually anonymous, so perhaps Walther's model is applicable to other media.

4.2 Self-disclosure and computer-mediated communication

Both experimental and anecdotal evidence suggest that CMC and general internet-based behaviour can be characterised as containing high levels of self-disclosure. Rheingold (1993) claims that new, meaningful relationships can be formed in cyberspace because of, not despite, its unique features. He further argues that people will reveal more intimate details about themselves in this medium. Similarly, Wallace (1999) argues that, 'The tendency to disclose more to a computer ... is an important ingredient of what seems to be happening on the internet' (p. 151). Self-disclosure has been studied in a number of different settings using computers. For example, in the medical field:

- Psychiatric patients have reported more symptoms and undesirable behaviours when interviewed by computer rather than face-to-face (Greist *et al.*, 1973).
- Clients at a sexually transmitted disease clinic reported more sexual partners, more previous visits to an STD clinic, and more symptoms to a computer than to a doctor (Robinson and West, 1992).
- Pre-clinical psychiatric interviews conducted using CMC compared with face-to-face yield more honest, candid answers (Ferriter, 1993).

Other contexts also suggest similar findings:

- People report high levels of self-disclosure to online friends and romantic partners (Parks and Floyd, 1996).
- Rosson (1999) analysed 133 stories posted by internet users on a resource called 'Web Storybase'. Overall, 81 of the stories contained personal information of some sort.
- In a study of 'coming out on the internet', McKenna and Bargh (1998) argue that participation in online newsgroups gives people the benefit of 'disclosing a long secret part of one's self' (p. 682).
- Compared with a pencil-and-paper survey, answers to an electronic survey are less socially desirable and lead to the disclosure of more information about the self (Kiesler and Sproull, 1986).

Box 3.3 describes how self-disclosure can be investigated.

3.3 *Self-disclosure, anonymity and self-awareness*

Joinson (2001) conducted three studies to answer the questions:

- Is self-disclosure higher when people interact by CMC rather than face-to-face?
- Does self-disclosure increase when those communicating cannot see each other?
- What is the role of private and public self-awareness in self-disclosure during CMC?

The methodology was virtually identical for each experiment: participants who had not previously met arrived separately at the psychology laboratory, and were seated in a cubicle with a 'chat' program running on a computer. In pairs, they were then given a dilemma to discuss ('Which five people should be saved in the event of a nuclear war?'). Face-to-face participants sat opposite each other in the same room and discussed the same dilemma. Their conversations were recorded and subsequently transcribed. Two independent raters (who were blind to group status) examined the transcribed discussions and measured the extent of participant self-disclosure.

Experiment 1: In this experiment there were two conditions: 20 pairs discussed the dilemma, either face-to-face or using the computers. In this experiment, the CMC participants disclosed four times as much information about themselves as the face-to-face participants.

Experiment 2: In this experiment, there were again two conditions: 20 new pairs discussed the dilemma using CMC, while either visually anonymous or when they could see the other participant via a video link. As predicted, very little was disclosed in the video link condition (0.63 disclosures per condition on average), while those in the visually anonymous condition disclosed significantly more (3.05 disclosures on average).

Experiment 3: In this experiment, participants' level of self-awareness was manipulated. Public self-awareness (concern about others' impressions) was either increased by using a video link and an expectation that the pairs would meet or reduced by using a darkened corridor and lack of video link. Private self-awareness (focus on your own self) was either increased by showing participants pictures of themselves or reduced by showing them a cartoon. The results showed that the highest level of self-disclosure was when participants experienced increased private self-focus alongside reduced public self-awareness, implying that when people use CMC to disclose large amounts of information they might be experiencing these states interacting together. Another striking aspect of these studies was that they have all the elements – limited time, lack of anticipated interaction, synchronous communication – that Walther argues would tend to reduce social communication.

Joinson concluded that one of the major causes of hyperpersonal interaction during CMC is heightened self-disclosure, which is likely to be caused by CMC leading to reduced public self-awareness and increased private self-awareness (Matheson and Zanna, 1988). Because self-disclosure tends to be reciprocated, and is the foundation of trust and intimacy in a relationship, Joinson argues that high levels of self-disclosure will lead to high levels of affiliation and liking in CMC groups.

Activity 3.5

Make a list of the people to whom you disclose intimate information about yourself. Next to each person's name, write: (a) the type of information you disclose (e.g. about your feelings, problems, and so on); and (b) whether you would be happy to tell that person everything about yourself, or would be selective about your choice of what to disclose.

Comment

Looking at your list, the first thing you might consider is the number of people you self-disclose to. Presumably people in your family or close friends are on the list. There might even be someone to whom you'd be happy to tell everything. We would also guess that, although you might be willing to disclose some information about yourself to acquaintances, you would be less likely to reveal intimate details of your life to them. However, there are other factors to take into account – people are sometimes very willing to disclose information about themselves (e.g. to strangers) if there's little chance of them ever meeting the person to whom the disclosure is being made again. Although disclosing intimacies about yourself usually requires a high level of trust between you and the other person, not all self-disclosure is intimate, and its power comes from your vulnerability – so if you disclose to a stranger, you may not feel vulnerable because you do not expect them to be able to use that information to harm you. If we disclose too early in a social relationship, it can make the other person feel uncomfortable, partly because they feel that they should reciprocate – that is, disclose something intimate back to you.

In this section, we have seen that the affordances new technology provides influence how we interact using that technology – the lack of visual cues has been posited as key in determining the social presence conveyed by a medium, and it has also been implicated in both reduced social communication and increased social communication and affiliation. The study of CMC is just beginning to consider why the unique properties of CMC can promote both task-oriented and socially oriented communication, both antisocial and overly social behaviour, both increased self-disclosure and increased control over one's self-presentation. In the following section, we look at an area, education, where the design of software and CMC environments, as well as the balance between task-oriented and social communication, are crucial.

Summary Section 4

- The social information processing model argues that CMC and face-to-face interaction differ only in the rate of social information exchange, not the quantity. Thus, if given extra time, CMC will be like face-to-face communication.
- An increasing body of work suggests that CMC is more social than face-to-face, right from the word go, and does not support the social information processing model.
- The hyperpersonal communication model suggests that this overly social communication is because of four key factors: shared social categorisation, optimising self-presentation, format of CMC, and the feedback loop.
- However, hyperpersonal CMC might not even be constrained by these limits, and might occur in synchronous CMC. For instance, the evidence of heightened self-disclosure in various different CMC formats suggests that hyperpersonal communication might occur in 'one-shot' experimental groups and in a variety of medical and other settings.

5   Education and computers

Since the mid-1970s, computers have become an increasingly important part of people's experience of education. Governments across Europe are attempting to increase access to computer technology in schools and, in the UK, the appropriate use of this technology is one of the features being built into a definition of student 'graduateness'.

Over the years there have been a variety of visions for the use of computers in educational settings. Initially, many of these focused on the potential of computer technology to support *individual* learners, perhaps because the technology was seen as perfect for matching the teaching to the existing level of performance and perceived needs of the learner, so called *contingent instruction.*

Psychologists and educationalists who advocated an associationist model of learning (based around conditioning theory – see also Chapter 2, Section 6.1) believed that the computer had the potential to deliver carefully tailored contingent instruction which enabled individual learners to be taught at their own pace and at an appropriate level. Software designers set about producing programs that guided learners through educational activities by breaking them down into small, incremental steps. Such programs rely heavily on repetition and schedules of reward and feedback, which is why this particular kind of software became known as 'drill and practice software'. This software was, and continues to be, popular for teaching skills such as basic arithmetic where practise is seen as being necessary if the requisite skills are to be acquired.

However, there are other ways, besides providing opportunities for practise, in which computer technology can be used to support the individual learner – as you are no doubt discovering through this course's Virtual Learning Environment (VLE).

Much of this chapter has been about the potential of new technologies to support both social and task-oriented interactions. How does this apply in educational settings? There is evidence to suggest that, whilst it is not a panacea, interacting around the computer can be a particularly productive way of learning (Light and Littleton, 1999). For example, Neil Mercer's analyses of children interacting around a historical simulation package demonstrated how the computer can provide a valuable focus for learners' joint activity and discussion (Mercer, 1995). However, the computer is also capable of mediating learning relationships in new ways. It is not only capable of *supporting* collaborative endeavour, it also has the potential to *transform* the ways in which collaborative activity is organised, creating new educational opportunities and environments. A good example of this is the opportunities for learning that arise within CMC.

A student participating in a computer conference

Computer technology enables large numbers of learners to communicate with one another despite being separated in time and space. At university level, for example, the possibilities offered by CMC have resulted in the development of VLEs where tutors and students interact using electronic conferencing systems, discussions boards and forums. Using internet connections they can log on to discussion zones to take part in ongoing debates or initiate ones of their own. They can read and digest the comments of other participants in the conference and then 'post' their own contribution for others to respond to in due course. Such discussions can extend over a period of days or weeks because the record of their progress is available whenever participants are able to access them.

These VLEs have become increasingly popular, in the UK at least. One practical reason for this is the growth in student numbers in higher education and the need to provide alternatives to face-to-face teaching. In addition, CMC is also seen to offer pedagogic and psychological benefits by encouraging peer-to-peer communication. In the rest of this section we will outline these benefits as well as highlighting some of the problems which may arise.

5.1 Computer-mediated communication in education

The traditional face-to-face university tutorial has been described as having an 'Initiation-Response-Evaluation' (I-R-E) structure (Beattie, 1982). The tutor asks a student a question, the student replies, and the tutor comments on that answer. In this model, the tendency is for the tutor to dominate the discussion, and opportunities for other forms of interaction – for instance, with other students – are thus minimal. A number of researchers (e.g. Tolmie and Boyle, 2000) have argued that, by contrast, CMC encourages higher levels of peer-based interaction and that this type of interaction is particularly valuable for learning. However, while CMC may well *enable* such interactions to take place, whether or not they actually do may depend on the expectations of the students and their previous learning experiences.

Learning can be seen as a process of **enculturation**: as children, students, have to 'learn how to learn' in school contexts. They have to learn how to participate in the practices of the school and use forms of 'schooled discourse'. So, given that much school classroom talk conforms to the classic I-R-E structure described above (Edwards and Mercer, 1987), it is perhaps not surprising that many students in UK higher education appear to be accustomed to having the tutor or teacher in control of what they say and do, and expect them to 'take the lead'.

Enculturation
A process through which people adopt specific cultural practices and act in accordance with cultural norms.

Even when CMC systems are set up explicitly to encourage interaction between students, it is not uncommon for the tutor to contribute the majority of items to the discussion and for the I-R-E model to establish itself in CMC environments. For example, Light *et al.* (2000) observed that students who were given the opportunity to engage in peer discussion in an innovative computer environment nevertheless waited in expectation of the 'proper answer' from the lecturer.

It is also clear that the same issues of self-presentation and social comparison, which are significant in face-to-face contexts, are also important to students engaged in CMC discussions. Light and Light (1999) noted how the psychology students they studied felt exposed putting their ideas or questions into writing, and the permanent visibility of their contributions within the computer conference associated with the module was a source of anxiety for many. They feared that they might be criticised: 'Trying to express an opinion on something you don't know much about anyway can be a bit daunting when the whole world can see you making a real wally of yourself' (Light and Light, 1999, p. 171). The notion of personal criticism was not clearly distinguished from criticism of ideas. The students were also intensely interested in, and sensitive to, their own ability and the quality of their work relative to their peers. Messages posted to the conference were often used as a source of informal 'feedback' or a means of gauging 'what level everyone is on'. Such social comparison is unsurprising. From a very early age learners are highly skilled at making sense of educational contexts and activities. They talk about learning experiences in terms of ability and effort (Bird, 1994) and are motivated to understand what it means to be a learner and what it means to do and succeed at educational tasks. The social climate of comparison, competition, success, failure, and issues of relative status in the classroom rapidly becomes established within the early years of schooling (Crocker and Cheesman, 1988) and remains with students throughout their educational careers.

So, whilst computers undoubtedly have the potential to reorganise learning interactions in a variety of significant ways, the established culture of learning can have a significant impact on the prospects for new CMC initiatives. Existing practices clearly offer resistance to the 'bolting on' of new forms of educational technology (Crook and Light, 1999).

One challenge associated with CMC is how to promote the desired interaction between learners. For example, in a study of Open University students using a CMC system, only a third were classified as actively participating (Mason, 1995). And in another study of 3000 online students, in any one month there were only about 100 who were active contributors to the CMC-based discussions (Morris and Naughton, 1999). Similar low participation rates are reported across a range of CMC experiences (Tolmie and Boyle, 2000).

It is interesting to note that lack of participation seems to be a real problem, not only in educational CMC but also in the workplace. On the other hand, organisations take many steps to reduce social use of email and chat. Perhaps educators and companies need to encourage social communication, while at the same time using the increased levels of participation to achieve learning or workplace objectives.

Despite these problems, many researchers point to the pedagogical benefit of CMC for promoting collaborative learning. For instance, Tolmie and Boyle (2000) argue that disagreements amongst peers mean that, because there is not an authority source, students have to 'make explicit the basis for their ideas' (p. 121). This type of discussion may lead to 'conceptual growth'. Tolmie and Boyle (2000) conclude that, 'This framework pinpoints the value of asynchronous e-mail exchange: it is not just that it facilitates discussion between students, but that any disagreements which occur will promote growth in understanding ...' (p. 121).

Whilst there is evidence that students often learn vicariously, by observing other people's discussions (McKendree *et al.*, 1998), it has also been suggested that CMC systems can be used to improve students' *argumentation skills* – for example, by reviewing arguments. In discussing the importance of argumentation, Reader and Joinson (1998) point out that what students usually take from a tutorial discussion are just the conclusions, which are considered to be important. Of greater pedagogical importance, however, is an understanding of the actual processes which led to these conclusions (McKendree *et al.*, 1998). The advent of CMC could thus bring with it a sense of an academic discipline as *process* rather than *product*, promoting a shift away from the 'school ethos' (Light *et al.*, 2000) to something much more egalitarian between tutor and student. Challenging existing conceptions of the processes of teaching and learning is thus a recurrent theme in studies of CMC. The emphasis is on the desirability of moving away from established 'delivery models of education, so that "the tutor's" task becomes that of structuring challenging conversations among a community of learners rather than channelling expertise or knowledge to the student ...' (Light *et al.*, 2000, p. 199).

5.2 Improving educational computing

Many applications of computing to education have been aimed at teaching academic content rather than the critical analysis, evaluation and synthesis of knowledge. Yet if we think about typical examination questions, they usually require students to 'critically evaluate' or to 'compare and contrast', rather than to 'write down everything they know about a topic'.

The use of educational CMC raises different concerns, however. Whilst in theory students should achieve 'conceptual growth' through text-based discussions, this requires participation and discussion between peers in the first place. One way to encourage this is to bring in assessment of educational CMC, but then fresh problems arise such as 'What exactly do you assess?' An alternative way of promoting participation involves allowing contributors to remain anonymous, thus overcoming the fear of appearing foolish. This has been used with mixed results. For example, in Australia, Chester and Gwynne (1998) allowed students to use pseudonyms to try to create 'hyperpersonal' interaction in a learning environment. They reported that anonymity 'allowed students to find a strong and confident voice', and that, 'two-thirds of the students rated their participation in the subject as greater than face-to-face classes' (1998, p. 6). Whilst in general there was a strong sense of community and a relative lack of antisocial behaviour among these students, there were also some problems. For example, one student using the pseudonym 'Hashmann' adopted the persona of a rapper with Black American slang who 'swore', wrote in capitals, and flamed other students who made moderate and sensible suggestions (1998, p. 8).

One lesson from the work of Chester and Gwynne is how educators beginning to use CMC in teaching can use the psychological processes that occur online to encourage (or discourage) certain types of behaviour.

Activity 3.6

How might online psychological processes have been used to discourage the kind of behaviour exhibited by Hashmann? Reflect a moment upon the implications of your suggestions for the more positive behaviours Chester and Gwynne report.

Comment

The easiest way to discourage behaviour like that exhibited by Hashmann would be to remove the anonymity allowed to students. However, Chester and Gwynne report that the anonymity they allowed their students was beneficial most of the time. This dilemma mirrors one faced by most people involved in policing internet behaviour – discouraging negative, antisocial behaviour by making people accountable also risks removing the positive behaviours encouraged by anonymity. There are ways in which it might be possible to retain anonymity and encourage 'right' behaviours (for instance, by prompting certain social identities or norms of behaviour). The importance of social identity in CMC is discussed in the next section of this chapter.

Summary Section 5

- There have been different visions relating to the use of computers in educational settings.
- Some of these visions focus on the potential of the computer to support individual learners, whilst others focus on opportunities for promoting collaboration between peers.
- The computer is not only capable of supporting collaborative endeavour, it has the potential to transform the ways in which collaborative activity is organised, creating new educational opportunities and environments.
- Whilst the computer has the potential to reorganise learning interactions in various ways, the established culture of learning can impact significantly on the prospect for new CMC initiatives.
- There are still important lessons to be learned if students are to be empowered to learn through participation in online interactions with their peers.

6 Group dynamics on the internet

The use of CMC in education illustrates the importance of understanding group behaviour on the internet for enhancing learning. While CMC would seem to be ideally suited to group work (whether educational or in the workplace), actual implementations are often disappointing. As we outlined earlier in this chapter, a common approach to mediated communication is to argue that a decrease in social cues leads to the medium (and therefore the communication that happens via the medium) being less social. So, it would be expected that group behaviour via a medium such as the internet should be hampered. This is certainly one explanation for some of the problems outlined in the previous section. However, work on group polarisation during CMC suggests that communication on the internet is anything but 'de-socialised'.

6.1 Group polarisation and conformity online

A consistent finding from studies of telephone use has been that groups became more extreme in their decision making when discussing using audio or computer links (Reid, 1981; Spears and Lea, 1992). As we have seen, one theory is that CMC encourages more uninhibited, anti-normative behaviour, which leads to a group's decision becoming more extreme because the balance of persuasive information leans that way.

Spears and Lea (1992) note, however, that many theories of social influence in groups rely, not on the amount and balance of information exchanged, but on the social processes that occur within a group. These processes are called 'normative influence' because people are changing their attitudes not because of the strength or number of arguments, but because they are conforming to the group norm. Box 3.4 explores the effects of both group membership and anonymity on this shift in attitudes.

3.4 Social identity, anonymity and group polarisation

Spears et al. (1990) used a computer-mediated conferencing system to examine the role of anonymity and group membership on group polarisation. Groups of three students discussed a series of topics (e.g. 'All nuclear power stations should be phased out') using the CMC system. Group membership was manipulated by making salient throughout the experiment either that participants were members of a group or that they were individuals. Visual anonymity was manipulated either by seating the three participants together in a room or by seating them in separate cubicles. Before the experiment, all participants completed initial measures of their attitudes to the discussion topics. Before the discussions, participants were also given a booklet that gave the results of a survey of their peers in response to the topics. So, for the first issue they discussed (whether or not 'Nationalised industries should be sold off'), the participants were informed that '32.2 per cent supported the sale of nationalised industries, and 67.8 per cent were against the sale'. Once participants had discussed the topics, they completed the same attitude measure, so that any shift in opinion could be measured.

The results of the experiments were as follows. In the visually anonymous condition, increasing the salience of the group led to a move towards the group norm, while increasing the salience of personal identity led to a shift away from the group norm. It is difficult for the reduced social cues model to account for such findings – in the visually anonymous condition, social context (in the form of group salience) had a marked effect on group polarisation. This is not what the reduced social cues approach would predict – for advocates of that approach, visual anonymity is all that should really matter, because their model of group polarisation relies solely on people making more extreme arguments. What Spears et al. showed was that CMC does not occur in a social vacuum – instead, people's reliance on the norms of their group are heightened when a social identity is activated.

Spears and Lea argue that the visual anonymity inherent in most CMC will, when a social identity is salient, strengthen the impact of social norms, and hence the normative influence. However, the crucial element here is whether or not the social or normative context supports the salience of a personal or social identity. When a social identity is salient, visual anonymity will increase adherence to group norms. When a personal identity is salient, the same anonymity will reduce the impact of social norms, and increase the person's adherence to their own personal norms and standards. This model is illustrated in Figure 3.4.

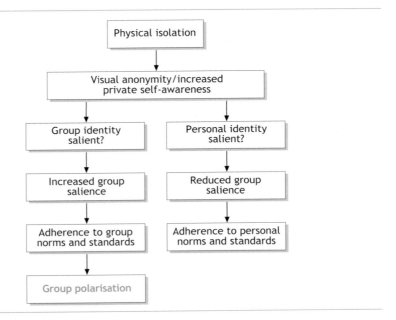

Figure 3.4   Social identity and group polarisation (Source: adapted from Spears and Lea, 1992, Figure 2.5, p. 53)

Much of the time the internet is ripe for high levels of conformity. For many people who use the internet, the codes or norms of behaviour are uncertain. Imagine you go into a café that has just opened, and you sit down to be served. You look over to the other patrons, and see that they are queuing with trays. The likely outcome is that you'll follow their lead – in a new environment you use other people as a guide to how to behave.

There is plenty of evidence that when new internet users, referred to as 'newbies', enter 'cyberspace', there is a concerted effort by experienced users to make them conform to the types of behaviour expected (Wallace, 1999). There are 'netiquette' guides with suggested modes of behaviour and newbies are criticised for 'wrong' behaviour (e.g. sending personal replies to a mass mailing list, or excessive quotation during discussions). Usually, it takes very little time for new internet users to grasp the conventions and norms of the new environment, and to behave in accordance with those norms. People who violate the norms of the group are often reprimanded by more experienced users.

Try to think of the last time you entered a new environment where you were uncertain how to behave. It might have been for a new activity, a new job, somewhere on holiday, or beginning an Open University course. Often these occasions cause people a considerable amount of anxiety – and in these situations we're usually acutely aware that we are using other people to guide our behaviour. Even when in familiar environments we use others' behaviour to guide us. Box 3.5 describes how norms were developed over time when a group of students started to communicate via email.

3.5 The development of norms in electronic communication

Postmes *et al.* (2000) examined the development of norms in groups of students communicating using an electronic mail system. They argued that one of the oversights of social identity approaches to CMC is that the social identities and norms are assumed to pre-exist and to be activated through associating oneself with a group label. The students in their study were taking part in a voluntary computerised statistics course called 'Dr Stat'. The computer system also provided an email facility to contact other users, something students soon discovered and began using. Postmes *et al.* hypothesised that, for the students using this email system, the norms they applied to their interactions would develop over time, and would only be applied within a group of students, and not to communication with members of staff at the University.

When they analysed the messages sent by students, their hypotheses were supported. First, over time, the typical type of communication (e.g. humorous or flaming) that characterised a group became more pronounced. So, if a group began by adopting a certain type of communication, this became more marked over time. This suggests that the norms within a CMC group are dynamically socially constructed during the interaction. The second hypothesis, that these norms would be constrained to the participants' own group, was also supported. When Postmes *et al.* looked at communication between students and staff, there was no evidence that students applied the norms developed within their own group to their communication with staff members. This finding suggests that the use of normative communication styles within a group was based on social contexts and shared group identity, rather than just learned responses.

6.2 Electronic communities

Spears and Lea's work indicates that being a member of a computer-based social group can have important psychological consequences. As we have seen, there is pressure toward conformity on the internet both from the enforcement of codes of behaviour by experienced internet users and from the increased adherence to group norms when one is visually anonymous. When we add to this the tendency for people with shared interests to group together on the internet, it should come as no surprise that electronic communities readily spring up in cyberspace.

The traditional notion of a community is usually based on geographical proximity or, in some cases, similar interests or expertise (e.g. the academic community, student community, bridge players). This led to an initial questioning of whether or not a community can exist online, and later whether an online 'community' provides the same psychological support as a real-life community (Kraut *et al.*, 1998).

According to Haythornthwaite *et al.* (1998), 'The question of whether or not one can find "community" on-line is asked largely by those who do not experience it' (p. 212). Instead, the issue is now how online communities differ from 'real-life' (i.e. face-to-face) ones, and in particular whether the benefits of membership of an online community are similar to those of 'real-life' community membership.

The most obvious difference between being a member of an electronic and a real-life community is the nature of the membership, both demographically and geographically. While being a Bonsai tree enthusiast may give one a sense of 'groupness' in real life with other enthusiasts around the globe, the internet allows this group to become more than a mental representation of shared interests. Being a member of such a community has a whole series of advantages for its members: it provides a sense of belonging, a support and advice source, and gives its members access to a shared social identity. However, some research from the USA has questioned whether members of online communities benefit in the same way that real-life community members do. In 1998 a group of researchers led by Robert Kraut and Sara Kiesler published the preliminary findings from the HomeNet project at Carnegie Mellon University (Kraut *et al.*, 1998). The HomeNet project gave computers with an internet connection to 256 people in 93 households in Pittsburgh, Pennsylvania (following withdrawals, the sample was reduced to 169 people in 73 households). They tracked the internet use and mental well-being of participants in the project over two years. Their conclusion was that: 'Greater use of the internet was associated with small, but statistically significant declines in social involvement ... and with increases in loneliness ... Greater use of the internet was also associated with increases in depression' (Kraut *et al.*, 1998, p. 1028).

Activity 3.7

Write down some of the reasons why using the internet might make some people more depressed. Keep these reasons in mind when you read the discussion of Kraut *et al.*'s findings below, and see if your initial thoughts have changed.

These findings drrew not only a large amount of media coverage (e.g. 'Sad, lonely world discovered in Cyberspace': headline in the *New York Times*, 30 August 1998), but also a large amount of scrutiny and criticism from psychologists involved in internet research. It seemed paradoxical that a medium used mainly for social ends seemed to be de-socialising. One possibility is that the internet is another technology that tends to 'privatise' leisure time (as with other essentially private forms of entertainment like watching television or reading a book), so people have less time for social activities and involvement. However, Kraut *et al.* rejected this argument because the 'major use of the internet is social' (1998, p. 1029). Moreover, research by the Pew internet American Life study suggests that internet use increases social communication within a home, and reduces television watching (Pew internet and American Life March 2001 Survey). So, using the internet might replace a private activity with a more sociable one.

Kraut and his colleagues went on to suggest that the ties created between people on the internet might be generally weak, whereas ties built in real life tend to be strong. A strong tie is characterised by 'frequent contact, deep feelings of affection and obligation ... that generally buffer people from life's stresses and that lead to better social and psychological outcomes' (Kraut *et al.*, 1998, p. 1019). Conversely, weak network ties are characterised by 'superficial and easily broken bonds, infrequent contact and narrow focus' (ibid.). Thus, although the main use of the internet in the HomeNet project was for interpersonal communication, the ties that bound the people communicating were weak, and so did not offer the same psychological support as a strong (i.e. face-to-face) tie. For instance, the HomeNet researchers point out that few of their sample made new friends online (although the researcher only seemed to count people as friends if they met face-to-face at some point). They also argue that because online friends aren't physically close at hand, they are unable to offer tangible support, nor are they likely to understand the 'context' for conversation, making discussion more difficult. They present two case studies from their sample which imply that the internet is not suitable for more delicate/emotional subjects, with participants reverting to the telephone in these situations. In the first case, one participant noticed how, although she liked email contact with her daughter at college, she tended, if she needed to support her daughter when homesick or depressed, to revert to the telephone. In the second case, a clergyman used the internet to swap sermon ideas, but used the telephone for advice about negotiating his employment contract.

Upon reading the last paragraph, you might be feeling a sense of déjà vu. As we discussed earlier in the chapter, the 'loss' approach to the study of mediated communication has a relatively long history. Indeed, Sara Kiesler, one of the key HomeNet researchers, was one of the main proponents of the reduced social cues approach to CMC in the 1980s and early 1990s. However, the HomeNet researchers didn't expect, or predict, a negative effect of internet use.

However, the picture is not quite so clear-cut. First, Kraut *et al.* tend to confuse correlation with causality. It is just as reasonable to suggest that people who were already feeling depressed turned to the internet, rather than that the internet caused depression (Shapiro, 1999). For instance, lonely people tend to watch television more than the average non-lonely person (Canary and Spitzberg, 1993), although it is again difficult to disentangle which is cause and which is effect. Without a control condition in the HomeNet project, the experimenters could not tell whether increased internet use was a cause or an effect of the increased incidence of depression. A second problem was that the HomeNet study involved families with children who were due to enter college. It would be expected that, if your child went to college, there would be both reduced social contact in the home (they have, after all, moved away), while the family might communicate by email more to keep in touch.

A similar problem occurs with the selection of their sample: parents involved in the running of a local school. People who are at an extreme end of a continuum (in this case, community involvement) tend to reduce their involvement over time (a phenomenon called regression to the mean). So, the HomeNet participants would be expected to reduce their involvement in the local community whether they had computers or not. Again, there was no control condition, so it is impossible to say.

Similar criticisms of the HomeNet research were proposed by McKenna and Bargh (2000). They noted that new technology is often associated with fear stories (e.g. there was once a movie called *Murder by Television*). They also noted that an earlier study, from the same group of researchers (Rimm, 1995), which claimed that the internet was 'awash with pornography', was not only based on false premises and quickly discredited, but the ramifications of the initial press coverage of these faulty results were still being felt (e.g. in the Computer Decency Act in the USA).

There is a clear link here between the importance of psychologists disseminating their findings, and a recognition that public policy can be influenced by the (often superficial) coverage of these findings. Notions such as 'internet addiction' often enter public discourse, and even influence government policy, encouraged by extensive coverage by the press, but supported by little empirical evidence. In the case of internet addiction, the term was coined by a medical doctor as a tongue-in-cheek swipe at the burgeoning number of addictions sponsored by mental health professionals. In a (so far) unsuccessful attempt to rein in the internet addiction bandwagon, Walther published his own tongue-in-cheek study of 'Communication Addiction Disorder', which he claimed led to people 'talking too much'. While no one would suggest that psychologists resist reaching a wider audience through the press, the role of psychologists in helping to set the public agenda is coming under considerable scrutiny. It is also worth noting that, although psychological methods often strive for objectivity through carefully controlled designs and sophisticated statistical analysis, the choice of hypotheses and the interpretation of results may nevertheless be heavily influenced by the researchers' own preconceptions. As we've also seen, the design of the typical CMC experiment (use of visually anonymous strangers; one-shot, time-limited groups) can have implications for the patterns of interaction that are normally attributed to the medium.

McKenna and Bargh point out in relation to the strength of the results of the HomeNet study that 'for the entire group of participants, the average reported level of depression after 2 years of being on the internet was less than it had been before being on the internet' (2000, p. 59). They also note that, although Kraut *et al.* are correct in noting that their participants' local social circle decreased (from 24 to 23 people), their wider social network increased from 25 to 32. So, overall, internet use seems to be associated with a widening in the number of friends and acquaintances. It is also worth questioning whether a small change (e.g. from 24 to 23) is meaningful even if it is statistically significant.

What are we to make of the HomeNet findings and subsequent criticism? On the one hand, this study neatly illustrates an ideological stance taken by researchers in discussing the psychological impact of new technology (see Box 3.6). It also highlights the methodological problems of conceptualising the nature of a 'strong' tie on the internet. If a romance develops on the internet, this stronger tie will quite likely lead to a meeting face-to-face. For instance, America Online (AOL) estimates that 10,000 marriages have come about through its online dating service. Once a relationship leads to marriage or cohabitation, it is extremely likely that internet contact diminishes between the two parties. So, in that sense, the internet is an enabling technology rather than a replacing one.

In a non-romantic setting, the prevalence of 'weak' ties is likely to be relatively high because most groupings on the internet are based on shared interest, so the focus of any interpersonal communication is likely to be limited. But, as we saw earlier, the combination of shared group membership and visual anonymity can create highly socially motivated behaviours. Perhaps the social network ties are weak in a traditional sense, but the ties that bind a group together in a shared sense of identity are high. Indeed, the impact of a virtual community's dissolution on the members, discussed in Section 6.3, suggests that this might be the case.

3.6 Utopian and dystopian visions of the internet

While the existence of online communities is little questioned any more, the impact of the internet on society in general has been the focus of much controversy. Just as CMC theories tend to stress either the benefits (warm models) or the costs (cool models) of CMC, so theorists of the social impact of the internet tend to stress the potential benefits of the internet or its dangers. Utopian approaches to the internet tend to stress its role in bringing together people into communities, increasing opportunity and openness and even accountability and democracy. Meanwhile, dystopian approaches to the internet stress its potential negative effects for the user (e.g. addiction, attracting paedophiles, cyber affairs, fragmentation of selfhood), and for society as a whole (the disintegration of community, increased depression, cyber terrorists), and conjure up images of lonely internet users who never leave the house and cannot cope with normal (by which they mean face-to-face) social interaction.

Undoubtedly, both visions of the internet betray more about the views of the protagonists rather than any 'real' or 'objective' truth about the future.

6.3 The disintegration of an online community

Elizabeth Reid (1998) has documented the downfall of a virtual community, called JennyMUSH, which was set up for abused women – and relied heavily on trust and intimacy. On one occasion, when the community's controllers (called 'Wizards' because the technology emerged for supporting Dungeons and Dragons games) were offline, one person changed their persona to 'Daddy' and began verbally abusing the other members. When the 'Wizards' logged on they found all the members of the community collected together in one 'room'. The

Wizards 'toaded' the member called 'Daddy' (i.e. they removed his or her ability to speak), whereupon the remaining members of the community turned to a vitriolic assault on their tormentor. Reid points out the similarity of this treatment to medieval notions of justice, and concludes by stating that the community never really recovered after this breaking of trust.

A similar breaking of trust is reported by Marc Feldman (2000) in the form of cases of 'Munchausen by internet', where people in online support groups claim illnesses that they do not have. Feldman outlines four such cases. In one, a woman called Barbara posted to a cystic fibrosis support group. Barbara claimed that she was waiting at home to die, and was being cared for by an elder sister (Amy). The group sent many supportive messages to Barbara, and were distressed to learn from Amy that she died a few days later. It was only when the group noticed that Amy shared Barbara's spelling errors that they questioned the story. Amy admitted to the hoax, and taunted the group for their gullibility. Feldman warns that a common reaction to such cases is for the online group to split into believers and doubters of the claims, or for people to leave the group in disgust.

Box 3.7 comments on the multiple identities that may be developed by some participants in online communities.

3.7 Virtual communities and identity

Elizabeth Reid (1998), who researches and participates in online communities, observes that some users adopt 'a different persona for every mood and every day of the week' (p. 36). However, Reid sees these multiple selves as operating on a 'very limited psychological and social plane' (ibid.). She also notes that a revealed deception within an online community can lead to a feeling of betrayal, especially from those who have formed intimate relationships with the deceiver. She further argues that the tendency to develop an online persona leads to rather sterile communities with a limited range of expression – play-acting a person does not give you access to the range of expression available in real life.

Projecting multiple, fragmented selves into virtual reality is a popular activity on the internet, and may indeed allow people to explore previously hidden aspects of themselves (Turkle, 1995). But Reid cautions that multiple selves can be damaging to online interaction and the development of meaningful relationships. However, the trend for developing online personae tends to be context dependent, and, whatever the number of multiple selves, they are all in some way linked to an embodied self. In Section 7.2 of this chapter we consider what impact virtual life might have on people's identities.

Rheingold (1993) suggests that the breaking of trust is the most damaging aspect of virtual communities, and the behaviour most likely to lead to their disintegration. It is interesting to note that many real-life communities seem to survive an act of betrayal by an erstwhile member – suggesting that, on the internet, trust is particularly important. It also gives some support to the contention of the HomeNet researchers that electronic communities are characterised by weak ties. Box 3.8 explores a related issue, namely the ethics of conducting research on electronic communities.

3.8 Ethics and researching online communities

As in most participant observation studies, the key ethical consideration in researching online communities is the issue of consent and whether or not to inform people of their unwitting involvement as research participants. A number of early studies took the approach that behaviour on the internet was a public broadcast, and as such the participants had effectively given up the right to be informed of a study. This approach has obvious benefits for the researcher, but when a number of online communities objected to being the guinea pigs for research there was a change in procedure. Now, researchers conducting observation studies online must request the consent of the members. Although this may influence the behaviour of the participants, the need to avoid exploiting such a rich source of data, and potentially breaking the trust of community members, is paramount.

Summary Section 6

- Research on social identity suggests that normative influence can be heightened during CMC when group members are visually anonymous and group membership is salient.
- Although it is accepted that electronic communities exist, they may lack the solidity and psychological benefits of real-life communities.
- The impact of the internet on mental health is unclear: the work of Kraut *et al.* showing a negative impact has been strongly criticised, and there is little evidence for internet addiction.
- Codes of ethics need to be fully developed for internet research.

7   Looking to the future

We began this discussion of CMC with the telephone. We did this for two main reasons: first, because theories developed to account for telephone use have been applied to CMC; and, second, to illustrate the dangers of predicting the impact of new technology on behaviour. Today, it is difficult to imagine that the telephone was first conceptualised as an 'electric toy' with little use beyond one-way broadcasting. In the future, it may be that our present conceptions of the possible implications and uses of computer technology are similarly laughable. With that warning in mind, we will now consider the impact of new technology on the person and society, and plot potential developments and possible psychological effects. Our key assumption is that, despite the internet becoming ubiquitous, effects of the medium will remain – just as we communicate differently when interacting face-to-face or on the telephone, despite many years of experience of both.

7.1   The role of the environment

In the past, psychology has tended to ignore the physical environment in favour of laboratory studies which take place in, by definition, a 'non-environment'. This tendency was noted by Brunswik (1956) who argued that, 'Both historically and systematically psychology has forgotten that it is a science of organism–environment relationship, and has become a science of the organism' (p. 6). However, the role of the physical environment in influencing behaviour has been well documented (e.g. Bell *et al.*, 1996). We would argue that the virtual environment has a similarly profound impact on our behaviour. This impact takes two forms: a direct influence via the affordances a system offers for social interaction and behaviour; and an indirect impact via mediating psychological processes. As such, the design of a virtual environment needs to be as carefully planned as the design of any physical environment. Just like the design of the built environment, so the design of a virtual environment will have similarly profound implications, not only for what we perceive as possible, but also for how we behave within the boundaries of the technological affordances.

7.2   Computers and the self

Some post-modern thinkers have argued that the essentially modernist vision of the self as a unified, essential, internal construct is ill suited to the post-modern world of uncertainty, new media and accelerated access to information (e.g. Gergen, 1992). Gergen argues that the growth of communication technology has led to a multitude of voices being heard, and a 'fragmented' sense of self. According to Gergen, the issue is not how we re-establish a core sense of self and identity, but rather how we learn to use new technology to 'play' with our identity. Similarly, Turkle (1995) argues that the development of the internet has led to a 'distributed' self.

However, as the internet develops, it has been argued that even the notion of an embodied self might become redundant. The development of both virtual reality and artificial intelligence suggests that we might be able to send avatars (virtual representations of the self) to interact in cyberspace on our behalf (or, indeed, consciously controlled by us). Will this have implications for our sense of self? Certainly, although what these might be is open to debate. What is likely, however, is that there will be an increasing convergence between reality and virtual reality. To an extent this is already happening. For example, a refrigerator that accesses the internet to order new milk is already on the production line (although whether anyone will want one is another thing entirely). In this sense, a particular focus on the 'psychology of the internet' is likely to become meaningless as increasingly the internet and computers become an integral, unnoticed part of everyday life.

7.3 Computers, work and learning

Computers, and particularly the internet, are beginning to change our notion of both work and education, and the artificial boundary between the two. Already in this course, you will have realised that the use of information technology in education has both costs and benefits. You lose flexibility of study (unless you take a laptop computer on to the bus, and/or can access the internet using a mobile device), and swapping from book to screen can be frustrating. On the other hand, you can interact with the course material in a wholly new way. For example, by using ICT you can access video images and audio material to enhance the information printed in this book, you can look up further information on the internet, and you can participate in additional activities using the VLE.

More fundamentally, the growth of the internet (and intranets) has encouraged the notion of 'lifelong learning'. As organisations encourage the management of knowledge, they are also recognising the notion of organisational learning – that is, not just individuals taking courses, but rather the whole culture of an organisation being focused on acquiring, developing and applying knowledge. The development of corporate universities, as well as increasingly close collaborations between universities and the industrial sector, illustrates this development of thinking. Technology, particularly computers and the internet, are not only making this possible, but also driving its development.

Fundamentally, the introduction of computer technology into schools, colleges and universities is challenging how we conceptualise learning and education. This has been recognised by the Royal Society for the Arts (RSA) in a report *Redefining Work*:

> *In the knowledge age, there will be no premium to be gained from the acquisition of information, for people will have easy access to quantities of information beyond our present ability to grasp. What will be important is the development of critical skills (in all senses) to use information and to evaluate it.*

> *(Bayliss, 1998, p. 53)*

7.4 Final thoughts

Throughout this chapter we have seen that interaction with, and via, technology involves not just the psychological processes of the individual(s) involved, but also much wider issues such as the role of technology in society, the nature and norms of CMC and our notions of what it means to be human. Admittedly, psychological research into the internet has tended to be fine-grained – especially when looking at communication. This is to be expected – most of the early work was conducted from a cognitive and experimental social psychology perspective. Unfortunately, the emphasis on measurement has tended to leave the (often more important) wider issues to sociologists, cultural and media studies and philosophers. However, in tandem with the changing role of technology in society and our lives, psychologists are beginning to address issues like the social impact of the internet and the nature of the 'information society'. In light of the role psychologists played in the development of, for instance, the traditional computer interface, this trend bodes well for a strong voice for psychology, whatever the future brings.

Further reading

Norman, D.A. (1988) *The Psychology of Everyday Things*, New York, Basic Books.

Norman discusses the design of everyday objects, and the psychology behind our interactions with them, in a very readable and accessible way. If you ever wondered why you can't work some seemingly simple objects, this book will tell you.

Johnson, S. (1997) *Interface Culture*, New York, Basic Books.

In this book Johnson discusses the development of computer interfaces and their cultural and psychological impact. Again, very readable.

Wallace, P. (1999) *The Psychology of the Internet*, Cambridge, Cambridge University Press.

This was one of the first textbooks on psychology and the internet. Wallace covers many of the key studies in this developing area, mixing anecdote, observation and experimental evidence adroitly to produce an interesting and well-researched read.

 # References

Adrianson, L. and Hjelmquist, E. (1999) 'Group processes in solving two problems: face to face and computer-mediated communication', *Behaviour and Information Technology*, vol. 18, no. 3, pp. 179–98.

Argyle, M. and Dean, J. (1965) 'Eye-contact, distance and affiliation', *Sociometry*, vol. 28, pp. 289–304.

Bayliss, V. (1998) *Redefining Work*, London, Royal Society for the Arts.

Beattie G.W. (1982) 'The dynamics of university tutorial groups', *Bulletin Of The British Psychological Society*, vol. 35, April, pp. 147–50.

Bell, P., Greene, T.C, Fisher, J. and Baum, A. (1996) *Environmental Psychology*, London, Harcourt Brace.

Bird, L. (1994) 'Creating the capable body: discourses about ability and effort in primary and secondary school studies' in Mayall, B. (ed.) *Children's Childhoods: Observed and Experienced*, London, Falmer Press.

Brunswik, E. (1956) *Perception and the Representative Design of Psychological Experiments*, Berkeley, University of California Press.

Canary, D.J. and Spitzberg, B.H. (1993) 'Loneliness and media gratification', *Communication Research*, vol. 20, pp. 800–21.

Chester, A. and Gwynne, G. (1998) 'Online teaching: encouraging collaboration through anonymity', *Journal of Computer Mediated Communication* [online], vol. 4, no. 2. Available from: http://jcmc.huji.ac.il/vol4/issue2/chester.html [Accessed 18 December 2001].

Chilcoat, Y. and DeWine, S. (1985) 'Teleconferencing and interpersonal communication perception', *Journal of Applied Communication Research*, vol. 18, pp. 14–32.

Crocker, T. and Cheesman, R. (1988) 'The ability of young children to rank themselves for academic ability', *Educational Studies*, vol. 14, no. 1, pp. 105–10.

Crook, C. and Light, P. (1999) 'Information technology and the culture of student learning' in Bliss, J., Light, P. and Säljö, R. (eds) *Learning Sites: Social and Technological Contexts for Learning*, Oxford, Pergamon.

Edwards, D. and Mercer, N. (1987) *Common Knowledge: The Development of Understanding in the Classroom*, London, Methuen.

Exline, R.V., Gray, D. and Winter, L.C. (1965) 'Affective relations and mutual glances in dyads' in Tomkins, S.S. and Izard, C.E. (eds) *Affect, Cognition and Personality*, New York, Springer.

Faulkner, C. (1998) *The Essence of Human–Computer Interaction*, London, Prentice Hall.

Feldman, M.D. (2000) 'Munchausen by internet: detecting fictitious illness and crisis on the internet', *Southern Medical Journal*, vol. 93, pp. 669–72.

Ferriter, M. (1993) 'Computer aided interviewing and the psychiatric social history', *Social Work and Social Sciences Review*, vol. 4, pp. 255–63.

Furnham, A. (2000) 'The brainstorming myth', *Business Strategy Review*, vol. 11, pp. 21–8.

Gergen, K. (1992) *The Saturated Self: Dilemmas of Identity in Contemporary Life*, New York, Basic Books.

Greist, J.H., Klein, M.H. and VanCura, L.J. (1973) 'A computer interview by psychiatric patient target symptoms', *Archives of General Psychiatry*, vol. 29, pp. 247–53.

Haythornthwaite, C., Wellman, B. and Garton, L. (1998) 'Work and community via computer-mediated communication' in Gackenbach, J. (ed.) *The Psychology of the Internet*, New York, Academic Press.

Johnson, S. (1997) *Interface Culture*, New York, Basic Books.

Joinson, A.N. (2001) 'Self-disclosure in computer-mediated communication: the role of self-awareness and visual anonymity', *European Journal of Social Psychology*, vol. 31, pp. 177–92.

Kiesler, S., Siegal, J. and McGuire, T.W. (1984) 'Social psychological aspects of computer mediated communication', *American Psychologist*, vol. 39, pp. 1123–34.

Kiesler, S. and Sproull, L.S. (1986) 'Response effects in the electronic survey', *Public Opinion Quarterly*, vol. 50, pp. 402–13.

Kraut, R., Mukhopadhyay, T., Szczypula, J., Kiesler, S. and Scherlis, B. (2000) 'Information and communication: alternative uses of the internet in households', *Information Systems Research*, vol. 10, pp. 287–303.

Kraut, R., Patterson, M., Lundmark, V., Kiesler, S., Mukopadhyay, T. and Scherlis, W. (1998) 'Internet paradox – a social technology that reduces social involvement and psychological well-being?', *American Psychologist*, vol. 53, no. 9, pp. 1017–31.

Lea, M., O'Shea, T., Fung, P. and Spears, R. (1992) '"Flaming" in computer-mediated communication' in Lea, M. (ed.) *Contexts in Computer-mediated Communication*, Harvester Wheatsheaf.

Light, P. and Light, V. (1999) 'Reaching for the sky: computer supported tutorial interaction in a conventional university setting' in Littleton, K. and Light, P. (eds) *Learning with Computers: Analysing Productive Interaction*, London, Routledge.

Light, P., Light, V., Nesbitt, E. and Harnad, S. (2000) 'Up for debate: CMC as a support for course related discussion in a campus university setting' in Joiner, R. (ed.) *Rethinking Collaborative Learning*, London, Routledge.

Light, P. and Littleton, K. (1999) *Social Processes in Children's Learning*, Cambridge, Cambridge University Press.

McKendree, J., Stenning, K., Mayes, T., Lee, J. and Cox, R. (1998) 'Why observing a dialogue may benefit learning', *Journal of Computer Assisted Learning*, vol. 14, pp. 110–19.

McKenna, K.Y.A. and Bargh, J. (1998) 'Coming out in the age of the internet: identity "demarginalization" through virtual group participation', *Journal of Personality and Social Psychology*, vol. 75, pp. 681–94.

McKenna, K.Y.A. and Bargh, J. (2000) 'Plan 9 from Cyberspace: the implications of the internet for personality and social psychology', *Personality and Social Psychology Review*, vol. 4, pp. 57–75.

Mason, R. (1995) *Computer Conferencing on A423: Philosophical Problems of Equality*, Internal Report 210, Open University, Centre for Information Technology in Education (CITE).

Matheson, K, and Zanna, M.P. (1988) 'The impact of computer-mediated communication on self-awareness', *Computers in Human Behaviour*, vol. 4, pp. 221–33.

Mercer, N. (1995) *The Guided Construction of Knowledge*, Clevedon, Avon, Multilingual Matters.

Morris, D. and Naughton, J. (1999) 'The future's digital, isn't it? Some experience and forecasts based on the Open University's technology foundation course', *Systems Research and Behavioural Science*, vol. 16, no. 2, pp. 147–55.

Norman, D.A. (1988) *The Psychology of Everyday Things*, New York, Basic Books.

Parks, M.R. and Floyd, K. (1996) 'Making friends in cyberspace', *Journal of Computer-mediated Communication*, vol. 1, no. 4. [online] http://jmc.huji.ac.il/vol1/issue4/parks.html [Accessed 10 December 2001].

Postmes, T., Spears, R. and Lea, M. (2000) 'The formation of group norms in computer-mediated communication', *Human Communication Research*, vol. 26, pp. 341–71.

Reader, W. and Joinson, A.N. (1999) 'Promoting student discussion using simulated seminars on the internet' in Saunders, D. and Severn, J. (eds) *The Simulation and Gaming Yearbook: Games and Simulations to Enhance Quality Learning*, vol. 7, pp. 139–49, London, Kogan Page.

Reid, A.A.L. (1981) 'Comparing telephone with face-to-face contact' in Ithiel de Sola Pool (ed.) *The Social Impact of the Telephone*, Cambridge, MA, MIT Press.

Reid, E. (1991) *Electropolis: Communication and Community on the Internet*, unpublished thesis, Department of History, University of Melbourne.

Reid, E. (1998) 'The self and the internet: variations on the illusion of one self' in Gackenbach, J. (ed.) *The Psychology of the Internet*, New York, Academic Press.

Rheingold, H. (1993) *The Virtual Community*, New York, Addison-Wesley.

Rice, R.E. (1984) *The New Media: Communication, Research and Technology*, Newbury Park, CA, Sage.

Rice, R.E. and Love, G. (1987) 'Electronic emotion: socioemotional content in a computer-mediated network', *Communication Research*, vol. 14, pp. 85–108.

Rimm, M. (1995) 'Marketing pornography on the information superhighway', *Georgetown Law Review*, vol. 83, pp. 1839–934.

Robinson, R. and West, R. (1992) 'A comparison of computer and questionnaire methods of history-taking in a genito-urinary clinic', *Psychology and Health*, vol. 6, pp. 77–84.

Rosson, M.B. (1999) 'I get by with a little help from my cyber-friends: sharing stories of good and bad times on the Web', *Journal of Computer-Mediated Communication*, vol. 4, no. 4. [online], http://jcmc.huji.ac.il/vol4/issue4/rosson.html [Accessed 10 October 2001].

Rutter, D.R. (1987) *Communicating by Telephone,* Oxford, Pergamon Press.

Rutter, D.R. and Stephenson, G.M. (1979) 'The role of visual communication in social interaction', *Current Anthropology*, vol. 20, pp. 124–5.

Shapiro, J.S. (1999) 'Loneliness: paradox or artefact', *American Psychologist*, vol. 54, pp. 782–83.

Shirani, A.I., Tafti, M.H.A. and Affisco, J.F. (1999) 'Task and technology fit: a comparison of two technologies for synchronous and asynchronous group communication', *Information and Management*, vol. 36, no. 3, pp. 139–50.

Short, J., Williams, E. and Christie, B. (1976) *The Social Psychology of Telecommunications* London, Wiley.

Siegal, J., Dubrovsky, V., Kiesler, S. and McGuire, T. (1983) unpublished manuscript, cited in Kiesler *et al.* (1984).

Spears, R. and Lea, M. (1992) 'Social influence and the influence of the "social" in computer-mediated communication' in Lea, M. (ed.) *Contexts in Computer-mediated Communication*, London, Harvester Wheatsheaf.

Spears, R., Lea, M. and Lee, S. (1990) 'De-individuation and group polarization in computer-mediated communication', *British Journal of Social Psychology*, vol. 29, pp. 121–34.

Sproull, L. and Kiesler, S. (1986) 'Reducing social context cues: electronic mail in organizational communication', *Management Science*, vol. 32, pp. 1492–512.

Stafford, L. and Reske, J.R. (1990) 'Idealization and communication in long-distance pre-marital relationships', *Family Relations*, vol. 39, pp. 274–9.

Standage, T. (1998) *The Victorian Internet*, London, Phoenix Books.

Tolmie, A. and Boyle, J. (2000) 'Factors influencing the success of computer mediated communication (CMC) environments in university teaching: a review and case study', *Computers and Education*, vol. 34, pp. 119–40.

Turkle, S. (1995) *Life on the Screen: Identity in the Age of the internet*, New York, Simon and Schuster.

Utz, S. (2000) 'Social information processing in MUDs: the development of friendships in virtual worlds', *Journal of Online Behavior*, vol. 1, no. 1. [online], http://www.behavior.net/JOB/v1n1/utz.html [Accessed 15 October 2001].

Wallace, P. (1999) *The Psychology of the Internet*, Cambridge, Cambridge University Press.

Walther, J.B. (1992) 'Interpersonal effects in computer-mediated communication: A relational perspective', *Communication Research*, vol. 19, pp. 52–90.

Walther, J.B. (1994) 'Anticipated ongoing interaction versus channel effects on relational communication in computer-mediated interaction', *Human Communication Research*, vol. 20, pp. 473–501.

Walther, J.B. (1995) 'Relational aspects of computer-mediated communication: experimental observations over time', *Organization Science*, vol. 6, pp. 186–203.

Walther, J.B. (1996) 'Computer-mediated communication: impersonal, interpersonal and hyperpersonal interaction', *Communication Research*, vol. 23, pp. 3–43.

Walther, J.B. (1999) 'Visual cues and computer-mediated communication: don't look before you leap', paper presented at the annual meeting of the International Communication Association, May, San Francisco.

Walther, J.B., Anderson, J.K. and Park, D.W. (1994) 'Interpersonal effects in computer-mediated interaction: a meta-analysis of social and antisocial communication', *Communication Research*, vol. 21, pp. 460–87.

Walther, J.B., Slovacek, C. and Tidwell, L. (1999) 'Is a picture worth a thousand words? Photographic image in long term and short term virtual teams', paper presented at the annual meeting of the International Communication Association, May, San Francisco.

Williams, E. (1972) 'Factors influencing the effect of medium of communication upon preferences for media, conversations and persons', Communications Studies Group paper number E/72227/WL.

Williams, E. (1975) 'Coalition formation over telecommunications media', *European Journal of Social Psychology*, vol. 5, pp. 503–7.

Zimbardo, P.G. (1969) 'The human choice: individuation, reason, and order vs. deindividuation, impulse and chaos' in Arnold, W.J. and Levine, D. (eds) *Nebraska Symposium on Motivation*, pp. 237–307, Lincoln, NE, University of Nebraska Press.

Telling and detecting lies

Aldert Vrij

Contents

This chapter offers a review of issues relating to the processes of telling lies and detecting deception in everyday and forensic contexts. You may find some personal resonance with issues and experiences discussed in the chapter, such as infidelities, false accusations, sexual and violent offences, and polygraph examinations.

Aims

This chapter aims to:

- give an insight into the psychological processes involved in deception
- demonstrate the contribution of different psychological approaches, including social constructionist, cognitive and behavioural, to an explanation of detecting lies
- show how psychological theories can be applied to real-life settings
- help demonstrate how to critically evaluate the contribution of different methodologies and research findings to this area
- give an insight into the difficulties of conducting good applied research when investigating lying.

1   Introduction

Try to remember the conversations you had yesterday. Did you, at any time, tell a lie? If you don't think you did, please reconsider this. Did you not even tell a 'white lie'? It is very likely that you did lie at some point yesterday, since people typically lie every day, as this chapter will reveal.

Many relationships could become awkward if people told each other the truth all the time. Clearly, though, some lies are not desirable (for example, those told during police investigations) and some can even lead to a custodial sentence (e.g. perjuries). In such instances officials will try to detect lies, and psychologists have been investigating how to do this in three different ways. First, they observe people's nonverbal behaviour (body movements, smiling, eye contact, voice pitch, speech rate, stuttering, and so on). Second, they analyse the content of what people say. Third, they examine physiological responses (blood pressure, heart rate, sweating of the fingers, and so on). Are there systematic differences between liars and truth tellers in nonverbal behaviour, speech content and physiological responses? Are people able to detect lies by paying attention to these aspects? This chapter attempts to answer both questions by reviewing the relevant literature, but attention is also given to ethical issues in deception research and the **ecological validity** of research findings. These findings reveal that people are, to some extent, able to detect lies by examining behaviour, speech content or physiological reactions. This makes lie detection a useful tool in police investigations (for example, to eliminate potential suspects or to examine contradictory statements). However, as this chapter will show, no perfect lie detection test exists and lie detection experts regularly make wrong judgements. Lie detection assessments are

Ecological validity
The extent to which a research study represents the real-life situation under investigation. The better the representation, the higher the ecological validity.

therefore not suitable for use as substantial evidence in court cases, although this sometimes happens, as we shall see.

Throughout the chapter, examples of everyday lying and lying in forensic settings are intertwined, and this is for a good reason. Obviously, lying to a friend about one's reasons for not going out with them differs in several ways from lying to a police detective about one's involvement in a crime (for example, from a moral standpoint). However, there are apparent similarities. Factors which may affect an individual's nonverbal behaviour, speech content and physiological responses when lying, such as fear of getting caught, attempting to make a convincing impression and having to think of a plausible lie, might be present in both everyday lies and forensic settings. Hence similar deceptive responses might result.

Although psychologists have investigated a variety of deception issues over a substantial time period, there are some remarkable gaps in their research activities. For example, research has almost exclusively been conducted with white European and North American participants and the findings in this chapter therefore mainly represent that cultural perspective. This may be a limitation. Lying might be seen as more negative in some cultures than in others, and the frequency of lying might therefore differ in different cultures. In other instances, cultural differences are less likely to occur. Regardless of ethnicity, guilty suspects might fear that their lies will be detected by police detectives, and they might therefore exhibit signs of anxiety when being questioned.

In Section 2, deception is defined, together with a description of the different types of lies that people tell, the reasons why they do it, how often people lie, and methods psychologists use to examine lying (throughout this chapter the terms 'deception' and 'lying' are used interchangeably). The section will demonstrate the complexities of lying in daily interactions, and will question the conventional view that lying is necessarily undesirable.

2   General issues

2.1 Definition of deception

Deception can be defined in many ways. Some researchers have adopted Mitchell's definition of deception (1986) as '*a false communication that tends to benefit the communicator*' (Bond and Robinson, 1988, p. 295). Mitchell's definition is controversial, however, because it implies that unconsciously and mistakenly misleading others should also be classified as deception. A sales assistant who has not been informed by her boss that a product's price has been reduced and who therefore asks for too much money is lying according to

Mitchell's definition. Many people do not agree with this, and believe that deception is an act of *deliberately* not telling the truth.

Many researchers therefore define deception as 'an act that is *intended* to foster in *another person* a belief or understanding which the deceiver *considers* false' (Zuckerman *et al.*, 1981, p. 3, emphasis in original). Here, lying is an intentional act: someone who does not tell the truth by mistake is not lying. A woman who mistakenly believes that she was sexually abused in her childhood, and reports this to the police, has given a false report but she is not lying. This may sound obvious but it is not. Often, in court cases, two witnesses give different and contradictory accounts of the event they have witnessed. Which of the two witnesses is lying? It might well be that neither of the witnesses is lying, but that (at least) one witness misremembered the event (see Chapter 7 on witness evidence).

There is now growing evidence that people are able to 'remember' highly emotional incidents which never occurred. Although very young children may be disproportionately vulnerable to these kind of errors (Ceci *et al.*, 1994a; Ceci *et al.*, 1994b), adults make such errors, too (Porter *et al.*, 1999).

In the Porter *et al.* (1999) study, 77 students were interviewed. During these interviews, students were presented with events. They were told that, according to their parents, these events had occurred in their childhood. The interviewer gave further details about the events supposedly given by the parents. Unknown to the interviewees, the events were invented by the researchers and had never happened to the participants according to their parents. Guided imagery instructions were given to the participants to help them generate images for the false event (e.g. 'visualise what it might have been like and the memory will probably come back to you'). Results indicated that 26 per cent of participants 'recovered' a complete memory for the false event, and another 30 per cent recalled aspects of it. An example of a falsely remembered experience was 'falling on one's head, getting a painful wound, and being sent to an emergency room'. It is crucial to distinguish such so-called false beliefs from lying, as it can be very difficult to detect false beliefs while paying attention to behaviour, speech content or physiological responses (Ceci and Bruck, 1998). We shall return to this issue later in the chapter and consider why false beliefs are hard to detect.

Burgoon and Buller (1994) defined deception slightly differently. According to them deception is 'a deliberate act perpetrated by a sender to engender in a receiver beliefs contrary to what the sender believes is true to put the receiver at a disadvantage' (pp. 155–6). The main difference between this definition and Zuckerman *et al.*'s definition is the last seven words '*to put the receiver at a disadvantage*'. This extra wording is unfortunate. Sometimes people tell lies not to put 'receivers' in a disadvantageous position, but to make them appear better or to protect themselves, for instance, from embarrassment. We will return to this point later in this section.

However, Zuckerman *et al.*'s definition is not entirely satisfactory either, because it ignores another aspect of deception. Ekman (1992) argues that people are only lying when they do not inform others in advance about their intentions to lie. Magicians are therefore not lying during their performance, as people in the audience expect to be deceived. In Ekman's definition of a lie or deceit, 'one person intends to mislead another, doing so deliberately, without prior notification of this purpose, and without having been explicitly asked to do so by the target' (Ekman, 1992, p. 28).

Ekman's definition is not quite complete either, as liars sometimes do not succeed in misleading 'targets', although they have a clear intent to do so. For example, the target may know that the information the liar wants him or her to believe is untrue. In these cases, the attempt to deceive the target has failed, but such unsuccessful attempts can still be classified as lies. A more complete definition of deception is 'a successful or unsuccessful deliberate attempt, without forewarning, to create in another a belief which the communicator considers to be untrue' (Vrij, 2000, p. 6). This is the definition we will use throughout the chapter.

Notice that the issue as to whether someone is lying or not has been defined solely from the perspective of the deceiver. That is, a statement is a lie if the deceiver believes what they say is untrue, regardless of whether the statement is true. Strictly speaking, even an actual truth could be a lie. Suppose that, unknown to his mother, a child has eaten all the sweets. When he asks for more, his mother, in an effort to prevent him eating too much, tells him that he can't have any more because there are no sweets left. This truthful statement is a lie as long as the mother believes that there are still sweets left.

Lying does not necessarily require the use of words. The athlete who fakes a foot injury after a bad performance is lying without using words. It is also possible to lie by withholding or hiding information. Taxpayers who deliberately do not report a particular source of income on their tax form are lying.

People sometimes fool themselves – a process called self-deception. People can ignore or deny the seriousness of several bodily symptoms, such as a severe pain in the chest during physical exertion. According to the definition we are using in this chapter, however, deception is an act which involves at least two people. This definition excludes self-deception, which therefore will not be discussed further in this chapter.

2.2 Types of lies

DePaulo *et al.* (1996) distinguished between *outright lies, exaggerations and subtle lies.*

Outright lies (also referred to as falsifications) are lies in which the information conveyed is completely different from, or contradictory to, what the deceiver believes is the truth. If you say you were revising for your exam yesterday when you were actually shopping, that is an outright lie. Most lies people tell are outright lies (DePaulo *et al.*, 1996).

Exaggerations are lies in which the facts are overstated or information is conveyed that exceeds the truth. People can exaggerate their regret for arriving too late at an appointment with a friend, can embellish their remorse for committing a crime during a police interview, or can present themselves to be more diligent than is in fact the case during a job interview.

Subtle lying involves literal truths that are designed to mislead. The former president of the US, Bill Clinton, was telling such a lie in 1999 when he said to the American people that he 'did not have sexual relations with that woman, Miss Lewinsky'. The lie was subtle, because the statement implied that nothing of a sexual nature had happened between the two of them, whereas he was relying on the narrower definition that they did not have sexual intercourse. Another type of subtle lying involves concealing information by evading the question or omitting relevant details. Passengers who tell customs officers what is in their luggage are concealing information if they also have illegal drugs which they deliberately fail to mention.

Activity 4.1

Before reading any further, write down some lies you have recently heard, told or read about and try to cluster them into the three categories (outright lies, exaggerations and subtle lies) mentioned above. For each lie, also write down what you think was the reason for the lie before reading on.

2.3 Reasons why people lie

People lie for several reasons:

- People lie in order *to obtain personal advantage.* For example, applicants may exaggerate their current income during a selection interview in order to secure a higher income in their next job.
- People lie in order to *avoid punishment.* For example, children may deny any wrongdoing to their parents in order to avoid punishment. Guilty suspects may conceal important information during police interviews to avoid a possible conviction.

- People lie *to make a positive impression on others* or *to protect themselves* from embarrassment or disapproval. When Clinton admitted for the first time on television to the American people that he had had an 'inappropriate relationship' with Monica Lewinsky, the first reason he gave for having misled people was 'a desire to protect myself from the embarrassment of my own conduct' (he may also have wanted to avoid 'political punishment').

The earliest lies children tell are designed to escape punishment (Bussey, 1992). Lies generated to obtain rewards probably appear later (DePaulo and Jordan, 1982), followed by lies to protect one's self-esteem (Bussey, 1992).

The lies mentioned so far are *self-oriented*, and are intended to make the liar appear better or to gain personal advantage. Approximately half of the lies people tell are self-oriented (DePaulo *et al.*, 1996).

- People also lie *to make others appear better*, or lies are told *for another person's benefit*. An innocent mother may tell the police that she committed the crime in order to save her guilty son from a conviction. Such a lie is *other-oriented*. Unsurprisingly, many other-oriented lies are meant to protect those people to whom the liar feels close (Bell and DePaulo, 1996).
- People may lie *for the sake of social relationships*. Goffman (1959) pointed out that life is like a theatre and that people often behave as actors and put on a show. Conversations could become awkward and unnecessarily rude, and social interactions could easily become disturbed, if people told each other the truth all the time ('I didn't like the food you prepared', 'I don't like this present you've given me', and so on). Social relationships may depend upon people paying each other compliments now and again. Most people will probably appreciate it when others make positive comments about their latest haircut. Making deceptive but flattering remarks might therefore benefit mutual relations. Social lies serve both self-interest and the interest of others. For example, liars may be pleased with themselves when they please other people, or tell a lie to avoid an awkward situation or discussion. (You may like to consider links here to theory of mind, i.e. the ability to put oneself in another's place, as discussed in Chapter 5, 'The autistic spectrum: from theory to practice').

Return to Activity 4.1. Were the lies you mentioned self-oriented or other-oriented? Did all five reasons why people lie occur on your list?

2.4 How often do people lie?

Activity 4.2

How often do you lie and what types of lie do you tell? During one day record all your social interactions and all of the lies you tell during those interactions. For the purpose of this activity, a social interaction is 'an exchange between you and another person that lasts

10 minutes or more'. Please record all lies, no matter how big or small. Please make detailed notes of the social interactions and your lies as soon as possible after the interactions have taken place. If you are not able to do this immediately after the interaction, write short reminders of your social interactions and lies as a memory aid and record your social interactions and lies later in the day. For each lie, write down (1) whether or not you felt comfortable while telling the lie, (2) whether you considered the lie trivial or serious, (3) whether the lie was spontaneous or planned, (4) whether or not you think the other person believed your lie, (5) whether or not you think you would tell this lie again if you could relive this social interaction, (6) whether the lie was self-oriented or other-oriented and (7) the reasons why you told the lie. You may want to be careful not to let your notes be discovered.

What is your reaction to being asked to complete this activity? Do you feel negatively about lying and think that you never or hardly ever lie? After you have given the issue a second thought (and after completing the activity), however, the situation might seem different. For example, how would people respond if you really told them the truth all the time? And how would you react if people were always perfectly honest with you? This chapter argues that lying has its advantages and that the vast majority of people, perhaps everybody, lie sometimes. That was the experience of people participating in Backbier *et al.*'s study (1997). The researchers held group interviews in order to gain deeper insight into the way people view lying in everyday life. Initially people reacted negatively about deception. However, the same people reported many instances in which they lied themselves, and showed a great deal of understanding of their own lies. The authors concluded that 'the interviewees did not seem to be aware of having a somewhat dual attitude toward lying, and, when confronted with it, it did not seem to bother them' (pp. 1048–9).

Psychologists have developed different ways of investigating the extent and nature of people's lies. For example, Backbier and Sieswerda (1997) instructed participants to write down when they last lied. They were also asked to indicate to whom the lie was told, why they had told the lie, what they had said and whether or not the lie was detected. The attractive part of this method is that it is easy to apply. A disadvantage is that you run the risk that people forget the last lie they told, which is perhaps most likely to occur when the lie is trivial.

Probably the most thorough investigation to date into people's lies in daily life is that of DePaulo *et al.* (1996). Activity 4.2 is an adapted version of their study, in which they asked participants to complete a diary. In this (US) diary study, 77 college students and 70 community members kept records of all the lies they told during one week. The results showed lying to be a fact of everyday life. College students reported telling two lies a day and community members told one lie a day. Most lies were self-serving. Participants also said that their lies were generally not serious, that they did not put much effort into planning their lies, and that they generally felt comfortable while telling the lie.

The majority of participants (70 per cent) reported that they would tell the lie again if they were given a second chance. As far as the respondents were aware, about 20 per cent of their lies were detected. These findings suggest that people generally do not feel too bad about their lies.

2.5 Who do people lie to?

Further analyses of DePaulo's diary study, reported by DePaulo and Kashy (1998), revealed a relationship between telling lies and the emotional closeness of the relationship. By comparing the lies told by community members to spouses, best friends, friends, acquaintances and strangers, it was found that the lowest rate of lying occurred in conversations with spouses, while the highest rate occurred with strangers. However, the results made clear that deception occurs in all types of close personal relationships. Although participants said they were predominantly honest in social interactions with their spouses, lies still occurred in nearly one out of every ten social interactions they had with them. Many of those lies were minor. Perhaps a limited amount of trivial lying serves important privacy needs for individuals in such close relationships (DePaulo and Kashy, 1998). However, interactions with spouses are also the domain of serious lies. When people were asked to describe the most serious lies they ever told to someone else, they overwhelmingly reported that the target of these lies were close relationship partners (Anderson *et al.*, 1999). These lies were often told to cover serious issues, such as infidelities, and were told to save the relationship. Sometimes spouses believe that the truth cannot be told without threatening the relationship. In such instances, they may decide that telling a lie is preferable. They perhaps do so reluctantly. They often feel uncomfortable while lying to their spouses (DePaulo and Kashy, 1998), but it is in their view the best option they have, given the circumstances.

One reason why people lie less to their romantic partners (and also to friends) than to strangers is that they have the desire to be honest to people they feel close to, but there are also other reasons (Anderson *et al.*, 1999). The fact that our friends and partners know more about us limits the topics that are suitable or 'safe' to lie about. We can try to impress strangers at a cocktail party by exaggerating our cooking skills but this is useless with friends who have experienced our meals. So, we might lie less because we think that we will not get away with it.

Although people tend to lie less to those with whom they feel close, there are exceptions. For example, a consistent finding is that college students often lie to their mothers (Backbier and Sieswerda, 1997; DePaulo and Kashy, 1998; Lippard, 1988). DePaulo and Kashy (1998) found that students lied in almost half of their conversations with their mothers. Perhaps they are still dependent on their mothers (for example, with regard to money) and sometimes have to lie to secure financial resources. Another explanation is that they still care about what their mothers think of them. Therefore, they tell their mothers that they do not drink much alcohol, that they attend all lectures, that they study hard and that they regularly clean their room.

2.6 Situational factors

How often people lie also depends on the situation. Robinson *et al.* (1998) interviewed undergraduate students, of whom 83 per cent said they would lie in order to get a job. However, these students said that it was wrong to lie to best friends, but they saw nothing wrong in lying if this secured the job. They also thought that employers expected candidates to exaggerate qualities when applying.

Rowatt *et al.* (1998) found that 90 per cent of participants admitted being willing to tell a lie to a prospective date. About 40 per cent of men and women indicated that they actually had told a lie to initiate a date with an attractive member of the opposite sex (Rowatt *et al.*, 1999). Also, DePaulo's diary study revealed that people lied relatively often to their romantic partners in the early stages of their relationship (once in every three social interactions). One possible explanation is that people wondered whether their 'true self' was loveable enough to attract and keep these partners, and they therefore presented themselves as they wished they were, instead of how they actually were (DePaulo and Kashy, 1998).

2.7 Sex differences in lying

DePaulo *et al.* (1996) did not find sex differences in the frequency of lying. However, they found that men and women tend to tell different lies. Men told more self-oriented lies, whereas women told more other-oriented lies, particularly to other women. Rowatt *et al.* (1998) reported that men are more willing than women to use deception in order to get a date. Also, differences emerge in the types of lie men and women tell during a date (Eyre *et al.*, 1997; Tooke and Camire, 1991). Women more frequently engaged in deceptive acts to improve their physical appearance (e.g. 'sucking in' their stomach when around members of the other sex), whereas men tended to feign their earning potential (e.g. misleading members of the opposite sex about their career expectations).

These deceptive acts reflect sex differences in preferences in characteristics of potential partners. When 50 male and 50 female participants were asked what they look for in a potential partner, men were more likely than women to emphasise the importance of their partner's physical appearance, whereas women were more likely than men to emphasise the importance of their partner's earning capacity (Buss and Barnes, 1986).

You may wonder to what extent the findings of DePaulo's diary study reflect lying in daily life. To what extent might people's knowledge that they have to keep records of all their social interactions and lies during a certain period affect the frequency and nature of these conversations and lies? Another difficulty faced is in finding out whether people are honest and complete while keeping records.

So far, this chapter has demonstrated the complicated role of lying in daily interactions. The conventional view that lying is inherently bad is not true, and telling the truth all the time is not desirable. Conversations could become awkward and unnecessarily rude if people told each other the truth all the time. We tell lies even to people we feel close to. We tell many lies at the beginning of a romantic relationship, and we make many untruthful flattering remarks to people we like. Women tell more other-oriented lies than men, make more flattering comments, and more frequently avoid saying things that may hurt the other person.

2.8 Methods of investigating lying in real-life situations

How can we investigate people's deceptive responses in real-life situations? For example, how can we study the deceptive responses of suspects in police investigations? Possibilities are offered by videotaping police interviews and analysing suspects' behaviour and speech content whilst they are lying, or by conducting a polygraph test (see Section 5.1) and examining suspects' physiological reactions whilst they are lying.

Activity 4.3

Before reading further, write down what methodological problems you think a researcher has to address while analysing an alleged liar's responses? For example, what would you use as a comparison for a deceptive response?

Ground truth
The actual guilt or innocence of the interviewees.

Comparable truth
A truthful response which is subsequently compared with a target response in order to find out whether the target response is deceptive or not.

Field study
A field study is a piece of research which studies an issue in its naturally occurring context, rather than in the artificial confines of a laboratory.

While assessing people's responses two particular methodological problems occur: problems with establishing the **ground truth** and problems with selecting **comparable truths**. In deception **field studies**, researchers evaluate the accuracy of decisions made by lie detection experts in criminal cases – these experts are usually polygraph examiners (see Section 5) or evaluators who assess the speech content via the *statement validity assessment* (SVA) method (see Section 4). That is, researchers evaluate whether the decisions made by the lie detection experts (the suspect spoke the truth/the suspect was lying) were correct. In order to evaluate these decisions, only those cases where the ground truth is satisfactorily established can be used – that is, cases where there is no doubt about the actual guilt or innocence of the suspect. In order to establish the ground truth, researchers sometimes use evidence such as medical evidence, material evidence and/or DNA-evidence as the objective 'guilt–innocence' criterion and judge whether these objective criteria match with the decision made by the lie detection expert. However, this type of evidence is often not available, since the lack of this sort of evidence is exactly the reason why lie detection experts have been consulted. If strong evidence such as medical evidence is available, no further evidence is needed for the prosecution, as this is enough to press charges and is likely to result in a conviction. However, in cases where the available evidence is too weak to press charges, prosecutors might be inclined to ask for polygraph tests or SVAs in order to strengthen their case. In other words, the other evidence in cases where polygraph examinations or SVAs take place is typically weak, meaning that the ground truth is difficult or even impossible to establish.

An ideal field study would be one in which polygraph tests or SVAs are carried out in cases with other indisputable evidence. Although such lie detection assessments are not needed to solve these cases, they might be carried out just for the sake of evaluating the methods (that is, to establish the accuracy of decisions made by lie detection experts). Obviously, the lie detectors should not be informed about the indisputable evidence! Surprisingly, at the time of writing, such a study has not yet taken place.

In order to evaluate the accuracy of decisions made by lie detection experts, researchers may also use confessions as a criterion to establish ground truth. Here problems arise since suspects' decisions as to whether or not to confess are sometimes based upon the outcome of a 'lie detection test', such as the polygraph (see Section 5). On the one hand, innocent suspects who failed a lie detection test sometimes see themselves confronted with evidence against them (the lie detection test) and no evidence which shows that they are innocent. This might result in defendants falsely confessing, as they see no opportunity to prove their innocence and to obtain an acquittal, whereas a guilty plea often results in a reduced sentence (Gudjonsson, 1992; Steller and Köhnken, 1989). On the other hand, guilty suspects who passed the lie detection test are unlikely to confess, given the lack of evidence against them.

   A second problem is selecting comparable truths. In establishing whether suspects are lying, their responses while lying are usually compared with their responses while telling the truth. Suppose a colleague with whom you are on friendly terms initiates a casual chat. After a while he tells you that people at work have come to the conclusion that you are responsible for the breakdown of some expensive equipment yesterday, which made your boss extremely angry. You haven't touched the machine, so you know that the accusation is false, and that is what you immediately say to your colleague. However, the false accusation clearly upsets you and makes you react nervously. What makes them suspect you? Your colleague notices your nervous reactions and subsequently accuses you of lying. Your colleague makes a serious (but common) mistake. Indeed, you are nervous, but it is the accusation itself that makes you nervous! Comparing your current reactions with your reactions before the accusation is not legitimate. The situations before and after the accusation are not comparable, and changes in your behaviour caused by the accusation can say nothing about whether or not you are lying.

Unfortunately, this sort of comparison between someone's behaviour during small talk and their behaviour during an actual interrogation is common practice in police interviews (Moston and Engelberg, 1993). Police officers are even advised to establish comparable truths in this way (Inbau *et al.*, 1986). In sum, the problem for the lie catcher is that truth tellers, not just liars, may sometimes be emotional, and that lie catchers can misjudge the symptoms shown by emotional truth tellers (Bond and Fahey, 1987). Ekman (1992) labelled this phenomenon the *Othello error*, after Shakespeare's play. Desdemona (Othello's lover) is falsely accused of infidelity. Realising that she cannot prove her innocence, Desdemona reacts with an emotional outburst that seems to verify the accusation. Selection of comparable truths is a major problem in real-life deception research (and also probably the main problem in polygraph testing).

In summary, field studies examine examples of deception as they occur in real life. The benefit of such studies is that the examples selected are realistic and give us insight into real-life deception. The disadvantages are that it is often difficult to judge whether someone is really lying or telling the truth (ground truth), and that it is difficult to select instances of lying and truth telling which are comparable.

An alternative to field studies are laboratory studies. In such studies, researchers ask participants to lie or tell the truth and measure participants' responses during lying and truth telling. For example, in one type of experiment, half of the participants have an item (e.g. a set of headphones) in their possession, whereas the other half of the participants do not (Vrij *et al.*, 1997). All participants are subsequently interviewed by a police detective who asks them six standard questions about the possession of the headphones ('Have you got the set of headphones in your possession?', 'You forgot to mention the set of headphones, didn't you?', 'You don't have to show me, but tell me exactly what you have in your pockets', and so on). All participants are requested to deny the possession. This means that half of the participants have to lie, whereas the other half can tell the truth.

Laboratory studies have some advantages. Establishing the ground truth is not a problem in such a paradigm, as the researchers know who is lying (e.g. to whom they gave the set of headphones). Creating comparable truths is not an issue either, as the situation for liars and truth tellers is identical (except for the lying). Differences in responses between both groups of participants can therefore be attributed to the deception involved. However, there are problems in laboratory studies, too. For example, the deception involved might not be realistic. Participants are asked to lie for the sake of the experiment, and, unlike the case in many real-life situations, there are no real rewards for telling a successful lie, nor any punishment for being caught out (Malone and DePaulo, 2001). In other words, how realistic are laboratory studies? What do they say about deception in real life?

Notice that deception research might raise ethical concerns. As signs of deception are more likely to occur when the deceiver experiences strong emotions (see Section 3), researchers typically want to induce emotions in their participants. This could be fear of getting caught (by introducing some form of punishment when they are caught), or strong motives to be successful (by offering money when they get away with their lies). Alternatively, participants are asked to lie or tell the truth about films that induce emotions (sometimes films of amputations are shown), or are brought into an interview setting which induces emotions (being interviewed by a police detective). Typically, the ethical principles of psychologists and codes of conduct of psychological associations state that participants in studies should not experience more distress in a study than can reasonably be expected in daily life. If researchers would like to induce more distress, then they should justify this (We shall return to this issue later on; you may also like to refer to Section 2.3 of Chapter 7 which discusses how psychologists have studied the influence of stress on memory).

Summary Section 2

- Deception can be defined as: *a successful or unsuccessful deliberate attempt, without forewarning, to create in another a belief which the communicator considers to be untrue.*
- People tell both self-oriented lies (to appear better or to gain personal advantage) and other-oriented lies (to make others appear better or for another person's benefit).

- Telling lies is a daily life event, which varies in quite complex ways according to the situation and the person being lied to.
- The conventional view that lying is inherently bad has been questioned.
- There is some evidence that men and women tell different types of lie.
- In order to examine people's responses while lying, both laboratory studies and field studies can be conducted. Both types of study have advantages and disadvantages.

3   Nonverbal behaviour and deception

3.1 Introduction

Activity 4.4

Before reading any further, list those nonverbal behaviours that you think reveal that someone is lying.

You might have written down 'liars generally look away', 'liars fidget' or 'liars stutter'. These are, in fact, the three cues most often mentioned when people are asked how they think liars behave (Vrij and Semin, 1996). Or you might have written down other cues. What rarely happens is that people say 'there are no cues to deception' or 'I don't know'. Apparently, people generally believe that nonverbal cues to deception exist and that they 'know' which cues reveal deception. Are people correct in this assumption? We start this section by discussing how accurate people are at spotting lies.

Most research examining liars' nonverbal responses has been carried out in laboratories. DePaulo *et al.* (2000) reported the results of 119 laboratory studies, whereas probably less than a handful of field studies have been conducted. In these laboratory studies, people lied or told the truth about beliefs and opinions, about personal facts such as the course they study, about video films or pictures they had just seen, or about the possession of an object. In others, participants were induced to cheat and then to lie about it, or were given the opportunity to take money and, if taken, to lie about this in a subsequent interview. See Box 4.1 for more details about a typical and classic deception design, devised by DePaulo and Rosenthal (1979).

4.1 DePaulo and Rosenthal's experimental lie design (1979)

Participants were asked to take one minute to describe each of the following persons: someone they liked, someone they disliked, someone they felt ambivalent about and someone they felt indifferent about (ambivalence was defined as strong feelings of both liking *and* disliking; indifference was defined as *no* strong feelings of liking or disliking). To elicit deception, participants were also asked to describe the persons they liked as if they really disliked them and to describe the persons they disliked as if they really liked them. The experimenter remained behind a one-way mirror and videotaped the descriptions. The participants were urged to try to be very convincing in all of their descriptions.

Researchers have examined a variety of different nonverbal behaviours, as shown in Box 4.2.

4.2 Nonverbal behaviours in deception research

- gaze aversion (looking away from the conversation partner)
- smiling (smiling and laughing)
- illustrators (hand and arm movements designed to modify and/or supplement what is being said verbally)
- hand/finger movements (movements of hands or fingers without moving the arms)
- self-manipulations (touching or scratching body, face or hair, playing with objects)
- speech rate (number of spoken words in a certain period of time)
- pauses in speech (silent periods during speech)
- speech latency (period of silence between question and answer)
- speech fillers (use of the words 'ah', 'um', 'er', and so on)
- stutters (words and/or sentence repetition, sentence change, sentence incompletions, slips of the tongue, and so on)
- pitch of voice (as measured in hertz, also changes in pitch of voice, such as a rise or fall in pitch)

Before discussing to what extent the behaviours in Box 4.2 are related to deception, one more issue needs to be considered. The mere fact that someone lies will not affect his or her behaviour. However, liars may experience three different processes during deception, called '*emotional*', '*content complexity*' and '*attempted behavioural control*' processes (Vrij, 2000), and each of these processes may influence a liar's behaviour. Each process emphasises a different aspect of deception and deceptive behaviour. However, the distinction between them is artificial. Lies may well feature all three aspects, and the three processes should not be considered as mutually exclusive.

3.2 The emotional process and nonverbal behaviour

The *emotional process* proposes that deception can result in different emotions. The three most common types of emotion associated with deceit are guilt, fear and excitement (Ekman, 1992). A liar might feel *guilty* because s/he is lying, might be *afraid* of getting caught, or might be *excited* about having the opportunity to fool someone. The strength of these emotions depends on the personality of the liar and on the circumstances under which the lie takes place (Ekman, 1992; Vrij, 2000). Guilt, fear and excitement may influence a liar's behaviour. Guilt might result in gaze aversion because the liar does not dare to look the target straight in the eye while telling a lie. Fear and excitement might result in signs of stress, such as an increase in hand and body movements, an increase in speech fillers and stutters, or a higher pitched voice.

3.3 Content complexity and nonverbal behaviour

The *content complexity process* emphasises that lying can be a cognitively complex task (Vrij, 2000). Liars have to think of plausible answers, should not contradict themselves, should tell a lie that is consistent with everything which the observer knows or might find out, and should avoid making slips of the tongue. Moreover, they have to remember what they have said, so that they can say the same things when someone asks them to repeat their story. People engaged in cognitively complex tasks make more speech fillers and stutters, pause more, and wait longer before giving an answer (Goldman-Eisler, 1968). Cognitive complexity also leads to fewer illustrators and to more gaze aversion. The decrease in illustrators is due to the fact that a greater cognitive load results in a neglect of body language, reducing overall animation (Ekman and Friesen, 1972). Gaze aversion (usually to a motionless point in the distance) occurs because looking at the conversation partner distracts from thinking too much. It is easy to examine the impact of content complexity on movements and gaze aversion. Ask people what they ate three days ago, and observe their behaviour while they try to remember what they have eaten. Most people will look away and will sit still while thinking about the answer.

3.4 Attempted behavioural control and nonverbal behaviour

So far, the predictions of how liars behave have been straightforward. A liar may experience emotions and/or may find it difficult to lie, and this will result in behavioural signs of emotion and content complexity. However, the situation is more complicated than this. Liars may be afraid that several cues will give their lies away, and therefore will try to suppress such signs in order to avoid getting caught. This is emphasised in the *attempted behavioural control process*. Hocking and Leathers (1980) argued that liars attempt to control their behaviour according to the cultural stereotype of liars. For example, if there is a widespread belief that liars look away, increase their movements and stutter, then liars will try to maintain eye contact, refrain from making too many movements and will try to speak fluently. When people try to do this, they sometimes tend to overcontrol themselves, with behaviour that looks rehearsed and rigid and speech that sounds too smooth as a result (DePaulo and Kirkendol, 1989). The effort to make a convincing impression is called *impression management* (Krauss, 1981) – for an example of this see Box 4.3.

4.3   Clinton's impression management

(a)   (b)

Former US President Bill Clinton showed a clear example of impression management when he testified before the grand jury in 1998 about his alleged sexual affair with Monica Lewinsky. Betty Currie (who was Clinton's personal secretary) had gone to Monica Lewinsky's home to collect the presents she had received from Clinton. The question was whether or not Clinton instructed her to do this. This was an important question, as it would be a clear sign of 'obstruction of justice' if Clinton indeed gave such instructions. Prosecutor Kenneth Starr's team asked Clinton twice whether he gave Betty Currie these instructions. Clinton denied doing so both times, but each time he showed remarkable behaviour. The first time, he denied quickly, even before the interviewer had completed his question. This is very uncommon for skilled politicians such as Clinton. Conversational rules tell us that you should not interrupt another, and politicians are very well aware of this rule. Clinton then showed rigid behaviour and looked straight into the camera (see photograph (a)). He even continued doing this during the period of silence that followed his denial. It looks as if he expected more questions about this issue. However, more questions were not asked by Starr's team at that time. Impression management became even more striking when the question was asked for the second time. While answering the question, Clinton shifted position and started to lean forward while denying having given instructions to Betty Currie. Again he showed rigid behaviour and looked straight into the camera (see photograph (b)). His behaviour looked perhaps even more rigid than the first time. We cannot say with certainty that Clinton was lying during these two fragments – but we can say that he really wanted to make an honest impression on Kenneth Starr's team and the grand jury during that particular part of the interview.

Activity 4.5

Return to the list of nonverbal behaviours that you wrote for Activity 4.4, and to Box 4.2. For each behaviour on your own list, or for any of the cues in Box 4.2, write down which of the three processes (emotional, content complexity and attempted behavioural control) the nonverbal behaviour is linked to.

3.5 The nonverbal behaviour of a liar

The fact that deception in itself does not affect someone's behaviour, but that behavioural deceptive indicators are in reality signs of emotion, content complexity and attempted behavioural control, implies that deceptive behaviour may only become visible if a liar experiences one of these three processes. That is, if a liar doesn't experience any fear, guilt or excitement (or any other emotion), and the lie is not difficult to fabricate, behavioural cues to deception are unlikely to occur. Most lies in everyday life fall into this category (DePaulo *et al.*, 1996) and are therefore unlikely to reveal any behavioural signs. This also explains why false beliefs (introduced in Section 2.1) are difficult to detect: people are not afraid of getting caught, do not experience cognitive load (they have clear, although mistaken, memories of what happened), and they do not try hard to make an honest impression (there is no need to as they believe that they are telling the truth).

Figure 4.1 presents a schematic representation of nonverbal indicators of deception. After each behaviour is, in brackets, the number of studies in which the behaviour was examined (e.g. gaze behaviour was examined in 26 studies). The percentages refer to the percentage of studies which revealed an increase in the behaviour during deception (positive score) or a decrease in the behaviour during deception (negative score). Thus, a decrease in hand/finger movements was found in 70 per cent of the studies (7 out of 10 studies), whereas none of the studies found an increase in hand/finger movements during deception. The term 'indicator' is somewhat misleading, as it suggests that deception is related to a unique pattern of specific behaviours. This is not the case – there

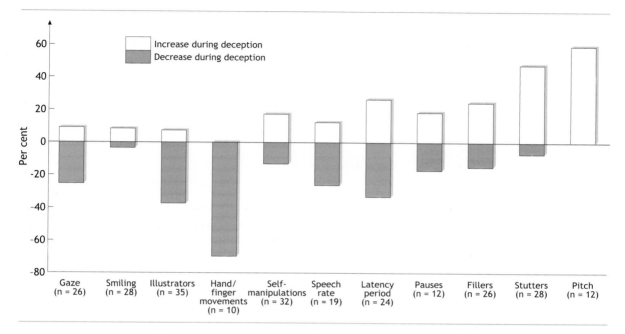

Figure 4.1 Summary of results of studies of nonverbal indicators of deception (Source: derived from Vrij, 2000)

is nothing comparable with Pinocchio's nose! It is simply not true, for example, that as soon as people start lying they raise an eyebrow, avert their gaze, develop a trembling voice, shuffle their feet or look away.

Despite the fact that there is no typical deceptive behaviour, some behaviours are more likely to occur during deception than others, particularly a decrease in hand/finger movements, a decrease in illustrators, an increase in stutters and an increase in pitch (see Figure 4.1). The higher pitched voice of liars might be the result of stress they experience (Ekman *et al.*, 1976). However, differences in pitch between liars and truth tellers are usually very small and therefore only detectable with sophisticated equipment. The decrease in illustrators and hand/finger movements during deception might be the result of lie complexity: perhaps liars have to think hard, resulting in a neglect of body language. Another explanation is that liars, in an effort to make an honest impression, move very deliberately and try to avoid those movements which are not strictly essential, resulting in an unusual degree of rigidity and inhibition. The increase in stutters might be the result of liars having to think hard or being nervous.

Contrary to widespread belief, gaze behaviour is unrelated to deception (Vrij and Semin, 1996). Both the emotional process and the cognitive complexity process predict that liars would show more gaze aversion. However, it is in fact relatively easy for people to control their gaze behaviour (Ekman and Friesen, 1972).

The attempted behavioural control approach suggests that liars from different cultures might try to show, or avoid showing, different behaviours, depending on what they think is suspicious behaviour. Indeed, there are cultural differences in nonverbal behaviour, as we shall see in Section 3.10 'Detecting lies across cultures'.

3.6 Methodological difficulties in measuring nonverbal indicators in experimental studies

Scoring of behaviours

It might be that some indicators are overlooked by researchers because the scoring systems they use to measure the occurrence of behaviours are not detailed enough. For example, some researchers do not measure the *frequency of occurrence* of behaviours (how many times a person shows each behaviour) during lying and truth telling, but instead measure the *duration* of these behaviours (for how many seconds a person shows each behaviour). Measuring duration is generally not refined enough. Vrij (2000) found that researchers who measured *duration* did not find differences in illustrators between truth tellers and liars, whereas others who measured the *frequency* of occurrence did find differences. To date no researcher has presented an alternative scoring method which revealed more nonverbal indicators of deception than the ones mentioned in Figure 4.1, with the exception of Ekman in his research concerning smiles (see Box 4.4).

4.4 Ekman's smiles as a different way of measuring differences in truthful and deceptive behaviour

Ekman and colleagues discovered that smiles are related to deception only when a distinction is made between felt and false smiles (Ekman et al., 1988). They found that truth tellers showed more felt smiles and liars more false smiles. Felt smiles include all smiles in which the person actually experiences a positive emotion and presumably would report that positive emotion. False smiles are deliberately made to convince another person that a positive emotion is felt whereas, in fact, it isn't. Felt and false smiles produce slightly different facial muscle actions and the skilled observer is able to spot these differences (Ekman, 1992).

Felt smile

False smile

Subtle differences

Differences between liars and truth tellers are often very small (Vrij, 1994), and so it is important to score people's behaviour in great detail. As mentioned earlier, lying is a daily life event. Most people are so practised and proficient in lying that they may be regarded as 'experienced liars' and we would therefore only expect weak links between nonverbal behaviours and telling lies. Weak links can also be predicted from an evolutionary perspective (Bond *et al.*, 1985). Obvious cues to deceit would have been recognised by human perceivers long ago and therefore would no longer be worthwhile to pursue. Moreover, any accusation ('I think that you are having an affair with your colleague', 'You drank alcohol during lunch time, didn't you?', 'You are suspected of having assaulted your child', and so on) might evoke similar emotions in both wrongdoers and those who are falsely accused (previously described in relation to the 'Othello error'). Wrongdoers might be afraid of getting caught, whereas those who are falsely accused might be afraid that they will not be believed by the accuser. Their behavioural responses might be similar.

Raising the stakes

Perhaps the weak link found between lying and nonverbal behaviour is nothing more than an artefact. Critics often mention that in experimental laboratory studies the stakes (the positive and negative consequences of getting caught) are not high enough for the liar to elicit clear nonverbal cues to deception (Miller and Stiff, 1993). Indeed, the deceivers in DePaulo and Rosenthal's study (1979) (see Box 4.1) faced a totally different situation from liars in some real-life situations, such as a suspect in a police interview, a smuggler at an airport, or a corrupt politician in a conversation with an interrogating journalist.

DePaulo and Rosenthal's study is perhaps more realistic than might at first appear (Malone and DePaulo, 2001). DePaulo's diary study (see Section 2.4 above) showed that people most often lie about their feelings, such as feigning greater liking than one really does feel, as did the participants in DePaulo and Rosenthal's study. Also, most daily lies, like those in experiments, are small lies of little consequence. In other words, many deception studies conducted in the laboratory do give an accurate insight into how people behave in the majority of everyday lies.

In order to raise the stakes in laboratory experiments, participants have been offered money if they successfully get away with their lies (Vrij, 1995). In other studies, participants are told that they will be observed by a peer who will judge their sincerity (DePaulo *et al.*, 1985). The results are mixed. Some of those 'high stake' studies do reveal behavioural differences, but others do not. However, when exposed to 'high' and 'low' stake lies, judges are consistently better at detecting high stake lies than at detecting low stake lies (Vrij, 2001).

The stakes in these experimental studies are still lower than those in certain real-life situations. Frank and Ekman (1997) therefore attempted to raise the stakes even further. In their study, participants were given the opportunity to 'steal' 50 dollars. If they could convince the interviewer that they had not taken the money, they could keep all of it. If they took the money and the interviewer judged them as lying, they had to give the 50 dollars back and also lost their 10 dollars per hour participation fee.

Moreover, some participants faced an additional punishment if they were found to be lying. They were told that they would have to sit on a cold, metal chair inside a cramped, darkened room labelled ominously 'XXX', where they would have to endure anything from 10 to 40 randomly sequenced, 110-decibel blasts of white noise over the course of one hour. These participants were given a sample of this punishment prior to engaging in the task. However, no participant who was judged to be lying actually received the punishment. Frank and Ekman found differences between liars and truth tellers, although they did not examine the behaviours listed in Figure 4.1. Instead, they measured and found differences between liars and truth tellers in the occurrence of facial expressions of fear or disgust. They could detect 80 per cent of truths and lies by looking for these emotions.

Although Frank and Ekman's laboratory experiment might be a good example of a high stake study, it also raises serious ethical concerns. To what extent is it ethically acceptable to threaten people so much, just for the sake of an experiment? Also, the threat of punishment by the researchers was a form of deceit. It was never their intention to apply this punishment. Deceiving participants may be regarded as an unethical research practice, as it is in conflict with the standard of informed consent. People have the free choice whether or not to participate in a psychology study and psychology associations therefore require researchers to obtain the consent of their participants before research with these participants can proceed. Prior to a study, participants should be properly informed about the research so that they can make a well-considered decision whether or not to participate. In cases where they are deceived about the nature of the study, a well-informed decision cannot be made. Psychology associations typically state that psychologists should not deceive participants about 'significant' aspects of the study. However, they typically do not rule out deception altogether: deception is allowed if the potential benefits from the study can be demonstrated to outweigh the undesirability of deception. In practice, this leaves room for deception. The term 'significant' is vague and therefore open to interpretation, and the American Psychological Association, for example, 'encourages its members to conduct a form of cost–benefit analysis to justify deception, weighing the benefits to science against the costs to the individual' (Clarke, 1999, p. 152).

3.7 Studying real-life nonverbal deception

Probably the best insight into deceptive behaviour in real-life situations will be obtained by examining people's behaviour in such situations. Mann *et al.* (2001) attempted to examine this by studying the behaviour of suspects during their interviews with police officers. The interviews were videotaped and the tapes were made accessible to Mann and colleagues for research purposes. All suspects in the sample were suspected of serious crimes, such as murder, rape and arson (that was the reason for their interviews being videotaped).

Statements were subsequently classified as lies on the basis of conclusive evidence (ground truth) and Mann *et al.* were also able to select comparable truths from the videotape. Also, the selected deceptive statements sometimes preceded and sometimes succeeded the selected truthful statements (i.e. sometimes the suspects lied, then later told the truth; on other occasions they first told the truth, then subsequently lied).

To give an example of a comparable truth, one man who was suspected of murder (a case described in detail by Vrij and Mann, 2001a), was asked: 'What did you do that day?' (the day of the killing). The man gave a detailed account of his activities during the morning, afternoon and evening. The police checked every single detail the man had provided. Several independent witnesses (including his employer) could confirm his story about his activities during the morning, but no confirmation could be obtained about his alleged activities during the rest of the day.

After a couple of weeks, conclusive evidence revealed that he met the victim in the afternoon and killed her later the same day. His truthful statements (about the morning) and deceptive statements (about the afternoon and evening) are comparable as there is no reason why someone should show different patterns of behaviour when describing different times of day.

The findings are remarkably similar to those found in laboratory studies. For example, while lying, the suspect made fewer illustrators and made more stutters (Vrij and Mann, 2001a). This is perhaps not surprising. One should keep in mind that liars in both experimental studies and in real-life situations may have to think hard while lying, may try to make an honest impression on others, and may be afraid of getting caught.

3.8 Sex and age differences in nonverbal behaviour and deception

Activity 4.6

Do you think that (1) males and females, and (2) children and adults, differ in their nonverbal behaviour when attempting to lie? If you think they do, list the differences that you think might exist before reading on.

Perhaps not surprisingly, no sex differences have been found in nonverbal cues to deception (DePaulo *et al.*, 2000). After all, there is no reason why emotional, content complexity and attempted behavioural control processes would differ between males and females while they are lying.

With regard to age, not much research has been conducted to date regarding children's deceptive behaviour. For ethical reasons, it is not easy to conduct child deception research. In order to examine children's deceptive responses in laboratories, they should be requested to lie. This creates ethical concerns, especially when the children are very young. In child deception research two paradigms are popular. In one paradigm (Lewis *et al.*, 1989), children are not requested to lie, but spontaneous lies are elicited instead. For example, before the experimenter leaves a child alone in a room, the child (sometimes as young as two years old) is instructed not to peek at a toy which is located behind him or her. Results of those studies show that most children do peek (their behaviour is secretly observed from a different room). After a while the experimenter comes back and asks the child whether or not he or she did peek. Most children in these studies denied that they have peeked and thus lied. In the second paradigm (Feldman *et al.*, 1979), children are asked to lie, but these lies are common white lies. Children taste two beverages, one drink is a pleasant tasting sweetened grape drink and the other drink is an unpleasant tasting unsweetened grape drink. After each sip the child is instructed that they should pretend to like (or dislike, depending on the experimental condition they are in) both drinks in order to 'fool' the interviewer in a game-like situation.

Not many researchers scored the actual nonverbal behaviours shown by the children in these studies, for example, one review was only able to include four studies (Vrij, 2002). Children younger than nine years old showed less smiling, longer and more frequent pauses, more self-manipulations and more illustrators while lying. It seems that children's deceptive behaviour better fits with the Western stereotype than adults' deceptive behaviour does, although gaze aversion was not a reliable cue to deception even in these young children.

So far, this section of the chapter has revealed that clear-cut nonverbal indicators of deception do not exist. This is in contrast to the stereotypical Western view that liars typically look away and fidget. The remaining part of the section deals with the issue of how good people are at spotting lies while paying attention to someone's nonverbal behaviour.

3.9 Detecting lies by looking at someone's nonverbal behaviour

In scientific studies concerning detection of deception, observers are typically given videotaped or audiotaped statements made by a number of people who are either lying or telling the truth. Statements of liars and truth tellers are usually taken from participants in laboratory studies, so that there is no uncertainty about the ground truth regarding these statements. After each statement observers are asked to judge whether the statement is truthful or false. In Figure 4.2 the first set of data ('Nonverbal behaviour') presents the percentages of lie detection (the 'accuracy rate'), derived from Vrij's review of 39 studies (2000). Included are studies in which the judges were college students who tried to detect lies and truths told by people they were not familiar with. (The results for 'CBCA' and 'Control Question Test', which are included for comparison, will be discussed later in the chapter.)

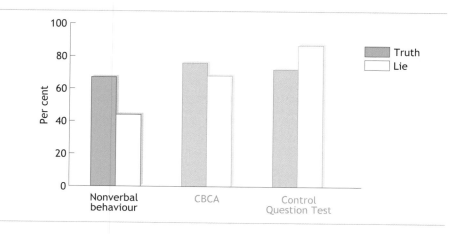

Figure 4.2   Accuracy rates for detecting truths and lies – nonverbal behaviour (Source: derived from Vrij, 2000)

The total accuracy rate was 56 per cent, which is a low score as 50 per cent accuracy would be expected by chance alone (guessing whether someone is lying or not gives a 50 per cent chance of being correct). Figure 4.2 further shows that people are to some extent capable of detecting truths (i.e. correctly judging that someone is telling the truth: 67 per cent accuracy rate) but particularly poor at detecting lies (i.e. correctly judging that someone is lying: 44 per cent accuracy rate). In fact, 44 per cent is below the level of chance. In other words, people would be more accurate at detecting lies if they simply guessed!

It could be argued that college students are not habitually called upon to detect deception. Perhaps professional lie catchers, such as police officers or customs officers, would obtain higher accuracy rates than lay people. It might be that their experience in interviewing people and catching liars has had a positive influence on their skills in detecting deceit. In several studies professional lie catchers' ability to detect lies was tested.

In a typical experiment (Ekman *et al.*, 1999), professional lie catchers watched video clips of 20 people who gave a statement about a number of current controversial issues which either was their true opinion (truth) or an opinion opposite to their true opinion (lie). For each statement, the professional lie catchers were asked to indicate whether it was a truth or a lie. In most studies, the professional lie catchers' accuracy rates were in the 45 per cent to 60 per cent range, which replicates what has been found in studies with college students. This suggests that professional lie catchers are no better at detecting deception than college students.

DePaulo and Pfeifer (1986) and Ekman and O'Sullivan (1991) directly tested this idea by including both lay persons and professional lie catchers as observers in their experiments. DePaulo and Pfeifer (1986) found that police officers were only as successful as college students in detecting deception (52 per cent and 54 per cent accuracy rates respectively). Ekman and O'Sullivan found that police officers (56 per cent accuracy) and polygraph examiners (56 per cent accuracy) obtained similar accuracy rates to college students (53 per cent accuracy), although members of the Secret Service (64 per cent accuracy) were better at detecting lies than college students. The latter finding suggests that some groups of professional lie catchers are better at detecting lies than others, a finding which was supported by a study conducted by Ekman *et al.* in 1999. The participating US Federal officers (police officers with a special interest and experience in deception and demeanour) and sheriffs (police officers identified by their department as outstanding interrogators) were considerably better at detecting lies (73 per cent and 67 per cent accuracy respectively) than mixed law-enforcement officers (officers who had not been chosen for their reputation as interrogators), who had 51 per cent accuracy.

Moreover, DePaulo and Pfeifer (1986) investigated how confident observers were in the decisions they made. They found that police officers were more confident than students, which suggests that being a professional lie catcher may increase confidence in the ability to detect deceit, but does not increase accuracy. Allwood and Granhag (1997) pointed out that the tendency to be overconfident is not unique to police officers, but that this is common amongst many different groups of professionals.

In some studies, individual differences in police officers' lie detection skills were examined. All these studies found that some officers were better lie detectors than others. Researchers have only just started to investigate what makes someone a good or poor lie detector. Ability to detect deceit is unrelated to age and gender, and, remarkably, unrelated to experience in interviewing suspects. Vrij and Mann (2001b) found that those officers endorsing popular stereotypical views on deceptive behaviour, such as 'liars look away' and 'liars fidget', were the poorest lie catchers. Perhaps good lie detectors employ less rigid rules than poor lie detectors. In their study with undergraduate students as lie detectors, Frank and Ekman (1997) found that good lie detectors are also good at spotting facial **micro-expressions** of emotions.

Micro-expressions
Remnants of interrupted or inhibited facial muscular movements, only present for a very short period of time.

Ekman has argued (Ekman, 1992; Ekman *et al.*, 1988) that high-stake lies may result in fraudulent facial emotional expressions, so-called 'micro-expressions' – time-reduced remnants of interrupted or inhibited facial muscular movements (Ekman and Friesen, 1974, p. 289). These are facial expressions that are displayed for only a fraction of a second but clearly reveal the liar's true feelings before being quickly covered with a false expression. Ekman also argues that fake facial expressions differ from genuine expressions (e.g. see discussion of false and felt smiles, in Section 3.6 above). The majority of the observers to whom lies are directed are unlikely to pick up on such subtle changes and therefore liars are able to mask their true feelings quite successfully.

How realistic are these detection of deception studies? Clearly, there are differences between lie detection in scientific deception studies and lie detection in real life. For example, when police officers try to detect lies in real life there is more at stake for the liars, probably making it easier to catch the liars, because the three processes (emotional, content complexity and attempted behavioural control) are likely to be more profound in these liars. Indeed, as we saw earlier, judges are better at detecting truths and lies when the stakes for the liar are high. However, this does not imply that detecting high-stake lies is always easy. For example, in Vrij and Mann's study (2001b), police officers watched videotaped press conferences of people who were asking the general public for help in finding their relatives or the murderers of their relatives. Some of them lied during these press conferences and were subsequently found guilty of killing the people they were appealing about. The accuracy score in this study (51 per cent) was not impressive either, suggesting that even liars who tell serious lies may get away with their deceit.

Also, in real life police officers can actually interview the suspect. Police officers, judges and prosecutors believe that it is easier to detect lies in real interviews than when they are watching a video (Granhag and Strömwall, 2001). However, researchers have compared the accuracy scores of interviewers who interviewed potential liars with those of observers who watched the interviews but did not actually interview the potential liars. The researchers found that observers were in fact more accurate in detecting truths and lies than interviewers were (Feeley and deTurck, 1997). Interviewers seemed to be more inclined to believe that the interviewees were telling the truth than observers (Feeley and deTurck, 1997), a phenomenon which is known as a *truth-bias*. In other words, interviewers are reluctant to accept that some people are convincing liars and are able to fool them. Such reluctance to believe that they might be fooled hampers lie detection.

3.10 Issues influencing nonverbal lie detection

Numerous factors affect observers' lie detection, including the following key issues:

- the 'wrong' cues
- the misleading power of the face
- young liars
- detecting lies across cultures
- familiarity with the liar
- the motivated lie detector
- implicit lie detection ('don't even think about it').

The 'wrong' cues

An important factor is that observers seem to have incorrect beliefs about how liars behave. Vrij (2000) reviewed more than 40 studies examining people's beliefs about deceptive behaviour. These studies were carried out in various countries, including the USA, the UK, Germany and the Netherlands, and with a variety of observers, including lay people, police officers and customs officers. Despite the variety in location and observers, the findings were highly similar. It appears that there is common understanding, at least amongst people from these countries, about how liars behave. Results showed that observers associate deception with a high-pitched voice, many speech fillers and stutters, a slow speech rate, a long latency period, many pauses, gaze aversion, a lot of smiling and many self-manipulations and illustrators. Vrij and Semin (1996) found that an increase in gaze aversion and an increase in speech disturbances (fillers and stuttering) were the most popular stereotypes, with almost 80 per cent of the observers (both lay people and police officers) endorsing them. All these behaviours are indicators of either nervousness or cognitive load. Apparently, the stereotypical belief is that liars are nervous and/or have to think hard, and will behave accordingly. As we saw earlier, most of these behaviours (such as gaze aversion) are not related to deception or are related to deception in a different way (for example, illustrators tend to decrease during deception and not to increase). To what extent do your own ideas (Activities 4.4 and 4.5) resemble the stereotypical belief?

There are at least two reasons why people have such poor insight into deceptive behaviour. First, people can be misled by perceptions based on their own behaviour. Vrij *et al.* (2001a) investigated participants' behaviour while lying and truth telling. They also asked the participants afterwards to indicate how they thought they behaved when they lied and when they were telling the truth. Results showed that participants had poor insight into their own behaviour and thought that they responded more stereotypically while lying (showing gaze aversion, an increase in movements, and so on) than they in fact did. In other words, it seems that during lie detection observers look for cues they mistakenly believe they themselves show while lying.

Second, people, including police officers, are taught to look for the wrong cues. In their influential manual *Criminal Interrogation and Confessions*, Inbau *et al.* (1986) describe in detail how, in their view, liars behave. This includes behaviours such as showing gaze aversion, displaying unnatural posture changes, exhibiting self-manipulations and placing their hand over their mouth or eyes when speaking. They based their view on their extensive experience with interviewing suspects. However, none of these behaviours are found to be reliably related to deception when investigated in deception research. Nor do Inbau and his colleagues provide empirical evidence for their claims.

In their deception detection study, Kassin and Fong (1999) trained half of their participants to look at the cues Inbau and colleagues claim to be related to deception. Although more confident in their ability to detect deceit than a control group who did not receive training, these trained judges actually performed worse in lie detection (46 per cent accuracy) than the control group (56 per cent accuracy).

The misleading power of the face

Zuckerman *et al.* (1981) presented research findings examining people's ability to detect lies while paying attention to different 'channels'; that is, when they pay attention to facial cues only, body language only, words only, or to combinations of channels, such as face plus body, body plus words plus voice, total picture, and so on. Results revealed that people became worse at detecting truths and lies as soon as facial cues were made available to them, clearly demonstrating the misleading power of facial information. A plausible explanation is that lie detectors pay particular attention to eye movements (gaze aversion), and as this behaviour is not actually related to deception they get fooled.

Young liars

Anecdotally, when people are asked whether they can detect lies, they commonly answer: 'at least in my children I can'. You would probably expect, however, that with increasing age, children will become better liars. Vrij (2002) reviewed studies examining adults' ability to detect children's lies and found that this is indeed the case. However, one should not think that it is particularly easy to spot children's lies. Most studies only revealed modest accuracy rates, rarely higher than 60 per cent, although, in general, parents are better than other adults at detecting their own child's deception.

In their experiment, Vrij and van Wijngaarden (1994) examined the effect of young liars' personality on judges' decision making. Adult observers watched 74 video recordings of children who each tasted a drink and then lied or told the truth about whether or not they liked the drink. For each video recording the observers had to indicate whether the child told the truth or lied. To investigate the social skills of the children, teachers were asked to fill out a social skills questionnaire for each of their pupils. Their findings demonstrated a *demeanour bias*. Introverted and socially anxious children showed a dishonest demeanour bias and were more often judged to be deceptive than were the other children, regardless of whether they were lying or not. Demeanour biases have been found previously in research with adults as well. Some individuals' nonverbal behaviour gives the impression that they are telling the truth (honest demeanour bias), whereas others' natural behaviour leaves the impression that they are lying (dishonest demeanour bias), regardless of whether they are actually lying or telling the truth (Riggio *et al.*, 1988). *Expressive people*, for example, exude credibility regardless of the truth of their assertions. It is not that they are particularly skilled at lying, but that their spontaneity tends to disarm suspicion, which makes it easier for them to get away with their lies (Riggio, 1986).

Introverts and *socially anxious* people, on the other hand, are said to impress others as being less credible. The social clumsiness of introverts and the impression of tension, nervousness or fear that is characteristic of socially anxious individuals are interpreted by observers as indicators of deception.

Detecting lies across cultures

Cross-cultural lie detection is prone to judgement errors. Nonverbal behaviours are culturally determined and do differ across cultures. For example, looking into the eyes of the conversation partner is regarded as polite in Western cultures but is considered to be rude in several other cultures (Vrij and Winkel, 1991). Afro-American people display more gaze aversion than white American people do, and people from Turkey and Morocco who are living in the Netherlands show more gaze aversion than native Dutch people do. In the Netherlands, Vrij and Winkel investigated the nonverbal behavioural patterns of white native Dutch and black Surinam citizens (citizens originating from Surinam, a former Dutch colony, but now living in the Netherlands) during simulated police interviews (Vrij and Winkel, 1991). Both a Dutch and a Surinamese interviewer were used, but this had no impact on the findings. Amongst other differences, Surinam people made more speech disturbances (speech fillers and stutters), exhibited more gaze aversion, smiled more often and made more self-manipulations and illustrators, regardless of whether they were lying or not. These behaviours show an overlap with the stereotypical view of liars' behaviours described earlier (Vrij and Semin, 1996), suggesting that typical 'Surinam' behaviour in experiments in Holland corresponds with behaviour that could be interpreted as indicating deception by native Dutch observers. This gives rise to possible *cross-cultural nonverbal communication errors* during cross-cultural police interviews. That is, nonverbal behavioural patterns that are typical for Surinam people in these settings may be interpreted by native Dutch observers as revealing attempts to hide the truth. This idea was tested in a series of experiments. Videotapes were made of simulated police interviews in which native Dutch and Surinam actors participated. Different versions were made of each interview. The actors showed typical 'Dutch' behaviour in one version of the interviews (for example, showed a moderate amount of gaze aversion) and typical 'Surinam' nonverbal behaviour in another version of the interviews (showed more gaze aversion). Dutch white police officers were exposed to one version of each interview and were asked to indicate to what extent the man made a suspicious impression. The outcomes are presented in Figure 4.3.

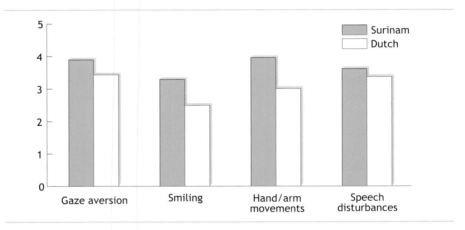

Figure 4.3   The cross-cultural nonverbal communication error (the scores indicate the degree to which the behaviours were judged to be suspicious) (Source: derived from Vrij *et al.*, 1991; Vrij and Winkel, 1992, 1994)

Ethnic background did not have an impact on police officers' impression formation. That is, they found native Dutch 'suspects' as suspicious as Surinam 'suspects'. However, suspects consistently made a more suspicious impression when they showed 'typical Surinam behaviour' than when they exhibited 'typical Dutch behaviour'. These findings support the prediction that cross-cultural nonverbal communication errors can occur during cross-cultural police interviews, and that nonverbal behavioural patterns that are typical for one ethnic group can be misinterpreted as signs of deception by observers from other ethnic groups.

Familiarity with the liar

In most studies concerning the detection of deception, observers are asked to detect lies told by people they do not know. In daily life, many situations involve detecting lies told by people with whom we are familiar. It seems reasonable to suggest that it should be easier to detect lies in people we know than in strangers. For example, we are more familiar with the normal behaviour of people we know, and should therefore be able to detect even minor changes in their behaviour. Research has consistently indicated that people become better at detecting truths and lies when they are familiar with the truthful behaviour of the person they have to judge. For example, Feeley *et al.* (1995) showed some observers video fragments of truthful communications of the people they had to assess later in the lie detection task. Their accuracy rates were significantly higher (72 per cent) than the accuracy rates of observers (56 per cent) who were not exposed to the truthful communications prior to the lie detection task.

Perhaps surprisingly, there is no evidence to support the assumption that it is easier to detect lies in lovers than in strangers. It has been argued that this is because, as relationships become more intimate, partners develop a strong tendency to judge the other as truthful, the so-called relational truth-bias heuristic (Levine *et al.*, 1999). McCornack and Parks have developed and tested a model to explain this (described in Levine and McCornack, 1992). As soon as the relationship between two people intensifies, they will become more confident that they can detect each other's lies ('I know the other person very well, I am able to tell whether he or she is lying'). High levels of confidence will then result in the belief that the other person probably would not dare to lie ('S/he had better watch out, I will detect every lie s/he tells me'). This will result in putting less and less effort into trying to discover whether someone is lying ('I don't have to worry that much, s/he does not lie to me anyway') (Stiff *et al.*, 1992). The less effort someone puts into trying to detect deceit, the easier it will be to dupe that person.

These findings seem to contradict the findings of DePaulo and Kashy's diary study (1998). They found that lies told to people to whom individuals felt close were more often discovered than lies told to people to whom they did not feel close. A possible explanation for this is that in experimental studies (such as those conducted by McCornack and by Levine), the observers could not verify the stories told by their partners and thus primarily had to focus on their partner's nonverbal behaviour in order to detect lies.

However, in real life, people are not restricted to observing someone's behaviour – they often have the opportunity to check whether what people say is actually true. It may well be that the participants in DePaulo and Kashy's study discovered the lies told by people to whom they felt close by actually checking the information given by these liars. Liars may realise that their partners do this. Also, liars tend to tell different types of lies to their partners than to people they know less well (Metts, 1989).

As mentioned earlier, the majority of lies that people tell are outright lies. However, people are much *less* likely to tell outright lies to their partners, as they believe that the risks are too high and that the partner will eventually find out that they are lying. Moreover, they can expect repercussions as soon as the lie is detected; also, how do they explain to their partner that they lied to them? Lies told to partners are therefore usually subtle lies, such as concealments. This type of lie is usually difficult to detect, because the liar does not reveal information that can be checked. The lie is also easier to justify if it emerges. It is always possible for liars to say that they simply forgot to tell their partner the information, or to say that they did not mention the information before, because they did not realise that their partner was interested in it, and so on.

Anderson *et al.*'s study (2000) used a different research design from previous studies. All previous studies used a 'between-participants' design: people had to detect truths and lies in either strangers or friends/lovers. Anderson *et al.* (2000) carried out a longitudinal study using a 'within-participants' design of same-sex pairs (males–males and females–females). In the first month of their psychology course, pairs of students who had only recently become friends (and therefore could be considered almost 'strangers') had to detect truths and lies told by each other (the truths and lies were contrived for the experiment). They were asked to do this again five months later (it was assumed that by this time the friends knew each other better). As the relationship progressed, female students, but not male students, became better at detecting lies. Apparently, females, but not males, became increasingly insightful about their friend's deceptiveness. These findings seem to challenge previous findings that the ability to detect deceit is unrelated to sex.

The motivated lie detector

Sometimes lies are not detected because observers do not want to detect them, as they judge it to be not in their best interest to learn the truth. People generally like it when others compliment them about their body shape, their hairstyle, the way they dress, what they have achieved, and so on. So why bother trying to discover whether those who make these compliments actually mean what they are saying? Also, more serious lies remain undetected for the same reason. A spouse will not always try to find out whether his partner is having an adulterous affair. As soon as a husband tells his adulterous wife that he has found out about her and her lover, she may feel compelled to choose between him and the other man, possibly resulting in a divorce, which may be something he does not want. Hence, communicating what he has discovered may have undesirable consequences for him and, on realising this, he may decide not to investigate this issue. However, in other daily life situations and in experimental studies the situation is different and people *do* want to detect lies. If in those situations people try harder, do they then get better? The evidence seems to suggest that the answer is no. When

DePaulo *et al.* (1999) compared studies in which no special incentives were offered to judges with those in which incentives (for example money) were given, they found that judges who were given some extra reason to try harder actually did worse.

Implicit lie detection ('don't even think about it')

There is evidence that people know more about deception than it appears they do when they are asked directly whether they think someone is lying (DePaulo, 1994). For example, in some studies, observers watched video fragments of people who gave truthful or deceptive descriptions of other persons they liked or disliked (see Box 4.1 for more information about this procedure). Observers were asked to detect deception both in a direct way ('Is the person lying?') and in an indirect way ('Does the speaker sincerely (dis)like the person s/he just described?'). These studies found greater accuracy on the indirect measures (Anderson *et al.*, 1999). This might be explained in terms of conversation rules which regulate politeness. Observers are often unsure as to whether someone is lying to them. In such instances it may be impolite, or undesirable, to accuse someone of being a liar, but it might be possible to challenge the words of a speaker more subtly. In other words, it is more difficult to say 'I think you lied about liking that person' than to say 'Do you *really* like that person so much?' Alternatively, people might look at different cues when detecting lies than when applying an indirect method. In Vrij *et al.*'s study (2001b), police officers watched a number of videotaped interviews with truth tellers and liars. Some participants were asked whether each of these people was lying, others were asked to indicate for each person whether that person 'had to think hard' (they were not informed that some people were actually lying). Police officers could distinguish between truths and lies, but only by using the indirect method. Moreover, only in the indirect method did they pay attention to the cues which actually discriminated between truth tellers and liars on the videotape, such as a decrease in hand movements.

Summary Section 3

- Typical deceptive behaviour does not exist, but emotions, content complexity and attempted behavioural control may affect a liar's behaviour.
- Examining high-stake lies is difficult, as they cannot be introduced in laboratory studies for ethical reasons.
- Both lay persons and professional lie catchers are generally not good at detecting lies when they observe someone's behaviour. However, the studies on which this conclusion is based have methodological limitations.

- Several factors affect lie detection, including people's tendency to rely on cues that are unreliable.
- There are individual differences in the ability to detect deceit. Researchers have only just begun to investigate what makes someone a good lie detector.
- There is evidence that people know more about deception than it appears, and that they might become better lie detectors if they try to detect lies in an indirect way.

4   How liars phrase their lies

4.1 What verbal cues do we expect?

For decades, psychologists have looked at verbal criteria that might distinguish truths from lies. *Statement validity assessment* (SVA) is the most popular technique to date for measuring the veracity of verbal statements. The technique has been developed in Germany to determine the credibility of child witnesses' testimonies in trials for sexual offences. It is perhaps not surprising that a technique has been developed to try and verify if sexual abuse has taken place with a child. It is often difficult to determine the facts of a sexual abuse case, as there is often no medical or physical evidence. Frequently the alleged victim and the defendant give contradictory testimonies and there are often no independent witnesses to say what has happened. This means that the perceived credibility of the defendant and alleged victim are important. The alleged victims are in a disadvantageous position if they are children, as adults have a tendency to mistrust statements made by children (Ceci and Bruck, 1995). To date, SVAs are accepted as evidence in criminal courts in several countries, such as Germany, the Netherlands and the USA.

The SVA method has been developed through German psychologists' clinical experience (rather than via experimental research) since the 1930s. The first comprehensive description of SVA was published by Undeutsch (1967) in German. SVA was further developed and refined by Steller and Köhnken who published an English version in 1989.

One part of SVA is what is known as *criteria-based content analysis* (CBCA), a systematic assessment of the credibility of a verbal statement. In order to extract a statement, children are interviewed following a 'structured interview' procedure. Strict guidelines for interviewing children have been laid down (Bull, 1998). They include the importance of building a good rapport with the child, endeavouring for as full a free narrative regarding the event as possible (particularly important for SVA), and questioning that begins with very open-ended questions and becomes increasingly narrowed to obtain more specific details. However, each statement must stand up in a court of law and therefore should contain a minimal number of leading questions (see Chapter 7 on witness testimony).

SVA interviews are audiotaped and then transcribed for CBCA. The assessment takes place on the basis of these written transcripts, with 19 criteria used in the assessment. Trained evaluators examine the statement and judge the presence or absence of each of the 19 criteria. The presence of each criterion in the statement enhances the quality of the statement and strengthens the hypothesis that the account is based on genuine personal experience. This idea was originally stated by Undeutsch (1967), and is therefore known as the *Undeutsch Hypothesis* (Steller, 1989).

Activity 4.7

What criteria would you look at when trying to decide whether a statement of a child is truthful? Try to write down three criteria you might consider relevant, such as the statement length, amount of detail or structure, and so on. Would you use the same criteria in evaluating the truthfulness of adult statements?

Vrij (2000) gives a detailed overview of the 19 criteria used in CBCA assessments, some of which will be described here.

- First of all, observers look at the *logical structure* of the statement. This criterion is concerned with whether the statement fits together.
- A second criterion is *unstructured production*. Liars tend to tell their stories in a more chronological manner (this happened first, and then this, and then that, and so on), whereas truth tellers tend to give their account in unstructured and incoherent ways, particularly when they talk about emotional events. You might have experienced this yourself. You might remember that someone comes to you, clearly upset, and tells you what has happened in a chaotic and incomprehensible way. In fact, the story can be so incomprehensible that you have to ask the person to sit down for a while, to calm down, have a cup of tea and tell you again exactly what has happened, beginning with the start of the event.
- A third criterion is the *number of details* mentioned in a statement. It is hypothesised that liars include fewer details in their accounts than truth tellers do. The type of details CBCA experts are looking for include:

  '*contextual embedding*' (does the statement contain details about times and locations?)

  '*reproduction of speech*' (did the interviewee recall literally what was said during the event?)

'*unusual details*' (are there any details mentioned which are 'odd' but not unrealistic?)

'*accounts of subjective mental state*' (does the statement include details about how the interviewee actually felt during the event?).

The criteria mentioned so far might differ between truth tellers and liars because it is believed to be too difficult for people to fabricate them (Steller, 1989). This is similar to the cognitive complexity approach described earlier. The other criteria are less likely to occur when people are lying, for motivational reasons (Steller, 1989), and are related to the attempted behavioural control approach described earlier. These criteria include:

- '*spontaneous corrections*' (when the person spontaneously admits that the previous description was incorrect and modifies that description)
- '*admitting lack of memory*' (spontaneously admitting to have forgotten some (crucial) details)
- '*raising doubts about one's own testimony*' (spontaneously admitting that the description sounds odd or implausible).

Liars will try to construct a report which they believe will make a credible impression on others, and will leave out information which, in their view, will damage their image of being a sincere person (Köhnken, 1999).

4.2 Do the predictions hold true?

In order to test whether the CBCA approach actually works and can discriminate between truthful and fabricated accounts, both field studies and laboratory studies have been conducted. In field studies, researchers have evaluated CBCA assessments in actual sexual abuse cases where the ground truth is often based on confessions; that is, whether or not the person accused by the child of sexual abuse confessed to having committed the crime. Of course, basing the ground truth on a confession generates the problems previously discussed in Section 2.8 of this chapter. Laboratory studies have problems as well. In real life, CBCA assessments are made solely on statements given by alleged child victims of sexual abuse. In other words, this involves statements describing highly emotional events. Obviously, laboratory studies can never simulate those types of experiences. Many CBCA experts therefore believe that laboratory studies are of little use in testing the accuracy of SVAs.

Some authors describe CBCA as a technique solely for evaluating the statements of children who are alleged victims in sexual abuse cases, as the technique was developed for this purpose (Raskin and Esplin, 1991). Others have advocated the additional use of the technique to evaluate the testimonies of suspects or adult witnesses who talk about issues other than sexual abuse.

What is your view on this? Do you think that deceptive statements made by children have a fundamentally different structure from deceptive statements made by adults? (What did you say in Activity 4.7?)

Vrij (2000) reviewed 17 studies related to CBCA. Twelve of the studies were laboratory studies, and in nine of these the statements that were assessed were given by adults. As with nonverbal behaviour and deception, there is no typical deceptive verbal behaviour. That is, not all liars say certain things or avoid saying specific things. However, the criteria discussed above (with the exception of admitting lack of memory) are more often found to be present in truthful statements compared with deceptive statements (in both adults and children), supporting the Undeutsch Hypothesis.

Some researchers have reported accuracy rates, that is, the number of correct classifications of truth tellers and liars based on CBCA assessments. Unfortunately, in only one of the field studies (see Box 4.5) were accuracy rates reported, so the scores are based solely on laboratory studies. The average accuracy rate in CBCA studies was about 70 per cent (see Figure 4.4; data for 'Nonverbal behaviour' and 'Control Question Test' are shown for comparison), with slightly higher scores for detecting truths (76 per cent) than for detecting lies (68 per cent). No differences in accuracy rates were found when assessing the statements of adults and children.

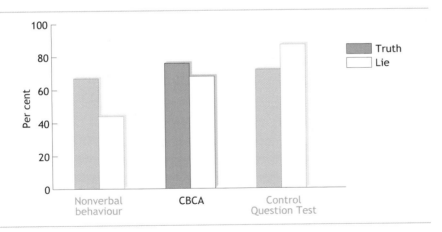

Figure 4.4   Accuracy rates for detecting truths and lies – CBCA (Source: derived from Vrij, 2000)

These accuracy rates are simply too low to justify CBCA assessments being used as the main piece of evidence in court. In particular, the substantial number of incorrect classifications of lies is worrying, assuming that they reflect how decisions in real-life court cases are made. The incorrect decision to believe fabricated stories made by alleged victims would have serious consequences. Such an error could result in somebody who is innocent being falsely accused of a crime and may lead to an unjustified conviction in a case where a judge (or jury) based their decision on the opinion of the SVA expert. False convictions of innocent suspects are seen as serious mistakes in Western legal systems, which are founded on the principle that it is better to acquit 10 guilty people than to convict one person who is innocent.

4.5 A field study with adult statements

Parker and Brown (2000) conducted a field study in which the SVA method was used in the assessment of the veracity of adult rape allegations. Each alleged victim was interviewed by specially selected and trained police officers, known as Sexual Offence Investigative Techniques officers. The transcripts were submitted to CBCA analyses. On the basis of 28 CBCA assessments, 88 per cent of the truthful and 92 per cent of the false reports were correctly classified. Even higher accuracy rates were found after the CBCA outcomes were reassessed following the *validity checklist* procedure (see Section 4.3 below for a description of this procedure).

Reporting on this field study, a UK newspaper, *The Independent* (31 October 2000), reported that a 'lie-detector' test to help uncover false allegations of rape is being developed. However, this might be something of an exaggeration.

First, description of the ground truth criteria is vague, which makes it impossible to check whether the ground truth had been satisfactorily established. For example, cases were classified as 'true' on the presence of 'convincing evidence of rape' (no information is given as to what that means), corroboration in the legal sense and with a suspect being either identified or charged. These criteria might not be valid, as they might not be independent case criteria. For example, why has the suspect been charged? Perhaps the alleged victim gave a statement which sounded convincing enough for the prosecution to press charges. This is, however, no guarantee that the statement was actually truthful. Conversely, cases were classified as 'unfounded' when, for example, there were 'substantial grounds to believe that the allegation has no basis in fact' (Parker and Brown, 2000, p.241). Consider the following example. Suppose that, for whatever reason, the police officer who interviewed the alleged victim believed that the allegation was false. This might have affected the interview. The officer might not have put so much effort into encouraging the interviewee to recall all details she could possibly remember. A low CBCA score and 'substantial grounds to believe that the allegation has no basis in fact' would have been the result.

Second, the reported accuracy rates were based upon 28 adult rape allegations, although 43 cases were assessed in that study – only partial results were reported. Perhaps these 28 cases were clear-cut cases, which might have inflated the CBCA accuracy scores.

Many CBCA experts would challenge the accuracy rates reported in Figure 4.4 by saying that they are merely based upon statements given by adults in unrealistic laboratory experiments. A realistic laboratory study (although not without ethical concerns) has been conducted by Tye *et al.* (1999).

In the first deception condition, a parent had taken a book which belonged to a student while their child (aged between 6 and 10) was watching. The theft occurred when the student was out of the room, leaving the child, his/her parent and two researchers behind. Later, when the child and parent were alone in the room, the parent asked the child to blame one of the researchers for the theft. After this instruction, the student (the owner of the book) returned and noticed that the book was missing. A dramatic scene then followed with the student apparently becoming very distressed and asking the child if he or she knew who took the book. Regardless of the answer given by the child, the student told the group (child, parent and two researchers) that the police had been called and that no one should leave the room because the police would want to talk to each person, starting with the child. A police officer then interviewed the child. Nine of the 16 children who were allocated to this condition accused the researcher of the theft and were therefore lying.

In a second deception condition the child did not see anyone take the book, but the book disappeared. The student then accused the parent of stealing the book. Later, when the child and parent were alone, the parent asked the child to lie and to protect the parent from the allegations and to accuse the researcher of stealing the book. In this condition, 11 of the 16 children did what they were told and accused the researcher of stealing the book.

In the truthful condition, a researcher (i.e. not the parent) had stolen the book while the child was watching. The researcher asked the child to keep the theft secret. Thirteen of the 16 children who were allocated to this condition nevertheless told the police officer in the subsequent interview that the researcher took the book. They were therefore telling the truth. The deceptive statements from the two deception conditions and the truthful statements from the truthful condition were assessed by CBCA evaluators who were blind to the actual experimental condition the child was allocated to. On the basis of these assessments, all false statements and 75 per cent of true statements were correctly classified. The CBCA evaluators performed better than a group of 115 lay people who classified 65 per cent of the true and about 50 per cent of the false statements correctly.

4.3 Problems with CBCA evaluations

Some people are highly critical about CBCA assessments and would like such evaluations to be abandoned as pieces of evidence in courts (Rassin *et al.*, 1997; Ruby and Brigham, 1997). Indeed, it is possible to identify several problems concerning CBCA evaluations, and two of these will be discussed below.

The nature of the test

What CBCA score should be obtained in order to judge a statement as truthful? This question is impossible to answer, as CBCA is not a standardised test. A standardised test has clear norms, which gives the test psychological meaning and makes interpretation possible (Kline, 1993). An intelligence test is a standardised test. If a person obtains a score of 130, then we know that s/he is well above the average expected for that person's age range. This is not the case with CBCA assessments. A child with a low CBCA score is not necessarily fabricating. Other factors (for example low mental capability of the child) may have influenced the CBCA outcome. Similarly, a child with a high CBCA score is not necessarily telling the truth (for example, the child might have been coached by a parent). Without any norms the meaning of a test score is impossible to gauge. Therefore, standardisation of a test is essential. In an effort to standardise CBCA assessments, the validity checklist has been developed (Steller, 1989). This contains a set of topics which SVA experts address (such as 'age of the child', 'cognitive abilities of the child', and 'susceptibility to suggestion'). By systematically addressing each topic, the evaluator can explore and consider alternative interpretations for the CBCA outcomes. The problem is how to determine the effect of those factors on the quality of the statement. For example, if a particular child is considered to be susceptible to suggestion in normal daily life situations, how then do we determine that this child was also suggestible in the particular interview, and if so, to what extent has this affected the quality of the statement? This can never be determined, it can only be estimated, and the answers experts give are therefore not more than their own (substantiated) opinion. If, for example, two experts disagree about the truthfulness of a statement in German criminal cases, they often also disagree about the likely impact of such factors (e.g. age, cognitive abilities of the child, susceptibility to suggestion) on that statement (Köhnken, personal communication). (See Chapter 7 for a further discussion of suggestibility and child witnesses.)

One of the factors that may influence the quality of a statement is the age of the child. CBCA studies have demonstrated that statements made by younger children include fewer criteria than the statements of older children (Vrij, 2000). Cognitive abilities and command of language develop throughout childhood, making it gradually easier to give detailed accounts of what has been witnessed. Being able to tell in detail what you have actually witnessed is one thing, being able to tell a convincing lie is another matter. Are young children capable of telling lies which sound convincing? It has been argued that as soon as children are able to consider the listener's mental state they will become better liars (Leekam, 1992). This idea is linked with the 'theory of mind' (see Chapter 5 on autism for a detailed discussion of this). From that stage, children will realise that in order to lie successfully they must convince another of the veracity of a false statement (Oldershaw and Bagby, 1997). A girl who has broken a toy may simply accuse her brother of this transgression. She may also actually try to make her mother believe that her brother has broken the toy, for example by arguing that she is not strong enough to do this herself. Very young children might not be very skilful verbal liars.

Observational data in daily life settings have revealed that four-year-olds' lies typically take the form of one-word responses rather than the more sophisticated elaborations of older children and adults (Bussey, 1992). Polak and Harris (1999) conducted a 'peek study' similar to the study conducted by Lewis *et al.* which was described earlier. If children successfully want to conceal that they have peeked, they should do two things: (1) deny that they have peeked and (2) feign ignorance about what the object looks like that they have secretly observed. Polak and Harris's findings showed that many three- to five-year-olds denied that they had peeked but did not feign ignorance about the object they had seen.

Cultural factors can also be influential. Ruby and Brigham (1998) examined cultural differences in verbal statements. In their laboratory study, both white American and African-American participants took part. They found that certain CBCA criteria were stronger predictors of truth for one ethnic group than for the other, and none of the criteria was a predictor of truthfulness for both ethnic groups.

No theoretical basis

The fact that SVA is a truth-verifying rather than a lie detection method is a second problem worthy of further discussion. This issue raises the question: 'What is the truth?' It is possible that witnesses believe that they have witnessed a particular event, and have detailed and vivid memories of this event, although the event may never have taken place. This phenomenon was earlier defined as 'false beliefs'. These false beliefs, although untrue, are likely to achieve high CBCA scores. Also, a story might be true except for one important detail. Suppose that someone has been sexually abused and provides a rich account of his/her experiences, but misidentifies the perpetrator and accuses an innocent person of being the culprit. Such an account may lead to high CBCA scores (most of the statement is truthful) and might subsequently result in experts believing his/her story. If courts base their decisions on these evaluations, innocent people could be convicted.

The problems for CBCA evaluators in distinguishing between memories of real events and false beliefs might be caused by the fact that, in the development of SVA, psychological theories about memory were not taken into account (Sporer, 1997; Tully, 1999). In that respect, *reality monitoring* might be a useful additional tool in making truth assessments on the basis of verbal statements (Johnson and Raye, 1998). The core of reality monitoring is the claim that memories of experienced events differ in quality from memories of imagined events. Memories of real experiences are obtained through perceptual processes and are therefore likely to contain, amongst others, perceptual information (visual details and details of sound, smell, taste or touch). Accounts of imagined events are derived from an internal source and are therefore likely to contain cognitive operations, such as thoughts and reasonings (e.g. 'I remember thinking about what my friend would like to have for a present'). Looking for these criteria might therefore be an aid to distinguishing between real experiences and false beliefs. Researchers have only just started investigating this.

Summary Section 4

- Research findings have indicated that verbal statements of truth tellers and liars differ on several criteria which form the basis of criteria-based content analysis (CBCA).
- One problem with making statement validity assessments (SVAs) is that factors other than lying or telling the truth (e.g. age) might influence the quality of verbal statements.
- SVA has difficulty in distinguishing between lies and false beliefs, due to the fact that psychological theories about memory were disregarded in the development of the method.

5 What goes on in the liar's body

5.1 The polygraph: how does it work?

Throughout history it has often been assumed that the act of lying is accompanied by physiological activity within the liar's body. For example, the Chinese used to force suspected liars to chew rice powder and then to spit it out. If the resultant powder was dry, then the person was judged to have been lying (Kleinmuntz and Szucko, 1984).

The modern way of detecting physiological activity in liars is by using a **polygraph** (from two Greek words, *poly* meaning 'many', and *grapho*, 'to write'). This is a scientific measuring device which can display, via ink pens on to charts or via a computer's visual display unit, a direct and valid representation of various types of bodily activity (Bull, 1988). The most commonly measured activities are sweating of the fingers, blood pressure and respiration (breathing). The polygraph accurately records even very small differences by amplifying signals picked up from sensors attached to different

Polygraph
A machine that can simultaneously monitor the activity from a number of physiological systems, typically by plotting responses onto moving graph paper.

parts of the body. In the typical use of the polygraph, four sensors are attached to the individual. Pneumatic gauges are stretched around the person's chest and abdomen in order to measure changes in the depth and rate of breathing. A blood pressure cuff placed around the upper arm measures changes in blood pressure, and metal electrodes attached to the fingers measure sweating.

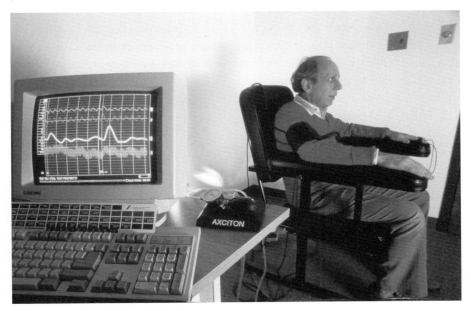

Using a polygraph to measure physiological activity when studying lying

The polygraph measures physiological activity and can record changes in these activities associated with arousal. It is assumed that liars will be more aroused than truth tellers. This may be the result of feeling guilty or, and in a polygraph context more likely, because examinees will be afraid that the polygraph will detect their lies.

Polygraph tests are currently used in criminal investigations in countries all over the world, including Israel, Japan and the USA (Lykken, 1998). In the UK, polygraph trials have been conducted (with sex offenders) to establish the possible benefits of employing the technique (Wilcox *et al.*, 2000), although (at the time of writing) polygraph testing is not currently in police use.

The use of the polygraph is the subject of lively debate. Two leading scientific polygraph researchers, David Raskin (a supporter of the polygraph) and David Lykken (an opponent), have engaged for several decades in prolonged controversy over the reliability and validity of various polygraph tests. They have come into conflict in the scientific literature, as expert witnesses in court and as opponents in legal process against each other. More recently, others such as John Furedy and William Iacono (opposed to the polygraph) and

Charles Honts (supporter of the polygraph) have taken over the Lykken–Raskin dispute.

People sometimes call a polygraph a lie detector, but this term is misleading. A polygraph does not detect lies: it merely detects physiological activity, related to arousal, which may accompany telling a lie. As was the case with nonverbal behaviour and verbal behaviour, a pattern of physiological activity directly related to lying does not exist (Saxe, 1991). This puts the polygraph examiner in the same difficult position as other lie detectors: how to distinguish between arousal caused by 'honest concern' (for example because of being falsely accused) and arousal caused by deception.

There are several polygraph tests. The *control question test* (CQT) is the one most commonly used in criminal investigations, and is the test on which supporters and opponents of polygraph testing generally disagree. The CQT compares responses to relevant questions with responses to control questions. *Relevant questions* are specific questions about the crime. A relevant question in a murder investigation could be: 'On March 12, did you shoot Scott Fisbee?' (Iacono and Patrick, 1997). *Control questions* deal with acts that are related to the crime under investigation, but do not refer to the crime in question. They are general in nature, deliberately vague, and cover long periods of time. They are meant to embarrass the suspects (both guilty and innocent) and to evoke arousal. This is facilitated by, on the one hand, giving the suspect no choice but to lie when answering the control questions, and, on the other hand, making it clear to the suspect that the polygraph will detect this lie. Examiners formulate a control question for which, in their view, a denial is deceptive. The exact formulation of the question will depend on the examinee's circumstances, but a control question in an examination regarding a murder might be: 'Have you ever tried to hurt someone to get revenge?' (Iacono and Patrick, 1997), where the examiner believes that the examinee did indeed hurt someone in his life.

Under normal circumstances, some examinees might admit this wrongdoing. However, during a polygraph examination they will not do this because the examiner will tell the examinee that admitting this would cause the examiner to conclude that the examinee is the type of person who would commit the crime in question and would therefore be considered guilty. Therefore, the examinee has no other choice than to deny this earlier wrongdoing and thus to be untruthful in answering the control questions. Obviously, there is no way that an examinee can be found guilty for having committed a crime by answering control questions untruthfully. In this respect, the examiner's statements are deceptive, which makes the test illegal in many European countries, including the UK where it is forbidden to lie to suspects.

The CQT is based on the assumption that control questions will generate more arousal than the relevant questions in the innocent suspect. First, the *innocent suspect* gives deceptive responses to the control questions but honest responses to the relevant questions. Second, because (1) the examiner puts so much emphasis on the control questions to which the examinee will respond deceptively, and (2) the examinee knows he or she is answering the relevant questions truthfully, the examinee will become more concerned with regard to his or her answers to the control questions. However, the same control questions are expected to elicit less arousal in *guilty suspects* than the relevant questions. A guilty suspect gives deceptive responses to both types of question, which in principle should lead to similar physiological responses to both types of question. However, relevant questions represent the most immediate and serious threat to the examinee, which will lead to a stronger physiological response than the control questions.

A typical CQT consists of about ten questions, of which three are relevant questions, three are control questions and four are filler items that are not used in chart interpretation (Iacono and Patrick, 1997). The set of ten questions is usually repeated three times. The CQT is typically applied in criminal cases in which all other evidence against the suspect is inconclusive. If an examiner concludes that the examinee has failed the CQT, a post-test interrogation typically takes place in which the examinee is pressured to confess. Examinees often do confess, thereby resolving a crime that otherwise possibly would have been unresolved.

This confession-inducing aspect of the CQT is considered very important. US government agencies justify the use of the CQT based on this utility (Iacono and Patrick, 1997). Do you think that this justifies introducing polygraph testing elsewhere?

Activity 4.8

Do you think it is possible to beat the CQT polygraph test and, if so, how? Write down any suggestions and keep your notes to check against Section 5.3 in a moment.

5.2 The polygraph: does it work?

There is a lot of anecdotal evidence in favour of CQT polygraph testing. For example, *The Independent* newspaper reported on 11 October 1999 that polygraph trials in the UK, commenced after evaluations in the USA, showed that they were 97 per cent accurate at detecting deception. Obviously, whether or not the polygraph works should be tested utilising valid and proper scientific tests. However, supporters and opponents of polygraph testing disagree on many issues, including which tests are valid tests of its accuracy. Scientific laboratory studies in polygraph testing often use a 'mock crime' paradigm (see Box 4.6 for an example). 'Guilty participants' are instructed to commit a mock crime and 'innocent participants' are told that they are suspected of such a crime. Both 'innocent' and 'guilty' participants are then submitted to a polygraph test.

4.6 A realistic polygraph study

A unique attempt to conduct a polygraph study in a realistic setting and maintaining certainty about the ground truth was made by Ginton *et al.* (1982). The participants in this study were 21 Israeli policemen who took a paper-and-pencil test that was presented as a requirement for a police course in which they were enrolled. They were asked to score their own tests, which provided an opportunity to cheat by revising their initial answers. However, the test answer sheets were chemically treated so that cheating could be detected.

It turned out that 7 of the 21 participants cheated. Later, all 21 were told that they were suspected of cheating. They were offered a polygraph examination, and were told that their future careers in the police force might depend on the outcome of this examination. (Note that the option to allow the police officers to refuse to take the test was realistic: in most jurisdictions where polygraph testing is used, taking a polygraph test is an option and not an absolute requirement for a suspect.) Although initially all 21 policemen agreed to undergo a polygraph examination, one guilty officer did not turn up for the actual examination, and two (one guilty and one innocent) refused to take the polygraph test. Three other guilty subjects confessed just before the polygraph interrogation, so the final sample included only 2 guilty and 13 innocent participants. The CQT was used, and the outcomes were moderately accurate. Both guilty officers were accurately detected. However, 2 of the 13 innocent officers were mistakenly judged to be lying.

These studies, which generally show favourable results for polygraph testing (although not 97 per cent accuracy!) are fiercely attacked by polygraph opponents. Amongst other things, they argue that the guilty participants have little incentive to try to beat the test (the consequences of being found guilty would not be serious, unlike real-life situations where conviction and imprisonment could be the result), and that innocent participants are unlikely to be concerned about the relevant questions, so that responses to control questions are not suitable for comparison (Iacono and Patrick, 1997).

Numerous field studies have been carried out to date, but they are also subject to debate. One issue is the extent to which studies are methodologically adequate. In their review, Iacono and Patrick (1997), opponents of polygraph testing, included three studies. So did Caroll (1991), another opponent, in his review. Honts and Perry (1992), supporters of polygraph testing, included 'three recent studies' in their review. Perhaps unsurprisingly, Honts and Perry's review (1992) reported the most favourable outcomes. Saxe *et al.* (1985) attempted to provide 'an objective description, to the extent that is possible, of current psychological knowledge of polygraph testing' (p.356). They presented a review which was initiated by the US Congressional Office of Technology Assessment (OTA) to advise President Reagan about polygraph testing. They found 10 studies that met the OTA standards.

The results presented in Figure 4.5 are based upon a review by Vrij (2000) that included more CQT field studies than any previous review (including the 10 OTA studies). This review will not satisfy the polygraph critics as they will say that it includes some 'improper' studies in which the ground truth is not satisfactorily established. It should be noted that the ground truth in most of the studies which were included was confession-based (as was the case in the OTA review). However, given the fact that it is the most comprehensive review so far, it at least gives an accurate review of the results of field studies conducted to date. As can be seen in Figure 4.5, accuracy rates were 72 per cent for truths and 87 per cent for lies (data for 'Nonverbal behaviour' and 'CBCA' are shown for comparison). These accuracy rates are above the level of chance but too low to justify presenting polygraph outcomes as main evidence in courts.

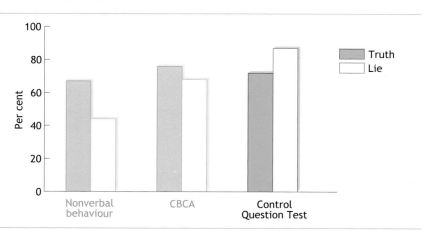

Figure 4.5   Accuracy rates for detecting truths and lies – Control Question Test (Source: derived from Vrij, 2000)

Notice that because the suspect's decision on whether or not to confess is sometimes based upon the polygraph outcome and not on their actual guilt or innocence (see Section 2.8), accuracy scores might be inflated. For example, if an innocent suspect who failed the polygraph test falsely confessed (in order to obtain a reduced sentence), then the incorrect polygraph outcome (guilty) will be classified as a correct decision by the researchers (because the suspect confessed). Alternatively, a guilty suspect who passed the polygraph test is unlikely to confess (due to the lack of evidence against him) and the case is likely to be dismissed due to a lack of sufficient evidence in this case. The incorrect polygraph outcome will not be noticed by the researcher because this case will not be included in the review since there is no confession.

5.3 Can suspects beat the polygraph test?

Polygraph test outcomes have potentially serious consequences for suspects, as they may eventually lead to their conviction. Examinees might therefore try to influence polygraph outcomes and try to produce physiological responses which may lead the examiner to conclude that they are telling the truth. Methods to achieve this are called 'countermeasures'. It is probably easier for examinees to increase their arousal while answering control questions than to lower their arousal while answering relevant questions. Therefore, countermeasures are generally meant to increase arousal during control questions. Different countermeasures can be distinguished, such as foot tensing (pressing your toes against the sole of your shoe) or tongue biting while answering the control questions.

Reid and Inbau (1977) did not seem to worry about the effectiveness of countermeasures. They argued that it is highly improbable that countermeasures can succeed, because properly trained examiners would notice that the examinee is trying to fool them. However, several studies, some conducted by polygraph supporters, have shown that the use of countermeasures can be very effective in defeating polygraph tests, and that they sometimes remain unnoticed by polygraph examiners (Honts *et al.*, 1994).

The most famous countermeasures test has probably been conducted by Floyd 'Buzz' Fay, a man who was falsely convicted of murder on the basis of a failed polygraph examination. He took it on himself to become a polygraph expert during his two-and-a-half years of wrongful imprisonment. He coached 27 inmates, who all freely confessed to him that they were guilty, in how to beat the control question polygraph test. After only 20 minutes of instruction, 23 of the 27 inmates were successful in defeating the polygraph examination (Kleinmuntz and Szucko, 1984).

You may wonder whether this case provides compelling evidence against the value of polygraph testing.

Summary Section 5

- A polygraph is a machine that can accurately measure changes in physiology associated with arousal within a person's body.
- Changes in arousal during a polygraph test are expected to occur when a person is lying but may also occur when people are not lying.
- One crucial element of the CQT is to deceive examinees (about the importance of control questions), which makes the test illegal in the UK where it is forbidden to deceive suspects.
- Examinees are able to fool polygraph examiners by using countermeasures.

6   Conclusion

This chapter has discussed the extent to which people are able to detect lies by paying attention to someone's behaviour, speech content and physiological responses. Results have demonstrated that observers are to some extent able to detect lies by paying attention to these aspects. However, mistakes in lie detection are inevitable. Will people ever become perfect lie detectors? Researchers continue their work to develop the foolproof lie detection test, but it seems unlikely that they will ever succeed. This is probably bad news for professional lie catchers, but perhaps not for others. Do we really want to know the truth all the time? It might well leave us with low self-esteem (Anderson *et al.*, 1999) or a wrecked relationship (Sagarin *et al.*, 1998). Professional lie catchers should keep in mind that a perfect lie detection test already exists: obtaining hard evidence which indisputably links the person to the suspected lie. However, this usually means that the police have to be out and about in order to find hard evidence (with all the resource implications that entails), instead of measuring suspects' responses inside the police station.

Further reading

Ekman, P. (1992) *Telling Lies: Clues to Deceit in the Marketplace, Politics and Marriage*, New York, W.W. Norton.

This book offers an account of how facial expressions of emotion and other nonverbal cues can reveal deception, and provides guidelines on how to spot these cues.

Lykken, D.T. (1998) *A Tremor in the Blood: Uses and Abuses of the Lie Detector*, New York, Plenum Press.

This text offers an accessible and critical view on the use of the polygraph.

Vrij, A. (2000) *Detecting Lies and Deceit: The Psychology of Lying and the Implications for Professional Practice*, Chichester, John Wiley and Sons.

This book provides more information about nonverbal, verbal and physiological indicators of deceit, and more about how to detect deceit.

 # References

Allwood, C.M. and Granhag, P.A. (1997) 'Feelings of confidence and the realism of confidence judgements in everyday life' in Juslin, P. and Montgomery, H. (eds) *Judgement and Decision Making: Neo-Brunswikian and Process-Tracing Approaches*, Mahwah, NJ, Lawrence Erlbaum.

Anderson, D.E., Ansfield, M.E. and DePaulo, B.M. (1999) 'Love's best habit: deception in the context of relationships' in Philippot, P., Feldman, R.S. and Coats, E.J. (eds) *The Social Context of Nonverbal Behaviour*, Cambridge, Cambridge University Press.

Anderson, D.E., DePaulo, B.M. and Ansfield, M.E. (2000) 'The Development of Deception Detection Skill: A Longitudinal Study of Same Sex Friends', *Journal of Nonverbal Behavior*, vol. 23, pp. 67–89.

Backbier, E., Hoogstraten, J. and Meerum Terwogt-Kouwenhoven, K. (1997) 'Situational determinants of the acceptability of telling lies', *Journal of Applied Social Psychology*, vol. 27, pp. 1048–62.

Backbier, E. and Sieswerda, S. (1997) 'Wanneer en waarom liegen we eigenlijk?', *Nederlands Tijdschrift voor de Psychologie*, vol. 52, pp. 255–64.

Bell, K.L. and DePaulo, B.M. (1996) 'Liking and lying', *Basic and Applied Social Psychology*, vol. 18, pp. 243–66.

Bond, C.F. and Fahey, W.E. (1987) 'False suspicion and the misperception of deceit', *British Journal of Social Psychology*, vol. 26, pp. 41–6.

Bond, C.F., Kahler, K.N. and Paolicelli, L.M. (1985) 'The miscommunication of deception: an adaptive perspective', *Journal of Experimental Social Psychology*, vol. 21, pp. 331–45.

Bond, C.F. and Robinson, M. (1988) 'The evolution of deception', *Journal of Nonverbal Behavior*, vol. 12, pp. 295–307.

Bull, R. (1988) 'What is the lie-detection test?' in Gale, A. (ed.) *The Polygraph Test: Lies, Truth and Science*, London, Sage.

Bull, R. (1998) 'Obtaining information from child witnesses' in Memon, A., Vrij, A. and Bull, R. (eds) *Psychology and Law: Truthfulness, Accuracy and Credibility*, Maidenhead, McGraw-Hill.

Burgoon, J.K. and Buller, D.B. (1994) 'Interpersonal deception, III. Effects of deceit on perceived communication and nonverbal dynamics', *Journal of Nonverbal Behavior*, vol. 18, pp. 155–84.

Buss, D.M. and Barnes, M. (1986) 'Preferences in human mate selection', *Journal of Personality and Social Psychology*, vol. 50, pp. 559–70.

Bussey, K. (1992) 'Children's lying and truthfulness: implications for children's testimony', in Ceci, S.J., DeSimone Leichtman, M. and Putnick, M. (eds).

Carroll, D. (1991) 'Lie detection: lies and truths' in Cochrane, R. and Carroll, D. (eds) *Psychology and Social Issues: A Tutorial Test*, London, The Falmer Press.

Ceci, S.J. and Bruck, M. (1995) *Jeopardy in the Courtroom*, Washington, DC, American Psychological Association.

Ceci, S.J. and Bruck, M. (1998) 'Reliability and credibility of young children's reports', *American Psychologist*, vol. 53, pp. 136–51.

Ceci, S.J., Huffman, M.L., Smith, E. and Loftus, E.F. (1994a) 'Repeatedly thinking about a non-event', *Consciousness and Cognition*, vol. 3, pp. 388–407.

Ceci, S.J., Loftus, E.F., Leichtman, M.D. and Bruck, M. (1994b) 'The possible role of source misattributions in the creation of false beliefs among preschoolers', *The International Journal of Clinical and Experimental Hypnosis*, vol. 17, pp. 304–20.

Clarke, S. (1999) 'Justifying deception in social science research', *Journal of Applied Philosophy*, vol. 16, pp. 151–65.

DePaulo, B.M. (1994) 'Spotting lies: can humans learn to do better?', *Current Directions in Psychological Science*, vol. 3, pp. 83–6.

DePaulo, B.M., Anderson, D.E. and Cooper, H. (1999) *Explicit and implicit deception detection*, paper presented at the Society of Experimental Social Psychologists, St. Louis, October.

DePaulo, B.M. and Jordan, A. (1982) 'Age changes in deceiving and detecting deceit', in Feldman, R.S. (ed.) *Development of Nonverbal Behaviour in Children*, New York, Springer-Verlag.

DePaulo, B.M. and Kashy, D.A. (1998) 'Everyday lies in close and casual relationships', *Journal of Personality and Social Psychology*, vol. 74, pp. 63–79.

DePaulo, B.M., Kashy, D.A., Kirkendol, S.E., Wyer, M.M. and Epstein, J.A. (1996) 'Lying in everyday life', *Journal of Personality and Social Psychology*, vol. 70, pp. 979–95.

DePaulo, B.M. and Kirkendol, S.E. (1989) 'The motivational impairment effect in the communication of deception' in Yuille, J.C. (ed.) *Credibility Assessment*, Dordrecht, the Netherlands, Kluwer.

DePaulo, B.M., Lindsay, J.L., Malone, B.E., Muhlenbruck, L., Charlton, K. and Cooper, H. (2000) 'Cues to Deception', *Psychological Bulletin*, vol. 129, pp. 74–118.

DePaulo, B.M. and Pfeifer, R.L. (1986) 'On-the-job experience and skill at detecting deception', *Journal of Applied Social Psychology*, vol. 16, pp. 249–67.

DePaulo, B.M. and Rosenthal, R. (1979) 'Telling lies', *Journal of Personality and Social Psychology*, vol. 37, pp. 1713–22.

DePaulo, B.M., Stone, J.I. and Lassiter, G.D. (1985) 'Telling ingratiating lies: effects of target sex and target attractiveness on verbal and nonverbal deceptive success', *Journal of Personality and Social Psychology*, vol. 48, pp. 1191–203.

Ekman, P. (1992) *Telling Lies: Clues to Deceit in the Marketplace, Politics and Marriage*, New York, W.W. Norton.

Ekman, P. and Friesen, W.V. (1972) 'Hand movements', *Journal of Communication*, vol. 22, pp. 353–74.

Ekman, P. and Friesen, W.V. (1974) 'Detecting deception from the body or face', *Journal of Personality and Social Psychology*, vol. 29, pp. 288–98.

Ekman, P., Friesen, W.V. and O'Sullivan, M. (1988) 'Smiles when lying', *Journal of Personality and Social Psychology*, vol. 54, pp. 414–20.

Ekman, P., Friesen, W.V. and Scherer, K.R. (1976) 'Body movement and voice pitch in deceptive interaction', *Semiotica*, vol. 16, pp. 23–7.

Ekman, P. and O'Sullivan, M. (1991) 'Who can catch a liar?', *American Psychologist*, vol. 46, pp. 913–20.

Ekman, P., O'Sullivan, M. and Frank, M.G. (1999) 'A few can catch a liar', *Psychological Science*, vol. 10, pp. 263–6.

Eyre, S.L., Read, N.W. and Millstein, S.G. (1997) 'Adolescent sexual strategies', *Journal of Adolescent Health*, vol. 20, pp. 286–93.

Feeley, T.H. and deTurck, M.A. (1997) *Perceptions of Communication as Seen by the Actor and as Seen by the Observer: The Case of Lie Detection*, paper presented at the International Communication Association Annual Conference, Montreal, Canada.

Feeley, T.H., deTurck, M.A. and Young, M.J. (1995) 'Baseline familiarity in lie detection', *Communication Research Reports*, vol. 12, pp. 160–9.

Feldman, R.S., Jenkins, L. and Popoola, O. (1979) 'Detection of deception in adults and children via facial expressions', *Child Development*, vol. 50, pp. 350–5.

Frank, M.G. and Ekman, P. (1997) 'The ability to detect deceit generalizes across different types of high-stake lies', *Journal of Personality and Social Psychology*, vol. 72, pp. 1429–39.

Ginton, A., Daie, N., Elaad, E. and Ben-Shakhar, G. (1982) 'A method for evaluating the use of the polygraph in a real life situation', *Journal of Applied Psychology*, vol. 67, pp. 131–7.

Goffman, E. (1959) *The Presentation of Self in Everyday Life*, New York, Doubleday.

Goldman-Eisler, F. (1968) *Psycholinguistics: Experiments in Spontaneous Speech*, New York, Doubleday.

Granhag, P.A. and Strömwall, L.A. (2001) 'Detection deception based on repeated interrogations', *Legal and Criminological Psychology*, vol. 6, pp. 85–101.

Gudjonsson, G.H. (1992) *The Psychology of Interrogations, Confessions and Testimony*, Chichester, Wiley & Sons.

Hocking, J.E. and Leathers, D.G. (1980) 'Nonverbal indicators of deception: a new theoretical perspective', *Communication Monographs*, vol. 47, pp. 119–31.

Honts, C.R. and Perry, M.V. (1992) 'Polygraph admissibility: changes and challenges', *Law and Human Behavior*, vol. 16, pp. 357–79.

Honts, C.R., Raskin, D.C. and Kircher, J.C. (1994) 'Mental and physical countermeasures reduce the accuracy of polygraph tests', *Journal of Applied Psychology*, vol. 79, pp. 252–9.

Iacono, W.G. and Patrick, C.J. (1997) 'Polygraphy and integrity testing' in Rogers, R. (ed.).

Inbau, F.E., Reid, J.E. and Buckley, J.P. (1986) *Criminal Interrogation and Confessions*, Baltimore, Williams and Wilkins.

Johnson, M.K. and Raye, C.L. (1998) 'False memories and confabulation', *Trends in Cognitive Sciences*, vol. 2, pp. 137–45.

Kassin, S.M. and Fong, C.T. (1999) '"I'm innocent!": Effects of training on judgements of truth and deception in the interrogation room', *Law and Human Behavior*, vol. 23, pp. 499–516.

Kleinmuntz, B. and Szucko, J.J. (1984) 'Lie detection in ancient and modern times: a call for contemporary scientific study', *American Psychologist*, vol. 39, pp. 766–76.

Kline, P. (1993) *The Handbook of Psychological Testing*, New York, Routledge.

Köhnken, G. (1999) *Statement Validity Assessment,* paper presented at the pre-conference programme of applied courses 'Assessing credibility' organised by the European Association of Psychology and Law, Dublin, Ireland, July.

Krauss, R.M. (1981) 'Impression formation, impression management, and nonverbal behaviours' in Higgins, E.T., Herman, C.P. and Zanna, M.P. (eds) *Social Cognition: The Ontario Symposium* (vol. 1), Hillsdale, NJ, Lawrence Erlbaum Associates.

Leekam, S.R. (1992) 'Believing and deceiving: steps to becoming a good liar' in Ceci, S.J., DeSimone Leichtman, M. and Putnick, M. (eds).

Levine, T.R. and McCornack, S.A. (1992) 'Linking love and lies: a formal test of the McCornack and Parks model of deception detection', *Journal of Social and Personal Relationships*, vol. 9, pp. 143–54.

Levine, T.R., McCornack, S.A., and Parks, H.S. (1999) 'Accuracy in detecting truths and lies: documenting the "veracity effect"', *Communication Monographs*, vol. 66, pp. 125–44.

Lewis, M., Stanger, C. and Sullivan, M.W. (1989) 'Deception in three-year-olds', *Developmental Psychology*, vol. 25, pp. 439–43.

Lippard, P.V. (1988) '"Ask me no questions, I'll tell you no lies": situational exigencies for interpersonal deception', *Western Journal of Speech Communication*, vol. 52, pp. 91–103.

Lykken, D.T. (1998) *A Tremor in the Blood: Uses and Abuses of the Lie Detector*, New York, Plenum Press.

Malone, B.E. and DePaulo, B.M. (2001) 'Measuring sensivity to deception' in Hall, J.A. and Bernieri, F. (eds) *Interpersonal Sensivity: Theory, Measurement and Application*, Hillsdale, NJ, Lawrence Erlbaum Associates.

Mann, S., Vrij, A. and Bull, R. (2001) 'Suspects, Lies and Videotape: An Analysis of Authentic High-Stake Liars', *Law and Human Behavior*, vol. 26, pp. 365–76.

Metts, S. (1989) 'An exploratory investigation of deception in close relationships', *Journal of Social and Personal Relationships*, vol. 6, pp. 159–79.

Miller, G.R. and Stiff, J.B. (1993) *Deceptive Communication*, Newbury Park, CA, Sage.

Mitchell, R.W. (1986) 'A framework for discussing deception' in Mitchell, R.W. and Mogdil, N.S. (eds) *Deception: Perspectives on Human and Nonhuman Deceit*, Albany, NY, State University of New York Press.

Moston, S.J. and Engelberg, T. (1993) 'Police questioning techniques in tape recorded interviews with criminal suspects', *Policing and Society*, vol. 3, pp. 223–37.

Oldershaw, L. and Bagby, R.M. (1997) 'Children and deception' in Rogers, R. (ed.).

Parker, A.D. and Brown, J. (2000) 'Detection of deception: statement validity analysis as a means of determining truthfulness or falsity of rape allegations', *Legal and Criminological Psychology*, vol. 5, pp. 237–59.

Polak, A. and Harris, P.L. (1999) 'Deception by young children following noncompliance', *Developmental Psychology*, vol. 35, pp. 561–8.

Porter, S., Yuille, J.C. and Lehman, D.R. (1999) 'The nature of real, implanted and fabricated memories for emotional childhood events: implications for the recovered memory debate', *Law and Human Behavior*, vol. 23, pp. 517–37.

Raskin, D.C. and Esplin, P.W. (1991) 'Statement Validity Assessment: interview procedures and content analysis of children's statements of sexual abuse', *Behavioral Assessment*, vol. 13, pp. 265–91.

Rassin, E., Merckelbach, H. and Crombag, H. (1997) 'De Criteria Based Content Analysis (CBCA) als instrument om de geloofwaardigheid van getuigenverklaringen te bepalen', *Nederlandse Justitiele Betrekkingen*, vol. 42, pp. 1923–9.

Reid, J.E. and Inbau, F.E. (1977) *Truth and Deception: The Polygraph (Lie Detector) Technique*, Baltimore, Williams & Wilkins.

Riggio, R.E. (1986) 'Assessment of basic social skills', *Journal of Personality and Social Psychology*, vol. 51, pp. 649–60.

Riggio, R.E., Tucker, J. and Throckmorton, B. (1988) 'Social skills and deception ability', *Personality and Social Psychology Bulletin*, vol. 13, pp. 568–77.

Robinson, W.P., Shepherd, A. and Heywood, J. (1998) 'Truth, equivocation/ concealment, and lies in job applications and doctor–patient communication', *Journal of Language and Social Psychology*, vol. 17, pp. 149–64.

Rowatt, W.C., Cunningham, M.R. and Druen, P.B. (1998) 'Deception to get a date', *Personality and Social Psychology Bulletin*, vol. 24, pp. 1228–42.

Rowatt, W.C., Cunningham, M.R. and Druen, P.B. (1999) 'Lying to get a date: the effect of facial physical attractiveness on the willingness to deceive prospective dating partners', *Journal of Social and Personal Relationships*, vol. 16, pp. 209–23.

Ruby, C.L. and Brigham, J.C. (1997) 'The usefulness of the criteria-based content analysis technique in distinguishing between truthful and fabricated allegations', *Psychology, Public Policy, and Law*, vol. 3, pp. 705–37.

Ruby, C.L. and Brigham, J.C. (1998) 'Can Criteria-Based Content Analysis distinguish between true and false statements of African-American speakers?', *Law and Human Behavior*, vol. 22, pp. 369–88.

Sagarin, B.J., Rhoads, K.L. and Cialdini, R.B. (1998) 'Deceiver's distrust: denigration as a consequence of undiscovered deception', *Personality and Social Psychology Bulletin*, vol. 24, pp. 1167–76.

Saxe, L. (1991) 'Science and the CQT Polygraph: a theoretical critique', *Integrative Physiological and Behavioral Science*, vol. 26, pp. 223–31.

Saxe, L., Dougherty, D. and Cross, T. (1985) 'The validity of polygraph testing: scientific analysis and public controversy', *American Psychologist*, vol. 40, pp. 355–66.

Sporer, S.L. (1997) 'The less travelled road to truth: verbal cues in deception detection in accounts of fabricated and self-experienced events', *Applied Cognitive Psychology*, vol. 11, pp. 373–97.

Steller, M. (1989) 'Recent developments in statement analysis' in Yuille, J.C. (ed.) *Credibility Assessment*, Deventer, the Netherlands, Kluwer.

Steller, M. and Köhnken, G. (1989) 'Criteria-Based Content Analysis' in Raskin, D.C. (ed.) *Psychological Methods in Criminal Investigation and Evidence*, New York, Springer-Verlag.

Stiff, J.B., Kim, H.J. and Ramesh, C.N. (1992) 'Truth biases and aroused suspicion in relational deception', *Communication Research*, vol. 19, pp. 326–45.

Tooke, W. and Camire, L. (1991) 'Patterns of deception in intersexual and intrasexual mating strategies', *Ethology and Sociobiology*, vol. 12, pp. 345–64.

Tully, B. (1999) 'Statement validation' in Canter, D. and Alison, L. (eds) *Interviewing and Deception*, Darmouth, Ashgate.

Tye, M.C., Amato, S.L., Honts, C.R., Kevitt, M.K. and Peters, D. (1999) 'The willingness of children to lie and the assessment of credibility in an ecologically relevant laboratory setting', *Applied Developmental Science*, vol. 3, pp. 92–109.

Undeutsch, U. (1967) 'Beurteilung der Glaubhaftigkeit von Aussagen' in Undeutsch, U. (ed.) *Handbuch der Psychologie vol. 11, Forensische Psychologie*, Göttingen, Germany, Hogrefe.

Vrij, A. (1994) 'The impact of information and setting on detection of deception by police detectives', *Journal of Nonverbal Behavior*, vol. 18, pp. 117–37.

Vrij, A. (1995) 'Behavioural correlates of deception in a simulated police interview', *Journal of Psychology: Interdisciplinary and Applied*, vol. 129, pp. 15–29.

Vrij, A. (2000) *Detecting Lies and Deceit: The Psychology of Lying and the Implications for Professional Practice*, Chichester, John Wiley and Sons.

Vrij, A. (2001) 'Telling and detecting lies as a function of raising the stakes' in Breur, C.M., Kommer, M.M., Nijboer, J.F. and Reintjes, J.M. (eds) *New Trends in Criminal Investigation and Evidence II*, Antwerp, Belgium, Intersentia.

Vrij, A. (2002) 'Deception in children: a literature review and implications for children's testimony' in Westcott, H., Davies, G. and Bull R. (eds) *Children's Testimony*, Chichester, Wiley and Sons.

Vrij, A., Akehurst, L. and Morris, P. (1997) 'Individual differences in hand movements during deception', *Journal of Nonverbal Behavior*, vol. 21, pp. 87–103.

Vrij, A., Edward, K. and Bull, R. (2001a) 'People's insight into their behaviour and speech content while lying', *British Journal of Psychology*, vol. 92, pp. 373–89.

Vrij, A., Edward, K. and Bull, R. (2001b) 'Police officers ability to detect deceit: the benefit of indirect deception detection measures', *Legal and Criminological Psychology*, vol. 6, pp. 185–96.

Vrij, A. and Mann, S. (2001a) 'Lying when the stakes are high: deceptive behaviour of a murderer during his police interview', *Applied Cognitive Psychology*, vol. 15, pp. 187–203.

Vrij, A. and Mann, S. (2001b) 'Who killed my relative? Police officers' ability to detect real-life high-stake lies', *Psychology, Crime, and Law*, vol. 7, pp. 119–32.

Vrij, A. and Semin, G.R. (1996) 'Lie experts' beliefs about nonverbal indicators of deception', *Journal of Nonverbal Behaviour*, vol. 20, pp. 65–80.

Vrij, A. and van Wijngaarden, J.J. (1994) 'Will the truth come out? Two studies about the detection of false statements expressed by children', *Expert Evidence*, vol. 3, pp. 78–84.

Vrij, A. and Winkel, F.W. (1991) 'Cultural patterns in Dutch and Surinam nonverbal behavior: an analysis of simulated police/citizen encounters', *Journal of Nonverbal Behavior*, vol. 15, pp. 169–84.

Vrij, A. and Winkel, F.W. (1992) 'Crosscultural police–citizen interactions: the influence of race, beliefs and nonverbal communication on impression formation', *Journal of Applied Social Psychology*, vol. 22, pp. 1546–59.

Vrij, A. and Winkel, F.W. (1994) 'Perceptual distortions in crosscultural interrogations: the impact of skin colour, accent, speech style and spoken fluency on impression formation', *Journal of Cross-Cultural Psychology*, vol. 25, pp. 284–96.

Vrij, A., Winkel, F.W. and Koppelaar, L. (1991) 'Interactie tussen politiefunctionarissen en allochtone burgers: twee studies naar de frequentie en het effect van aan- en wegkijken op de impressieformatie', *Nederlands Tijdschrift voor de Psychologie*, vol. 46, pp. 8–20.

Wilcox, D.T., Sosnowski, D. and Middleton, D. (2000) 'Polygraphy and sex offenders', *Forensic Update*, vol. 61, pp. 20–5.

Zuckerman, M., DePaulo, B.M. and Rosenthal, R. (1981) 'Verbal and nonverbal communication of deception' in Berkowitz, L. (ed.) *Advances in Experimental Social Psychology, Volume 1*, New York, Academic Press.

The autistic spectrum: from theory to practice

Ilona Roth

Contents

This chapter offers a review of psychological research and practice aimed at understanding and explaining autistic spectrum disorders (ASDs) and helping people who have them. The discussion ranges from problems of identification and diagnosis, through theoretical research into causes, to an evaluation of selected therapeutic approaches. The chapter highlights the diversity of perspectives that exist in this area. It draws on the personal testimony of people with autism and their families, as well as on more formal sources of evidence. It will be of relevance to all those who are interested in autism, whether from an academic, practical or personal perspective. The coverage is necessarily selective: it poses many questions for consideration, but does not claim to offer definitive answers.

Aims

This chapter aims to:

- provide an understanding of autistic spectrum disorders (ASDs)
- illustrate a range of theoretical and practical perspectives on this area and the links and contrasts between them
- consider the principles and problems of diagnosing autistic spectrum disorders
- highlight the theoretical and practical implications of treating autistic disorders as a spectrum
- emphasise the developmental trajectory of autistic spectrum disorders, and its implications
- outline and evaluate socio-cognitive and biological explanations of autistic spectrum disorders
- outline and evaluate a range of therapeutic and educational approaches, within an evidence-based framework.

1 Introduction

Christopher was born a normal, healthy baby, or so we thought ... Chris always preferred objects to people – his first smile was directed at the cat, always a firm favourite. The only time he really laughed was when tickled or thrown up into the air. At the time we didn't think anything was wrong. After our daughter, who was hyperactive and only slept a few hours here and there, we welcomed this placid little soul who never demanded anything.

At about 10 months of age a dramatic change came over our docile little boy. It was just as if somebody had turned on a switch. In the space of a week he crawled, walked and climbed – to the top of the wall units. He had absolutely no sense of danger and usually came down the quick way, head first ... By the time Chris was eighteen months old the speech that he had had, disappeared ...

My sister-in-law ... was visiting and picked Chris up ... She said 'Do you know, I can't get this baby to look me in the eyes.' It was only at this point that we realised that Chris had never looked us straight in the eyes.

(The National Autistic Society, Annual Report, 1987, p. 3, parent of a child with autism)

Alison was a happy, chubby, lively little girl, totally dependent on us for all her needs. Living in a world of her own, she took little notice of her surroundings, but was used to the routine we had formed. We noticed that she would constantly rock herself backwards and forwards, and seemed to get some sort of relief or comfort from this ...We also bought her a little rocking chair which she really loved, and because she responded to music, the radio used to please her, and the record player was in constant use.

(*Cole, 1987, p. 3*)

To me it's not the big misunderstandings, the ones you read about in books on autism, that has been most difficult. Like for example misinterpreting 'Give me your hands' and think they want you to chop them off.

What has been very confusing and often hurtful are the more subtle ones, the ones that no-one ever could explain. Like when someone said 'It's getting better' or 'Of course you will get that job', and I thought this meant they actually knew this.

(*Gerland, 1997, p. 15, writing about herself*)

I must mention that the boy loved to watch the different calendars of different rooms and then recall the numbers. He also compared them. He thus spent a lot of time, gazing at the numbers. He wanted to know what they meant. He found a kind of pattern in them. He wondered how the figures bent and straightened up, curled and sometimes broke!

(*Mukhopadhyay, 2000, p. 19, writing about himself*)

These extracts are about children and adults with autism. If you know someone with autism, the descriptions may well be familiar. For those of you have not had such close contact, they are designed to give an initial insight into what it is like to have autism or a related condition such as Asperger's syndrome (see Section 3.2 for a definition of this). One reason for including parental accounts is that parents can often pinpoint a particular moment in their child's infancy at which they started to have anxieties. Another is that, even as they grow older, most people with severe forms of autism appear to lack the capacity for self-reflection and the communication skills necessary to describe their own experiences. Though a few researchers (e.g. Grayson, 1997, p. 231–42) believe that the communicative competence of profoundly autistic people is underestimated, impairments in this area are generally considered to be key features of autism. The minority of individuals like Gunilla Gerland and Tito Mukhopadhyay, who can describe the problem in their own terms, have played an invaluable role in enhancing understanding in recent years.

1.1 Key concepts for this chapter

The word autism comes originally from 'autos', the Greek word for 'self' and means, literally, being absorbed in oneself. In 1943, the psychiatrist Leo Kanner adopted the term to describe some of his child patients: they appeared isolated from the world, withdrawn from social contact, and most had severe intellectual difficulties (Kanner, 1943). Kanner became convinced that these and other features of the children's behaviour reflected a **syndrome**, a specific disorder with a characteristic set of symptoms. Increasingly in recent years, the idea of an autistic syndrome has been elaborated to allow for a spectrum – a range or constellation of disorders reflecting slightly different patterns of symptoms, and collectively known as **autistic spectrum disorders**. The terms 'autism' and 'autistic spectrum disorders' (ASDs for short) will be used interchangeably throughout this chapter, as they are in much clinical work, as generic descriptions of this spectrum. Where the discussion deals specifically with the core or prototypical autistic syndrome, this will be referred to as **classic autism**; the terminology relevant to other sub-types of ASD will be introduced as necessary.

   Despite individual variation in symptoms, ASDs are usually considered to involve a three-way pattern of impairment originally described by the psychiatrist Lorna Wing (Wing and Gould, 1979). This so-called **triad** consists of impairments in:

- reciprocal social interaction
- reciprocal communication
- scope and range of activities and interests

Figure 5.1 illustrates key symptoms in the three areas of the triad. The central triangle gives examples of non-triad skills that may accompany the impairments.

   A consistent finding is that males are more likely to be affected by ASDs than females: the ratio ranges from 4:1 for classic autism to as much as 10:1 for 'milder' conditions within the spectrum. This is a typical feature of developmental disorders where communication is a central component.

Syndrome
A psychological or medical condition characterised by a specific set of symptoms that regularly occur together forming a recognisable pattern.

Autistic spectrum disorders
Collective term for the group of closely related conditions all of which share some or many of the symptoms of classic autism.

Classic autism
The most typical type of autistic spectrum disorder, characterised by impairments in social interaction, verbal and non-verbal communication, and restricted scope of activities and interests.

Triad
Characteristic three-way pattern of impairments in autistic spectrum disorders.

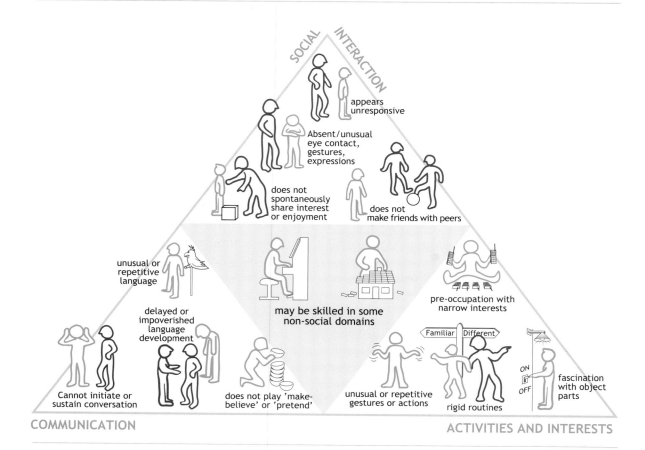

Figure 5.1   The triad of impairments in ASDs

1.2 Discussing people with autism

Research and clinical literature often refers to 'autistic individuals' or 'autistic children', terms that many, including people with autism themselves, see as undermining their humanity. **The National Autistic Society** (NAS) advocates the use of the terms 'people with autism' or 'people with an autistic spectrum disorder', and this chapter will use such terminology as far as possible. However, Clare Sainsbury, who herself suffers from an ASD, has written:

> *I object to the insistence on using 'people-first' language ... We are not people who 'just happen to have' autism; it is not an appendage that can be separated from who we are as people, nor is it something shameful that has to be reduced to a sub-clause.*

(*Sainsbury, 2000, p. 12*)

Issues of 'labelling' are clearly complex ones, as we have previously seen in relation to PTSD, and will be further discussed in Section 2 below.

National Autistic Society
Organisation for people with ASDs, their families and carers. Acts as a forum for exchange of ideas and information, spearheads national and international initiatives and raises public consciousness.

1.3 A framework for this chapter

The different perspectives explored in the chapter are linked by several explanatory threads:

- theory–practice interplay
- multidisciplinary approaches
- different levels of analysis
- different kinds of evidence
- the question of 'difference'.

Each of these 'threads' is introduced briefly below.

Theory–practice interplay: The psychological work on autism discussed in this chapter represents a variety of professional perspectives that share the twin goals of establishing effective theoretical understanding, and of harnessing this understanding to provide effective support and therapy. The perspectives vary in their theoretical assumptions and in the extent to which they emphasise research or practical advances in diagnosis, therapy and education. As you will see, there is no clear-cut division between 'pure research' and 'practical application', and the narrative throughout the chapter highlights the close interplay between theoretical and applied activities.

Multidisciplinary approaches: Theoretical and applied activities may involve the same people, or different individuals within one team. Such team work is therefore *multidisciplinary*. Autism can result in problems in family, school and social settings, as well as involving medical complications such as epilepsy. So, while this chapter features the work of research, clinical and educational psychologists, it also includes the work of **psychiatrists**, **neurologists**, and other medical specialists, teachers and health visitors. Families and carers of people with autism also make important contributions to this team work.

Different levels of analysis: The three level framework proposed by Frith (1999) suggests that there are three main perspectives on any developmental condition: behavioural, cognitive and biological. Each of these perspectives must also consider the role of the individual's environment. Frith's framework provides a key organising dimension of this chapter, with one modification: we shall extend the cognitive to include the social. As you progress through the different sections, you will find that the major focus shifts between these levels as outlined below:

Behavioural level: Work on the identification, diagnosis and mapping of ASDs, discussed in Sections 2 and 3, is extensively (though not exclusively) informed by descriptions of the observable behavioural manifestations of autism. Some of the therapeutic work discussed in Section 6 is also targeted at altering behaviour, rather than dealing with 'underlying' problems.

Socio-cognitive level: This level is termed socio-cognitive to emphasise that it embraces *all* of the person's mental functioning – the processes by which a

Psychiatrist
Medical doctor specialising in the diagnosis and treatment of psychological problems or disorders.

Neurologist
Medical doctor specialising in the diagnosis and treatment of disorders of the nervous system.

person with autism makes sense of the social world are as much affected as those used to recognise objects and events; emotional functioning is affected as well as more intellectual thought processes. This level is the focus for Section 4, and it also informs the diagnostic advances and therapeutic work discussed in Section 6.

Biological level: This level comprises several sublevels: damage or faults in the genes that a person inherits may in turn affect the biochemical and physiological functioning of neurons and other cells, body organs and endocrine (hormonal) systems, and the structure and functioning of brain areas and circuits. There may even be evolutionary factors to consider. Section 5 considers the role of such biological influences in autism while some of the therapeutic work discussed in Section 6 is informed by biological ideas.

Remember that the individual's *environment* provides a context that can influence (or be influenced by) each of the levels we have identified. This may be the biological environment in which the nervous system develops, the physical environment in which we operate as living organisms, or the social environment in which we function as human beings. It is important to think of autism as involving a **developmental trajectory** – a process that unfolds across time, in interaction with these multiple environmental contexts. Current understanding of these interactions is limited, but they are considered at the end of Sections 3, 4 and 5.

Developmental trajectory
The notion that development occurs over an extended time span and takes a particular pathway, in interaction with multiple environmental contexts.

Different kinds of evidence: Much of the work represented in this chapter necessarily approaches autism from an outside perspective whereby the researcher or practitioner seeks to describe, explain and address a psychological problem within a framework of dispassionate observation, theorisation and therapy. But as we saw at the beginning of this section, personal or insider accounts offer a different type of evidence that can inform and enrich outsider perspectives. Arguably, parents' understanding of their children has something of this 'inside' status, so parental accounts are treated as a further special source of evidence.

The question of 'difference': At each stage of the chapter we will encounter some of the tension between highlighting differences between people and stressing their similarities. In particular, the difficulties of clearly demarcating the boundary between the autism spectrum and 'normality' will be apparent.

Section 2 opens this account of work on autism by considering the diagnostic process. Remember that most of the features of behaviour described will be shown by all children at some time or another. A psychologist or psychiatrist will make a careful evaluation of a wide range of evidence before making a diagnosis of autism.

Summary Section 1

- The term 'autism' was originally introduced by the psychiatrist Kanner to describe a syndrome he observed in some of his child patients.
- People with autistic spectrum disorders have a moderate to profound inability to make sense of, and engage 'normally' with, everyday events and situations, particularly those with a 'human' content.
- They have particular difficulties in three areas: social interaction, language and communication, and rigid adherence to narrow interests, routines and activities.
- Current thinking favours the idea of autism as a spectrum of difficulties.
- Males are more frequently affected than females.
- Psychological work on autistic spectrum disorders embraces a variety of interacting perspectives and disciplines, all of which seek understanding of the condition and effective approaches to support and treatment.
- This work is characterised by different levels of analysis and the use of different kinds of evidence.

2 Identifying and diagnosing autistic conditions

The starting point for all systematic work on ASDs, whether in the field of research, therapy or education, is a clear and agreed description of characteristic patterns of symptoms for use in diagnosis. Accurate diagnosis is necessary to ensure shared understanding about the nature and implications of an individual's problem, and serves as the first step in establishing an appropriate basis for care and support for the individual and his or her family.

2.1 Principles of diagnosis

Underlying the use of systematic descriptions of autism in diagnosis is a framework of assumptions known as the **diagnostic approach** – an important tool in general medicine as well as in clinical psychology and psychiatry. Research and practice within this framework has provided evidence that particular psychological symptoms consistently group together to form identifiable clusters or syndromes, and has helped to elucidate the underlying causes of some of these clusters. Though the diagnostic approach assumes that syndromes are separable, it also accommodates overlap between their

Diagnostic approach
Approach within clinical psychology and psychiatry involving the systematic description and classification of symptom patterns, and their use in the identification and treatment of psychological problems.

Differential diagnosis
Use of diagnosis to distinguish between problems or conditions that have similar or overlapping sets of symptoms.

respective symptoms. For instance, lack of responsiveness to human voices could be a symptom of autism or of a hearing impairment. **Differential diagnosis** between these conditions depends on weighing up the overall pattern of symptoms. This is a necessary prerequisite for establishing therapeutic needs: a hearing impaired child has different needs from a child with autism.

2.2 Diagnostic criteria for autism

Diagnostic criteria
A formally agreed profile of symptoms and characteristics, typifying a syndrome or disorder, used in diagnosis.

Profiles of characteristics necessary for a diagnosis of classic autism or an ASD are called **diagnostic criteria**. These criteria appear within general systems for the classification and diagnosis of psychological problems such as the Diagnostic and Statistical Manual prepared by the American Psychiatric Association (last revised in 2000 and known as DSM-IV-TR™), and the International Classification of Diseases, prepared by the World Health Organisation (currently in its tenth edition and known as ICD-10).

We will first look at the diagnostic criteria for 'classic' autism. In Section 3 of this chapter we will highlight the way this 'classic' picture must be modified to take into account varying symptom patterns across the spectrum.

> **5.1** *Diagnostic criteria for classic autism according to DSM-IV-TR™*
>
> **A**   A total of six (or more) items from (1), (2) and (3), with at least two from (1), and one each from (2) and (3):
> 1   Qualitative impairment in social interaction, as manifested by at least two of the following;
>
>   (a) Marked impairment in the use of multiple nonverbal behaviours such as eye-to-eye gaze, facial expression, body postures, and gestures to regulate social interaction.
>
>   (b) Failure to develop peer relationships appropriate to developmental level.
>
>   (c) A lack of spontaneous seeking to share enjoyment, interests or achievements with other people (e.g. by a lack of showing, bringing or pointing out objects of interest).
>
>   (d) Lack of social or emotional reciprocity.
> 2   Qualitative impairments in communication as manifested by at least one of the following:
>
>   (a) Delay in, or total lack of, the development of spoken language (not accompanied by an attempt to compensate through alternative modes of communication such as gesture or mime).
>
>   (b) In individuals with adequate speech, marked impairment in the ability to initiate or sustain a conversation with others.

(c) Stereotyped and repetitive use of language or idiosyncratic language.

(d) Lack of varied, spontaneous make-believe play or social imitative play appropriate to developmental level.

3 Restricted repetitive and stereotyped patterns of behaviour, interests and activities, as manifested by at least one of the following:

(a) Encompassing preoccupation with one or more stereotyped and restricted patterns of interest that is abnormal either in intensity or focus.

(b) Apparently inflexible adherence to specific, non-functional routines or rituals.

(c) Stereotyped and repetitive motor mannerisms (e.g. hand or finger flapping or twisting, or complex whole-body movements).

(d) Persistent preoccupation with parts of objects.

B Delays or abnormal functioning in at least one of the following areas, with onset prior to age 3 years: (a) social interaction, (b) language as used in social communication, (c) symbolic or imaginative play.

C The disturbance is not better accounted for by Rett's Disorder or Childhood Disintegrative Disorder.*

(American Psychiatric Association, 2000, DSM-IV-TR^{TM}, p. 75)

*Rett's Disorder and Childhood Disintegrative Disorder are syndromes with some symptoms overlapping with autism. Discussion is beyond the scope of this chapter.

Activity 5.1

Consider the four personal accounts of autism at the beginning of this chapter in light of the diagnostic criteria outlined above. Make a list of those diagnostic criteria represented in the different accounts, and compare your list to that given at the end of this chapter.

2.3 Other points for diagnostic consideration

Besides having 'criterial' symptoms, many people with autism have additional difficulties. For instance, they may experience perceptual distortions such as perceiving normal noises as extremely loud and disturbing. These features are not always present, and are not specific to autism. For example, dyslexia and ADHD share some features with autistic spectrum disorders. Omitting such shared features from criteria helps to ensure that they discriminate autism from other disorders.

Peeters and Gillberg (1999) state that 80 per cent of children who meet the criteria for classic autism score below 70 on psychometric tests of intelligence (IQ tests), which places them in the range associated with severe intellectual impairment. Most of the remaining children with this diagnosis score in the range 70 – 100, which is still at the low end of the range statistically defined as normal.

Activity 5.2

Given the communication problems in autism, why might there be difficulty interpreting these IQ findings?

Comment

It is difficult to know how far autistic children's performance on IQ tests is independent of their language difficulties. Many IQ tests include specific tests for verbal skills, and all IQ tests require an understanding of verbal instructions. Some researchers and practitioners argue that it is difficult or impossible to provide a measure of IQ that is uncontaminated by language difficulties.

Some people with autism have exceptional skills in one particular area. For instance, children whose overall level of IQ performance is low are often exceptionally good at particular sub-tests such as the 'block design' and 'embedded figures' tests shown in Figure 5.2. In the block design test (a), the task is to select blocks as necessary to make up the same design as is shown at the top. In the embedded figures test (b), the task is to locate a shape within the pram pattern that matches the separate triangle.

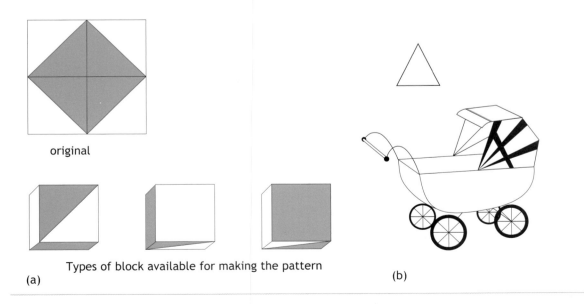

original

Types of block available for making the pattern

(a)

(b)

Figure 5.2   Examples of the block design and embedded figures tests from the Wechsler Intelligence Scale for Children

A small proportion of people with autism have outstanding talents known as **savant skills**. Some are musically gifted, while others can accomplish astonishing feats of memory or mental arithmetic. These will be discussed further in Section 3.

To make a full evaluation of such complex and varied manifestations, diagnosis is typically a multi-stage process in which a system such as DSM-IV-TR^{TM} is just one of many tools employed. Practitioners will draw on multiple sources of information, including face-to-face encounters, discussions with family and the family doctor, and detailed observation of behaviour. They may use a specially structured schedule of observations and questions that enables them to chart communication, social behaviour and other activities, using standardised tasks, to ensure that all areas of the diagnostic criteria are assessed.

Savant skills
Exceptional talents, typically in an area such as music, art or mathematics, possessed by a person who is otherwise intellectually disabled.

2.4 Problems and benefits of diagnosis

The checklist format of the criteria is specifically designed to accommodate individuals who have different numbers and patterns of criterial symptoms, as well as difficulties that also occur in other disorders. Nonetheless diagnosis must involve placing an individual's profile of difficulties within a category and, inevitably, one concern is that such diagnosis could sometimes be unreliable, with serious consequences for individuals and their families. In practice, however, research suggests that clinicians are reliable in differential diagnoses between the autistic spectrum and other disorders. Box 5.2 describes how Klin *et al.* (2000) investigated this.

5.2 *Evaluating diagnostic reliability (Klin et al., 2000)*

Klin *et al.* studied the measure of agreement (inter-rater reliability) between different clinicians (including psychiatrists, clinical psychologists and speech and language pathologists) when diagnosing the problems of over 900 participants. A substantial number of these were thought to have autistic spectrum disorders. Experienced clinicians showed a very high measure of agreement on differential diagnoses, not only when using the DSM-IV-TR^{TM} criteria, but also when basing their diagnoses solely on experienced clinical judgement. For the less experienced clinicians, judgements were extremely reliable when directly based on DSM-IV criteria, but less so when based exclusively on the clinicians' judgement. All clinicians agreed strongly in deciding which participants had symptom patterns within the autistic spectrum and which called for alternative diagnoses. However, the level of agreement dropped for differential diagnoses of 'sub-types' within this spectrum. The reasons for this uncertainty in diagnosing 'sub-types' will be considered further in Section 3.

Another possible criticism of the diagnostic approach is that it involves an inappropriate application of 'the medical model' to autism and thus 'pre-judges' the causes of the condition as biological. Yet medicine includes many different ideas about cause, ranging from the notion that biological organisms cause diseases such as the common cold, to the notion that psychological stresses may contribute to high blood pressure (Roth and Kroll, 1986). Similarly the diagnostic approach to autism embraces a variety of explanatory perspectives. Most of these agree that biological influences play a role in causing autism (discussed in Section 5), but they vary widely in how they link these biological influences to functioning at socio-cognitive and behavioural levels.

A further concern is whether a diagnosis of autism serves as a 'label' from which a person cannot escape, even if his or her symptoms have ameliorated or disappeared. However, the balance of arguments for and against labelling may be different for different disorders. ASDs tend to be pervasive disorders, involving most areas of the person's psychological functioning. Arguments for highlighting these difficulties by labelling may be stronger than for other less pervasive conditions.

Specialists and parents frequently argue that the decision to diagnose a child or adult with autism represents the first step towards helping them. Parents may have experienced years of perplexity, distress and frustration because the problems of their children are misunderstood. The diagnosis provides an explanation for their children's behaviour, helps them to understand and cope with their special and distinctive difficulties, and facilitates access to special educational and therapeutic facilities.

Despite these practical benefits, there remains the ethical issue of whether labels serve to place people in 'pigeon holes' that deny their individuality and their humanity. There are some sharply contrasting views about this. Clare Sainsbury (2000) points out that the concern to avoid labelling is often linked to a belief in 'normalisation' – the belief that the best way to revalue people with disabilities is by denying or de-emphasising their difference. She points out that:

> *Instead of starting with the needs, choices and values of a disabled individual, [normalisation] starts with the unchallenged standards of 'normal' people …*
> *Far from seeming radical or positive, the philosophy of normalisation seems painfully familiar to those of us whose very disability lies in our 'differentness'.*

(*Sainsbury, 2000, p. 33*)

For Sainsbury, then, the label 'autistic' validates the right of individuals to be different.

Yet the expression of difference can be 'normalist', too. Diagnostic systems such as DSM-IV-TR™ are intentionally expressed in 'normalist' language to highlight the ways in which the behaviour and experience of people with autism departs from statistical norms. The distress that this can cause is well expressed by the writer Valerie Paradiz, the mother of a child with autism:

> *In the DSM-IV, there are words which I cannot bring myself to say about Elijah. Words like 'lack', 'deficiency', 'impairment', and 'failure'. Condescension litters the DSM-IV and betrays a burdensome psychiatric history.*
>
> (*Paradiz, 2002, p. 59*)

There is no easy remedy for the difficulties expressed by Paradiz. All discussions of clinical problems, including the present chapter, must engage with formal and normalist language to some extent. But this needs to be balanced by a respect for people with autism as individuals with the same variability of personality and outlook as everyone else. Some approaches to differentiating across the autistic spectrum, in order to express peoples' differences, are evaluated in the next section.

Summary Section 2

- Diagnosis is a complex process that plays an important role in identifying individual therapeutic and educational needs, and in placing theoretical research on a sound footing.
- The diagnostic approach involves the description of autism in terms of symptoms, and is primarily focused at the level of observable behaviour.
- The characteristics of ASDs are summarised within formal systems of diagnostic criteria, such as the DSM-IV-TR™ and the ICD-10.
- For a diagnosis of classic autism, a person must show a specified number and pattern of difficulties in each of the triad areas, and certain key difficulties must have appeared before 36 months.
- Many people with autism have additional cognitive difficulties, while some have special skills, and a few have outstanding talents.
- The diagnostic approach has theoretical and practical benefits, but also reflects ethical issues that are difficult to resolve.

3 Mapping the autistic spectrum

Many individuals have autistic-like symptoms that do not meet the requisite number or profile of features for a diagnosis of classic autism. In this section we will consider the background to the spectrum concept and some different interpretations of the variations that it includes. The section concludes by setting these ideas in a developmental context: different patterns of symptoms in infancy may result in qualitatively different outcomes for individuals later.

3.1 History of the spectrum concept

An intriguing fact in the history of autism research is that while Kanner's work in America led him to introduce 'early infantile autism' as a clinical entity in 1943, another doctor, Hans Asperger, working at the same time in Vienna, described a very similar syndrome, which he called 'autistic psychopathy' (Asperger, 1944). Asperger described children with unusual or impoverished use of gesture, strangely formal or pedantic use of language, and difficult relations with their peers, parents and teachers. Quite often these children had been referred to Asperger because of their 'anti-social' or unfeeling behaviour towards others. But some of them were exceptionally able academically. Asperger worked with a number of his patients into adulthood. Here is an extract from one of his cases studies:

> It was as if he never took any notice of other people. He behaved so absent-mindedly that he often did not recognise his closest acquaintances. He was extremely clumsy and gauche, and there were all the difficulties we described earlier in learning to deal with the practical chores of everyday life. He remained awkward and socially unconcerned with his demeanour ... When he was at school there were constant serious difficulties ... For languages he had no talent at all. In secondary school ... he was able to get by only on the basis of his other abilities ... Even as a toddler, one could see in him a most unusual and spontaneous mathematical talent. Through persistent questioning of adults he acquired all the necessary knowledge from which he then worked independently ... Not long after the start of his university studies, reading theoretical astronomy, he proved a mathematical error in Newton's work ... In an exceptionally short time he became an assistant professor at the Department of Astronomy.

> (Asperger, 1944. Translated by Frith, 1991, pp. 88–9)

Not all of Asperger's patients fitted the pattern of milder social disability and outstanding intellectual talents represented by this case study. However, his observations indicated that autism might be a heterogeneous category, and this variability was further documented in 1979 by Lorna Wing and Judith Gould (see Box 5.3).

5.3 The incidence of autistic spectrum disorders (Wing and Gould, 1979)

Wing and Gould carried out an *epidemiological study* in which they screened 35,000 children under the age of 15 for the presence of one or more symptoms within the main autistic triad. Of all these children, 17 (or just under 5 children in 10,000) matched accepted criteria for 'classic' autism. However, a considerably larger group had *some* difficulties in reciprocal social interaction, usually coupled with communication problems and an impoverished range/scope of activities. Including this wider group, the overall estimate of prevalence was more like 21 children in 10,000 (equivalent to 0.2 per cent). Wing and Gould's conclusion – that the autistic syndrome embraces a core set of symptoms and variations on this core pattern – established the spectrum concept.

Epidemiological study
Large-scale study of the incidence and distribution of a disorder within a population.

More recent studies have suggested even higher rates of incidence for the broad spectrum: between 0.6 and 1 per cent of all school-age children. A likely explanation is that diagnostic practices have changed since the Wing and Gould study to include more borderline cases. However, some researchers have recently argued that there is an increase in the actual incidence of autistic spectrum disorders, claiming that it is diagnoses of classic cases that have increased. The evidence for this claim is currently unclear.

3.2 Continuum or sub-types?

One interpretation of cases like Asperger's astronomer is that they represent the typical lifespan development of an autistic person who, because they are less intellectually disabled, develops more successful living strategies. Some clinical practitioners use the term **High Functioning Autism** (HFA) to denote this group, implying that autism is a **continuum**, spanning individuals with different levels of intellectual and social disability and including individuals with 'borderline' autistic symptoms. This might be seen as suggesting, in turn, an ill-defined boundary between ASDs and 'normality'. In keeping with this, you perhaps know someone who, without having attracted any clinical label, is extremely 'driven' in one field, while seeming eccentric and lacking in social graces. Marian Glastonbury (1997) has argued that the unusual lifestyle of prominent writers and philosophers such as Kafka, Beckett and Wittgenstein,

High Functioning Autism
A sub-area of the autistic spectrum, characterised by less severe symptoms and/or higher intellectual level.

Continuum
A dimension of continuous variation, without breaks or discreet steps.

coupled with the eccentric genius and prolific nature of their work, is consistent with an autistic-type condition.

Whether these examples really demonstrate that autistic spectrum disorders 'shade' into normality partly depends on how we define 'disorder' and 'normality'. Some researchers refer increasingly to a broad **cognitive phenotype for autism**, that is, a distinctive way of engaging with the physical and social world, shaped by both genetic and environmental influences, that only manifests as a disorder in more extreme cases. This fits well with the continuum model.

Other practitioners have argued that the difficulties of individuals such as Asperger's astronomer patient are *qualitatively* distinct from classic autism and constitute a separate sub-type. In the early 1990s, this widespread shift in thinking stimulated the introduction of separate diagnostic criteria for **Asperger's syndrome**.

The criteria currently proposed for Asperger's syndrome in DSM-IV-TR^{TM} are identical to those proposed for classic autism (see Box 5.1) in two of three main triad headings: 'Qualitative impairments in social interaction' and 'Restricted repetitive and stereotyped patterns of behaviour, interests and activities'. They differ most significantly in omitting the triad area 'Qualitative impairments in communication', suggesting instead that:

1   There is no clinically significant general delay in language development.
2   There is no clinically significant delay in cognitive development, in normal everyday skills (other than social ones), or in curiosity about the environment.

Cognitive phenotype for autism
A distinctive profile of cognitive skills or strategies characteristic of the autistic spectrum that is the outward (phenotypic) expression of genetic attributes (genotype), in interaction with environment.

Asperger's syndrome
A sub-type of autistic spectrum disorder similar or identical to High Functioning Autism. Clinicians disagree about whether it involves language difficulties, and how far it is qualitatively distinct from other autistic spectrum disorders.

Activity 5.3

Look at the extract from Asperger's account of the astronomer. Do the DSM-IV-TR^{TM} criteria revised as above for Asperger's syndrome, match better with the astronomer's difficulties than the original criteria for autism given in Box 5.1?

Comment

In keeping with the Asperger's criteria, the astronomer showed impairments in social interaction, a restricted range of activities and interests, and, arguably, no delay in cognitive development. However, he *did* seem impaired in his communication and everyday skills, had difficulty learning a new language, and was described as extremely clumsy and gauche.

Peeters and Gillberg (1999) point out that, contrary to the implications of DSM–IV–TR^{TM}, it is extremely rare for any person with autistic spectrum symptoms to have entirely normal use of language. In 'Asperger-type' autism,

expressive language may be grammatically and syntactically perfect, and yet it may be excessively formal and pedantic. **Receptive language** may be far too literal and concrete, as illustrated by Gunilla Gerland in Section 1. It is typically these pragmatic aspects of language understanding that people with Asperger-type autism seem to find difficult. The omission of communication difficulties from the diagnostic criteria is therefore controversial. Peeters and Gillberg also argue that clumsiness, or lack of motor co-ordination, *is* a distinctive feature of 'Asperger-type' autism, and should be included in the diagnostic criteria.

Most clinicians agree that Asperger's syndrome is a recognisable sub-type of autism, yet there is disagreement about what distinguishing features should be enshrined in diagnosis. This is not as surprising as it might seem: diagnostic systems such as DSM-IV-TR^{TM} are constantly revised and updated by expert working groups, in the light of new research and clinical findings.

It might seem that continuum and 'sub-type' approaches are contradictory, since one implies a continuous dimension of variation, shading into 'normality', while the other assumes clinical entities that are, at least to some extent, discreet from one another and from 'normality'. In practice both approaches have some validity in different contexts. The continuum approach draws attention to shared features of all ASDs such as social difficulties and preference for a highly structured environment. It is useful to highlight such generic problems for people like teachers who may be encountering people with ASDs for the first time. The 'sub-type' approach serves to highlight more specific educational and therapeutic needs of different subgroups. For instance, children with Asperger's syndrome are typically capable of integrating into a mainstream school, while those with profound autism are more likely to flourish in a specialised educational environment.

3.3 Savant skills

Savant skills – exceptional talents in a specific area – pose a particular puzzle for attempts to map the autistic spectrum. They may occur with Asperger's syndrome, as with the early mathematical skills of Asperger's astronomer, but, as noted in Section 2, they also occur with classic autism. No diagnostic sub-group has been proposed for people with such skills, possibly because they are very rare and 'cross-cut' other subgroupings. However, these skills are so striking that it does not seem right to classify them just as an atypical manifestation of ASD.

The young artist Stephen Wiltshire has attracted much interest with exceptionally detailed architectural drawings such as the one in Figure 5.3.

Expressive language
Competence in the
production of language.

Receptive language
Competence in
understanding language
produced by others.

Figure 5.3   Stephen Wiltshire's drawing of the Kremlin Palace and a photograph taken from the same view

Stephen first demonstrated his talent at an early age, when he was also showing symptoms of classic autism. It is not just the accuracy, detail and perfect perspective of his finished drawings which has attracted such wonder and admiration, but also the manner in which he executes them, as described in this extract from an article by Oliver Sacks:

> Stephen bestowed a brief, indifferent glance at my house – there hardly seemed to be any act of attention – glanced then at the rest of the road, the sea, then asked to come in ... Stephen started at one edge of the paper (I had a feeling he might have started anywhere at all), and steadily moved across it – as if transcribing some tenacious inner image or visualisation. It was not quite like 'ordinary' drawing, but as if he had a camera lucida in his head which every so often he would pause over and consult.

(Oliver Sacks' foreword to Cities by Stephen Wiltshire, 1989, p. 6)

Another 11-year-old boy, Tito Mukhopadhyay, has recently confounded experts by showing savant skills that involve not only an outstanding grasp of vocabulary but the ability to write poetry and reflections that are full of imaginative images:

Wish my legs had the wings of a bird

And fly me to afar

I would gather the raindrops from every cloud

To wash my every tear

(Beyond the Silence, Mukhopadhyay, 2000, p. 55)

Tito's autobiography documents how he struggled to overcome his problems and express his talents. This underlines the importance of considering what factors may influence outcomes when people with ASDs grow up.

3.4 Growing up with ASD

Follow-up studies of people with ASDs suggest that most have lifelong difficulties of some kind. Peeters and Gillberg (1999) estimate that about two-thirds of those diagnosed before school age remain dependent on others for support and housing as adults. However, for some individuals at least, the pattern of symptoms changes and becomes less severe with age.

Follow-up studies
Longitudinal studies of individuals, typically focusing on the outcome of early difficulties.

Kanner (1973) traced the progress of 96 individuals in their twenties and thirties, whom he had seen as child patients. Twelve had made reasonably good social adjustments, and were leading fairly successful independent lives. Of these, 11 had jobs (though usually not commensurate with their qualifications) and one was still at college. Seven had their own homes (others lived with parents) and one, a successful musical composer, was married with a child.

Prognosis
Prediction of outcome,
especially in relation to
whether a psychological
problem ameliorates,
persists or worsens.

In a review of outcome studies, Howlin and Goode (1998) suggest that the **prognosis** is best for children with 'high functioning' or 'Asperger's type' symptoms, which is perhaps not surprising, since they seem to be less seriously affected in the first place.

Kanner commented that, in most of the 'successful' cases, during the mid-teens 'a remarkable change took place ... Unlike most autistic children they became uneasily aware of their peculiarities and began to make a conscious effort to do something about them' (1973, p. 209). It seems that these children had spontaneously attained some awareness of self and others.

In one respect, however, this enhanced awareness may accentuate problems: it brings with it a recognition of being different, of 'missing out' on the richness of others' social experience, or of making unintentional social 'gaffes' that lead to further isolation:

> To us, most normal people ... are social Mozarts who intuitively learn to employ
> a very complex set of rules and standards fluidly and creatively, seemingly
> with little or no effort; we, on the other hand, are stuck with the sheet music,
> trying to memorise scales and plonking out simple tunes one note at a time.

(*Sainsbury, 2000, p. 88, Joseph, writing about himself*)

This awareness of difference can occasionally have devastating consequences including depression and, in a few cases, attempted suicide (Howlin and Goode, 1998).

Another predictor of outcome is having a specialised skill or interest. Kanner (1973) observed that several of the group of 12 had used their special interests to identify a niche and 'open a door for contact'. It seems that they used their skills to define themselves as individuals, and to provide a basis for social exchange with others. In the case of Stephen Wiltshire, his special interest and talent have been a powerful force for personal and social development even though his disability is profound. It is also interesting that both Stephen and Tito had determined and resourceful mentors who helped them to channel their talents and transcend their problems. This highlights the potentially important role of the child's interactions with his/her social context in fostering positive development.

Studies of outcome point up quite sharply the scope for 'outsider' and 'insider' viewpoints to shed different light on a question. Outsider studies evaluate success in terms of indices such as independent living, employment, number of social contacts, whereas insider accounts tell us about the feelings and experience of the individual. What counts as 'success' from the outside may nonetheless be experienced by the individual as loneliness and isolation.

Summary Section 3

- Asperger worked independently of Kanner during the 1940s. His case studies, including intellectually able children, highlighted variations in severity and in specific symptoms among children identified as autistic.
- Wing and Gould's population study established the spectrum concept.
- The term Asperger's syndrome is used for symptom patterns similar to autism, but less pervasive. The significance of language and communication difficulties in this group is currently uncertain.
- Savant skills present a particular challenge to understanding the spectrum.
- Continuum and subgroup approaches to autism have complementary explanatory, diagnostic and practical functions.
- Follow-up studies of autism suggest lifelong consequences in most cases. Many individuals achieve considerable social and personal adjustment, but may continue to experience difference and isolation.

4   Explaining autistic conditions: the socio-cognitive level

An important challenge for psychologists working on autistic spectrum disorders is to explain *why* characteristic impairments occur in three different areas of functioning (social interaction, communication, activities and interests). One strategy for explaining this three-way pattern is to identify a single underlying problem that links the different symptoms. This section considers such 'core deficit' approaches. They all address autism at the socio-cognitive level, but make different assumptions about how cognitive and social functioning interrelate.

4.1   Do people with autistic spectrum disorders lack a theory of mind?

The most influential, and perhaps the most compelling, socio-cognitive model argues that people with ASDs have a diminished capacity to understand the thoughts, beliefs, intentions and emotions of other people, and perhaps themselves. Indeed, people with autism may be unaware that others have such

Theory of mind/mind reading
A person's capacity to understand the thoughts, intentions, beliefs and feelings of others (and themselves), sometimes known as 'mind reading'.

a 'mental life'. It has been argued that such **theory of mind** (ToM) was fundamental to the evolution of our species as advanced social animals (e.g. Humphrey, 1976), as it allows people to make predictions and inferences about the behaviour of others. Making a similar point from a philosophical perspective, Daniel Dennett (1978) suggested that if a person was unable to understand the thoughts or intentions of another person, much of social interaction and communication would be a mystery. Hence a ToM deficit could explain the autistic difficulties in both of these areas. The following anecdote illustrates this point. An autistic child was asked by his teacher 'Go and ask Mr Smith (another teacher) if he would like a cup of coffee.' The child went and found Mr Smith and delivered the question, but then came straight back without waiting for the reply: he did not realise that the *intention* of these communications was to find out whether Mr Smith wanted a drink. Most conversation is inherently ambiguous, and to make sense of it, we use context and behaviour to work out the intentions behind what people say.

Dennett reasoned that the most stringent test of ToM was whether a person could understand that someone else's belief about a situation was different from their own, and from reality – the so-called **false belief test**. Imagine the following scenario:

False belief test
Experimental test of theory of mind requiring a person to demonstrate understanding that another person's belief may be different from their own or from reality.

You and a friend drive to the shops in your car. You park your car in a particular street (Mount Street) and as you both have different shops to visit you arrange to meet back at the car in an hour's time. Shortly after parting from your friend, you realise you have left your wallet at home, so you take the car home to fetch it. When you get back to where you parked before, it is full up, so you have to park in a different street (Park Street). You *know* that when your friend goes to meet you she will assume that the car is where you originally parked it. Unless you can find her first, she will go to meet you in Mount Street.

In this situation you understand that your friend's belief about the location of the car is false, and that she will act on the basis of this false belief. Developmental studies suggest that children typically develop similar understanding at the age of four. Simon Baron-Cohen and colleagues (Baron-Cohen *et al.*, 1985) designed an experimental test of whether children with autism could understand false belief, called the 'Sally-Anne False Belief Task', described in Box 5.4.

5.4 The Sally-Anne False Belief Task (Baron-Cohen et al., 1985)

The child sits at a table on which there are two dolls (Sally and Anne), each placed facing a lidded container (a basket and a square box). The experimenter names the dolls for the child, and then checks that the child has understood which is which. The experimenter enacts a scenario of hiding a marble in the basket using one doll (Sally) to 'hide' the marble with the other (Anne) looking on. Sally then 'leaves the room' and the marble is re-hidden in the box. Sally then returns and the experimenter asks the child three questions.

1 'Where will Sally look for her marble?' (belief question: the correct answer is 'in the basket')
2 'Where is the marble really?' (reality question: the correct answer is 'in the box')
3 'Where was the marble in the beginning?' (memory question: the correct answer is 'in the basket')

Three groups of children were tested (one at a time) on the task:

Experimental group	20 autistic children with an average age of 11 years 11 months
Control group 1	14 children with Down's syndrome with an average age of 10 years 11 months
Control group 2	27 typically developing children with an average age of 4 years 5 months

The children with autism selected for the task had an average mental age of nine years and three months, as tested on a non-verbal IQ test, and five years and five months as tested on a verbal test. The participants were selected such that both these mental age scores would be higher than those of the children with Down's syndrome and of the typically developing children (whose mental age would approximate their chronological age).

The children in all groups answered the reality and memory questions correctly. 85 per cent of the typically developing children and 86 per cent of the children with Down's syndrome also answered the belief question correctly. In contrast 80 per cent of the children with autism answered the belief question incorrectly. That is, when asked 'Where will Sally look for her marble?' they pointed to the marble's current location rather than to where the marble had been re-hidden in Sally's absence.

Figure 5.4   The Sally-Anne False Belief Task

Activity 5.4

Why do you think the experimenter had selected autistic children with a higher mental age than the other two groups of children? Why do you think there were two different control groups of participants?

Comment

The higher mental age among the autistic participants was designed to ensure that the way they tackled the task was not simply due to lower intellectual level. The reason for including both typically developing children and children with Down's syndrome as control groups was to ensure that any differences in the experimental group are specifically associated with autism, and not with learning difficulties in general. Similar design features are common to many experimental studies of children with autism.

Why do autistic children fail on the 'belief' question in this experiment? They are intellectually as able as the other two groups of children. Also they had no difficulty in remembering where the marble was originally hidden or in understanding where it had been relocated: they were able to answer both the memory question and the reality question correctly. One explanation is that since children with autism have difficulties with pretend play, they misunderstood the pretend 'drama' that was being 'enacted' by the dolls. However, this was ruled out by later experiments that replicated the task using real people to enact the scenario.

Baron-Cohen *et al.* argued that autistic children tend to fail on the 'belief' question because, instead of 'putting themselves in Sally's shoes', they assume that her belief about where the marble is hidden is the same as their own knowledge of where the marble really is. In short, the study appears to show that children with autism lack the capacity for understanding another person's mental state. This now classic study stimulated a massive wave of research that has examined and refined the ToM hypothesis and tested its predictions. Autistic children have been found to have difficulties in many areas that are consistent with a ToM deficit. For instance, children with ASDs make little use of 'mental state' language (words like 'think', 'know', 'believe', 'feel') in their speech. They have difficulty understanding or engaging in deception. Irony (saying 'what great weather' when it is pouring with rain) and metaphor ('that will keep the wolf from the door') are lost on them. Problems like these make young people with autism very vulnerable to deception or exploitation.

However, 20 per cent of children with autism pass experimental ToM tasks like the Sally-Anne test. It is also only possible to test participants who can understand task instructions, which precludes testing profoundly autistic participants. Finally, the approach addresses *ongoing* behaviour and skills in individuals diagnosed as autistic, but it does not explain the *process* of development that leads to these outcomes. We will consider how the ToM approach has been elaborated to address this developmental trajectory, before considering other approaches that complement or challenge it.

4.2 Developmental origins of theory of mind

The critical skills for engagement in the social world, which Baron-Cohen (1995) calls *mind reading*, appear to be both complex and subtle. Certain early infant behaviours, which autistic children fail to acquire, are thought to provide the basic 'building blocks' for this mind reading.

Gaze following and proto-declarative pointing

Consider how behaviour might provide one person with cues to what another person is thinking. For instance, how do you know that someone you are talking to is interested in what you are saying? They may open their eyes wide, sit up straight or make noises like 'hmmm'. Such gestures and expressions are *cues to thoughts*, which we monitor all the time without being aware of it. Baron-Cohen (1995) provides evidence that the ability to use subtle behaviours, such as picking up where someone is looking and looking there too (**gaze following**) typically develops very early, around eight months. Similarly the capacity to look at something to which another person is pointing, or to point in order to indicate an object of interest (**proto-declarative pointing**), develops at around 12 months. Both types of behaviour enable a child to coordinate their own mental state (attention) with another person's.

Seeing leads to knowing

Think back to the car parking example. Your judgement that your friend will go back to the original car parking place in Mount Street is actually a well-informed 'guess' based on evidence from your friend's behaviour. For instance, your friend *saw* you parking the car and walked off *without* seeing you moving the car. We don't consciously run through such information before 'calculating' other peoples' states of mind. However, we are capable of making rapid, direct and non-conscious judgements of what other people are likely to know or believe, in part at least, from what perceptual information they have had access to. Baron-Cohen (1995) suggests that this **seeing leads to knowing** principle is grasped by typically developing children between 36 and 48 months of age.

Metarepresentation and pretend play

Alan Leslie (1991) has suggested that understanding mental states such as false belief requires the sophisticated skill of 'de-coupling' or disengaging (mentally speaking) from the truth of a situation (e.g. 'The car is in Park Street'), in order to hold in mind an idea that differs from this reality ('Jane thinks the car is in Mount Street'). This capacity is known as **metarepresentation**, and it is seen as a crucial element of language understanding. Leslie argues that typically

Gaze following/gaze monitoring
The skill of following where someone is looking and looking there, too, in order to share attention. Infants typically develop this behaviour at around eight months.

Proto-declarative pointing
The skill of pointing to indicate an object of interest, as opposed to pointing in order to ask for an object to be fetched. Infants typically develop this behaviour at around 12 months.

Seeing leads to knowing
The principle that a person's belief/knowledge about a situation depends partly on what perceptual information has been available to them. Children typically grasp this between 36 and 48 months.

Metarepresentation
Process of disengaging from reality in order to think about one's own, or another person's, thoughts. Considered necessary for false belief, pretence, etc.

developing children display simple de-coupling at around 18 months, when they start enacting pretend play. In his words, when a child puts a banana to his/her ear, pretending that it is a telephone, s/he is temporarily disengaging from the reality ('This object in my hand is a banana') in order to indulge in the pretence (I'll pretend that 'this object is a telephone'). This 'simpler' metarepresentational skill may act as a developmental precursor for understanding that one's own or other people's thoughts can be hypothetical or different from reality. Figure 5.5 illustrates how acts of both pretending and false belief about a situation can be seen as metarepresentations. Leslie's primary emphasis is on characterising what thought processes are necessary for pretence – whether solitary or social.

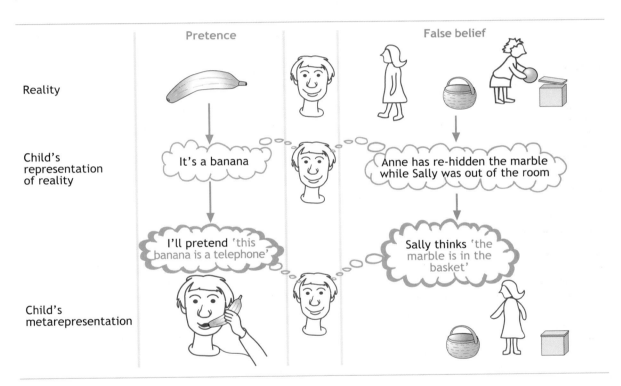

Figure 5.5   Pretending and false belief as metarepresentation

There is much experimental and observational evidence that children with autism fail to develop early 'pre-mind-reading' skills. Box 5.5 summarises some of this evidence in relation to gaze following, proto-declarative pointing and pretend play.

5.5 *Developmental pre-cursors of theory of mind (Leekam et al., 1997; Baron-Cohen, 1987, 1989; Baron-Cohen et al., 1992)*

Leekam *et al.* (1997) tested whether children with autism would spontaneously follow, with their eyes, an experimenter sitting opposite them, who changed her head direction to look at a toy. The children showed significant impairment in this gaze monitoring task compared with control participants. In another study, Baron-Cohen (1989) tested whether children with autism would use proto-declarative pointing to indicate an object of interest, with similar results.

Baron-Cohen (1987) gave autistic children a range of toys and observed how they played with them. The children engaged in as much 'functional' play, such as ordering or stacking bricks, as a control group, but showed much less 'symbolic' or pretend play than the control group, such as using a brick as a cup, a box as a car.

These experimental results were confirmed by a survey conducted by Baron-Cohen *et al.* (1992). A questionnaire asking about the presence of the above behaviours was completed by the health visitors and parents of three groups of children: 20 autistic children; 20 younger siblings, aged around 18 months; and another group of 50 toddlers aged 18 months old. All of the 50 'normal' toddlers had the key behaviours, while a majority of the autistic children lacked them. Among the younger siblings, who were considered genetically 'at risk' of developing autism (see Section 5 below), one child lacked the key behaviours, and subsequently received a diagnosis of autism.

The ToM ideas considered here provide an introduction to an extensive body of related theories and research findings. We now turn to some key difficulties.

4.3 A distinctive subgroup?

The fact that around 20 per cent of children with autistic spectrum disorders regularly pass tasks such as the Sally-Anne test fits well with the notion of an autistic spectrum including different profiles of skills and deficits. But it questions the idea of a *core* ToM deficit that all people with ASDs share. So is the theory inadequate, given that it its predictions are not always supported?

Francesca Happé (1994) suggests that some of those passing tests such as the Sally-Anne test may have relied upon simple 'problem solving' strategies that avoid the need for genuine mind reading. Many of these individuals fail more complex false belief tasks, in which participants have to show understanding of one character's false belief about a second character's belief about a situation. As an illustration, suppose that, in the car parking example in section 4.1, unbeknown to you, your friend *saw* you *re-parking* the car in Park Street. You would then believe (falsely) that your friend believed that you were parked in

Mount Street. Understanding this kind of situation involves understanding **second-order false belief**. Failures on such second-order false belief tasks suggest that most people with autistic spectrum disorders have *some* degree of ToM difficulty.

On the other hand, some intellectually able individuals with ASDs also pass these second-order tasks. The fact that these individuals remain socially disabled questions whether the somewhat contrived experimental tests of ToM are really a good guide to the presence or absence of everyday mind-reading skills. Happé (1994) devised a more naturalistic and subtle probe for everyday mind-reading skills, described in Box 5.6.

Second-order false belief
One person's false belief about another person's belief about a situation.

5.6 The 'Strange Stories' task (Happé, 1994)

Participants were presented with stories such as the following:

Irony

Ann's mother has spent a long time cooking Ann's favourite meal: fish and chips. When she brings it in, Ann is watching TV, and she doesn't even look up or say thank you. Ann's mother is cross and says 'Well that's very nice isn't it! That's what I call politeness!'

The participants were asked:

    Q1.   Is it true what Ann's mother says?

    Q2.   Why does Ann's mother say this?

Figure 5.6   Ann and her mother

Similar stories were presented for situations requiring an understanding of underlying intentions, such as a white lie, a deliberate lie, persuasion.

Happé tested three groups of autistic participants:
- Those failing 'first-order' ToM tasks
- Those passing 'first-order' ToM tasks
- Those passing first-order and second-order ToM tasks

There were marked differences between the three groups in accuracy on Question 1 and in the justifications given on Question 2. The third, most able, group performed quite well, yet less accurately than an appropriately matched control group. Their attributions of mental states to the story characters were often wrong. For example, one participant said that Ann's mother said what she said 'not to shock her daughter'.

Happé offers an explanation of why the third group of individuals – who are both intellectually able *and* have substantial ToM skills – remain disabled nonetheless. She argues that people in this subgroup have come by their social and mind-reading skills after a delay, such that the normal developmental context in which these skills are embedded is absent. As a result their skills are somewhat atypical and do not serve the individuals well in all situations. Yet the development of even moderate ToM skills may bring about another striking change, as we will consider next.

4.4 Theory of mind and self-awareness

One of my most recurrent problems throughout middle childhood was my constant failure to distinguish between my knowledge and that of others. Very often my parents would miss deadlines or appointments because I failed to tell them of these matters. For instance my parents missed the school's Open House in my fifth grade and my mom asked me afterward, 'why didn't you tell us about it?' 'I thought you knew it,' I replied.

(*Sarah, in Sainsbury, 2000, p. 60*)

Sarah's lucid comment on her childhood highlights the way ToM deficits can lead to communication difficulties resulting from failure to understand another person's state of knowledge. However, it also reflects Sarah's capacity, now, to reflect accurately on how her communication problems arose. This emergence of *self-awareness* in parallel with ToM is consistent with the suggestion that children acquire a sense of self through taking the role of others. Note that such developing self-awareness could also be seen as enhancing one of the dimensions of consciousness (Mead, 1934).

Capacity for 'mind reading' and enhanced self-awareness are both characteristics that may help diagnosticians to define the 'Asperger's' subgroup more adequately than the current problematic diagnostic criteria, and to establish specific therapeutic needs. As we have seen, the benefits of having insight into self and others can be accompanied by feelings of pain and isolation for 'high-functioning' individuals, calling for sensitive therapy.

4.5 Central coherence and cognitive style

Despite variations in ToM performance between subgroups, the approach as a whole provides a compelling explanation for problems in the areas of social interaction and communication. However, it offers no obvious explanation for symptoms in the third 'triad' area, such as impoverished imagination, restricted interests and repetitive behaviour. Frith (1989) and Happé (1999) have proposed that these behaviours reflect a different kind of atypical functioning: a distinctive **cognitive style**, characterised by difficulty in 'global processing', that is, in coordinating aspects of reality to form 'coherent' wholes. Global processing is a strategy we use for selecting, perceiving and remembering the meaningful and relevant elements from disorganised masses of information. The cognitive style in autism relies, instead, on good visual and rote memory to process the details of the information rather than the overall gist or meaning.

Cognitive style
A set of cognitive or information processing strategies which characterise how an individual approaches the world.

This approach challenges an image of autism as a disorder characterised exclusively by impairments, and draws attention to skills that have beneficial features. For instance, tolerance of repetition and sameness, and the capacity for accuracy have potential uses in therapy and education (see Section 6). Obsessive attention to detail may foster special talents. The work of Stephen Wiltshire (Figure 5.3), for instance, displays a grasp of precision and detail way beyond the scope of most artists. Pring and Hermelin (1997) have studied the development of Stephen's gift, and argue that his capacity to 'filter out' global impressions of his surroundings fosters his talent for producing perfect perspective drawings from memory.

Frith and Happé's central coherence model can be seen as *coexisting* rather than *conflicting* with the ToM approach, since it uses different concepts and explains different symptoms. However, Baron-Cohen *et al.* (2002) propose that ToM deficits and idiosyncratic information processing are essentially *complementary* aspects of a broader socio-cognitive style, characterised by poor social and emotional understanding, coupled with efficient skills in certain 'non-social' domains.

4.6 Emotions, relatedness and the developmental process

Cognitive style and ToM approaches both draw extensively on cognitive concepts to explain why functioning in autism is atypical. ToM has typically assumed that successful social interaction and communication involves *processing information* about other people in the form of social stimuli such as gestures, expressions, language and behaviour. The processes that promote emotional understanding and relatedness between people have been seen as essentially akin to the more 'rational' processes involved in understanding a person's factual knowledge or beliefs.

Peter Hobson (1993) approaches social understanding from a philosophically different standpoint. He proposes that, rather than 'processing information' to derive 'theories' about the thoughts and emotions of others, people's primary emotional relatedness to others promotes **empathy** or direct understanding. Similarly, people's awareness of self is not a theory-like representation of their thoughts, but a sense of self as a 'subject' who is in relations with other 'subjects'.

The basis for these ideas is Hobson's view that humans are first and foremost social beings, with an 'innate' capacity for personal relatedness – a view prefigured by Kanner (1943). From this, Hobson elaborates an account that contrasts how typically developing and autistic infants engage with the world from birth. Key features are outlined in Box 5.7, followed by a summary of relevant evidence.

Empathy
A direct or intuitive way of understanding other people's feelings and desires. Contrasts with the more rational or inferential understanding implied by 'theory of mind' or mind reading.

5.7 *Hobson's approach (Hobson, 1993)*

The following key features of typical development are missing in autism:

- *human primacy*: the infant engages emotionally and socially with humans in ways that are distinct from how he/she engages with the rest of the physical world.
- *reciprocity*: the infant's early behaviour is 'pre-programmed' to elicit responses from his/her carer, and to respond to those responses. This triggers a continuous cycle of interaction in which each affects the other – a *transaction* that promotes emotional bonding.
- *inter-subjectivity*: through the sharing of experience involved in such transactions the child acquires 'direct' knowledge of others as subjective beings with their own feelings, thoughts, intentions and beliefs.
- *reflexivity*: the child acquires an understanding of self via his/her developing aware-ness of others as subjective beings.

Key predictions for the behaviour of children with ASDs are:

1 *Difficulty in recognising self and others as distinct human 'subjects'.* In support, Hobson (1993) highlights difficulty in using the personal pronoun 'I'. For instance, a child

with ASD asked 'Do you want a biscuit?' might respond 'You want a biscuit', meaning 'Yes, I want a biscuit.' Hobson interprets this as evidence that the child does not distinguish himself from other subjects, or from inanimate objects.

2 *Atypical engagement with carers from birth.* Lord (1993) provided evidence that infants later diagnosed as autistic have offered fewer and 'poorer' opportunities to their parents for engagement and interaction. Hobson also interprets failure to develop behaviours such as gaze following and proto-declarative pointing (see Section 4.2) as supporting this prediction and as showing a failure to develop inter-subjectivity.

3 *Difficulty in recognising and expressing emotions.* Hobson et al. (1989) studied the ability of children with autism to supply appropriate emotional terms in response both to pictures of faces and to voices depicting different emotions. Compared with appropriately matched control groups, these children showed a grasp of the vocabulary terms, but applied them haphazardly to the stimuli, suggesting they did not understand which expression was which.

While the evidence illustrated in Box 5.7 is broadly consistent with Hobson's model, none of it is conclusive. For instance:

1 Atypical pronoun use could equally be part of wider pragmatic language difficulties, rather than reflecting specific problems of self-recognition.

2 Evidence for atypical engagement with carers *from birth* depends on retrospective reconstructions, or on extrapolating from later behaviour. Failure to develop behaviours such as gaze following does not necessarily imply atypical behaviour at birth, since these typically only appear at eight months. In a survey by Frith and Soares (1993) two-thirds of the mothers of children with ASDs had not been disturbed by their children's behaviour in the first year. A surprising number of such children are also later rated as 'securely attached' (Rogers and Pennington, 1991).

3 Deficits in emotional understanding do not necessarily reflect a *lack* of emotional experiences. Sigman *et al.* (1995) studied the performance of 'high-functioning' young people on a whole range of emotion tasks. In one task, the participants had to relate an occasion when they had experienced emotions such as pride, happiness, embarrassment, etc. The children were able to give responses, albeit slowly, but these tended to be atypical: for instance, while food was given as a source of happiness, birthday presents or parties were not. Hence the children did not lack emotional experiences, but had made 'odd' connections between these and social contexts. Again these results do not clearly favour Hobson's account.

In general, it has been difficult to find clear evidence that favours Hobson's theory. A number of its predictions are similar to those of the ToM model: both assume that people with ASDs may fail to take a distinctive 'stance' towards the human world; both predict early impoverishment in use of gestures, and later difficulties in understanding other minds; both are consistent with evidence of genetic influences in autism (to be discussed in Section 5). Even so, Hobson's emphasis on the direct, inter-subjective quality of much social and emotional understanding is appealing. In a more recent paper, Baron-Cohen (Baron-Cohen *et al.* 2002) also moved from the rational connotations of 'mind reading' to a more relational notion of 'empathising'. Hobson also provides a framework for considering how autism might 'unfold' developmentally, as a process involving both the infant and 'significant others' in his/her environment, such as carers and siblings. Yet like the other models discussed in this section, the main focus of Hobson's model remains individual: it has relatively little to say about how an atypical developmental trajectory might affect parents and family. We will conclude this section by briefly considering this contextual interplay.

4.7 The family context

Whether or not children with autism behave atypically from the moment they are born, the effects of their atypical way of relating to others must inevitably be felt by parents and others in the family:

> *Jane would allow herself to be cuddled, but only if I didn't look at her. She always resisted sitting on my lap unless she was facing away. And I could go to her with my arms out, just as I had a million times with my boys, but she would never reach out to me in return ... One day I found my husband ... smiling at her, the tears rolling down his face, begging her to smile back.*

(From Randall and Parker, 1999, p. 107)

This poignant account highlights what seems almost self-evident: that caring for a child with an autistic spectrum disorder will cause perplexity and, at times, distress. As the extract also illustrates, the unusual behaviour of the child may evoke equally unusual behaviour in the parent, which may in turn affect the child. This 'negative spiral', extended over a long period, may well account for a finding by Piven *et al.* (1994) that some parents of children with autism may seem to subtly emulate the symptoms of their child, for instance, appearing rather aloof. On the other hand, this finding is also consistent with genetic evidence, discussed in the next section, for attenuated forms of autism in relatives of affected individuals.

The effects of ASDs on families have been extensively documented. For instance, DeMyer (1979) described parents who expressed disappointment, depression and inadequacy, with consequent effects on their marital relationships. Randall and Parker (1999) suggested that siblings of a child with autism may feel overlooked, frustrated or embarrassed, and may even feel responsible for the autistic difficulties. All of these findings underline the importance of providing support for the family of autistic people wherever necessary.

Summary   Section 4

- Most socio-cognitive approaches to autistic spectrum disorders seek to unify different symptoms in terms of models of underlying functioning.
- Theory of mind approaches argue that difficulties in understanding mental states such as beliefs, intentions and desires are the 'core' problem.
- Experimental tests of theory of mind employ tasks such as testing the understanding of false belief.
- Baron-Cohen has identified early developmental milestones such as gaze following as 'pre-mind-reading' skills. Children with autism show less of these skills compared to controls.
- Some individuals with autism pass theory of mind tasks and have some capacity for everyday social understanding.
- Self-awareness is an important skill that goes with more advanced theory of mind performance.
- Frith and Happé have addressed symptoms such as repetitive behaviour and obsessive interests via a 'cognitive-style' approach.
- Hobson highlights a lack of innate emotional relatedness and a consequent deficit in inter-subjectivity as a key feature of autistic spectrum disorders.
- Effects of a child's autism on parents and siblings are well documented.

5 Explaining autistic conditions: the biological level

Section 4 focused on explaining the characteristic symptoms of ASDs in terms of socio-cognitive functioning. In this section the focus shifts to the biological level: what biological influences might both trigger and maintain atypical functioning in areas like theory of mind, global information processing and emotional relatedness?

As was emphasised in Section 1, biological perspectives on ASDs reflect several 'sub-levels'. These sub-levels offer a complex mix of complementary, conflicting or coexisting accounts, both within themselves, and in relation to other levels of explanation covered in the chapter. We start by considering genetic factors that might explain why ASDs often affect more than one member of the same family.

5.1 Are there genetic factors in autistic spectrum conditions?

Concordance rate
Measure of how frequently a phenomenon or condition co-occurs in two sets of individuals, particularly those who are related such as twins.

In investigations of whether genetic factors affect behaviour patterns, particular interest focuses on comparisons between identical twin (mono-zygotic or MZ) and non-identical (di-zygotic or DZ) twin pairs. If there is a genetic influence, the **concordance rate** for MZ twins should be particularly high, because both members of twin pairs have the same genetic material. For DZ pairs the genetic relationship between the twins is the same as that between ordinary siblings. Concordance rates for DZ twins and for other siblings should be similar: higher than in the general population, but much lower than for MZ twins.

Studies documenting higher rates of concordance for autistic spectrum symptoms among MZ twins compared to DZ twins, are described in Box 5.8.

> **5.8 *Twin studies of autism (Folstein and Rutter, 1978; Bailey et al., 1995)***
>
> Folstein and Rutter (1978) investigated 21 same-sex pairs of twins, including 11 MZ pairs and 10 DZ pairs between the ages of 5 and 23. Each pair included one member diagnosed as autistic. Of the 11 MZ twin pairs, 4 were concordant for classic autism (i.e. both twins had classic autism). Of the 10 DZ pairs, none were concordant for autism. However, the concordance rates rose considerably when all autistic spectrum symptoms were taken into account. Seven out of 11 MZ twins unaffected by classic autism had some autistic-type symptoms, particularly involving language. This was true for only one of the unaffected members of a DZ pair.
>
> Folstein and Rutter's findings have been extensively replicated. Bailey *et al.* (1995) re-contacted all participants in the earlier study. They re-checked diagnostic and medical assessments and augmented the overall sample, providing data on a total of 25 MZ and 20 DZ same-sex twin pairs. The findings, which are summarised in Table 5.1, confirmed and extended those of Folstein and Rutter. The overall MZ concordance rate for classic autism in this combined study is 60 per cent. However, this concordance rate rises to 92 per cent if twins showing a broader spectrum of autistic-type symptoms are taken into account. The autism concordance rate for DZ twins is 0 per cent but rises to 10 per cent when autistic spectrum symptoms are included.

Table 5.1   Concordance rates found by Bailey *et al.* (1995)

	MZ % concordance	DZ % concordance
Both twins autistic	60	0
One twin autistic; other with spectrum symptoms	32	10
Total	92	10

The markedly raised concordance for full autism in MZ twins has been interpreted as evidence for a genetic predisposition. The presence of autistic-type difficulties in most of the non-autistic identical twins, and one of the non-autistic DZ twins is consistent with the idea of an autistic spectrum, and suggests a genetic basis for this spectrum.

Activity 5.5

What other explanatory factors might be considered when interpreting these twin studies?

Comment

Some have argued that the concordant MZ pairs developed autism because they were exposed to damaging social influences during childhood, which did not affect the DZ pairs to the same extent. This argument is difficult to sustain. No convincing model has been offered to explain how such difficulties could arise purely from social influences that have such a profound and early impact on identical twins but not on non-identical twins.

If the genetic interpretation of MZ concordance rates is correct, one puzzling question is 'why are there so many identical twin pairs who are not fully concordant?' (i.e. they share spectrum difficulties but are not equally severely affected). Folstein and Rutter proposed that the more profoundly affected member of these pairs might have been exposed to additional 'environmental' hazards in the womb or during birth. They examined birth records for all twin pairs in their study, looking for evidence of problems such as a delay in breathing of more than five minutes, or a convulsion, which would be likely to cause brain damage. In a majority of cases the more seriously affected twin had suffered an additional birth hazard. This led Folstein and Rutter to propose a 'threshold' model of causation in which a genetic abnormality makes a child vulnerable to developing an autistic spectrum condition, and a birth hazard interacts with this predisposition to 'push' the child over the threshold into full-blown autism. Pursuing this argument further, Folstein and Rutter speculated that in some cases (for instance non-concordant DZ twins), brain damage caused by a birth hazard alone might be sufficiently strong to produce autism.

This is an important but controversial model, since it suggests that different cases of autism might arise from different causal influences, working either together or separately. This has been accepted by researchers such as Peeters and Gillberg (1999), who argue that the biological causes of different cases of ASDs are multiple, with only a proportion being genetically triggered.

However, Bailey et al. (1995) provided arguments for a different interpretation of Folstein and Rutter's data showing an effect of birth hazard. They produced evidence that birth hazards such as a delay in breathing are a *result* of earlier 'sub-optimal' development due to autism, not a cause of autism. In other words, the members of twin pairs who experienced birth traumas did so *because* damage that would later result in autism was already affecting robustness and responsivity in the womb. They concluded that autism is a 'strongly genetic disorder', in which an initial genetic fault triggers atypical development of the brain and nervous system, which in turn leads to the observed behavioural symptoms and socio-cognitive deficits.

This discussion highlights two different models that identify genetics and brain damage as separable biological influences. Folstein and Rutter's model sees these influences as 'adding together' or interacting, whereas Bailey *et al.* see them as part of a single chain of influence leading from genes to brain damage to behaviour. Both models allow for environment: the first sees an unfavourable environment in the womb as something that adversely influences the baby before birth; the second sees the baby's own 'sub-optimal' development as influencing his/her environment, for instance, by reducing the baby's intake of oxygen before birth. But this model begs the question of why MZ twins with the same genetic material (and therefore the same genetic 'faults') should differ in their foetal robustness. It seems difficult to avoid the conclusion that a two-way interaction between the foetus and his/her pre-natal environment leads to more or less severe outcomes. This indicates the complexity existing among models at the biological level of explanation.

Another question raised by the twin studies is how to interpret the concordance rate for the DZ twins. According to a genetic hypothesis, the rate of concordance in DZ twins should, like that for family members, be higher than predicted by the incidence of ASDs in the general population. Bailey *et al.*'s data support this prediction. Extrapolating further, families with one autistic member should be relatively likely to have others with ASDs in the immediate or wider family tree.

This has been investigated in a range of research studies. For instance, Bolton *et al.* (1994) compared the incidence of ASDs in the families of individuals with autism and in control families. The results indicated a significant clustering of autism and autistic-type conditions in relatives of individuals with autism, with an overall rate of 20 per cent, very similar to that quoted for DZ twins in the twin studies. Once again, the distribution of symptoms within family members supported the idea of a spectrum ranging from classic autism in some family members to extremely subtle symptoms in others. Gillberg (1991) carried out a similar study in which he looked at the incidence of Asperger's syndrome and ASDs across three generations of certain families. One of the family patterns is shown in Figure 5.7.

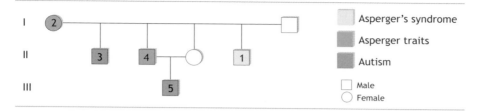

Figure 5.7   A family tree showing distribution of ASDs (Gillberg, 1991, p.125)

(1) was the original patient. He is an unmarried man of 33 with Asperger's syndrome. He works as a lawyer. (2) is the mother of (1). She is described as highly intelligent with borderline Asperger's symptoms – pedantic and friendless. (3) is the eldest brother of (1). He was diagnosed with classic autism at the age of four and lives in a group home. (4) is the middle brother of (1). He has borderline Asperger's symptoms, including odd pedantic speech. He is married despite his social gaucheness. (5) is the first-born son of (4), aged three. He is described as showing signs of classic autism.

Controversially, Baron-Cohen *et al.* (2002) suggest a possible evolutionary basis for family patterns of ASDs. Their model embraces the notion, introduced in earlier sections, of a cognitive phenotype for autism. This is characterised by poor understanding of how minds work, coupled (at least in high-functioning individuals) with very good understanding of domains governed by physical laws, such as physics and engineering. Baron-Cohen *et al.* point to the obsessions that many autistic children have with machines, and provide evidence for precocious understanding, among children with ASDs, of how mechanisms work. They also cite survey evidence that professions such as engineering and science predominate among the parents of people with ASDs. They argue that, expressed *in a mild form*, this way of engaging with the world might have had selective evolutionary advantages. The drawbacks of one or more members of a community having poor social understanding would be offset if these individuals had an enhanced understanding of physical causality, since this would enable them to fulfil useful functions such as constructing robust dwellings, or predicting the path of approaching storms. The full implications of these intriguing ideas have yet to be evaluated.

Overall, the discussion in this section points strongly to a genetic influence in ASDs, but probably does not imply that there is a 'gene for autism'. Although certain inherited disorders such as **phenylketonuria** are known to be due to a single gene fault, the twin and family pattern in ASDs are most

Phenylketonuria
A metabolic disorder in which excessive amino acid levels in the blood cause brain damage if untreated. Caused by a known fault on a single recessive gene.

Polygenetic
The combined influences
of a number of different
genes acting together, as
opposed to the influence
of a single gene.

likely to indicate influences that are **polygenetic**, due to the combined effects of multiple genes. Ideas about which genes, on which chromosomes, might be involved, and whether these are the same genes in all cases of autism are extremely controversial. Equally, the mechanisms by which genetic and/or chromosomal abnormalities play a predisposing role in autism are not understood. However, it is highly likely that genetic influences have **organic effects** – particularly on the early development and functioning of the brain and nervous system.

Organic effects
Generic term for
influences affecting body
organs and systems.

5.2 Do organic influences play a role in autistic spectrum conditions?

Much of the evidence for organic influences comes from subtle or non-specific types of dysfunction that may vary from one autistic individual to another. Steffenburg (1991) conducted a study of 52 children with ASDs. There was evidence for atypical functioning of the brain and/or nervous system in over 90 per cent of the participants, but in just under 50 per cent these symptoms were non-specific. For instance, a substantial number of this latter group had epileptic symptoms and/or abnormal **electro-encephalograms** or **EEGs**. While deviations from characteristic EEG patterns usually reflect brain malfunction, they do not necessarily indicate what this malfunction is. Other individuals within this 50 per cent group showed atypical composition of the cerebro-spinal fluid (CSF) which circulates around the brain. Samples of CSF, which can be painlessly withdrawn by a small needle inserted into the spinal cord, contain breakdown products from neuro-transmitters (natural chemicals which enable communication between brain cells), nerve cells and synapses (the connections between brain cells). Atypical concentrations may indicate over-production of nerve cells and abnormal functioning of synapses. In a further 38 per cent of Steffenburg's cases, autism was accompanied by an additional organic or **chromosomal syndrome** known to involve brain damage. However, in these cases it is not clear whether the brain damage was specifically linked with the autism or with the accompanying syndrome.

**Electro-encephalogram
(EEG)**
Recording of the overall
pattern of electrical activity
in the brain, made by
attaching electrodes
superficially to the scalp.
Sometimes used to identify
brain dysfunction.

**Chromosomal
syndrome**
Syndrome caused by
chromosomal damage or
anomaly. May comprise
both psychological and
physical symptoms.

Other studies have attempted to investigate specific brain areas involved in autism. Some of the different brain areas suggested by these studies are shown in Figure 5.8 (a) and (b). Relevant findings are discussed here in Box 5.9 and later in Box 5.10.

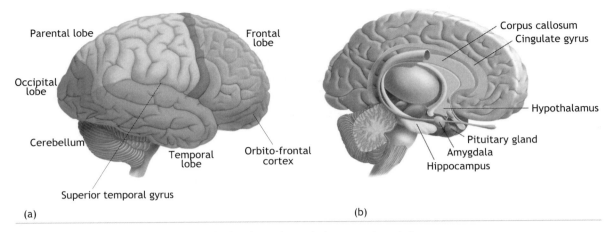

Figure 5.8   (a) Exterior view of the brain showing main cortical areas and cerebellum
              (b) Interior view of the brain showing the structures forming the limbic system

5.9 Major brain areas implicated in autism

Frontal lobes Many researchers (e.g. Ozonoff, 1995) claim that autistic symptoms such as repetitive, inflexible behaviour and social inappropriateness resemble the behaviour of people who have suffered accidental frontal lobe lesions. The frontal lobes are thought to play a major role in **executive function** – planning or programming behaviour to achieve long-term goals. Patients with frontal lobe lesions lose the capacity to plan their behaviour; at times they seem impulsive or uninhibited, making irrelevant, inappropriate or thoughtless responses to a situation; at other times, they go on making the same response long after it has been proved ineffective. Evidence to support this frontal lobe link to autism comes from neuropsychological tests used in diagnosing frontal lobe lesions. Both frontal lobe patients and people with ASDs perform poorly on tests of flexibility in adopting new rules to solve problems. However, there is no evidence of major frontal lobe lesions being implicated in autism.

Cerebellum One set of studies using sophisticated brain scanning equipment (e.g. Courchesne *et al.*, 1988) reported underdevelopment within this area, which is known to play an important role in the control of motor movements, particularly those with a social function such as gestures, posture and expression. An abnormality in the cerebellum could play a role in the impoverished or idiosyncratic non-verbal communication usually associated with autism, but it is not clear how this explanation could be generalised to other symptoms. Ozonoff (1995) offers an alternative interpretation: since the cerebellum is one of several brain areas richly connected to the frontal lobes, primary damage to the cerebellum could be interrupting normal information flow to the frontal lobes, producing executive-type deficits as a 'secondary' effect.

Frontal lobes
Major area of the cerebral cortex, involved in a variety of cognitive functions, particularly co-ordinating and planning behaviour.

Executive function
Programming or planning behaviour in order to meet particular goals. Frontal lobes are thought to play a major role in this.

Cerebellum
Brain structure located under the occipital lobes, involved in posture, movement and balance and in information processing.

Temporal lobes
Major area of the cerebral cortex, involved in a variety of cognitive functions including understanding speech and memory.

Limbic system
Structures internal to the temporal lobes. Evolutionarily 'early' part of the brain that instigates 'survival' behaviours, including emotions and appetites, as well as relaying information to the cortex.

Amygdala
Small structure in limbic system of the brain. Particularly involved in emotion.

Temporal lobes Several brain scan studies suggest atypical functioning in the temporal lobes. The temporal lobes are the most common site for epileptic seizures associated with autism. They are known to play a crucial role in understanding language, a focus of core difficulties in autism, as well as in memory. Atypical functioning of the **limbic system**, internal to the temporal lobes, and especially the **amygdala**, which plays a key role in emotion, has also been implicated in autism (Baumann and Kemper, 1988).

5.3 Causal links and models

There seems little doubt that genetic factors and atypical functioning of one or more areas of the brain and nervous system accompanies some or all ASDs. However, this tells us little about the role of these influences in a 'causal chain' leading to autism.

As we saw, genetic defects may play a major initiating role, perhaps affecting the development of specific brain areas and systems, which in turn hinders the development of specific socio-cognitive functions. The idea that similar brain damage may result from birth hazards, as suggested by Folstein and Rutter, or even from other sources, has not been conclusively disproved. Shattock and Savery (1997) maintain that brain damage in autism is secondary to metabolic disorders in which the chemical breakdown and digestion of certain food substances releases poisonous bi-products into the blood stream, and ultimately into the brain. Shattock further suggests that the rising incidence of autism noted in Section 2 is due to the effects of raised toxin levels in the environment and foods. Currently such causal claims are highly controversial, though this does not rule out atypical metabolism as a side effect of autism. Rutter *et al.* (1999) have documented a striking incidence of autistic-like symptoms in children adopted from Romanian orphanages, who were subjected to extreme emotional and physical deprivation in the early months of their lives. It is conceivable that this deprivation affected brain function. However, unlike children with classic autism, many of these children showed marked diminution of symptoms once in a nurturing environment.

Equally challenging is to explain how organic influences affect functioning at the biological, socio-cognitive and behavioural levels. Section 5.2 identified a number of major and distinct brain areas. Can these different areas be meaningfully linked, given that each has multiple functions, and given the difficulties pointed out by Ozonoff in identifying primary and secondary influences? How do you extrapolate from such biological links to the difficulties that people with autism experience and manifest? The need for explanations to traverse levels is a key issue, but making the right connections is problematic.

Baron-Cohen and colleagues (1999, 2000) have offered a model that attempts to address some of this complexity, building on Baron-Cohen's developmental account of mind reading in Section 4. As we saw, early developing behaviours such as following someone's gaze or looking where they are pointing are thought to constitute a mechanism that 'kick starts' the capacity to 'read' mental states such as beliefs and emotions from people's behaviour, and particularly from their eyes. Baron-Cohen *et al.* suggest that in typically developing children, this mechanism is served at the biological level by an integrated brain system involving the amygdala, together with specific sub-areas of the temporal lobe (the **superior temporal gyrus**) and of the frontal cortex (the **orbito-frontal cortex**). These structures were shown in Figure 5.8. The theoretical rationale for these ideas derives from a proposal by Brothers (1990) that these parts of the brain have evolved as a 'module' specialised for the processing of socially significant stimuli. The essential idea is that part of the brain is specialised for 'social intelligence'. The researchers draw on a wide range of evidence to argue that early influences on this system result in atypical brain functioning that produces the characteristic 'mind-reading' deficits seen in autism. An experimental test of the model is featured in Box 5.10.

Superior temporal gyrus
A folded area on the outside of the temporal lobes. Thought to have an active role when a person is monitoring another's direction of gaze.

Orbito-frontal cortex
The area on the under surface of the frontal lobes. Thought to have a role in exercising judgement.

5.10 **Testing predictions of the 'amygdala model' (Baron-Cohen et al., 1999; 2000)**

The experiment involved two participant groups:
- ASD group: six adult participants with a diagnosis of high-functioning autism or Asperger's syndrome.
- Control group: 12 non-autistic control participants.

The participants in both groups were matched for mean age, IQ, educational level, handedness and socio-economic status.

Participants were presented with a series of photographs of eyes such as those shown in Figure 5.9, and asked to perform the following tasks. Brain scanning was carried out while each participant performed the tasks.
- Task A: press one of two buttons to indicate whether the person shown is male or female (sex judgement).
- Task B: press one of two buttons to indicate which of two emotions shown at the bottom of the photograph is portrayed by the eyes (a 'mind-reading' task).

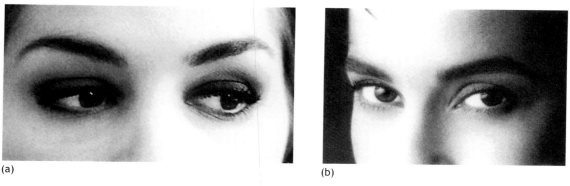

(a)   (b)

Figure 5.9   Examples of test stimuli used in Baron-Cohen's experiment

Both faces in Figure 5.9 are female. The emotions portrayed are (a) concerned and (b) sympathetic.

Both participant groups performed the two tasks with considerable accuracy, though the control group performed better than the ASD group on the 'mind-reading' task. The main interest of the researchers lay in the areas of the brain that were activated while performing the 'mind-reading' tasks. In the non-autistic group, the areas activated included the left amygdala. In the participants with ASDs, the amygdala was not activated at all, and other areas, such as the superior temporal gyrus, were activated more strongly than in the control participants.

The experimenters concluded that the different parts of the brain used by ASD and control participants when responding in task B reflected the use of different processing strategies. In particular, failure to activate the left amygdala meant that the ASD participants were not engaging with the faces as emotional stimuli. Their reliance on brain areas such as the superior temporal gyrus meant that they were treating the task as a kind of face recognition: they were assessing the emotional expressions in an atypical 'non-emotional' way.

As a theoretical model, Baron-Cohen's approach has several appealing features:

- it focuses on specific sub-areas of the brain known to have specialised functions, rather than on global areas that have multiple functions
- it builds on anatomical knowledge of neuronal connections to integrate different sub-areas of the brain into a single functional system
- it builds on neuropsychological findings to predict how atypical system functioning will affect the socio-cognitive skills of people with ASDs.

Such experimental results as those in Box 5.10 also provide a biological basis for Happé's finding (1994) that some people with 'high-functioning' autism or Asperger's syndrome pass theory of mind tasks without having full social understanding. The suggestion that they learn 'solutions' in an atypical way is

supported by the present findings suggesting that different brain functioning is
involved. A difficult challenge for such an approach is to explain differences in
functioning across the spectrum: on the one hand, the majority of people with
autistic spectrum disorders fail theory of mind tasks, and the Baron-Cohen *et al.*
result does not bear directly on their failure. On the other, the notion that
elements of the cognitive phenotype for autism are present in 'normal'
individuals outside the spectrum (see Section 4.5) begs the difficult question of
whether their brain function is also atypical.

Another problem is that the amygdala model makes no mention of structures
such as the cerebellum and frontal lobes, which have been implicated in autism
by other researchers. Does this mean that separate models are required to
explain the role of these structures? Answers to these questions are beyond the
scope of this chapter, but they indicate that current understanding of brain
functioning in autism is provisional.

The problem of reconstructing the developmental trajectory also re-surfaces
here. Studies of adult brain dysfunction do not tell us what biological influences
were at play before or at birth, how they might have altered the typical course of
brain development and the individual's interactions with his/her environment.
Observed atypicalities of brain function may even develop as a *result* of autism.
Though the notion of **neural plasticity** is usually associated with beneficial
change to the nervous system as a result of experience, it can also imply
detrimental change. In an elegant and wide-ranging article, Schore (2001) argues
that healthy development of brain structures like those in Baron-Cohen's model
occurs during a critical period in the child's infancy *subject to* the regulating
effects of the child's interactions with his/her caregiver. It is therefore possible
that the impoverished social interaction experienced by autistic children over
time induces negative plastic changes, as the neural pathways associated with
social interaction are underused and therefore become weakened. This
controversial idea does not preclude the infant entering the world with an innate
difficulty in social engagement. However, it does echo Hobson's idea (1993) that
such a starting point could trigger a 'negative spiral' in which the capacity for
social engagement becomes progressively more flawed. According to Schore's
model, this spiral constitutes a complex cycle of interaction involving behaviour,
social cognition and brain function.

Neural plasticity
A process by which the
strength of specific
connections between
brain cells (neural
pathways) is altered.
Connections can become
stronger or weaker,
depending on whether
they are used frequently
or infrequently.

Summary Section 5

- Twin and family studies provide strong evidence for genetic influences in
  ASDs, and for a spectrum ranging from classic autism to subtle borderline
  symptoms.
- One model linking genetic influences to organic dysfunction sees genetic
  influences as triggering a single causal chain; another suggests that

organic dysfunction may occur independently and add to or interact with genetic vulnerability.

- Evidence for brain and neuronal dysfunction ranges from non-specific EEG findings to neuropsychological evidence and scanning techniques highlighting specific brain areas including the frontal and temporal lobes, cerebellum, limbic system and amygdala.
- The amygdala model of autism suggests links between findings at biological and socio-cognitive levels, but is currently speculative.
- Impaired social interactions between the infant and his/her caregiver may have a detrimental effect on organic functioning.

6   Helping people with autistic spectrum disorders

In this section we will consider approaches to providing help and support for people with ASDs. Most interventions are designed for children, but we will also touch on the developing range of interventions aimed at adults. Another dimension to consider is the extent to which such interventions target the specific needs of the different sub-areas or groups highlighted throughout this chapter.

Practical developments in diagnosis, therapy and education span the three levels of explanation, from observable behaviour to socio-cognitive functioning and biology. Most of the work is directly or indirectly informed by the account of symptoms in Sections 2 and 3, and by the theoretically oriented work represented in Sections 4 and 5. One 'behavioural' approach considered here is intentionally more pragmatic in its rationale, illustrating a different theory–practice relationship. As before, the various perspectives may contradict, complement or just coexist with one another.

First we will consider some approaches that appear to 'fly in the face' of both theoretical and practical understanding by claiming to 'cure' autism. This preliminary discussion will provide an assessment of the therapeutic and ethical principles that should guide practical interventions.

6.1 The myth of 'miracle' cures

Over the years since Kanner's first description of autism, a number of practitioners have claimed, dramatically, that particular therapeutic procedures effectively amount to 'cures'. To the parent or family of a person with autism, these approaches have understandable appeal, even if only on the principle of 'try anything if it might help'. However, careful scrutiny has invariably raised serious doubts about the claims, and has suggested that in some cases these approaches may be actively harmful.

The psychoanalyst Bettelheim described his approach in his book *Empty Fortress: Infantile Autism and the Birth of Self* (Bettelheim, 1967). He maintained that cold and rejecting behaviour on the part of parents, and particularly mothers, was responsible for the 'autistic withdrawal' of their children. His 'treatment' involved separating children from their parents and caring for them in a special 'therapeutic' environment, designed along psychoanalytic lines. His book describes apparently dramatic improvements in the emotional adjustment, speech and behaviour of children treated in this way. However, the claims did not stand up to critical evaluation (Jordan, 1999; Rutter, 1999). Indeed, as Paradiz (2002) notes, Bettelheim probably exaggerated his credentials as an academic and psychoanalyst, and falsified his data. A visitor to the centre in the 1970s stated:

> ... there were locked doors everywhere – it is claimed 'to keep the world out' – and I caught only a brief glimpse of a pupil ... For the first year the child is completely separated from his parents and after that only limited visiting is allowed – perhaps 2 or 3 times a year.

> (Roth, personal communication, 1976)

This procedure caused untold distress to parents, and the stigma and guilt that they experienced as the original 'perpetrators' of their children's problems lasted for many years. Several decades on it seems astonishing that involuntary separation of children from their families could be justified and implemented following one specialist's unconfirmed theoretical perspective.

Another controversial approach, introduced in the 1980s, was known as 'holding therapy'. It was enthusiastically endorsed by the ethologist Tinbergen (Tinbergen and Tinbergen, 1983) and the clinical psychologist Richer (Richer, 1987). They believed that the origins of autism lie in profound anxiety that prevents children from establishing appropriate social bonds with parents and others. The therapy itself, pioneered by the psychiatrist Welch (1983), aimed at overcoming fear of emotional contact by close and sustained physical contact between the child and his/her mother, usually with the child sitting on the mother's lap and facing her. The role of the therapist was to help the mother initiate and maintain the hold, and to develop direct eye contact. As the child would typically find such close and prolonged contact disagreeable or frightening, considerable force was often needed to maintain it. Welch claimed some striking therapeutic successes in individual cases (Welch, 1983). But both parents and professionals have cast serious doubt on these claims and suggested that the procedure was actively harmful (Rutter, 1999). Hocking (1987) tried the technique with her son over a three-year period:

After I stopped the therapy, it took me a long time before I could see the whole experience in perspective and was appalled by some of the things we had done ... my son's response to our attempts to blast a way through his protective wall was to withdraw even further.

(Hocking, 1987, p. 15)

Such failures highlight the importance of establishing sound guidelines for evaluating proposed interventions.

6.2 Evidence-based practice

Activity 5.6

Imagine that, as a practitioner, you need to evaluate claims made for the success of a particular therapy. What would you want to know before you were prepared to accept the claims? Note down some ideas before reading on.

Box 5.11 sets out a framework of relevant questions for evaluating practice. There is a considerable overlap with the design considerations for an appropriately controlled and ethically sensitive experimental study. There are, of course, difficulties in applying rigorous experimental standards in the complex real-world setting we are considering here. However, given what is at stake, sound theoretical grounding, valid claims about efficacy, and ethical procedures are necessary standards for practice. Rutter observes 'It has become generally accepted that all of us, as clinicians, need to base what we do on solid empirical research findings' (1999, p. 169). This approach, which is widely advocated in clinical psychology, is known as **evidence-based practice**.

Evidence-based practice
An approach that advocates the importance of basing therapeutic practice on sound empirical evidence.

We will evaluate Bettelheim's and Welch's approaches in light of the criteria in Box 5.11, and refer back to them in subsequent discussion.

5.11 Criteria for evaluating practical interventions

I   Theoretical rationale

Is there either a theoretical or a sound practical rationale for predicting success? For both Bettelheim's and Welch's approaches the answer would have to be 'no'. As this chapter has shown, there is no evidence (research or otherwise) to suggest that autism is **psychogenic** in origin (in the sense that it arises from deep emotional conflict engendered by the child's social or familial environment), indeed there is extensive evidence for the role of other influences. In fairness, Bettelheim and Welch clearly believed in psychogenic causes for autism, and the overwhelming evidence favouring genetic and neuropsychological influences did not exist when they devised their therapies.

Psychogenic
Influence on the development of psychological problems that originates 'in the mind', rather than from known biological factors.

2 Methodological considerations

Do tests of the procedure employ a relevant group of participants?
Participants involved in a proposed therapeutic procedure for autism/ASDs must be
shown to have an appropriate diagnosis. Otherwise the fact that it succeeds says
nothing about its application to autism. There was no evidence that Bettelheim
employed widely accepted diagnostic criteria for autism. His participants may well
have been emotionally disturbed, or have come from emotionally dysfunctional
families, but this is not the same thing. Similarly, Welch explicitly offered her therapy
for a wide category of childhood emotional disturbances. Since there was apparently
no attempt to secure differential diagnoses for participants, it would be unjustified to
draw any specific conclusions about effects on autism. This illustrates the benefits of
systematic diagnosis following agreed criteria, as outlined in Section 2.

**Can reported successes clearly be attributed to the intervention as
opposed to other factors or chance?** Once again, neither Bettelheim nor Welch
carried out their work in the kind of systematic way that would permit answers to
these questions. For instance, no attempt was made to compare the efficacy of the
therapeutic procedure with that of an alternative 'control' procedure.

**What are the criteria for success? For example, does the effect last?
Does it generalise to a range of situations or to individuals beyond the
participants?** Again, both Bettelheim's and Welch's work was flawed by the fact
that success was based on the therapist's subjective evaluation of single cases, that
there was no proper follow-up and no clear effects on the well-being of the
children.

3 Ethics

**Can the intervention be carried out in an ethically acceptable way that
does not cause distress to the child with autism or his/her family?**
Bettelheim's approach clearly raised serious ethical questions. Holding therapy is also
ethically questionable. For instance, it advocates deliberately distressing the child in
order that the parent can overcome emotional negativity, and persisting in holding
even though this is disagreeable.

Most practitioners these days are extremely wary of therapeutic procedures that
are presented as 'cures'. Some effects of autistic spectrum disorders are seen as
'lifelong'. However, there is much scope for improving the life situation of
people with ASDs, employing sounder principles for intervention.

6.3 Developments in early identification

Section 2 indicated that securing a diagnosis for a child can be a complex
process. People with Asperger's syndrome are especially likely to remain
undiagnosed and to grow up considered eccentric or socially aloof.

Therefore, improving identification techniques offers one way to address practical needs.

Is it necessarily better for individuals to receive a diagnosis that 'labels' them as early as possible?

For children with severe autism, the benefits of early identification almost certainly outweigh the drawbacks. They are more likely to receive treatment for any medical problems and to gain access to specialist services and appropriate educational support. For children with mild or borderline ASDs, there may be arguments for keeping the boundaries blurred. Yet Clare Sainsbury writes:

> *Finally getting the right label was one of the best things that has ever happened to me. By my teens I was seriously depressed after years of being different and not knowing why, and believing that, since no-one gave a name to my problem, I must just be imagining it, or not trying hard enough (after a decade of trying very hard and failing very hard to be like everyone else). This experience was shared by many other people with Asperger's.*

> (*Sainsbury, 2000, p. 31*)

Significant progress in early identification comes from instruments such as the CHAT (*Checklist for Autism in Toddlers*, Baron-Cohen *et al.*, 1992, 1996, see Box 5.12). This instrument seeks to shift the focus of diagnosis from outward signs towards symptoms that are part of the core socio-cognitive deficit, and this illustrates the fruitful interplay between theoretically driven research and practice.

5.12 Developing and using the CHAT (Baron-Cohen et al., 1992, 1996)

The CHAT consists of a questionnaire for parent and health visitor about behaviours thought to serve as early 'building blocks' for the development of mind-reading skills, in particular gaze monitoring, proto-declarative pointing and pretend play (see Box 5.5). These questions are mixed with questions about other developmental milestones, for example:

'Does your child ever use his/her index finger to indicate *interest* in something?' (Proto-declarative pointing.)

'Does your child like climbing on things, such as up stairs?' (General motor development.)

Baron-Cohen *et al.*'s first CHAT study (1992), mentioned in Box 5.5, established that the three key behaviours were present in typically developing children by 18 months. They were absent from the behavioural repertoire of a group of older children diagnosed with autism, and from some 18-month-old siblings identified as genetically 'at risk'.

Baron-Cohen *et al.* (1996) collaborated with health visitors and GPs on the screening of 16,000 children in Southeast England. The CHAT was administered during a routine developmental check-up at 18 months. Out of all children screened, 12 failed on all three critical items from the CHAT. On further assessment, using a range of the diagnostic instruments described in Section 2, 10 of these children were diagnosed as autistic. The remaining two received a diagnosis of 'developmental delay'. This means that they were markedly late in achieving significant developmental milestones, particularly in the area of language and communication. Further delay in this pattern might meet criteria for a spectrum disorder. Another 22 children failed to show either or both proto-declarative pointing and pretend play. Fifteen of this group also received a diagnosis of developmental delay.

From this study the researchers concluded that the CHAT is successful in screening for the absence of a core group of behaviours, which carries an 83.3 per cent risk of autism. The CHAT was seen as making a useful contribution to early identification of autism, though not as a diagnostic tool in itself.

We can evaluate this study in light of the criteria in Box 5.11.

Theoretical rationale: The approach is extensively grounded in the empirically well-supported ToM framework.

Methodological considerations: The approach includes many methodological checks: the questionnaire was 'pre-screened' to identify key indicators; the study included a very large population; children initially identified by the CHAT were extensively assessed using diagnostic tools such as DSM-IV. However, the test is not 100 per cent reliable. It is, in principle, possible for children to pass the test and yet later develop the symptoms of autism (known as a 'false negative').

Ethics: The procedure is conducted in a sensitive way, involving the child with parent and health visitor at a routine check-up. However, children who fail on the three 'target' behaviours automatically become part of the group further assessed for autism. If children so assessed turn out not to meet diagnostic criteria (known as a 'false positive') this could be a needlessly upsetting experience. In this study, 10 of the children picked up by the CHAT *did* receive a diagnosis of autism, and the remaining two received a diagnosis of developmental delay.

A second ethical problem is that parents did not know that the checklist included with the routine 18-month check-up was actually screening for autism. Had they known, some parents might have withheld their consent.

The 'false negative' and 'false positive' problems have both been addressed in a follow-up study (Baird *et al.*, 2000). In current use of the CHAT, the false positive rate is almost zero, and the false negative rate has been substantially reduced by a second administration of the questionnaire after an interval. The CHAT is one of a developing range of screening questionnaires aimed at improving early identification across the autistic spectrum: others have been developed for the specialised problem of identifying older individuals with 'high-functioning' symptoms.

6.4 Treating behavioural symptoms

The *Lovaas approach* focuses specifically on changing 'autistic' behaviour (rocking, obsession with objects, idiosyncratic speech or no speech). The approach, elaborated and practised by Lovaas and colleagues for more than 30 years, rejects the notion of explaining autism in terms of underlying or core problems – whether these are at the socio-cognitive or biological level. It has its roots in the behaviourist tradition in psychology, which focuses on externally observable behaviours. We describe the key assumptions of the Lovaas approach in Box 5.13

5.13 *The Lovaas approach (Lovaas, 1987, 1996)*

Key assumptions are:
1   Autism is characterised by behaviours that are detrimental or destructive to the child and/or to those around him or her.
2   The search for 'underlying causes' of autism may be theoretically misguided and is irrelevant to developing effective therapy.
3   Learning plays a central role in the autistic child's failure to acquire 'desirable' behaviours (such as physical contact with others), and in his/her acquisition of 'undesirable' behaviours (repetitive behaviours that may be injurious or anti-social, such as head banging, destruction of objects, taking clothes off in public, etc.). Therefore behaviour modification is an appropriate technique for changing these behaviours.
4   The key to behaviour modification therapy is to analyse the child's behaviour into 'manageable' components that can be individually tackled.
5   An important extension of this approach (introduced in the 1980s) is training parents to carry out the therapy themselves at home.

In a typical application of these principles, the parent or therapist might decide to focus on a child's use of compulsive questioning. By consistently refusing to acknowledge or pay attention to these questions, the parent seeks to avoid providing reinforcement for them. However, if the child seeks the parent's attention without resorting to compulsive questioning, he or she is positively reinforced by receiving attention. In this way, the therapist aims to 'extinguish' undesired behaviour, and increase and 'shape' desired behaviour (refer back to Chapter 2 for a discussion of behavioural learning theory in relation to PTSD).

Lovaas's approach has been reasonably effective in helping children with ASDs to control undesirable behaviours, especially those that are self-destructive, or anti-social to family members. It has also enabled impassive children to learn gestures such as smiling and waving, and previously mute children to acquire elementary language responses. Involving parents as the key providers of therapy obviates the need for therapy to be carried out in the unfamiliar environment of hospital or clinic, and this emphasis on home-based therapy has been emulated in many other therapeutic approaches.

Lovaas (1996) claimed that an intensive home-based programme during the pre-school years can 'normalise' functioning in about two-fifths of children with autism, and argued that these findings were inconsistent with neuropsychological models of autism. Note that in this instance the flow of ideas is from clinical practice to theory, rather than from theory to clinical practice.

Despite its benefits, criticisms of Lovaas's approach arise when we apply the criteria in Box 5.11:

Theoretical rationale: the approach is intentionally 'atheoretical' in addressing symptoms and rejecting the need to understand 'causes'. However, the idea that autism is purely a problem of faulty learning is difficult to reconcile with substantial evidence for genetic and organic dysfunction, which in turn are linked to deficits in planning behaviour and in social understanding.

Methodological considerations: critics have argued that Lovaas's selection of participants is ill-defined, and that the design of the interventions cannot exclude improvements due to other factors. Lack of generalisation is a key problem: while children can be trained to make responses such as 'Can I have a biscuit?', this behaviour does not generalise into the command of syntax, semantics and pragmatics that is required to use language flexibly in different social situations. Similarly, though a child can be taught social responses such as smiling or waving, he/she may not have acquired an understanding of the subtle significance of these gestures in complex social interactions.

Ethics: Lovaas's approach requires a tremendous commitment of time (40 hours per week for the intensive programme) and emotional strength. These are likely to be beyond many parents' capabilities and may accentuate the kinds of family tensions mentioned in Section 4. Lovaas's approach also gives therapist and family the power to decide what behaviour is 'undesirable'. This carries the danger of requiring a child to conform to his/her family's particular cultural stereotypes of what behaviour is socially acceptable, as opposed to helping the child to overcome behaviour that is actually damaging to self or others.

In its 'pure' form then, Lovaas's approach is controversial. However, elements of behaviour modification are included as a complementary feature of many educational and home-based therapy programmes. Some parents appear naturally gifted therapists: Tito's autobiography (Mukhopadhyay, 2000) describes subtle forms of behaviour modification that his mother intuitively combined with other strategies to help him to control problematic behaviour and develop his potential.

6.5 Developing socio-cognitive skills

Some recent approaches are directed at helping people with autism to establish theory of mind-type skills. The rationale, in contrast to behaviour modification, is that this will bring about relatively fundamental psychological change and social adjustment rather than tackling 'surface' symptoms. Experimental work by Hadwin *et al.* (1996) demonstrated a way of teaching mental state understanding to children with ASDs. Patricia Howlin and colleagues (Howlin *et al.*, 1999) elaborated this as a programme for practitioners and carers to use with children (see Box 5.14).

5.14 *Teaching mind-reading skills (Howlin et al., 1999)*

The approach offers detailed materials and instructions for helping children tackle three main areas of mind-reading skills: understanding emotions; understanding 'informational states of mind', such as beliefs and pretend play. In each of these areas the training materials are arranged in order of difficulty so that the child progresses from learning about simple mind-reading skills to more complex ones. For instance, the training material for emotions is arranged to tackle the following skill levels:

Level 1: ability to recognise from photographs facial expressions such as happy, sad, angry, afraid.

Level 2: ability to recognise expressions as in Level 1, but from facial cartoons.

Level 3: ability to predict how a character will feel given a situation depicted in a picture (e.g. fear when an accident is about to happen).

Level 4: ability to identify a character's feelings (happy or sad) according to whether their desires (e.g. to go to the cinema) are satisfied.

Level 5: ability to recognise emotions caused by a character's belief about a situation (e.g. a child wants to go to the cinema and thinks their mother is taking them).

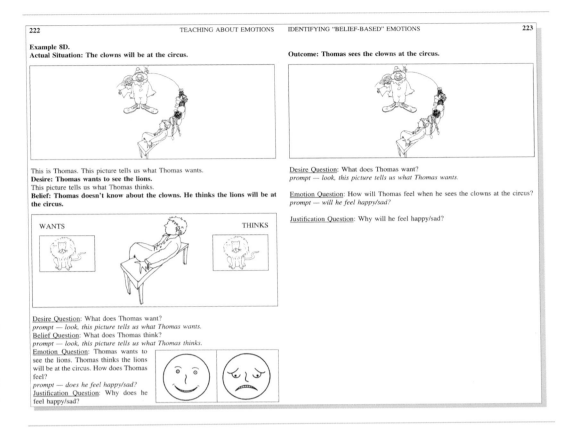

222   TEACHING ABOUT EMOTIONS   IDENTIFYING "BELIEF-BASED" EMOTIONS   223

Example 8D.
Actual Situation: The clowns will be at the circus.

This is Thomas. This picture tells us what Thomas wants.
Desire: Thomas wants to see the lions.
This picture tells us what Thomas thinks.
Belief: Thomas doesn't know about the clowns. He thinks the lions will be at the circus.

WANTS   THINKS

<u>Desire Question</u>: What does Thomas want?
prompt — look, this picture tells us what Thomas wants.
<u>Belief Question</u>: What does Thomas think?
prompt — look, this picture tells us what Thomas thinks.
<u>Emotion Question</u>: Thomas wants to see the lions. Thomas thinks the lions will be at the circus. How does Thomas feel?
prompt — does he feel happy/sad?
<u>Justification Question</u>: Why does he feel happy/sad?

Outcome: Thomas sees the clowns at the circus.

<u>Desire Question</u>: What does Thomas want?
prompt — look, this picture tells us what Thomas wants.

<u>Emotion Question</u>: How will Thomas feel when he sees the clowns at the circus?
prompt — will he feel happy/sad?

<u>Justification Question</u>: Why will he feel happy/sad?

Figure 5.10 Example of page used in teaching Level 5 'mind-reading' skills

Figure 5.10 illustrates a teaching page for Level 5. In each area, the teacher works through a whole series of such pictorial examples with the child and tests that the child has understood the principle being taught, before moving on to a different example. In this way the approach seeks to ensure generalisation of the skill across different examples and to the next level of difficulty. The situations illustrated are as near as possible to real-life situations that the child might experience. However, as Figure 5.10 shows, the approach could be seen as encouraging a 'pictures in the mind' notion of how other people think.

Some success has been achieved with these materials, including the key step of helping children to generalise from the materials to situations they have not previously encountered (e.g. Hadwin *et al.*, 1996).

Again, we can use the criteria in Box 5.11 to evaluate this approach.

Theoretical rationale: The programme has a firm grounding in ToM research, which predicts that children will benefit from techniques designed to enhance mental state understanding.

Methodological considerations: Hadwin *et al.*'s study (1996) constituted an acceptable 'pilot', employing appropriate participants and evaluation of the success of the measure. However, it may be that what the child learns here is a set of rather 'wooden' or theoretical skills for interpreting social situations that will not generalise into skills for entering social interactions.

Ethics: The fact that the child is taught a somewhat 'mechanical' view of how minds work could be seen as an ethical problem. This concern is tackled in an interesting, though small-scale, study by Chin and Bernard-Opitz (2000). In an intervention with three boys diagnosed with 'high-functioning' autism, they focused not on theory of mind per se, but on the conversational skills that are a practical manifestation of theory of mind. They taught the boys the skills of initiating and maintaining a conversation, taking turns and listening attentively, and changing conversational topic. The intervention was moderately successful: one child showed particular improvement, and the parents/carers of all three children rated the training as very effective. Yet the children's performance on experimental tests of false belief showed no improvement as a result of the training, suggesting a dissociation between experimental 'mind reading' and practical, everyday skills associated with understanding other minds.

This once again highlights the complex implications of the ToM approach. Theoretical insights are translated here into practical applications, but these applications may in turn call for modifications of theory or further revision of the applications.

6.6 Biological treatments?

Evidence that biological influences play an important role in autistic spectrum disorders might suggest that the most effective therapies would be biological. In practice, therapeutic approaches targeted at biological functioning are particularly problematic. Genetic and neuropsychological influences in autism are not reversible, given the techniques of medical science available at the time of writing. Though studies in the field of molecular genetics have begun to offer provisional insights into which genes might be involved, there is no immediate prospect of interventions that could reverse these effects. In addition, we saw that influences at the biological level are only part of a complex causal and developmental process. An effective biological therapy would need to intervene in this process from a very early stage.

Despite the lack of therapies that address core biological influences, there are some important therapeutic interventions for symptoms that may accompany autism. Steffenburg's study, mentioned in Section 5, indicated that autism often occurs with epilepsy and/or may occur alongside another major medical syndrome that needs treating. Excessive hyperactivity and repetitive symptoms such as head banging need to be managed to avoid self-injury. While behavioural modification techniques described earlier are preferable, it may be necessary to prescribe drug treatments that influence brain function. One theory is that hyperactivity and repetitive behaviour is caused by the abnormal levels of the neurotransmitter called serotonin noted in some people with autism. A drug called fenfluramine, which reduces serotonin levels, has been quite effective in managing these symptoms. However, an earlier claim that it acts as a treatment for autism has, like other 'miracle therapies', been discredited.

This discussion would not be complete without mention of diet-based treatments for autistic spectrum disorders. A number of parents claim that special diets (especially those free of wheat-based or cow's milk-based products) alleviate their children's symptoms, and enhance their skills. However, sceptics (e.g. Rutter, 1999) argue that when such treatments are systematically evaluated, there is no evidence to support them. The theoretical rationale for such diets is not clear: the hypothetical effects of metabolic disorders on the brain (see Section 5) would occur early in development and would therefore not be reversed by a retrospective change of diet.

Activity 5.7

Consider such dietary approaches in light of the Box 5.11 criteria. Is there any theoretical rationale? Do anecdotal reports that they are effective in specific cases count as success? What ethical concerns might arise?

Comment

Turn to the end of this chapter for a discussion of these issues.

6.7 Integrated approaches

As we have seen, the individual needs of people with ASDs differ, depending on severity, age, life situation and coping strategies. At all stages, education and personal growth are as important as therapy per se. This section illustrates approaches that support and foster individuals within a broad educational and therapeutic framework. Such approaches seek to address key features of autistic disability (such as the need for structure, routine, and difficulty interpreting puzzling social messages), key features of autistic skill (for instance, precision, accuracy and tolerance of repetition) and the specific needs and outlook of the individual. The framework considered here is Treatment and Education of Autistic and related Communication handicapped Children (TEACCH), originally developed in North Carolina. It is widely used in UK school and home settings, and is one of several educational frameworks recommended by the NAS (see Box 5.15).

5.15 The TEACCH framework

Key principles are:

1 Provision of structure, both in the person's environment and in the approach to teaching, which is typically one-to-one.
2 Emphasis on identifying and harnessing skills, particularly visual perception and memory, precision, accuracy and tolerance of repetition.
3 Evaluation of individual therapeutic needs on a regular basis, and the use of socio-cognitive and behavioural therapies as necessary.
4 Empowering parents by encouraging their full participation.
5 Emphasis on developing independence, and generalising from learning experiences, in order to master a range of everyday situations.
6 Training for practitioners that emphasises a 'whole person' approach.

In implementing these principles a key technique is visual structuring of the person's environment and teaching. For instance, pictures, symbols or objects may be set out on a TEACCH board to help the person in structuring space, concepts, tasks and activities. The board may serve as a visual timetable by presenting photographs of activities in the order in which they are to be carried out.

An adult service manager reviewing the implications of TEACCH for different settings gives the following example of a home intervention.

A young lady living at home had become extremely anxious and nervous about changing her clothes, wanting to wear the same things all the time and seeming to find a security in doing so. Trying to encourage her to change had become a time of stress and tension for all concerned. TEACCH principles were applied as follows:

Establishing visual boundaries	Seven small coloured baskets were organised – one for each day of the week, and labelled.
How much?	One complete set of clothes was put into each of the daily baskets.
When have I finished?	Once she was dressed in the clothes each day the empty basket was upturned onto the other empty baskets.
What next?	At the end of the day the new basket of clothes was put out for the next day, and she put what she was wearing into the family laundry basket.

Once the system was understood this young lady took to using it without problems, and nightly traumas about changing clothes faded away. Her independence has been developed by involving her in the setting up of the baskets for the week at the weekends.

(Robinson, 1997, pp. 8–10)

We can again evaluate TEACCH against the criteria given in Box 5.11.

Theoretical rationale: The approach draws on a range of theoretical insights, particularly the need to interpret inappropriate behaviour and anxiety in the light of both central coherence and ToM-type difficulties. It also embraces established therapeutic principles from fields such as behaviour modification.

Methodological considerations: The success of TEACCH depends crucially on its adaptability to individual needs, and therefore documented cases of individual success – as illustrated by Box 5.15 – are relevant, as well as more systematic reviews of overall success. A recent longitudinal study by Persson (2000) tracked the progress of a group of autistic men living in a group home, who participated in TEACCH for the first time. Over a period of two years or more, there was clear evidence for improvement in behaviour problems, sense of independence and well-being, as well as a reduced need for staff monitoring.

Some practitioners express concern that TEACCH is an external 'prop' that, because it is not internalised, relies on the parent or carer to maintain it. Powell and Jordan (1997) state that children may regress in their behaviour and stress levels on moving away from a TEACCH-based system. As such, TEACCH is best suited to the needs of people with more extreme ASDs. However, Golding (1997) describes how TEACCH and other principles have been incorporated into an impressive programme for 'high-functioning' adolescents. The programme fosters the move from individual activity to group work in which participants provide each other with reflections and encouragement and offer mutual support. Golding's approach illustrates the benefits of a procedure tailored to the special therapeutic needs of 'high-functioning' individuals. They are encouraged to use their capacity for self-awareness as a basis for sharing experiences with similar others, thus offsetting a sense of isolation.

Ethics: Like other integrated programmes, TEACCH has many positive ethical features. In particular, it is flexible to individual needs, considers dignity and general well-being, and by empowering parents to administer the programme, reduces their feelings of helplessness.

Summary Section 6

- Bettelheim's and Welch's approaches to 'curing' autism do not stand up to scrutiny, and raise serious ethical problems.
- Key features of an 'evidence-based practice' approach are sound theoretical rationale, appropriate methodology and ethical standards.
- The CHAT provides a tool for improving early identification of ASDs; other screening tools are in development for older people.
- Lovaas's behaviour modification approach is controversial in its assumptions about cause, and its viability as a 'pure' approach, but has usefully informed a range of interventions.
- The ToM approach informs both Howlin *et al.*'s programme for teaching mental state understanding, and a more naturalistic intervention aimed at enhancing social understanding.
- Biological therapies may be necessary for particular symptoms, but do not currently tackle core biological influences.
- TEACCH offers an integrated, multi-perspective approach, and has been adapted to promote group work for 'high-functioning' individuals.

7 Conclusion

This chapter has introduced an extremely rich and complex area in which new approaches and findings are constantly appearing. The diverse activities of psychologists and others in this area have been illuminated.

Discussion throughout the chapter has maintained several different but interwoven threads. Think first of the original twin goals of work on ASDs: establishing theoretical understanding and providing support and therapy. It should now be clear why these goals and the means of pursuing them are inextricably connected. For instance, diagnostic practice has underlined characteristic groupings of symptoms but has simultaneously drawn attention to the variations among these groupings. This has fostered research into the ways in which different subgroups across the spectrum operate in ToM or global processing tasks, which has in turn suggested new ways of diagnosing ASDs, and highlighted the need for therapies 'tuned' to different groups. Research studies highlighting socio-cognitive deficits have also informed therapeutic practices, but these have in turn questioned theories about which *types* of social understanding are most relevant to an individual's adjustment in the real world.

The pursuit of the twin goals has a further theoretical 'spin-off'. Investigations of why people with ASDs behave or experience the world as they do tell us much about the foundations of more typical behaviour and experience. For instance, a crucial feature of Baron-Cohen's developmental mind-reading model is how skills such as gaze monitoring pre-figure the development of 'mind reading' within typical development. This 'information processing approach' to social engagement with others has been countered, and latterly modified, in the light of Hobson's radically different idea that people's interpersonal relations have an 'empathic' quality.

Here we have gained insights by contrasting typical and atypical development. Yet paradoxically, research on ASDs has also taught us to be wary of assuming clear-cut boundaries between what is typical and atypical. The notion that mild forms of autism are essentially variations on the 'norm' and are represented in the general population as a cognitive style or phenotype has surfaced at several points in the discussion. Indeed the characteristic 'cognitive style' associated with ASDs has been shown to have advantages and in some cases to go with exceptional talent.

All this poses a significant conundrum: that developments in autism research and practice are advancing simultaneously on two seemingly contradictory fronts. On the one hand there is a move to define, explain and support 'difference' – whether between people with ASDs and others, or among spectrum subgroups themselves. On the other hand there is growing emphasis on continuity – on shared features of behaviour and experience across and beyond the spectrum, and on our common needs as human beings. There is no easy way to reconcile these contrasting strands, but an analogy from another field may help. Think of the spectrum of visible light: for some purposes it is useful to consider it as a series of *quantitatively* different wavelengths that are on a continuum – not only with each other, but with other forms of energy such as X-rays and ultra-violet, which we don't see at all. At other times, it is more appropriate to think of this spectrum more as we actually perceive colour: as relatively discreet perceptual categories (red, blue, green, etc.) that are experienced as *qualitatively* distinct from one another and from energies that we don't see. Both approaches have their place in our conceptual and practical scheme of things. This duality occurs in many fields of human experience and it is a particular attribute of human cognition to be able to operate and flourish in both.

A second major thread has been the variety of perspectives that inform work on autism and the ways they interrelate. We have noted a valuable role for diverse research and practice within and across at least three different levels – symptomatic/behavioural, socio-cognitive and biological. We have also considered ways in which these different perspectives complement each other, and areas in which they conflict. Does this mean that all approaches on offer should be given equal weight? Not really. There is a clear argument for favouring models that offer a coherent theoretical framework, that are compatible with a range of empirical findings, and that guide further work along appropriate paths. If there are choices between such models, then it makes sense to favour those that offer the clearer, more cogent explanations. As we saw, very similar principles apply to practice.

Thus it would be misguided to deny that biological influences and socio-cognitive influences play key roles in the development of ASDs: there is much careful research providing evidence that cannot be explained in other ways. Explaining just how these influences interact with each other and with other levels of explanation is, as we saw, more difficult. While there are persuasive links between the functioning of some brain areas and ToM-type skills, this leaves other identified brain areas (such as the cerebellum) and other socio-cognitive skills (such as global processing skills) out of the frame. Models such as Baron-Cohen's, which seek to make these wider links, are at best provisional and leave the therapeutic implications unclear. A yet harder challenge is to build into such models a development trajectory in which biology, cognition and behaviour both influence and are influenced by the multi-faceted environment that surrounds the human organism. The chapter hinted at difficult tensions between this and known biological and cognitive constraints: in what ways can the child influence and be influenced by the immediate environment of his/her family? How might environmental privation influence biological mechanisms? How should the notion of such 'transactions' influence the design of interventions?

The chapter has also illustrated the important role of 'insider' accounts in modifying, extending and even challenging conclusions based on outsider evidence. In particular, insider accounts have echoed growing theoretical reservations about the idea that people with ASDs necessarily lack forms of social or self insight. The self insights featured in this chapter may be unusual, but they are striking and poignantly clear. They have done much to transform accepted stereotypes of what it is like to have an ASD, and practical approaches, such as Golding's, that seek to develop reflexivity and empathy are to be welcomed.

Finally, work on ASDs has come far since Kanner and Asperger, yet both contributed prescient insights: Kanner's notion of an 'innate inability to form the usual, biologically provided, affective contact with people' and both Kanner's and Asperger's emphasis on special or exceptional skills, informed their clinical practice and remain as central themes in current work.

▶ Comment on Activity 5.1

Christopher: lack of eye contact and loss of language indicating qualitative impairments in communication (area 2) and possibly a lack of social reciprocity (area 1). Symptoms developed below 36 months.

Alison: 'living in own world' suggesting qualitative impairments in both social interaction (area 1, particularly not sharing interests, lack of social reciprocity) and communication (area 2, apparently she does not speak). Rocking indicates repetitive activities, and musical interests could reflect a preoccupation (area 3).

Gunilla: her rather idiosyncratic understanding and use of language could reflect a subtle communication impairment (area 2). However, her difficulties, which are not well captured by the diagnostic criteria, probably reflect a less severe spectrum disorder – see Section 3.

Tito: fascination with calendars suggests a preoccupation (area 3). However, his command of language to describe this obsession seems at odds with several criteria in area 2. Tito also has areas of outstanding talent – especially poetry, which fits with the descriptions of 'savant' skills in Sections 2.3 and 3.3. He is almost certainly in the small minority of individuals whose autism goes together with 'savant syndrome'.

Comment on Activity 5.7

Since the discussion of dietary therapy given in this chapter is very limited, we can only tentatively apply the criteria in Box 5.11

1   Theoretical rationale: the causal mechanisms that might link a disorder of metabolism to an effect on brain function are unclear. Autism has an onset before 36 months of age, so any metabolic defect would have to be present at, or soon after, birth in order to affect developing brain function. Such a chain of events cannot be ruled out, but it cannot easily be verified, and it does not explain why a diet undertaken at a much later age should have any effect on autistic symptoms. The metabolic theory also appears incompatible with the large and robust body of evidence favouring other, particularly genetic, influences. Some researchers do claim, controversially, that it is genetic influences that render children vulnerable to metabolic disorders, which in turn cause autism. However, it is equally possible that metabolic defects are the *result* rather than the cause of autism.

2   Methodological considerations: there is little doubt that some parents of children with ASDs find special diets of help in reducing some of their children's symptoms. The journal of the National Autistic Society, *Communication*, has featured reports from parents who endorse the use of special diets. Individual success stories such as these should not be rejected, but must be balanced against the reports of parents who do not find special diets helpful. Since these claims are contradictory, it cannot be ruled out that any beneficial effects are not directly due to changing the child's diet. More systematic studies have been inconclusive.

3   Ethics: the effects of dietary treatments are at most modest, and therefore ethical issues arise if any exaggerated claims are made for the success of therapy. In addition, since such diets often entail omitting a major source of protein, such as milk, or a major source of carbohydrate, such as wheat, there is the risk of exposing the child to a poorly balanced diet.

Further reading

Autism spectrum disorders:

Baron-Cohen, S. (1995) *Mindblindness: An Essay on Autism and Theory of Mind*, Cambridge, MA and London, MIT Press.

Baron-Cohen excels in his capacity to unify complex arguments and extensive empirical findings within a clear and persuasive and accessible theoretical framework.

Mukhopadhyay, T.R. (2000) *Beyond the Silence: My Life, and the World of Autism*, London, National Autistic Society.

A fascinating, poignant and unique book: the biography of the 11-year-old poet, Tito.

Powell, S. and Jordan, R. (eds) (1997) *Autism and Learning: A Guide to Good Practice*, London, David Fulton.

An excellent collection of essays on how to enhance educational experiences for people with autism.

Focusing specifically on Asperger's syndrome:

Frith, U. (ed.) (1991) *Autism and Asperger Syndrome*, Cambridge, Cambridge University Press.

A fascinating collection of essays about Asperger's syndrome, including one of Asperger's original papers in translation. Frith's books are always worth reading for the author's wisdom and accessible style.

Attwood, T. (1998) *Asperger's Syndrome: A Guide for Parents and Professionals*, London, Jessica Kingsley.

A highly regarded book written by an expert who has worked in this area for 25 years.

Sainsbury, C. (2000) *The Martian in the Playground*, Bristol, Lucky Duck Publishing.

Clare Sainsbury has Asperger's syndrome. Her book offers excellent insights into life as a schoolchild with this problem, and includes a collection of first-person testimonies.

References

American Psychiatric Association (2000) *Diagnostic and Statistical Manual of Mental Disorders* DSM-IV-TR™ (4th edn), Washington, DC, APA.

Asperger, H. (1944) '"Austistic psychopathy" in childhood', translated in Frith, U. (ed.) (1991).

Bailey, A., Le Couteur, A., Gottesman, I., Bolton, P., Simonoff, E., Yuzda, E. and Rutter, M. (1995) 'Autism as a strongly genetic disorder: evidence from a British twin study', *Psychological Medicine*, vol. 25, pp. 68–77.

Baird, G,. Charman, T., Baron-Cohen, S., Cox, A., Swettenham, J., Wheelwright, S., Drew, A. (2000) 'A screening instrument for autism at 18 months of age: a six year follow-up study', *Journal of the American Academy of Child and Adolescent Psychiatry*, vol. 39, pp. 694–702.

Baron-Cohen, S. (1987) 'Autism and symbolic play', *British Journal of Developmental Psychology*, vol. 5, pp. 139–48.

Baron-Cohen, S. (1989) 'Perceptual role-taking and proto-declarative pointing in autism', *British Journal of Developmental Psychology*, vol. 7, pp. 113–27.

Baron-Cohen, S. (1995) *Mindblindness: An Essay on Autism and Theory of Mind*, Cambridge, MA and London, MIT Press.

Baron-Cohen, S., Allen, J., and Gillberg, C. (1992) 'Can autism be detected at 18 months? The needle, the haystack and the CHAT', *British Journal of Psychiatry*, vol. 161, pp. 839–43.

Baron-Cohen, S., Cox, A., Baird, G., Swettenham, J., Nightingale, N., Morgan, K., Drew, A. and Charman, T. (1996) 'Psychological markers in the detection of autism in infancy in a large population', *British Journal of Psychiatry*, vol. 168, pp. 158–63.

Baron-Cohen, S., Leslie, L. and Frith, U. (1985) 'Does the autistic child have a "theory of mind"?', *Cognition*, vol. 21, pp. 37–46.

Baron-Cohen, S., Ring, H.A., Bullmore, E.T., Wheelwright, S., Ashwin, C. and Williams, S.C.R. (2000) 'The amygdala theory of autism', *Neuroscience and Biobehavioural Reviews*, vol. 24, pp. 355–64.

Baron-Cohen, S., Ring, H.A., Wheelwright, S., Bullmore, E.T., Brammer, M.J., Simmons, A., Williams, S.C.R. (1999) 'Social intelligence in the normal and autistic brain: an fMRI study', *European Journal of Neuroscience*, vol. 11, pp. 1891–8.

Baron-Cohen, S., Wheelwright, S., Lawson, J., Griffin, R., Hill, J., (2002) 'The exact mind: empathising and systemising in autism spectrum conditions' in Goswami, U. (ed.) *Handbook of Cognitive Development*, Oxford, Blackwell.

Baumann M. and Kemper, T.L. (1988) 'Limbic and cerebellar abnormalities: consistent findings in infantile autism', *Journal of Neuropathology and Experimental Neurology*, vol. 47, pp. 369.

Bettelheim, B (1967) *Empty Fortress: Infantile Autism and the Birth of Self*, New York, The Free Press.

Bolton, P., MacDonald, H., Pickles, A., Rios, P., Goode, S., Crowson, M., Bailey, A. and Rutter, M. (1994) 'A case control family history study of autism', *Journal of Child Psychology and Psychiatry*, vol. 35, pp. 877–900.

Brothers, L. (1990) 'The social brain: a project for integrating primate behaviour and neurophysiology in a new domain', *Concepts in Neuroscience*, vol. 1, pp. 27–51.

Chin, H.Y. and Bernard-Opitz, V. (2000) 'Teaching conversational skills to children with autism: effect on the development of a theory of mind', *Journal of Autism and Development Disorders*, vol. 30, pp. 569–83.

Cole, B. (1987) 'The story of two little sisters', *Communication*, vol. 21, no. 3, pp. 1–5.

Courchesne, E., Yeung-Courchesne, R., Press, G.A., Hesselink, J.R. and Jernigan, T.L. (1988) 'Hypoplasia of cerebellar vermal lobules VI and VII in autism', *New England Journal of Medicine*, vol. 318, pp. 1349–54.

DeMyer, M.K. (1979) *Parents and Children with Autism*, New York, John Wiley.

Dennett, D. (1978) 'Beliefs about beliefs', *Behaviour and Brain Sciences*, vol. 4, pp. 568–70.

Folstein, S. and Rutter, M. (1978) 'Infantile autism: a genetic study of 21 twin pairs', in Rutter, M. and Schopler, E. (eds), *Autism: A Reappraisal of Concepts and Treatment*, New York, Plenary Press.

Frith, U. (1989) *Autism: Explaining the Enigma*, Oxford, Blackwell.

Frith, U. (1991) (ed.) *Autism and Asperger Syndrome*, Cambridge, Cambridge University Press.

Frith, U. (1999) 'Paradoxes in the definition of dyslexia', *Dyslexia*, vol. 5, pp. 192–214.

Frith, U. and Soares, I. (1993) 'Research into earliest detectable signs of autism: what the parents say', *Communication*, vol. 27 no. 3, pp. 17–18.

Gerland, G. (1997) 'A real person', *Communication*, spring, pp. 15–6.

Gillberg, C. (1991) 'Clinical and neurobiological aspects of Asperger syndrome in six family studies' in Frith, U. (ed.) (1991).

Glastonbury, M. (1997) "I'll teach you differences": on the cultural presence of autistic lives', *Changing English*, vol. 4, pp. 51–65.

Golding, M.M. (1997) 'Beyond compliance: the importance of group work in the education of children and young people with autism' in Powell, S. and Jordan, R., *Autism and Learning: A Guide to Good Practice*, London, David Fulton.

Grayson, A. (1997) 'Can the physical support given in facilitated communication interactions help to overcome problems associated with executive function?' in

Living and Learning with Autism: The Individual, the Family and the Professional, Sunderland, Autism Research Unit.

Hadwin, J., Baron-Cohen, S., Howlin, P. and Hill, K. (1996) 'Can we teach children with autism to understand emotion, belief or pretence?', *Development and Psychopathology*, vol. 8, pp. 345–65.

Happé, F.G.E. (1994) 'An advanced test of theory of mind: understanding of story characters' thoughts and feelings by able autistic, mentally handicapped and normal children and adults', *Journal of Autism and Developmental Disorders*, vol. 24, pp. 129–54.

Happé, F.G.E. (1999) 'Understanding assets and deficits in autism: why success is more interesting than failure', Spearman Medical Lecture, *The Psychologist*, vol. 12, pp. 540–5.

Hobson, R.P. (1993) *Autism and the Development of Mind*, Hove, Lawrence Erlbaum.

Hobson, R.P., Ouston, J. and Lee, A. (1989) 'Naming emotion in faces and voices: abilities and disabilities in autism and mental retardation', *British Journal of Developmental Psychology*, vol. 7, pp. 237–50.

Hocking, B. (1987) *The Independent*, 3 November.

Howlin, P., Baron-Cohen, S. and Hadwin, J. (1999) *Teaching Children with Autism to Mind-Read: A Practical Guide*, Chichester, John Wiley & Sons.

Howlin, P. and Goode, S. (1998) 'Outcome in Adult Life for People with Autism and Asperger's Syndrome' in Volkmar, F.R. (ed.) *Autism and Persuasive Developmental Disorders, Cambridge Monographs in Child and Adolescent Psychiatry*, Cambridge, Cambridge University Press.

Humphrey, N.K. (1976) 'The social function of intellect' in Bateson, P.P.G. and Hinde, R.A. (eds) *Growing Points in Ethology*, Cambridge, Cambridge University Press.

Jordan, R. (1999) *Autism Spectrum Disorders: An Introductory Handbook for Practitioners*, London, David Fulton.

Kanner, L. (1943) 'Autistic disturbances of affective contact', *Nervous Child*, vol. 2, pp. 217–50.

Kanner, L. (1973) *Childhood Psychosis: Initial Studies and New Insights*, Washington, DC, V.H.Winston.

Klin, A., Lang, J., Cicchetti, D.V. and Volkmar, F.R. (2000) 'Brief report: inter-rater reliability of clinical diagnosis and DSM-IV criteria for autistic disorder', *Results of the DSM-IV Autism Field Trial*, vol. 30, no. 2, pp. 163–7.

Leekam, S., Baron-Cohen, S., Perrett, D., Milders, M. and Brown, S. (1997) 'Eye-direction detection: a dissociation between geometric and joint attention skills in autism', *British Journal of Developmental Psychology*, vol. 15, pp. 77–95.

Leslie, A. (1991) 'The theory of mind impairments in autism: evidence for a modular mechanism of development?' in Whiten, A. (ed.) *The Emergence of Mindreading*, Oxford, Blackwell.

Lord, C. (1993) 'Early social development in autism' in Schopler, E., van Bourgondien, M.E., Bristol, M.M. (eds) *Preschool Issues in Autism*, New York, Plenum Press.

Lovaas, O.I. (1987) 'Behavioural treatment and normal educational and intellectual functioning in young autistic children', *Journal of Consulting and Clinical Psychology*, vol. 55, pp. 3–9.

Lovaas, O.I. (1996) 'The UCLA young autism model of service delivery' in C. Maurice (ed.) *Behavioural Intervention for Young Children with Autism*, Austin, TX, Pro-Ed.

Mead, G.H. (1934) *Mind, Self and Society*, Chicago, IL, Chicago University Press.

Mukhopadhyay, T. (2000) *Beyond the Silence: My Life, the World and Autism*, London, National Autistic Society.

National Autistic Society (1987) 'From the parents' point of view', *Annual Report*, Spring, National Autistic Society.

Ozonoff, S. (1995) 'Executive functions in autism' in Schopler, E. and Mesibov, G.B. (eds).

Paradiz, V. (2002) *Elijah's Cup: A Family's Journey into the Community and Culture of High Functioning Autism and Asperger's Syndrome*, The Free Press, New York.

Peeters, T. and Gillberg, C. (1999) *Autism: Medical and Educational Aspects* (2nd edn), London, Whurr.

Persson, B. (2000) 'Brief report: a longitudinal study of quality of life and independence among adult men with autism', *Journal of Autism and Developmental Disorders*, vol. 30, no. 1, pp. 61–6.

Piven, J., Wzorek, M. and Landa. R. (1994) 'Personality characteristics of the parents of autistic individuals', *Psychological Medicine*, vol. 24, pp. 783–95.

Pring, L. and Hermelin, B. (1997) 'Native savant talent and acquired skill', *Autism*, vol. 1, no. 2, pp. 199–214.

Randall, P. and Parker, J. (1999) *Supporting the Families of Children with Autism*, Chichester, John Wiley.

Richer, J. (1987) *The Treatment of Children with Autism*, paper given at the Child and Adolescent Psychiatry Specialist Section, Royal College of Psychiatrists Annual Conference, 26 September.

Robinson (1997) 'TEACCH in adult services: the practitioner's eye view', *Communication*, summer.

Rogers, S.J. and Pennington, B.F. (1991) 'A theoretical approach to the deficits in infantile autism', *Development and Psychopathology*, vol. 3, pp. 137–62.

Roth, M. and Kroll, J. (1986) *The Reality of Mental Illness*, Cambridge, Cambridge University Press.

Rutter, M. (1999) 'Autism: two-way interplay between research and clinical work', *Journal of Child Psychology and Child Psychiatry*, vol. 40, pp. 169–88.

Rutter, M., Andersen-Wood, L., Beckett, C., Bredenkamp, D., Castle, J., Groothues, C., Kreppner, J., Keaveney, L., Lord, C., O'Connor, T.G. and the English and Romanian Adoptees (ERA) study team (1999) 'Quasi-autistic patterns following severe early global privation', *Child Psychology and Child Psychiatry*, vol. 40, pp. 537–49.

Sainsbury, C. (2000) *Martian in the Playground*, Bristol, Lucky Duck Publishing.

Schopler, E. and Mesibov, G.B. (1995) (eds) *Learning and Cognition in Autism*, Plenum Press, New York.

Schore, A.N. (2001) 'Effects of a secure attachment relationship on right brain development, affect regulation and infant mental health', *Infant Mental Health Journal*, vol. 22, pp. 7–66.

Shattock, P. and Savery, D. (1997) *Autism as a Metabolic Disorder*, Sunderland, Autism Research Unit.

Sigman, M.D., Yirmiya, N. and Capps, L. (1995) 'Social and cognitive understanding in high functioning children with autism' in Schopler, E. and Mesibov, G.B. (eds).

Steffenberg, S. (1991) 'Neuropsychiatric assessment of children with autism: a population-based study', *Developmental Medicine and Child Neurology*, vol. 33, pp. 495–511.

Tinbergen, N. and Tinbergen, E. (1983) (eds) *Autistic Children: New Hope for a Cure*, London, Allen and Unwin.

Welch, M. (1983) 'Appendix I: Retrieval from autism through mother–child holding therapy', in Tinbergen, N. and Tinbergen, E. (eds).

Wiltshire, S. (1989) *Cities*, London, J.M. Dent.

Wing, L. and Gould, J. (1979) 'Severe impairments of social interaction and associated abnormalities in children: epidemiology and classification', *Journal of Autism and Developmental Disorders*, vol. 9, pp. 11–29.

World Health Organisation (1992) *International Statistical Classification of Diseases and Related Health Problems* (ICD–10) Geneva, World Health Organisation.

CHAPTER 6

Relationships at work

Rebecca Lawthom

Contents

This chapter offers an overview of theory and research concerned with relationships at work. You may find personal resonance with some of the issues raised here including negative experiences of teamwork, conflicts at work, bullying and unconscious processes influencing work relationships.

Aims

This chapter aims to:

- explore particular relationships within organisations: leaders and followers, relationships within teams, and bullying relationships at work
- demonstrate how psychological theory can be applied to the workplace and organisations
- contextualise the current position of occupational psychology by providing a brief historical overview
- reveal the possibilities for research within organisational settings and the constraints operating on researchers.

1 Introduction

1.1 Practical starting points

Why is psychological understanding in workplace settings necessary? All of us come into daily contact with organisations, whether as employees or clients, or consumers being served by organisations. Contact with organisations may take the form of telephone calls (to banks or insurance companies), complaints, letters from companies informing us of appointments or advertisements selling us products. The list is endless and the contacts need not be face-to-face, as they are in a doctor to patient consultation for example. Increased access to information communication technologies (ICTs), especially the internet, allows us more opportunity to interface with organisations. What all of these interactions have in common, however, is that we often relate or respond to an individual who is representing the organisation rather than to the organisation as a whole. Imagine you have taken a day off work to wait at home for a furniture delivery and it does not turn up. You begin the complaints process by ringing up the company. During a negative interaction when dealing with the individual on the phone (who is often following company procedure in what they say), you might feel frustrated or annoyed at what you perceive as stubbornness. We often forget that the individuals we deal with are part of networks of other relationships that affect how they respond to us. Issues which might be affecting them and their attitude include their relationship with their boss, the people in their team, the opportunities for promotion available to them and, of course, out of work commitments such as family and friends. Therefore, a seemingly random interaction takes on new meaning if we consider workplaces as potentially rich in psychological understanding. Occupational psychology takes up this challenge and explores behaviour in the workplace. It is a sub-discipline of psychology that covers topics ranging from training and staff development to human–computer interaction.

The field of occupational psychology is vast and so a comprehensive summary is inappropriate in this context. Rather, a selection of theories and questions will be used to frame the chapter. We focus on particular sets of relationships within the workplace: those of leaders within organisations, those within work teams, and the problem of bullying. The rationale for the choice of these topics will become clearer as we move through the chapter, although the main linking theme is *relationships*. However, as we explore the literature on how psychology has been applied in the workplace, it will become clear that very little of this work has itself directly explored relationships.

The terms 'occupational psychology', 'organisational psychology', 'industrial psychology' and 'work psychology' arise from different traditions in different countries. Historically, in Britain, 'occupational psychology' is the preferred term while in the US, 'organisational psychology' is commonly used. The Division of Occupational Psychology within the British Psychological Society has considered whether to change its name to encompass the terms 'work' and 'organisational psychology', although at the time of writing this has not yet occurred. Advocates claim that, in the 'new' world of work, psychologists trained in occupational psychology need to compete with other 'people practitioners' (such as management consultants or personnel managers), and retain a distinct identity.

Scientific management
This is an approach whereby work is broken down into clearly defined skills and pay is determined on the basis of productivity.

Human relations
This is a school of thought that argues that social needs, in addition to monetary rewards, are also met through work.

The overall aim of this chapter is to explore how psychological theory can be applied in the 'real-life' setting of the workplace. The chapter begins by providing a historical outline of the research traditions that inform occupational psychology, those of **scientific management** and **human relations**. This sets the context for understanding how relationships at work (the emotional interests of employees) were not taken into account in early studies concerning the workplace, but were later 'discovered' and researched. The chapter then explores three areas of interest within organisations: leaders, teams and bullying. Section 5 on unconscious processes explores the ways in which psychodynamic theory might be applied to each of these three areas. To conclude, we look at the context in which organisational research and practice is undertaken.

As adult learners at The Open University you should have organisational experiences to draw on, such as remote or face-to-face contact with tutors, staff based at Walton Hall, regional staff and fellow students. Moreover, you will undoubtedly have other organisational experiences to help put some of the theories covered here in context. In this chapter the terms 'organisations' and 'workplaces' are used interchangeably as this is in line with occupational psychology's focus on paid work. That said, workplaces encompass a variety of contexts from homes to institutions, so feel free to draw upon those experiences that seem the most fruitful when tackling the activities.

1.2 Theoretical starting points

There are three assumptions that underpin this chapter and require clarification. First, *organisations are dynamic contexts with histories*. In order to understand current practices within occupational psychology we need to engage with historical context. The notion of 'alternative histories' is also important because theorists have diverse and often very different constructions of how occupational psychology as a discipline has developed (for example, Hollway, 1991, versus Shimmin and Wallis, 1994). Hollway's claim is that knowledge from work and occupational psychology should be understood in the specific social and political context of the time and this can be illustrated by the concept of job satisfaction. Job satisfaction is a twentieth-century phenomenon, previously unthinkable in feudal times (where landowners held power) or in pre-industrial times, where craft workers controlled their own work.

Second, *organisations are interpersonal contexts*. They provide complex ways of linking people, technology and psychological processes, including social cognition, personality, memory, unconscious processes, learning and identity – some of which we will consider in this chapter. While occupational psychology has certainly engaged with some of these topics, areas such as language, 'race' and gender, have only recently been touched upon.

Third, *work takes many forms*. The domain of work might be an area that you have access to and an interest in. Although occupational psychology has engaged primarily with paid work, the experiences you may draw upon include paid and unpaid work, or contact with organisations in other capacities (e.g. voluntary work, parents' organisations, community settings). The narrative of this chapter recognises that 'work' (however defined) takes place in a variety of settings, from domestic to community. The challenge of this chapter is to enable you to explore how theories and approaches used in psychology can be extended to understandings of behaviour at work in general across these different settings.

Occupational psychology deals with organisational issues within the workplace. What exactly is an organisation and what constitutes work? While this question seems simple to answer, if you think about the different types of organisational setting you have come across and the different understandings of work then you will see that these concepts are rather complex. Box 6.1 illustrates how psychologists have viewed organisations.

6.1   Defining organisations

Organisations are difficult to define and, as in other areas of psychology, it becomes necessary to draw upon several perspectives to understand them. It is easier to label a petrochemical company as an organisation than to consider a church to be an organisation. Organisations can be defined as 'social arrangements for the controlled performance of collective goals' (Buchanan and Huczynski, 1991, p. 7). It is precisely this concern with performance and the need for control that distinguishes organisations from other forms of social arrangements, such as the family. We shall see in this chapter that control and power over resources are key issues for organisations. The social arrangements in organisations are rarely democratically distributed among members – certain members hold positions from which they can control and coordinate the activities of others in the interests of the organisation. The above definition is one view of organisations. Theorists such as Morgan (1986) argue that a multi-perspective view of organisations is necessary. In *Images of Organizations*, he presents eight metaphors to understand organisations as:

- machines
- biological organisms
- human brains
- cultures or subcultures
- political systems
- psychic prisons
- systems of change and transformation
- instruments of domination.

These metaphors can be used to classify organisations or view them in different ways. Metaphors can be useful devices, particularly when it is difficult to find satisfactory ways to understand ideas. These organisational metaphors help to critically evaluate the dominant ways of viewing organisations. The machine metaphor is probably the most widely used representation that people share when asked 'what is an organisation?' The concept of a machine with regulated inputs, running to clockwork efficiency is a common notion. Images of industrial organisations that manufacture products come to mind. In contrast, Morgan (1986) points out that other constructions or ways of viewing organisations can be useful. One of the metaphors, organisations as biological systems, draws upon biological theories to consider organisations as systems. Here, complex organisations are viewed in terms of aiming to self-regulate and return to homeostasis (a steady state). These metaphors encourage creativity amongst researchers and managers.

Car manufacturing plants (approximately 1930 and 2000)

1.3 Work psychology in an historical context

Wendy Hollway (1991) critiques and evaluates the dominant ways of viewing the person at work. In her analysis, she considers the way in which occupational psychologists and other professionals have intervened in the workplace. She notes that the interventions have gradually changed both in scope and in focus. At the beginning of the twentieth century the focus was solely on the individual, around the middle of the century concern shifted to the social level, and at the end of the century to the organisational level. In the first two phases 'factory hands' and the 'sentimental worker' were used to describe the model of the person being used within these different time periods.

Much of our understanding about people in workplace settings has been derived from research or consultancy work developed on behalf of managers, and therefore driven by the needs of managers in organisations. Some of the earliest research explored the impact of fatigue upon workers or how best to 'fit men [sic] to jobs'. While some of these questions may be of relevance to workers, it is primarily managers who are deciding the agenda and benefiting directly from the research (in terms of lower employee turnover and increased productivity). Therefore, occupational psychology could be viewed as essentially 'top-down': change is imposed from the top of an organisation downward. Baritz (1960) noted that organisational consultants and psychologists were effectively 'servants of power', in that they behaved at managers' bidding. This is clearly one construction or reading of the history of occupational psychology. We shall return to this in Section 6 when we explore research ownership in organisational settings. Others point out that, in Britain, the dominant contribution has been a focus on 'human factors', looking at safety, shift patterns, time and motion studies (e.g. Shimmin and Wallis, 1994). This approach differs from both 'scientific management' and 'human relations' (see Section 1.5).

1.4 Levels of analysis

The focus of occupational psychology has partially shifted from purely concentrating on the individual to wider issues such as groups and whole organisations. To understand behaviour in organisations fully, we must consider three levels of analysis of the processes occurring within individuals, groups and organisations:

- *Individual level.* We may be interested in what motivates people at work, how they perceive the workplace and their attitudes towards work.
- *Group level.* The picture becomes more complex as interpersonal processes occur. We may want to consider how people communicate, how they work successfully in teams and how groups of people coordinate work.
- *Organisational level.* Concern shifts to organisational structure, the operating environment, and organisational change and the impact on employees.

The notion that a multi-level analysis is necessary in order to understand human behaviour seems fairly obvious in the twenty-first century. You have already been introduced to the benefit of adopting a range of perspectives and levels of analyses when exploring other issues throughout the course.

'Levels of analysis' is a particular approach to viewing topics of interest within organisations. As you read this chapter, consider whether this is a useful structure. Can topics fit into discrete levels of analysis or is the picture more complex? Leadership, for example, is both an individual and group process. According to some theorists it is a property of the individual, but others believe that leaders can only be understood within a context, in interaction with those they lead and therefore using a group level of analysis.

1.5 Scientific management and human relations

One of the most influential approaches to studying organisations originated in the US. Frederick W. 'Speedy' Taylor (1911) introduced a philosophy of 'scientific management'. He was an engineer by training, in charge of maintenance at a steel company. He researched the piece rate system and postulated that people were motivated primarily by economic factors. He proposed that there was a link between performance and pay. He carried out 'time and motion' studies to ascertain the best way to cut metal and standardise work procedures based on this (hence Taylor's nickname 'Speedy'). Consequently, production workers in manufacturing were paid on the basis of productivity. Workers' roles were limited, repetitive and boring and managers held much of the system knowledge about manufacturing processes. Only managers had access to the bigger picture, the production line. Workers were confined to workstations, performing tasks that were limited in scope. Supervisors became an important part of the process as they were needed to monitor the system, allocate work and time the process. Taylor's brand of scientific management created the 'supramachine', such as Henry Ford's assembly line, that ran upon principles of rationalisation and, crucially, control.

'Taylorism' is inextricably linked with the history of the twentieth century, where workers needed little training to effectively become part of the machine of production. This approach to production, characteristic of a particular period of manufacturing and time within the development of capitalist economies has also been termed 'Fordism' (because of its association with Ford car production). Production as a process became detached from the skills and creativity of individual employees. Since jobs were transformed so that skills were not necessary, workers became more easily interchangeable and people were seen as replaceable commodities.

> *Owing to the extensive use of machinery and to the division of labour, the work of the proletarians has lost all individual character and consequently, all charm for the workman. He becomes an appendage of the machine, and it is only the most simple, monotonous, and most easily acquired knack, that is required of him.*
>
> (*Karl Marx,* The Communist Manifesto, *1985 [1848], p. 31*)

Human relations is a school of thought that emerged as a reaction to these early influential management theories. Elton Mayo (1880–1949) is regarded as the founder of the approach and he argued that individuals needed to fulfil social needs (in addition to pay) through work. Mayo's early research, which became known as the 'Hawthorne studies', emphasised the role of social and group factors in explaining motivation. These studies are outlined in Box 6.2.

6.2 The Hawthorne studies

This research was carried out between 1924 and 1932 at the Hawthorne works of the Western Electric Company in Chicago. It is credited with being a classic study in the field of workplace motivation and you may have heard references to the 'Hawthorne effect' – the notion that behaviour changes as a result of being observed. This extensive piece of research was carried out by three American industrial psychologists: Elton Mayo, Fritz Roethlisberger and William Dickson. It revolutionised social science thinking and paved the way for further research into the impact of social factors on workplace behaviour. Four main research phases can be identified.

Illumination experiments

This study utilised an experimental design (with experimental and control groups) to explore the effect of illumination on productivity. The researchers found that production output was not proportionately related to lighting. Indeed, production even increased when 'candle-power' (a measure of lighting) was reduced. The study concluded that lighting was only one factor among many and that studying large groups made isolating variables and the subsequent effect upon output very difficult to discern.

Relay assembly test room study

Six female workers were selected and placed in a room separated from the wider workforce. This enabled the research to be more focused. Being isolated from other workers made the researcher's task easier. The women could choose their co-workers and initially worked a 48-hour week. The researcher monitored the way in which the workers put together small telephone relays, through observation. Notes were made of their conversations and the researcher talked to the women and listened to their complaints. The research questions in this phase were:

- When do employees become tired?
- Are rest pauses useful?
- Is a shorter working day desirable?
- What is the impact of equipment changes?
- Why does production decline in the afternoon?

To address these research questions, changes were made to rest pauses, working hours and refreshment breaks. The length of breaks was initially lengthened and early finishes added to the day. These benefits were eventually withdrawn. With each successive change, productivity increased. Output increased when rest breaks were added, when early finishes were introduced and even when the women returned to a standard 48-hour week.

There is much controversy over the interpretation of these findings. The women may have felt special in a different room and built up a different relationship with the researcher. In addition, the opportunity to choose their own co-workers may have meant that they worked better as a team. The results of this phase led the researchers to conclude that motivation was not solely linked to money or working conditions but also to *group belonging*. This led the researchers to explore employee attitudes and the factors that impacted upon these attitudes became more apparent. What is interesting about this research study is the way in which the research developed over time. Having explored the impact of lighting upon productivity, researchers controlled the working environment further by placing a smaller group of workers under observation. In this phase, the experience of being in a group possibly confounds the independent variables such as timing and length of rest pauses. Here, the idea arose that belonging to a group (the social element of working) known as the 'informal organisation', might also impact upon productivity. To address this question a different methodology is required.

Female workers in the relay assembly test room study

Interviewing programme

Managers wanted to find out more about how their employees felt about working conditions, supervisors and their motivation to work. An extensive interviewing process consisting of 20,000 interviews was undertaken. At first, researchers asked highly structured questions on feelings towards work. Later, the questions became more open-ended and less directive, with the focus shifting to include non-work topics such as family and social issues. The information obtained surprised the researchers. Running alongside the formal organisation they discovered an *informal organisation* that consisted of a network of employees some of whom were in designated positions of authority. These workers who informally designated themselves as 'bosses', controlled the rate of production and imposed a strict hierarchy. Workers were told by these 'bosses' to control their rates of production.

In addition, the interviews revealed that job satisfaction was a function of many factors, which included the social organisation of the company, the status of the individual, the social demands on employees and company policies, the impact of technology and treatment by supervisors. This led the researchers towards a more sophisticated understanding of the employee at work. The discovery of an informal organisation also led to the last phase of the research – the Bank Wiring Observation Room study.

Bank Wiring Observation Room study

To further explore how social groups influenced behaviour, a group of men (bank wirers) were observed in detail. Three groups, each containing three wirers and a supervisor, were observed. Analysis revealed that across these formal groups, informal 'cliques' existed with informal leaders. In addition, the cliques developed informal 'norms' for work production. Figures given to the management did not tally with the actual work rate and researchers observed that the group worked well below their capacity. Workers were adhering to the following code of norms:

- You should not turn out too much work – 'rate busters' are people who turn out too much work.
- You should not turn out too little work – 'chislers' turn out too little work.
- You should not tell supervisors anything that might be harmful – 'squealers' tell on their workmates.
- You should not attempt to maintain social distance. Even inspectors should not act officiously.

(Roethlisberger, et al. 1964, p. 522)

The group had agreed explicitly amongst its members what constituted a fair day's work, since they feared lay-offs or cuts in incentives if work rate increased too much. The output norm was enforced through negative sanctions such as ridicule.

Conclusions

Overall, the Hawthorne studies suggest that a number of *interpersonal factors* are important in explaining work motivation. First, pay and conditions alone do not explain workers' motivation. Second, a sense of belonging and a need for recognition are important. Third, attitudes towards work are shaped by formal and informal groups. Fourth, the informal group or clique is powerful in motivating workers. It can be seen from the research above that one of the social elements of work – namely the groups individuals are assigned to – can affect motivation, satisfaction and ultimately production.

Historical analyses demonstrate that the development of theories is linked to the social and historical context in which they arise. This is evident in the short history of occupational psychology (around 100 years) in which two approaches can be traced. The first approach is 'Fordism' and a preoccupation with efficiency and productivity. The search for 'perfect' workers, 'men who fitted the job' [*sic*] aided by the growth of psychological testing and the desire to measure abilities, occurred around a time of social upheaval (First World War). The second approach is an interest in and concern for human relations within organisations. This is also motivated by a desire for increased productivity, but here employee relations are taken into account. The original 'Hawthorne effect' (Roethlisberger, et al., 1964), a US phenomenon, was a recognition that people had emotions and feelings which affected the pace of work. This research was progressed by the Tavistock Institute for Human Relations in London (see Box 6.3). Relationships at work were clearly not a prime concern of the scientific management school but they were an important feature of the human relations school. Despite this early focus on the working individual's interpersonal world, however, very little of the research which followed explicitly addressed the nature of relationships at work.

6.3   Organisations as systems

One of the most well-known ideas to come out of the Tavistock Institute was the notion of organisations as systems that contain a number of elements that interact with each other. Eric Trist, one of the researchers at the Institute, introduced the idea that organisations are open systems. In this model, organisations are seen as flexible and self-regulating, taking in inputs, transforming them and creating outputs. Furthermore, Trist observed that organisations are socio-technical systems. This means that any production system requires a technical system (the means of making, e.g. the technology) and a social system (the organisation of the people who make the system). For example, looking at The Open University as a socio-technical system, there are technical elements and social elements in place to provide good distance education. Technical system components include the planning of courses, the written materials, the timetable, technology such as the VLE, and the regional centres (appropriately located). The social system components include consideration of students' needs, support networks of students, communication between students, tutors and Walton Hall. Both systems need to be interrelated to provide optimum opportunities for education. When creating work systems, it is important to take both elements into account. One of the most famous studies developing socio-technical systems thinking is Trist and Bamforth's Longwall mining study (1951). This study, examining coal-mining practices, demonstrated that the introduction of new technology disrupted the self-regulating team ethos that miners were used to. The introduction of new work procedures enforced individual working, narrowed the mining task and disrupted the social element of work. The Tavistock researchers reintroduced work groups as these were more likely to provide meaningful work, develop responsibility and satisfy human needs. This was indeed the case.

Summary Section 1

- Psychological theories can be applied to interpret experiences in organisations.
- Historically, occupational psychology has taken many different forms.
- 'Scientific management' focused on the worker achieving efficient production.
- 'Human relations' explores workers' motivations and the informal organisation.
- The Hawthorne studies emphasised the social element of work and these ideas have progressed in Britain at the Tavistock Institute.

2 Leadership: relationships between leaders and workers

Historically, a considerable amount of research has been conducted on leadership by occupational psychologists. We will summarise and evaluate this research. Many different approaches have been taken and theories have developed in complexity. We will draw upon research on leadership as well as approaches that explore leadership behaviour as a function of different situations. Are there certain general characteristics or personality traits that make a good leader? Alternatively, is leadership a function not only of the leader, but also of the people who are led and of the situational context?

Activity 6.1

Consider some famous leaders in history. What do you think made them great leaders? How do we judge what constitutes good leadership?

Comment

Leaders you may have considered include Winston Churchill, Mohandas K. Ghandi, John F. Kennedy, Mother Theresa, Napoleon Bonaparte and Nelson Mandela. Good leadership qualities you might have come up with include charisma, power, compassion, determination and intelligence. However, what about qualities such as ruthlessness – would that be judged as a 'good' leadership quality? Did you consider physical qualities, such as height? In the next section, we will examine some of the qualities that have been considered indicators of leadership quality by some researchers.

John F. Kennedy (1917–63), Mother Theresa (1910–97) and Nelson Mandela (1918–)

2.1 Leadership traits

The earliest work in this area examined what are known as 'great man' theories (see comment on p. 322). Broadly, leadership was defined in this early work as the way in which an individual uses the process of influence over another individual or group. The theories suggested that leadership was concerned with strength of personality. The idea that leadership could be explained solely with reference to a particular type of personality dominated early leadership research. Much early work sought to discover which personality characteristics demarcated leaders from followers, or typified good leaders. The notion of leadership being associated with implicit qualities dominated the 1940s. While early research (later reviewed in Stogdill, 1974) suggested that leaders were taller and more intelligent, it failed to find consistent personality traits which set leaders apart. More recent work, based on meta-analysis, suggests that leaders may possess a small number of common traits, but effective leaders are those who can both create vision and implement it (which could potentially be a skill rather than a trait). Lord *et al.* (1986) carried out empirical research which suggested that leaders were more conservative, dominant, extrovert, intelligent, masculine and better adjusted than non-leaders. Other work indicates that the traits of cognitive ability, drive, honesty, integrity, motivation, persistence, self-confidence and knowledge of business are distinguishing features of great leaders (Kirkpatrick and Locke, 1991). These kinds of models espouse a very particular vision of leadership.

The references to 'great man' theories of leadership, and the dominance of men in early theories generally, is worth considering. Firstly, leadership has historically been linked with masculinity. Secondly, the historic gender imbalance in the workforce was taken for granted as men occupied paid work areas and women maintained the home. The gender segregation of work sees divisions between paid and unpaid work. These divisions contribute further to income and status inequality.

The 'great man' theories, while suggesting that certain traits are important, cannot provide conclusive evidence to explain what constitutes good leadership and how it works in practice. This is because individual characteristics (personality traits) are not necessarily expressed consistently across all studies and situations. Importantly, environments have an impact on the way in which personality is expressed. Features such as the leadership task and the group's characteristics may affect the way leaders emerge and behave. Furthermore, many of the studies rely upon self-report measures where leaders assess their own traits, bringing demand characteristics (the implicit nature of test-taking) and the unreliability of self-report measures into question (leaders, like most people, are likely to report socially desirable characteristics). There is also a design flaw inherent in the method. It is possible that some of the traits described have been developed by being in the leadership role, thus, the role itself demands the development of these traits. The early search for consistent leadership characteristics proved elusive. Would it be more valid to enquire about appropriate *leadership styles?*

2.2 Leadership styles

In contrast to the trait approach, the style approach identifies and describes the behaviour of leaders; that is, what leaders do rather than how they describe themselves. During the 1960s, research at Michigan University identified behavioural differences between effective and ineffective leaders. The studies indicated that effective leaders tended to be more employee-centred and more concerned about the welfare of subordinates, whereas ineffective leaders tended to employ a more task-centred approach (a concern with the job in hand). It was suggested that leaders employed *either* a person-centred *or* a task-centred approach (but not both). Meanwhile, at Ohio University, research explored the way in which subordinates described the leaders' style. Much of the work took place in relation to military leaders, asking subordinates to fill in questionnaires. Four main factors were identified by the research:

1 *Consideration.* The way in which leaders and subordinates related to each other.
2 *Initiating structure.* The extent to which leaders provided clarity regarding the demands of a role.
3 *Production emphasis.* The extent to which production targets influenced the leader's behaviour.
4 *Sensitivity.* The extent to which the leader displayed sensitivity to the needs of the followers.

Later studies have focused on two of these factors: (1) consideration (sometimes labelled as 'relationship-oriented' or 'employee-centred') and (2) initiating structure (labelled as 'task-oriented' or 'production-centred'). The studies mentioned above question whether leaders can employ more than one type of leadership style and which style is more effective. Can effective leaders be concerned with people *and* tasks? The Ohio study found that considerate leaders were keen to create a pleasant atmosphere and maintain high morale (Stogdill, 1963). However, superiors (those above the managers) saw considerate leaders as less effective because they did not emphasise discipline. In contrast, superiors viewed structuring leaders as highly effective because they were more concerned with production than employee satisfaction.

Developments of the style approach have combined a concern for people with a concern for tasks. The leadership grid in Figure 6.1 rates concern for people and concern for tasks on a scale (ranging from low to high). Managers can plot their styles on the grid. Blake and McCanse (1991) describe five major leadership styles: team management (focusing on people and task); middle-of-the-road management; impoverished or laissez-faire management (little focus on either); country club management (focusing only on people); and task management (focusing only on the task). The assumption here is that effective leaders combine 'task-concern' with 'people-concern'.

In evaluating the style approach, a number of problems arise. Implying causality between leadership style and work output is difficult as many studies are based upon correlational analysis. Describing leadership style (from the perspective of the subordinate) suggests that leaders employ a uniform style regardless of the person they are managing. It also implies that the subordinate's perspective is accurate. In contrast, attribution theory in psychology suggests that we explain our own behaviour in terms of context but, interestingly, explain others' actions using stable internal characteristics. For example, we might explain our own poor performance on a task as being due to tiredness or the difficulty of a task, but a colleagues' poor performance as being due to laziness or incompetence. In addition, earlier work such as the Hawthorne studies (see Box 6.2) indicated that informal leadership existed

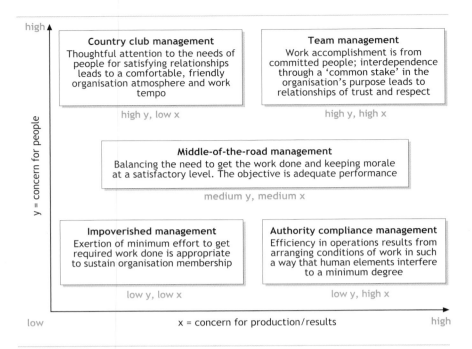

Figure 6.1   Leadership grid (Source: adapted from Blake and McCanse, 1991)

within groups, thus the explicit formally designated leaders within the group may not perform the leadership activities. Moreover, as in the trait approach, this kind of research ignores situational variations – can one style be effective across all situations?

Activity 6.2

Can you think of two incidents at work or in an organisational context that involved a leader/manager? Think of one that was handled well (in your opinion) and one that was handled badly. Did the leader/manager display a consistent style of leadership during both these distinct incidents? Could this style be characterised as task-centred or people-centred?

Comment

Thinking of leadership across different events is a useful way of contextualising leadership-style theories. Probably, the leader/manager displayed different styles across the incidents you considered. If the leader/manager displayed a consistent style, did it work well only in one incident? Styles are rarely effective across all circumstances and we will explore this issue in the next section.

2.3 Contingency theories

Contingency theories suggest that the style or behaviour employed by the leader is contingent upon (depends upon) the circumstances of the situation. We shall explore two contingency models that set out and describe how the situation and the leader's behaviour interact – Fred Fiedler's *contingency model* (1967) and Victor Vroom and Philip Yetton's *normative decision model* (1973).

Fiedler (1967) developed a model of the least preferred co-worker (LPC). The model proposes that leader performance depends on both the leader's personal characteristics *and* the degree to which the leader is able to control the situation. The key variable is the LPC and how the leader reacts to this individual. Leaders are asked to numerically rate the person they least enjoy working with on a number of dimensions such as friendliness and pleasantness (on a scale of one to eight). A high score (across the dimensions) indicates that the leader demonstrates a largely positive attitude towards their LPC (and from this, it can be hypothesised an even more positive attitude towards liked co-workers). A low LPC score suggests that the leader views the least preferred co-worker in negative terms. From this analysis, leaders can be identified as either high LPC leaders or low LPC leaders. High LPC leaders are relationship-oriented and tend to be more positive, even about people they don't like, whereas low LPC leaders are focused on task completion. Fiedler's model also takes into account three contingency variables which determine the amount of control exercised by the leaders in a given situation:

- *Group atmosphere.* The extent to which the group accepts the leader and therefore how likely the group is to be committed to the task.
- *Task structure.* The extent to which the group is clear about the tasks and goals of the group.
- *Position power.* The extent to which the leader can control and administer rewards and punishments.

The favourability of the situation is determined by rating each variable. Fiedler's model states that leadership situations are considered most favourable when subordinate relations are good, leaders have a strong position of power and the task is highly structured. The model suggests that in extreme situations (most and least favourable) task-oriented leaders (low LPC) will be more favourable. A moderate situation would be one in which subordinate relations are neither good or bad; leaders have neither a strong or weak position of power and the task is neither highly structured nor unstructured. Fiedler's model represents a complex way of mapping out both leader-like behaviours and situational contexts (see Figure 6.2). But how does the leader–LPC rating affect the performance of the group? Looking at the process of leadership alone does not tell us much about the outcome.

Contingency theories
Contingency theories of leadership argue that leadership behaviour is contingent upon (depends upon) the situational circumstances.

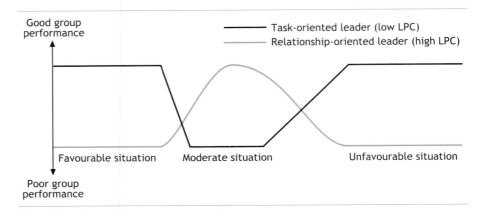

Figure 6.2   Fiedler's contingency model predictions (Source: adapted from Fiedler, 1967)

It is interesting to note the difficulties of doing this kind of research in naturalistic environments. Researchers either have to simulate leadership within a laboratory setting, which increases the reliability and internal validity of the study, or attempt to work in organisations, which increases ecological validity. One of the difficulties of the latter option is that managers, whose job is primarily to produce goods or services, are rarely interested in theories being tested since this will not have an immediate impact upon productivity.

Other contingency models focus on distinct aspects of leadership behaviour. The Vroom–Jago normative model (1988) builds on earlier work by Vroom and Yetton (1973) and explores decision making and the extent to which leaders involve subordinates in decision-making processes. Using a decision tree (see Figure 6.3), this model encourages leaders to address questions about the decision-making task such as time available, subordinates' commitment and likely acceptance of the decision. This model does not suggest one best style but provides a range of five styles, from autocratic to consultative to group-centred. These are:

- A1 Decide alone from personal knowledge without discussion.
- A2 Seek information from subordinates but reach a decision alone.
- C1 Consult with selected individuals, seeking information, and then decide alone.
- C2 Consult with the whole group, allowing them to decide.
- G2 Share the problem with the group and mutually decide what to do.

(Note: A – autocratic; C – consultative; G – group).

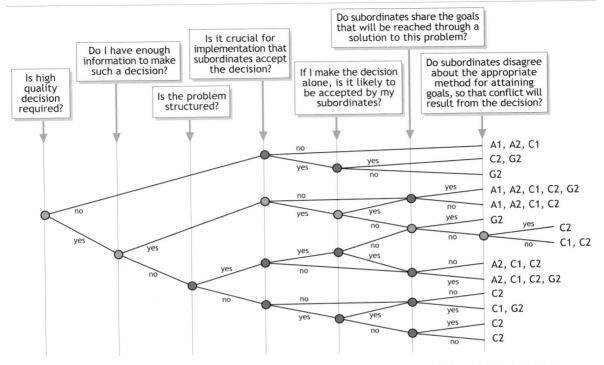

Note: By answering the relevant questions shown in the boxes above and tracing a path through this decision tree, leaders can identify the most effective approaches to making decisions in a specific situation. The possible decision-making styles reached through different paths are listed on the right of the tree (A1, A2, C1, C2, G2). The question 'Do subordinates disagree about the appropriate method for attaining goals, so that conflict will result from the decision?' is only relevant to the path highlighted in the tree.

Figure 6.3   Normative decision model (Source: adapted from Vroom and Yetton, 1973)

This model presents a continuum of autocratic to democratic decision-making behaviour. Furthermore, research has indicated that managers who use diverse methods of decision making (ranging from democratic to participatory methods) are viewed as more effective. This finding validates the idea that decision-making style can vary with situational demands (Field, 1982).

Contingency models in general address whether one style of leadership is more effective or appropriate than another. However, the models stress different aspects of the leader–subordinate relationship – motivation, least preferred co-worker and decision making – suggesting that no one style is entirely appropriate for all situations. Rather, behaviour is a complex interaction between the characteristics of the situation and the behaviour of people involved.

2.4 Transactional and transformational leadership

Many of the leadership theories outlined above assume a transactional model of interaction between leaders and followers. Within such a model relationships are seen in terms of exchange. Interactions or transactions take place where leaders reward, punish, initiate structure or show consideration only in return for worker effort and motivation. Bass (1985) distinguished between transactional and transformational leadership. The latter is seen as a process whereby leaders and followers are engaged in a process of transformation, potentially raising each other to higher levels of effort through shared values. Transformational leaders try to motivate workers by engaging them fully, participating in developing shared priorities, focusing on the personal development of the individual as well as reward structures. Broadly, transformational leaders are interested in the 'whole' employee (not just the work they can produce). Bass's model of transformational leadership has four components:

- *Individualised consideration.* Leaders individually consider followers' needs, providing opportunities for growth and training, to enhance self-esteem.
- *Intellectual stimulation.* Leaders inspire creativity and 'off the wall' thinking. Followers are persuaded to let their imagination run riot.
- *Inspirational motivation.* Leaders can envision the future and provide an optimistic and realistic portrayal to followers.
- *Idealised influence.* The leader is a role model and followers can easily trust and be impressed by the leader's charisma.

A final feature of Bass's model is laissez-faire management where leaders are not involved, largely absent and indifferent to followers: neither transactional nor transformational. The model has generated much empirical research using both measures of leadership effectiveness and follower satisfaction. The Multifactor Leadership Questionnaire (MLQ) allows followers to rate leaders on the dimensions listed above (Bass and Avolio, 1995).

Note the change in terminology from subordinates to followers in this model. Research terms reflect changing concepts and societal ideas.

Research suggests that laissez-faire leadership is undesirable and the two components most important for satisfaction and effectiveness are idealised influence and inspirational motivation. An issue with this kind of research is again the correlational design used. While idealised influence and inspirational

motivation are associated with satisfaction and effectiveness, no causality can
be implied.

It would appear that while leadership is important, it remains rather difficult
to define and even harder to measure. Meindl and Ehrlich (1987) make the
point that people romanticise leadership, seeing it as more influential than it
really is. By focusing on traits, styles or situational contingencies, research fails
to measure factors such as group performance or wider organisational
structures (such as organisational decision making) that affect effective
management. Meindl (1992) also argues that leadership should be examined in
terms of who the followers are rather than in terms of the features of individual
leaders. Leadership research is always changing and more recent theories
include the relationship process between leaders and their teams rather than
looking solely at leader behaviours. However, occupational psychology
research continues to search for leader-like qualities and many organisations
continue to use personality and cognitive ability testing to select particular
individuals to fit managerial jobs.

*This search within organisations to find 'our kind of manager' has implications
for the mix of individuals in organisational settings. Critics have argued that by
recruiting managers who are similar to present jobholders, diversity is not
enriched. This has clear implications for issues of class, 'race', gender, sexuality
and disability.*

One of the interesting things you may have noticed about leadership as an area
of research is the way in which it is studied and the wider historical context.
Despite the fact that leadership is all about relating (how leaders relate to
followers and vice versa) little of the research directly explores this. Rather, the
process of leadership is theorised as a static one, conceptualised in terms of
how leaders consider followers (or vice versa) or how leaders involve followers
in decision making or inspire them. While concepts such as transformational
leadership touch on the dynamic nature of the leader/follower relationship,
research has not explained the variability involved in managing others. Rather
like other relationships (parenting or friendship), the nature of working
relationships changes from day to day, and involves different experiences for
the parties involved. In addition, leadership research (as in other areas of
psychology) has failed to come up with the definitive model(s) of good
leadership. Yet, the notion of contingency is a useful one to draw upon. Good
leadership cannot be prescribed, though certain models of leadership
behaviour and decision making are preferred in certain conditions. In the next
couple of sections of the chapter, we focus on the behaviour of followers in
more detail, exploring teams and workplace bullying.

Summary Section 2

- Early research on leadership explored traits of good leaders.
- Research on the styles of leadership suggests that leaders employ management styles that are task-centred or person-centred.
- The contingency approach to leadership argues that appropriate leadership behaviour is dependent upon the situation. Characteristics explored include decision making and the least preferred co-worker.
- A model of leadership is transformational leadership. Here, motivation and rewards are related to the whole employee not just the work they produce.
- Leadership research is continuing but has so far failed to systematically define what makes a good leader.
- Very little leadership research directly explores the nature of the relationships between leaders and followers.

3 Groups in organisations

Groups or teams of people undertake much of the work in organisational settings. The course you are currently doing (DSE232) is a product of team-working, with collaboration between a core course team, academics at Walton Hall, external consultants and editorial teams. Groupings of people may be formalised, such as committees, project groups or course teams; or informal 'unofficial' groups and cliques that influence the pace, quality and output of work. The study of formal work groups has concentrated on the way in which the different sizes, structures and compositions of such groups can affect productivity and satisfaction, and the kinds of roles people play. Much research within groups has been in the area of group dynamics – why and how groups change over time. For example, the Hawthorne studies revealed that it was informal groups rather than management who actually structured work norms and output.

Activity 6.3

The terms 'group' and 'team' are used interchangeably in the literature although there are some distinct differences. Can you think of some differences? Try and draw up a list to compare with the suggestions in the following sections.

3.1 What are teams and why are they important?

What is a team? Unsworth and West (2000) suggest a number of conditions that need to be fulfilled prior to a group of people being identified as a team. First, people within the group need to have shared goals and need to interact with each other in order to achieve the completion of the goals. Second, each person within the team needs to have a clearly defined role and the team needs an identity within the organisation. For example, a production team in a clothing factory has shared goals – numbers of quality garments to produce, expressed in terms of shared production targets. They need to interact with each other as not all members have every skill needed to complete the garment – each has a specialist role or skill (pocket-making, zip-fitting) which relies upon a task being completed by another team member. The team also has a definite identity within the organisation. The common-sense notion of a team is one in which members are geographically close to each other, but new forms of technology, such as email and videoconferencing, allow teams to be distributed across the globe. The old adage 'two heads are better than one' suggests that creativity is enhanced by having more than one individual on a task. The restructuring of work based on a team is one of the most common job design interventions in organisations. Managers often introduce teamworking in order to improve productivity. Gordon (1992) found that 82 per cent of companies with 100 or more employees had implemented teamworking.

One of the issues with research in this area is: when does a group of people become a team? One aspect is that teams need to feel they are a team, and share work interdependently.

Despite the popularity of teamworking, does it have any effect on outcomes such as productivity and member satisfaction? Mohrman et al. (1995) suggest that teamworking offers the following benefits:

- Enables companies to develop and produce services and goods in a cost-effective manner, while maintaining quality.
- Facilitates more effective organisational learning (and the retention of that learning in terms of skill and training).
- Jobs that used to be performed in sequence by individuals are performed simultaneously by people working in teams, thus saving time.
- Allows information to be linked and integrated in ways not possible for individuals.

Much research has been carried out into the effects of teamwork on productivity. Applebaum and Batt (1994) reviewed 12 large-scale studies and 185 case studies, concluding that organisational performance had improved in terms of efficiency and quality after the introduction of teamworking. However, teams can also generate difficulties. The productivity of a team is often compromised due to 'process losses' – the problems associated with coordination of a team and motivating a team (Stroebe and Frey, 1982). Coordination problems occur as task allocation and communication processes are shared and transmitted (or not) across many members. Motivational process losses are effects revealed by social psychologists studying groups of people, often in laboratory settings. As an example, Latané et al. (1979) revealed that people clapped more loudly when measured individually than in a group. This phenomenon is termed **social loafing** and refers to the process whereby individuals exert more effort when measured individually than when working in a group.

Social loafing
This term refers to the behaviour in groups whereby individuals exert less effort (because they are part of a group) than they would as individuals.

Social loafing is a well-documented phenomenon. It can be demonstrated particularly well during brainstorming sessions with laboratory groups. Brainstorming involves a group of people contributing ideas. The ideas are first generated without judgement and later evaluated. Findings show that while individuals enjoy being innovative with others, they put less effort into that task when responsibility for a task is shared. The number of ideas generated is less and quality is often compromised when individuals brainstorm in groups as opposed to brainstorming on their own. Erez and Somech (1996) explored social loafing by comparing real work teams in kibbutzim and urban settings. Kibbutzim are collective living arrangements where people work together on shared projects and where group identity is valued. Traditional practices, such as parents having sole responsibility for their children, are not followed. In Erez and Somech's study, a range of variables were manipulated including goal setting, communication and rewards. They found that social loafing occurred only with the urban participants who were given a 'do your best' goal. It did not happen in kibbutzim settings where goals were clear and shared, open communication was encouraged and teamwork was the norm. Their research suggested that specific goals, good communication and incentives for teamwork can eradicate social loafing. Interestingly, further research conducted in diverse cultural contexts has suggested that the social loafing effect is primarily Western and not found universally. For example, studies in China and Israel (Earley, 1987, 1993) found that in these countries participants worked harder in a group than alone.

Unsworth and West (2000) propose a useful model for examining teams. The model, shown in Figure 6.4, illustrates that inputs (such as the task, the composition, the organisational context and the cultural context) affect the process of the team (defined in terms of leadership, communication, cohesion and decision making) and the effectiveness of the team (outputs). We will briefly explore each of these in turn.

Figure 6.4   An input–process–output model

3.2 Team inputs

Task

The actual task that a team tackles will influence the effectiveness of the team. Some tasks are clearer than others. A car production team, for example, has a more clearly defined task than a team given the job of designing a new magazine. Research on individual motivation theory suggests that tasks can be classified in terms of five core job dimensions: autonomy, variety, significance, identity and feedback (Hackman and Oldham, 1976). This theory has also been used to predict how well teams work together and research suggests that it successfully predicts effectiveness in professional jobs (Campion et al. 1996) and technical, clerical, management and customer service teams (Cohen et al. 1996).

Composition

Team composition refers to the diversity of individual members who comprise the team. The way in which individuals categorise themselves can affect the performance of the team. Social psychological research in the area of person perception and cognition notes that people regularly classify things, attitudes, people and themselves into identifiable groups for ease of understanding and rapidity of processing. People often differentiate between their group (the in-group) and other groupings (out-groups) based on diverse features such as gender, 'race', functional role, and so on.

A group of assembly workers may demarcate themselves (the in-group) from the supervisor's group (the out-group) who are perceived as working for management. Social identity theory (Tajfel, 1978; Tajfel and Turner, 1979) proposes that in-groups not only identify themselves as belonging to the in-group but evaluate themselves using dimensions that maximise the difference between themselves and the out-group, and compare themselves favourably with the out-group. Therefore, the ways in which team members perceive identities can enhance or impede team functioning.

Activity 6.4

Consider a group or team you have been a member of. How did you classify group members, both individually and as a group identity? Did you use a salient dimension (to you) such as age, parent/non-parent, job role, or gender? Did this have any implications for the way in which you interpreted individual contributions or behaviour, or how you dealt with 'out-group' members?

Comment

You may have been a member of a parent/teacher association (PTA) where the parental identity was seen as particularly salient. In such a case, rather than there being one group (the PTA), there may have been an in-group (parents) and an out-group (teachers) – of course, if you are a teacher, then the in-groups and out-groups would be reversed. If you were a member of the parent in-group, you may have found yourself giving other parents' opinions priority over teachers' views. Similarly, many working contexts lend themselves to an 'us-and-them' delineation where in-groups and out-groups can form. Examples might include 'officers and civilian staff' in policing, 'nurses and doctors' in healthcare, regimental rivalries in military service (cap-badge rivalry), 'plasterers and electricians' in the building trade, and so on.

If a team sees itself as an in-group, sharing a common characteristic, then smooth functioning may occur. However, if some other characteristic (e.g. gender diversity) results in exaggerated in-group/out-group behaviour *within* a team (such as 'you always side with the women') then the effectiveness of the team may be compromised. Research seems to suggest that diversity of skills and knowledge is generally good for organisations. For example, Wiersema and Bantel (1992) found that, in 100 top management teams within manufacturing companies, educational diversity correlated with adaptive organisations and effective strategic change (attributes that are associated with successful organisations). However, work on diverse attributes such as gender, age and 'race' suggests that perceived differentiation can cause prejudice and stereotyping and this may impact upon individuals within organisations (Tajfel, 1978). Overall, there is mixed evidence on the effects of gender and 'race' diversity within teams. What might be advantageous from an organisational perspective is not necessarily good from an individual's standpoint.

Organisational context

The organisational context in which the team works is a crucial determinant of team performance. Organisational features such as reward systems, technical support for the team, the wider organisational climate or culture, and internal and external competition can all affect the way the team behaves and works. Many teams operate with shared goals but are rewarded individually, with incentives for individual work. If, for example, individuals are structured within teams but paid individually on a performance basis (e.g. how much business the individual brings into an organisation) then this will have detrimental effects on teamworking. Organisational climate, the way in which employees perceive the organisation, may differ on dimensions such as concern for welfare. Organisations in which teamworking is to succeed need a climate characterised by skill development, well-being and support of employees (Mohrman *et al.*, 1995). Competition within the organisation also impedes effective teamwork, as teams are forced to expend energy competing with one another rather than working collectively on a task. West and Anderson (1996) found that factors such as support, sharing objectives, allowing participation in a safe way, and creating constructive outlets for diverse opinions are all predictors of good teamworking. The wider organisational context is also significant. When companies work in highly uncertain economic and legislative environments (such as the information technology sector), teams are a particularly effective way of working and greater benefits can accrue to organisations that make good use of teamworking (Cordery et al. 1991).

Overall, the context in which teams operate is important but consultants, managers and practitioners often continue to emphasise the importance of intra-team processes (such as assertiveness, negotiation or conflict resolution), or finding the right mix of people. Belbin (1981) shows one such example of this kind of work using research on roles and personality of individuals. Belbin's research proposes that the appropriate selection of individuals and the adequate development of skills can engineer effective teams (see Box 6.4). It is an approach that focuses on individual factors at the expense of contextual factors. There seems to be some resistance to research which proposes that training is needed to overcome some of the difficulties of working together. Perhaps this could be due to the way in which research findings are communicated to practitioners and managers.

6.4 Designing an effective team

Meredith Belbin and colleagues conducted a study exploring different management teams in action (Belbin, 1981). Teams consisted of managers from industry participating in a business game (involving strategic decision making) at a British management college. The research revealed:

- Distinct management styles could be identified. These eight distinct styles were known as eight 'team roles'.
- The managers routinely adopted one or two of the roles consistently.
- The particular role exhibited by the manager could be predicted through psychometric tests.
- Certain combinations of team roles produced more effective teams.
- Team roles did not necessarily map onto the managers' previous functional roles (such as accountant), but the mix of roles shared amongst members influenced group effectiveness.
- Contributory factors included individuals' recognition of their best role and self-awareness of the best contribution they could make.

The roles identified by Belbin were related to the personality and approach of individuals. As each role contributed to group effectiveness, good teams contained all roles. These were, in terms of role and function:

1 *Chair.* Coordinates the activities of the other team members. Tends to listen to contributions, encourage, focus and coordinate the task.
2 *Shaper.* Often the task leader (focusing on task completion), the main function of this individual is to direct the team. The person is outgoing and forceful. Their strength lies in energising others to perform.
3 *Plant.* This is the creative thinker in the team; however, this role needs to be drawn out. They are often the source of original ideas.
4 *Monitor–evaluator.* This is an analytical role and the individual provides critical thinking in the team. They are good at checking and piloting ideas.
5 *Company worker.* This is the person who focuses on getting the work done. They are practical organisers, transforming ideas into goals and timetables.
6 *Team worker.* Likeable and popular, this person encourages, supports and understands others. They focus on looking after personal relationships in the team.
7 *Completer–finisher.* Relentlessly driven by deadlines, this individual keeps the team on its toes.
8 *Resource investigator.* Keeps in touch with other teams and resources.

Cultural context

Cultural context is also a variable that affects team functioning. Hofstede's work (1980) amongst 117,000 IBM employees in 40 countries provides an interesting cultural analysis. From survey data, Hofstede classified countries along four dimensions:

- *Individualism–collectivism.* Refers to the way in which people define themselves within a society and the extent to which individualistic identities are favoured over collective identities.
- *Power–distance.* The formality of relationships between workers and bosses. High power–distance is characterised by managers being many levels away and hence quite distant from employees.
- *Uncertainty–avoidance.* The way in which ambiguity about the future is handled.
- *Masculinity–femininity.* Focuses on whether achievements (associated with 'masculinity') or relationships (associated with 'femininity') are valued.

Countries exhibited much variation in these dimensions. Spain demonstrated a culture of high power–distance and high uncertainty–avoidance with a collectivist, feminine culture. Britain was relatively low on power–distance, low in uncertainty–avoidance (therefore prepared to handle ambiguity about the future) and high on individualism and masculinity. Therefore wider cultural value systems existing within countries might influence team processes and change the definition of what it is to be a team. For example, in highly individualistic cultures, teamworking may be in opposition to wider cultural norms. Consequently, teamworking may be easier to implement in collectivist cultures (Smith and Noakes, 1996).

3.3 Team processes

Team processes can be affected by factors such as task and team composition, which in turn can affect outcomes and team effectiveness.

Leadership

Bass's typology of transactional versus transformational leadership (1990), outlined in Section 2.4, can be applied within teams. Transactional leaders work by reward and punishment, acting upon mistakes and reacting to problems rather than anticipating them. Transformational leaders work by motivating individuals as a team using charisma, inspirational motivation, intellectual stimulation and individualised consideration (developing individuals as well as teams). The latter style is more beneficial to teams. An alternative to conventional leadership is the concept of **self-managing work teams** where leadership may be rotated or distributed, depending on the task. Leadership

Self-managing work teams
Teams in which leadership is managed within the team. Specialist managers outside the teams are not needed as the teams manage workload independently.

processes, whether an individual role or managed by the team, are clearly important to consider. It is also worth considering the informal leadership processes, as discovered in the Hawthorne studies (see Box 6.2), which although not formally recognised, were shown to be powerful in regulating group norms of output.

Communication

Good communication is essential for effective team functioning (Unsworth and West, 2000). However, team communication brings the added difficulties of increased participation and sometimes communication from a distance (e.g. email, forums). Diversity of members (e.g. on gender) and the perceived status of who is giving information or chairing meetings can also affect communication processes.

Decision making

Decision making is another interpersonal process that can affect teams. The process of decision making, including identifying the problem, generating solutions, selecting a strategy and implementing it, highlights issues surrounding working collaboratively. Research on brainstorming (see Box 6.5) suggests that creativity may be impeded in groups and evaluating ideas may result in 'groupthink' (Janis, 1982).

6.5 Groupthink

Groups that are close can become closed. Groups can develop a collective view of their own and groupthink occurs when group members are so closed off to external or competing information, they incorrectly evaluate decision options:

> It is the psychological drive for consensus at any cost that suppresses dissent and appraisal of alternatives in cohesive decision-making groups.
>
> (Janis, 1982, p. 8)

Members' strivings for unanimity override the motivation to realistically appraise alternative courses of action. A famous example of groupthink is the Bay of Pigs disaster when US President John F. Kennedy and his expert advisors supported an invasion of Cuba using badly trained exiles. The decision to attack was made without reference to information that predicted failure. Janis (1982) studied the Bay of Pigs invasion plan through documentation and personal accounts, and noted the following symptoms of groupthink:

- *Illusions of invulnerability*. The notion that the group is invulnerable to the potential dangers which might arise if the risky action is followed.
- *Illusion of unanimity*. Participants play up areas of convergence and downplay divergent opinions.

Bay of Pigs, 1961

- *Excessive optimism*. Participants feel euphoria regarding the future and the safety of belonging to the group. A newly acquired 'we' feeling predominates.

- *Suppression of personal doubts*. Participants feel reluctant to voice concerns or break the consensus of the group. Members tend to self-censor and to discourage deviation from group consensus.

- *Self-appointed mindguard*. Members of the group take on the role of 'mindguard', whose job is to protect others from thoughts that might put them off the chosen course of action.

- *Docility fostered by suave leadership*. A suave leader who makes it difficult to question consensus can manipulate the agenda.

Janis also highlighted the consequences of this phenomenon, including poor-quality decisions, biased information, and the lack of contingency planning. Groupthink stimulated a body of social psychological research that explored decision making in groups. It proved largely inconclusive as a distinct phenomenon but decision making processes continue to be researched.

Research within groups suggests that participation in decision making is a key factor in implementing decisions and allowing minority dissent to be expressed. Minority dissent allows a voice of conflict to be heard that challenges team dogma (Nemeth and Owens, 1996).

Cohesion

Team climate
Team climate is commonly defined as the shared perceptions of the 'way things are done within the team'.

Another important team process is cohesiveness: the attraction, support and liking amongst team members. Mullen and Copper's work (1994) suggests that effective team performance is more likely to stimulate team cohesion rather than cohesion stimulating subsequent performance. **Team climate** is the atmosphere within the team. Using primary healthcare teams, Peiro et al. (1992) examined the way in which team climate affected members' stress and satisfaction. Individuals were asked to fill in measures of team climate, individual stress and job satisfaction. Team climate scores were aggregated across individuals within a team and then correlated with individual scores on stress and satisfaction measures. A good team climate defined in terms of support, respect for rules, goal-related information and innovation was positively related to happy, unstressed, satisfied team members.

3.4 Conclusions

From a brief assessment of the research findings, it can be seen that team-working is a complex phenomenon. Within organisational settings, teams are comprised of diverse individuals with often conflicting motivational needs and attitudes towards work. Teams are affected by the nature of the task, the composition of the team, the wider organisational framework and the culture in which the company operates. Teams are complex in terms of relationships and networks. Little of the research undertaken explores the *interpersonal nature* of working with others, however. Rather, individuals are defined by attributes such as gender, 'race', role and these aspects of identity are studied. While there is clearly scope for research which explores relationships at this group level of analysis, research access is a potential barrier. Practitioners and managers are so convinced by the benefits of teamworking (the implementation of teams is so widespread) that systematic evaluation is difficult. The issue of research access is discussed further in Section 6. Individuals are commonly placed in teams with little training or support in how to work together. Teams can be useful social groupings and can help protect employees from stress, but, as we shall explore in Section 5, teams can also add to stress. In the next section, we explore a set of problematic relationships that can cause distress to employees – bullying in the workplace.

Summary Section 3

- Teams can be seen as distinct from groups: they have a shared goal requiring interaction, individuals have distinct roles and teams need an identity.
- Teamworking is commonly believed to impact positively upon productivity and satisfaction but research shows that it depends upon the effectiveness of the team.
- Teams are affected by inputs such as the clarity of the task, the composition of the team, the surrounding organisational context (such as climate, reward systems) and the cultural context (such as the emphasis on individualism over collectivism).
- Processes within teams, such as groupthink, leadership and decision making, can affect team effectiveness.
- Relationships between team members are often considered in terms of team climate, how members perceive one another and their team as a whole.

4   Bullying in the workplace

The archetypal image of the bully is one we generally associate with schooldays. Children who wield power and torment others are powerful and feared peers. The study of school bullying has been ongoing over two decades, but the term 'adult bullying' has become associated with workplaces (Adams and Crawford, 1992; Bassman, 1992). There have so far been few academic studies exploring bullying at work. Identifying the incidence of bullying has been difficult due to the lack of legislation and case law that could define how it might appear in practice. Bullying shares similarities with sexual harassment where the 'victim' has to experience harassment and define it accordingly. In this section, we shall explore adult bullying within organisational settings and provide some explanatory frameworks.

4.1 Bullying: a brief overview

Dictionary definitions conceptualise bullying as intimidation, persecution and oppression (both physical and moral).

The way in which we use language and define concepts is clearly a product of culture. Research carried out in Scandinavia and Germany uses terms that translate into 'mob' and 'mobbing' to distinguish adult bullying from bullying in childhood. The term 'mobbing' in the English language tends to be associated with large groups rather than acts perpetrated by one individual.

The field of workplace bullying overlaps into related areas such as harassment, violence at work and discrimination. Most of the work on bullying has been undertaken in Scandinavia where the academic interest mirrors strong public awareness of the concept and laws passed specifically relating to it. In Britain, it is a newer field of study. All the work in this area draws parallels from childhood bullying.

Activity 6.5

How would you define bullying? Can you think of any differences that may distinguish adult bullying from childhood bullying?

Comment

Bullying behaviours you may have thought of include physical violence, verbal abuse, social exclusion and blackmail. Indeed in the childhood literature, there is a clear distinction between direct bullying, defined as physical/mental/verbal abuse and indirect bullying, associated with non-overt aggression and social exclusion. The bullying of adults is often different with even more verbal and indirect bullying occurring, and being reported, more often than physical violence.

The workplace is a backdrop against which many emotional battles are fought. This may happen consciously in the form of disputes between unions and management, within teams and between workers and managers. It may also happen unconsciously when emotions get projected onto other workers. Rayner and Hoel (1997) note that the workplace presents much scope for a far more diverse range of tactics and the parameters of what constitutes bullying are broad. They categorise bullying behaviours into the following groupings:

- *Threat to professional status.* Professional humiliation, belittling, accusing others of lack of effort.
- *Threat to personal standing.* Insults, calling of names, intimidation, devaluing with reference to age, gender, sexuality, 'race' and/or impairment.
- *Isolation.* Preventing access to opportunities, withholding information, physically or socially isolating.
- *Overwork.* Undue pressure, unrealistic deadlines.

- *Destabilisation*. Failing to give credit, reminders of previous failures, taking away responsibility, meaningless tasks.

While it is possible for anyone who works to experience some of these indicators, the experience of bullying must include three factors: a measure of frequency of the bullying; an impact upon work; and the victim must feel bullied. What is difficult about formally defining bullying (as distinct from general unhappiness at work) is how the bullying fits into the wider **organisational culture**. Generally, this refers to a shared view of the 'way things are done' within the organisation. It can therefore act as a screen through which the interpretations of behaviour are filtered. The hypothetical scenario described in Box 6.6 illustrates this.

Organisational culture
The way in which organisational practices, procedures and behaviours are perceived and interpreted.

6.6 Bullying or institutional loyalty?

John is a keen young management trainee in a leading food supermarket called Freshleys. He has been employed on a management training programme that eventually should lead to store managerial status. He works a 60-hour week, ostensibly shelf filling, which his boss claims is 'good for him'. For the first three years John is moved from department to department, shelf filling. He wears a badge with the title of management trainee but often has only one or no people to manage. John is keen to progress in the company but is aware that the Freshleys way is to start at the bottom doing long hours. The 'training' seems to be only on the job and narrow in focus. John is often put under enormous pressure and phoned at home on his days off regarding work-related matters such as stock levels. John, however, interprets his manager's behaviour as totally in keeping with the company way. John's brother is getting married and John asks for a Saturday off in three months' time. The manager denies permission for a Saturday off, saying John's section is a mess, if he cannot run it while he is there then what will happen when he is away. Moreover, he questions John's commitment to the company, wanting time off for a wedding. The manager further threatens John by stating if he has the day off, he may have to wait longer for formal training (which is imminent). This should take the form of learning how to merchandise, having full responsibility for a large section of the store and the secondment to other stores for periods of time. John weighs up his options. He can take the day off but he will potentially lose the opportunity to train further and progress in the company. It is only the manager who can put John's name forward and allow the training to happen. On the other hand, he can forfeit the wedding (missing a big family occasion) and stay on the manager's 'right side'. John is in a quandary but, considering the options and in consultation with his family, he interprets the manager's request as perfectly reasonable. John's family point out his relative powerlessness within the company and attribute the manager's behaviour to a 'personality clash' or to meeting store requirements. John misses the wedding and eventually gets promoted onto the next level nine months later.

The key issue in the scenario in Box 6.6 is the notion of interpretation. Different individuals are likely to have different thresholds of tolerance for the behaviour of others. This in turn affects their perceptions and subsequent reactions. If bullying behaviour is seen as somehow reasonable and acceptable within an organisation, then it will not be reported. These definitional issues, together with methodological problems (i.e. it would be almost impossible and highly unethical to manipulate bullying in an applied setting such as the workplace), mean that research into the incidence of bullying, the precursors of bullying and the effects of bullying is largely descriptive and based upon surveys (see Box 6.7).

6.7 Methods used to study bullying

In Sweden and Norway where public awareness of bullying is high, the government has funded much research in the area and trade unions have willingly participated in it. Leymann's research (1990) is dominated by the questionnaire method, whereby an interviewer uses highly structured questions. The research on incidence rates similarly uses victim self-reports through structured interviews. Other research uses postal questionnaires to both blue- and white-collar workers within the public and private sector. In Britain, Rayner (1997) reported on a large survey (1137 respondents) with only 1 per cent of the sample not responding. However, the characteristics of the sample – a group of part-time university students – make this a potentially biased sample.

A common characteristic across the research, whether interviewer administered questionnaires or structured interviews, is that the research explores the *experience* of being bullied. The voices heard are those of the bullied, with the data originating from those who claim to have been bullied. Certain researchers argue that the use of self-reports is too subjective a measure. The voices of the bullies themselves would enhance understanding. A few studies undertaken in penal establishments use a variety of different methods. Here, recorded hearings, staff interviews and inmate interviews permit triangulation of the data.

Box 6.7 details the kinds of methods commonly employed in bullying research. What conclusions can we draw from findings in this area? The two major studies (conducted in Scandinavia) indicate that 4 to 5 per cent of employees are bullied for an average period of three years. A British study suggests that 77 per cent of the sample (1000) had witnessed bullying at work (Rayner, 1997). Half the sample reported that they had been bullied at work (sometime in their working life) and most victims were in a non-managerial staff position at the time of being bullied. Exploring the gender and status of the bully, women were bullied equally by men and women while men were rarely bullied by women. Around three-quarters of the bullies were line managers or senior line managers. This suggests that bullying is related to power and is a function of status within organisations.

Rayner's study (1997) also explored the antecedents to bullying. Anecdotal evidence, supported in this study, suggests that most people experience bullying when they change jobs or get a new manager. While previous anecdotal evidence suggests that individuals are more likely to be singled out and bullied; in Rayner's study employees reported being bullied in groups (81 per cent). Responses to questions about subsequent action following being bullied suggested that people who had never themselves been bullied anticipated a more proactive reaction from people who had been bullied (such as confronting the bully or consulting with personnel) than people who had themselves experienced bullying. Moreover, 27 per cent of those who had been bullied subsequently left their jobs. However, the data for individuals in larger groups suggests that when groups are bullied, individuals are less likely to leave (12 per cent). Rayner's study clearly demonstrates the high incidence of workplace bullying. It is difficult to validate some of the findings within a British context due to the paucity of research. However, the findings bear similarities to studies conducted in school settings and in other countries. The finding that women were equally bullied by men *and* women replicates playground findings. Whether this is due to girls being unsuccessful at bullying boys, or boys not wanting to admit to being bullied by girls, is unresolved.

In organisational settings, the picture is complicated further since the ratio of men to women in managerial positions is unequal. The effects of bullying and subsequent responses such as leaving the organisation indicated an interesting psychological phenomenon. While bullied individuals are likely to leave their jobs, groups somehow are more resilient. Groups containing more than five individuals manage to protect themselves (or at least their job security). A number of explanations are possible here. One explanation, in line with what has been termed 'cognitive dissonance theory' (Festinger, 1957), is that individuals can see that others are coping with the bullying and subsequently change their perception of it. For example, upon observing that their colleagues do not perceive a manager's behaviour as bullying, the individual who initially felt bullied may come to view that behaviour as acceptable. It is also possible that 'groupthink' (see Box 6.5) is present, with members sharing perceptions of the bullying experience and therefore denying or ignoring its existence (or becoming less willing to interpret it as bullying).

4.2 The effects of bullying

Bullying affects individuals and organisations. Incidence studies suggest that bullying often results in individuals leaving organisations, with the added cost to the organisation of further recruitment, selection and training of new employees. Some of the Scandinavian research explores the relationship between bullying and the quality of the work environment. As these are correlational studies, they do not show cause and effect, nor predict bullying. There are reported relationships, however, between a high incidence of bullying and a certain leadership style (i.e. lack of leadership).

Predicting the causes or precursors of bullying is problematic, particularly in terms of research design. While childhood studies of school bullying have occasionally encompassed a longitudinal element, linking child bullies to subsequent adult bullying (Olweus, 1993), research in the adult bullying field is newer and less well developed. Looking at the immediate impact of bullying is more straightforward. Leymann (1990) proposes that one in seven adult suicides is attributable to bullying. There is also a 'ripple effect' of bullying, which incorporates friends and family being affected by the individual who is bullied. Victims of bullying often have difficulty retaining communication or social contact.

Activity 6.6

Having briefly considered workplace bullying, think about the psychological theories and concepts that you have come across in this course which seem relevant here. How can bullying be explained by psychology? Section 4.3 considers some possibilities.

4.3 Parallels between bullying and wider psychological literature

Some of the related research areas include those on aggression and attribution. Social psychology has a long history of exploring aggression, between groups and individuals. The typical experimental paradigm here is to manipulate frustration or aggression in the laboratory between strangers. Transferring this into the workplace poses problems as bullying takes place between people who know each other. However, aspects of behavioural learning theory (previously discussed in Chapters 2 and 5) may prove interesting in modelling bullying. Another useful area is that of attribution theory, which states that we explain our own negative behaviour with reference to the environment and our circumstances and the negative behaviour of others as being the result of their internal characteristics, such as personality traits. This may help explain the issue surrounding the subjective reports of bullying where victims perceive managers' actions as bullying, rather than associated with the job role. This does not mean that self-reports are invalid, rather that bullied employees construe bullying in a particular way.

A related area is that of workplace stress. The effects of stress on employee turnover and sickness are akin to the impact of bullying upon employees. Certain models of stress, such as the transactional model, view stress as a dynamic process between the person and the environment (refer back to Section 2.1, Chapter 1). Here, it is the discrepancy between the individual's perceived capability and the demands of the situation that results in stress. The bully can intimidate and undermine perceived competence and increase the demands of the job, thereby resulting in stress.

It has also been argued that one way of explaining bullying behaviour is in terms of personality traits, though others reject the individual approach that this explanation takes. Using a wider framework it can be seen that bullying is a social issue best understood as an interaction between individuals and characteristics of social settings.

You may have heard of, or read about, the 'Stanford Prison Experiment' (Zimbardo, 1975). In this study, a mock prison was created and undergraduate students were asked to play the roles of prison guards and prisoners. The experiment was prematurely halted because the 'prison guards' took on bullying roles. This occurred even though all participants knew that it was a mock prison. Bullying was considered by the participants to be an entirely natural part of the roles they were playing. Could it be that people expect certain roles to involve behaviours that might constitute bullying? This might explain both why the people in those roles exhibit bullying behaviours and why others accept those behaviours.

Taking a wider framework, one can situate workplace bullying in the historical context of human relations and social dynamics. Strong management and clear hierarchies, alongside the relative powerlessness of the unions, may have contributed to the increase in workplace bullying. Organisational structures and cultures are often microcosms of the world outside. The experiences of individuals in organisations are mediated by structures in society, such as economic growth, prosperity and the political climate. It is interesting to note that the first work in this field originated in Scandinavia, a country with a reputation for good employee relations.

4.4 Conclusions

One of the tensions in the literature on workplace bullying is 'where does the problem lie?' Is it an individual problem with bullies and victims displaying particular characteristics or vulnerabilities? Personality theory or psychodynamic insights would position traits or attachment as central to understanding the adult bully. Conversely, bullying can be seen as an organisational or societal problem, resulting from changing work conditions and economic structures. Certainly bullying behaviour occurs in work relationships that are breaking down or have failed. It is an example of a negative relationship. While the problem of bullying becomes an organisational issue when it has an impact on the organisation itself, for example in terms of employee turnover, the crux of the problem is again an interpersonal one. As we discovered with leadership and teams, the human element of relating poses problems that are rarely touched upon in psychological research.

Crawford (1997) argues that organisations should be liable for psychological distress caused by working with others. This is a key issue in interpretation – the way that bullying is viewed subsequently affects the intervention proposed. An individual model may propose individual counselling while social theorists may propose reorganisation of the workplace. As in other areas of psychology, there can be no clear answers, as perspectives vary in their analysis of the causes and impacts of behaviour.

Summary Section 4

- Research suggests that workplace bullying is an important issue that has only recently received recognition.
- The literature contains a mixture of anecdotal evidence, studies of incidence reporting, explanations of bullying behaviour and contextual frameworks.
- Definition and recognition are key issues in attempting to define bullying.
- Attitudes towards bullying are both an individual phenomenon (thresholds and attributions) and filtered through organisational cultures.

5 The unconscious processes in working relationships

5.1 Psychoanalysis

Psychoanalytical theories view individuals as constantly torn between internal unconscious forces and external social pressures. These unconscious forces include drives, urges and conflicts that have been built up from childhood. A key issue for individuals is how to manage these unconscious processes in order to relate appropriately to others. The workplace offers a social and psychical context for playing out these dynamic internal relationships.

Workplace norms and rules may well help the individual to confront their unconscious forces and this will be influenced by the reality of the organisational culture. Various psychological **defence mechanisms** may be employed in (un)sociable, (un)helpful and (un)healthy ways.

    Workplaces encompass a variety of social and interpersonal contexts. What happens within them is never purely harmonious and is open to conflicts. Moreover, the meanings we assign to and derive from these contexts may not always be apparent. Indeed, we form a variety of conscious and unconscious associations and meanings within organisations that may have profound influences on our daily lives and identities. A question often asked about a peer or ourselves at work in relation to an event is, '*Why* did they do that?' The answer to this question for the psychoanalyst would involve a deep analysis of unconscious processes that are triggered by and direct human behaviour in social and cultural contexts. To search for conscious, rational reasons for workplace behaviour is, according to psychoanalysis, a mistake made by many psychologists. Instead, we are asked to probe how workplace behaviours have their roots in our psychical apparatus, our internal conflicts and our unconscious processes.

Defence mechanisms
Largely unconscious processes for avoiding inner conflict and the anxiety it creates.

5.2 Unconscious processes in teams

In Section 3, we explored the processes between individuals in teams. These processes were explicit interactions, such as decision making and creativity. In Section 2 we focused on characteristics of individuals, such as traits. An underlying assumption of both these sections was one of *conscious* processing: that there are clear, conscious processes occurring in teams that can adequately be observed and described. However, from a psychoanalytic perspective, it is possible to address the interrelationships between team members at another level: the *un*conscious.

    Wilfred Bion (1961), a theorist interested in psychoanalytic aspects of group behaviour, discerned two group mentalities. Generally speaking these two mentalities work as processes within groups, represent the unconscious, coexisting though contradictory wishes of members and groups both to face reality (to get on with the task) *and* to avoid reality. The two mentalities are:

1 *Work group mentality.* A tendency to work on the primary task of the group (primary here defined as the reason the group is working together).
2 *Basic assumption mentality.* A tendency to avoid working on this primary task (perhaps because the conflict could potentially cause psychological distress).

Stokes (1994) gave an example of the staff of a day centre arguing about whether clients (with learning difficulties) should have access to an electric kettle in order to make themselves hot drinks. The argument was posed in terms of normal living (reality or work group mentality) versus the possibility of danger (avoidance, or basic assumption mentality). Stokes observed that the staff group negotiated a position in relation to the issue at hand that veered towards avoidance. Other (unrelated) policy and practice concerns were drawn upon in order to justify the avoidance position – for example, the current difficulties faced by staff when working with angry and potentially violent clients. General concerns about risk were used, such as the potential for clients to scald themselves while making themselves a mid-morning cup of tea. The 'normal living' argument increasingly became a difficult concept to embrace and just when an argument reached a near solution, a new objection would be raised.

In Bion's terms we have a case where the unconscious conflicts of staff wishing to avoid the issue (now bound up and associated with empowering clients and promoting potentially risky behaviours) were reduced by the group adopting a basic assumption/avoidance of reality position. Interestingly, Stokes reports on how a group analyst working directly with the group read the group's ambivalent feelings and encouraged the group to return to the primary task: to explore empowering working relations and practices in the day centre. This was done by an outsider (the analyst) recognising the harmful feelings and explicitly getting the group to both recognise and challenge their avoidance.

We can probably all think of examples where teams that we have experience of did not focus on the task in hand and other agendas came to the fore. Workload within teams is often an issue that can degenerate into bad feelings about the contribution of some individuals or a backlash against the wider organisation. Bion (1961) suggests that when a group is in work group mentality, the focus is on task-completion. However, in basic assumption mentality, unconscious needs of members are directing the agenda of the group. Here, the group veers off the task and focuses on the reduction of anxiety and internal conflicts. The way in which this is done varies according to the basic assumptions common to all members. Bion explicitly defines these basic assumptions:

- *Basic assumption dependency.* The group behaves as if the primary task is to provide for the needs and wishes of members. The leader's role is of protector, making the group feel good and protecting them from the actual primary task. The group can become dependent on the leader, fearing development and change. For example, instead of addressing difficult items on an agenda, debates are postponed and put off until the next meeting.
- *Basic assumption fight/flight.* The group focuses on a danger or enemy. The group sees its task as following the leader and waiting for appropriate action. For example, a team planning their work may spend time

complaining angrily about rumours of change within their organisation, putting off a focus on the planned workload.

- *Basic assumption pairing.* This is based on the collective, unconscious belief that a pairing (sometimes the leader and an external member, or two members) can bring about salvation. By focusing on the future and chosen pair's responsibilities, the group can deny the present. So, decisions are vague and futile, as the general argument emerges that better decisions can and will be made in the future.

What is interesting about these three assumptions is the way in which they can impede functioning. A team can become paralysed, in fear of or obsessed with a common enemy and unrealistically hopeful about the future. Moreover, the unconscious dilemmas of the team are transferred onto members who occupy positions of leadership. In Box 6.8 we look more closely at how notions of leadership are influenced in these unconscious conditions of avoidance.

6.8 *Leadership in basic assumption groups*

When groups are working with a basic assumption mentality there is often collusion between 'followers' and 'leaders': the latter who only become leaders when they can meet the basic assumption demands of the group (or followers):

- In basic assumption dependency the leader must provide for members' needs.
- In basic assumption fight/flight the leader must identify the enemy and attack or expel.
- In basic assumption pairing the leader must create a brighter future and prevent change happening.

When groups and leaders come together, the group's unconscious demands will be projected onto the leader so that they identify with the feelings experienced by the group:

- Basic assumption dependency leaders will feel resistance to change and a burden of status and hierarchy – the group feels dependent.
- Basic assumption fight/flight leaders are faced with aggression and suspicion from members – rules and procedures become the focus of the group.
- Basic assumption pairing leaders are asked for solutions, for alternative futures – the future dominates the present.

Bolton and Zagier Roberts (1994) used a case study to demonstrate how a team deals with absent leadership. A unit that provided services for people with learning difficulties had been without a consultant psychiatrist (the leader) for two years. With no leader to turn to, team members addressed all their concerns at management. The situation became difficult since the management viewed some of the issues to be inconsequential and they began to question the team's competence.

Eventually a consultant psychiatrist who had been external to the organisation was drafted in as leader and met with an extremely angry staff group who felt that the management had consistently ignored them. Indeed, the staff team had become so disenchanted that they had postponed important policy documents until the new psychiatrist arrived. Working with the team over a series of meetings, progress was made. Members began to draft a document and engage with their work. Interestingly, with these more comfortable working relationships a natural leader emerged from within the team (Daphne) and together the group produced some new initiatives. Meanwhile, the Health Authority was restructured and during the transition the meetings stopped. Shortly afterwards Daphne died suddenly. When the meetings restarted, the team felt outraged that the management had sent no note of condolence and a protest letter was drafted. The response from management was, 'That is what your staff support group is for', suggesting that this was not a management concern, employees already had avenues of support to pursue. The focus of the meetings once again became centred upon management. The consultant psychiatrist drafted a report outlining this crisis (having discussed the problem both with managers and the team), aiming to close down the consultation process whereby an external psychiatrist temporarily filled the role. Following his withdrawal, the long-standing vacant post was advertised.

In this example, the team is uncomfortable without leadership and the managers' covert aim was to provide leadership for the team. However, in working with the team (ostensibly on the primary task), the consultant psychiatrist is colluding with the team in denying the management vacuum. Only when the consultant formally withdraws from the organisation can the managers and the team admit their need for a leader (which is subsequently advertised). In order to deal with leadership and other such structures (for example teamworking), the authority structures need to be clear. The primary task should be shared and agreed upon. Moreover, leaders and followers need support systems to contain the anxieties arising from work, and deal with processes of change.

Box 6.8 illustrates the complexity of leadership and team processes. Working in organisational settings where we come into contact with others can stir up anxieties, pain and confusion. We may try to contain much of this (unconsciously) but often organisational practices and relationships between employees and managers are unconsciously structured to defend against anxiety. In the next section bullying is interpreted from a psychoanalytic perspective.

5.3 Psychoanalytic perspectives on bullying at work and beyond

Earlier, in Section 4, we explored the phenomenon of workplace bullying. Some research has applied the principles of psychoanalytic theory to workplace bullying (Crawford, 1997). For example, according to psychoanalytic readings, the workplace bully is likely to be someone who has failed to resolve childhood conflicts successfully. Crawford puts workplace bullying on a continuum that stretches from workplace homicide (a phenomenon in North America), to physical violence, through to sexual harassment and bullying. It is most likely to be aggression without violence – psychological aggression. Potential sites where bullying could occur include the beggar as bully, car driving as bullying (particularly road rage), and groups or gangs taking over public space and forcing others off. The domestic areana is *potentially* a site for bullying as part of domestic and child abuse. While bullying is widespread and possibly a symptom of wider societal dysfunction, Crawford sees workplace bullying as a sign of organisational dysfunction. It is evidence of conflict within organisations that cannot be contained, 'the conflict is either seeping to the surface or suddenly spills out' (Crawford 1997, p. 221). Certain types of organisations parade bullies and sanction them – the 'organisational hatchet man'. Crawford uses an example from the catering industry to demonstrate how the production of good food in highly rated restaurants can be associated with pressure. The well-known chef Raymond Blanc, who once had his nose, cheek and jaw broken when a colleague threw a heavy saucepan at him, comments:

> *I was thrown into an industry I hardly knew, and used violence not really to hurt people but to hurt their pride. I used verbal violence as well because I was so involved in what I was doing. I couldn't comprehend how someone could slaughter a dish, how someone could take short cuts. So I reacted to it. But I saw what I was doing and didn't like myself.*

> (Hillier, 1995, cited in Crawford, 1997, p. 27)

Here, verbal violence is justified with reference to 'slaughtering' good food. In the kitchen, the food and dishes are almost humanised in order to make the violence more justified. Cooking becomes a matter of life and death in this scenario. Catering is only one industry of many where bullying occurs. Anecdotal evidence seems to suggest that organisations with rigid hierarchical structures are likely to have disciplinarian cultures, where the power differentials between employees are handled inhumanely. Organisations as diverse as banks, the civil service, university departments and the Church show incidences of bullying (Crawford, 1997). Moreover, Crawford notes that even within the psychology profession (our own 'backyard') there can be an abuse of power (a form of bullying) between tutors and students or therapists and clients. The underlying assumption across all these organisational types is that while organisations continue to defensively distance themselves from the intangible, primitive elements of individuals, these elements often reappear in groups and organisations in the form of bullying. Crawford recommends that organisations need somehow to deal with the unconscious – where envy, rivalry, aggression, revenge and 'murderous' feelings become played out in real contexts. In terms of organisational liability therefore, it may be important to emphasise the potential psychological consequences of people working together:

> If no one has any liability for what transpires in the workplace, a free-for-all, you potentially condone organisational tyrannies, battlegrounds seeping with blood, legitimating the dictator, the fool and the weak to have a free hand in the lives of too many good people, with potentially devastating consequences – power exercised irresponsibly, where a workforce can find no peace and the primitive goes unchecked, a legitimate area for troubled human relations. These ideas are basically a discussion about the tension in organisations between the primitive and the mature and the consequence of a tilt in one direction or another.
>
> (Crawford, 1997, p. 224)

Psychodynamic insights into bullying suggest that this psychological violence is a sign of dysfunction, an eruption of the unconscious into the formal organisation. Crawford's suggestion for a remedy is a more explicit agenda that deals with anger and frustration. Crawford's particular psychoanalytic reading of bullying has focused more on the notion that bullies themselves have at some earlier point been the victims of bullying. The idea here is that the victim experiences the violence, observes the aggressor and then displaces this onto others. A different psychoanalytic reading of bullying might explore how bullies can 'use' victims to act out unresolved internal conflicts. One of the strengths of the psychoanalytic approach is the way in which it explicitly deals with relationships between people. For example, rather than explaining conflict in terms of roles or personality or structure, it turns to emotional (and often irrational) unconscious behaviour as an explanatory framework. This is an approach that takes the complexity of relationships and the way we make sense of them (unconsciously) and focuses on relationships as the issue to be tackled (rather than, for example, on team-building or management skills). The case study in Box 6.8 illustrates the benefit of having an external psychoanalyst who can interpret and work with the problem. However, this area does not lend itself easily to research for a variety of ethical reasons. From a practical viewpoint, many managers are likely to be sceptical of therapy as a valid intervention in the workplace.

Summary Section 5

- In this section the psychoanalytic perspective was examined in relation to organisational phenomena.
- Unconscious processes in organisations can be seen as operating within teams and between leaders and followers.
- Conflict (or lack of) between management and workers within organisations can be understood in terms of unconscious processes within and between these groups.

6 Ownership of research findings

Throughout this chapter one of the messages conveyed is the essential messiness and richness of organisations. This makes them difficult places both to access and to research. The traditional view (inspired by Taylor) that organisations run along mechanistic, rational lines is now very much outmoded. As organisations are recognised as dynamic collections of bodies and activities, with colliding agendas and differing needs, explicit tensions and difficulties can be recognised and dealt with. One of the tensions is the notion of ownership – who owns the process of organisational research and practice? There are a variety of stakeholders to consider.

First, in Britain, the sub-discipline of occupational psychology provides a recognisable route to status as a chartered occupational psychologist. Chartered occupational psychologists may choose to practise solely within consultancies and/or use consultancy work for both income and research. The research undertaken usually relies on instruments used in the consultancy, such as psychometric tests, career development profiling or team-building interventions. As consultancies are businesses with salaries, profit and loss accounts (and sometimes shareholders), it is questionable whether research can be neutral or value-free, particularly where evaluations of commercial products are undertaken.

A second stakeholder within research production is the researcher allied to higher education institutions who is carrying out independent or, more likely, funded research. Funding bodies that finance organisational work shape both the direction of research priorities and the way information is disseminated. Researchers working within these boundaries need to satisfy funding councils and participant organisations, while disseminating findings to an academic community. They also pursue academic careers that depend in part upon publication rates. Researchers within organisations have decisions to make regarding whose voice is heard. Lawthom (1997) points out that even where different organisational perspectives are represented within a research project, managers often shape or interpret the findings in a particular way (e.g. for shareholders or employees). Indeed, the contract negotiated at the beginning of research work is often with a senior manager who can choose if and how to disseminate findings. Therefore it is organisations and usually senior managers who are frequently the biggest stakeholders, acting as gatekeepers for both researchers and consultant/practitioners. As Hollway (1991) and Baritz (1960) noted, managers police the organisational boundaries. They control access to participants and shape research in line with organisational priorities. As a result research and consultancy priorities are more likely to be managerial in emphasis than worker-led. For example, a psychological issue of interest to employees might be negotiating fair salaries and benefit packages. However, senior managers may be more interested in downsizing (or 'rightsizing') the organisation to make it more economically viable. Box 6.9 highlights some of the issues that arise when conducting research in organisational settings.

Finally, a further less obtrusive stakeholder is the consultant who is not a psychologist but may work under the guise of organisational development, organisational consultancy, and personnel development. There are a growing number of practitioners in the 'people field', working as personal development consultants and trainers, personnel professionals, organisational development consultants or strategic consultants. These practitioners compete with chartered psychologists in the same domains: training and developing people; facilitating organisational change; creating learning organisations. Therefore chartered psychologists are paradoxically often creating tools and measures that are delivered by other professionals who are not necessarily trained researchers.

6.9 Designing appropriate research in organisational settings

If we wanted to systematically evaluate the service provision of nursing in hospitals by measuring patient satisfaction, the research design would be hampered by the nature of the nursing role and the need to give ethical consideration to patients. A methodologically rigorous design might employ manipulation of treatment and/or manipulation of nursing care to assess the felt impact upon patients. Clearly, as a piece of work this would be unacceptable in terms of the ethical commitments espoused by psychological bodies. One option would be to employ a quasi-experimental design investigating naturally occurring differences within, in this case, a hospital or trust. Alternatively, a design might employ an experimental method but use participants who were not real patients (e.g. student volunteers in laboratory-controlled settings). These different research settings pose particular problems of authenticity versus generalisability. The mock-up study where students enact patient roles might yield results that may not generalise to a patient population, or to nursing staff working with real patients. One of the reasons for this is that participants within real organisational settings have a set of emotional commitments and investments that are difficult to replicate in the laboratory. For example, nurses generally care about their real patients but probably would not have the same emotional investment in students playing the role of patients in a laboratory experiment. The dynamic nature of organisations brings with it difficult issues and tensions for the researcher and practitioner to work with, practically, morally and ethically.

7   Conclusion

In this chapter we have covered historical and contemporary debates in the application of psychology in the workplace. As organisations consist of people with diverse needs, they can be researched and explored at different levels. This chapter examined issues around leadership. Explanations at this level, however, often downplay the relational nature of workplaces. Two further topics, teamworking (and group processes) and bullying dealt more explicitly with relationships. For example, the phenomenon of groups of people needing coordination (as in teams) can bring individual needs into conflict with group goals. Considering the unconscious motivational processes occurring within groups provides an alternative framework. Lastly, the notion of intervention in terms of research and practice was examined in organisational settings. Questions of ownership, ethics, rights and power are key issues in considering working with individuals in real settings.

The focus of this chapter has been necessarily broad, ranging from traditional areas of occupational psychology, such as leadership and teams, to newer areas such as bullying. The study of workplace bullying and the practice of applying psychoanalytic understanding to organisations have been less common within occupational psychology. This shift, in both what constitutes occupational psychology and the way in which it is approached, has been paralleled by a shift in thinking. Critical thinkers have argued that our concepts of organisations, work and occupations are changing. Indeed, Sims, et al. (1993) argue for a shift from the concept of the 'organisation' to 'organising'. The latter is seen to embrace meaning-making and social processes where tensions exist between order and disorder, and where unpredictability and anxiety (as opposed to rationality) is 'managed' wherever possible. This much richer definition more easily incorporates the latter two topics covered – bullying and psychodynamic understanding. The management of anxiety, and tensions between order and disorder, are prevalent themes within these areas. Both bullying and the application of psychoanalytic theory deal with the social processes in organisations and the interpretation or meaning-making of behaviour.

   This chapter has outlined a number of theories that can be used to explain different facets of relationships at work. Hopefully, a good deal of the chapter resonates with your experiences of work and/or your dealings with organisations. One of the key issues to arise from this chapter is a more explicit recognition of the emotional impact organisations can engender in individuals. This chapter may have encouraged you to consider organisations (using Morgan's metaphors) not only as machines (running to clockwork efficiency), but also as instruments of control (bullying) or psychic prisons (containers of anxiety). The way in which you think about organisations will never be the same again!

Further reading

Chmiel, N. (2000) *Introduction to Work and Organizational Psychology: A European Perspective*, Oxford, Blackwell.
This text provides an excellent introduction to the main subject areas in occupational/work/organisational psychology.

Morgan, G. (1986) *Images of Organizations*, London, Sage.
This text uses metaphors to creatively explore various ways of 'reading organisations'.

Rayner, C., Hoel, H. and Cooper, C. (2001) *Workplace Bullying*, Hove, Psychology Press.
The authors explore the issues associated with bullying in the workplace; they introduce case material and consider real problems.

Warr, P.B. (2002) *Psychology at Work*, (5th edn), London, Penguin.
This edition of a classic text provides a collection of essays looking at psychological processes, the study of groups and work teams and the nature of organisations.

References

Adams, A. and Crawford, N. (1992) *Bullying at Work: How to Confront and Overcome it*, London, Virago.

Applebaum, E. and Batt, R. (1994) *The New American Workplace: Transforming Work Systems in the United States*, Ithaca, NY, Cornell University.

Baritz, L. (1960) *The Servants of Power: A History of the Use of Social Science in American Industry*, Middleton, CT, Wesleyan University Press.

Bass, B.M. (1985) 'Leadership: good, better, best', *Organizational Dynamics*, Winter, pp. 6–40.

Bass, B.M. (1990) *Bass and Stogdill's Handbook of Leadership: Theory, Research and Managerial Applications*, New York, Free Press.

Bass, B.M. and Avolio, B.J. (1995) *MLQ, Multifactor Leadership Questionnaire*, Redwood City, CA, Mind Garden.

Bassman, E.S. (1992) *Abuse in the Workplace: Management Remedies and Bottom Line Impact*, Westport, CT, Quorum.

Belbin, R.M. (1981) *Management Teams: Why They Succeed or Fail*, Oxford, Butterworth-Heinemann.

Bion, W. (1961) *Experiences in Groups*, New York, Basic Books.

Blake, R.R. and McCanse, A.A. (1991) *Leadership Dilemmas: Grid Solutions*, Houston, TX, Gulf Publishing.

Bolton, W. and Zagier Roberts, V. (1994) 'Asking for help: staff support and sensitivity groups reviewed' in Obholzer, A. and Zaiger Roberts, V. (eds) *The Unconscious at Work: Individual and Organizational Stress in the Human Services*, London, Routledge.

Buchanan, D.A. and Huczynski, A. (1991) *Organizational Behaviour: An Introductory Text* (2nd edn), Englewood Cliffs, NJ, Prentice Hall.

Campion, M.A., Papper, E.M. and Medsker, G.J. (1996) 'Relations between work team characteristics and effectiveness: a replication and extension', *Personnel Psychology*, vol. 49, no. 2, pp. 429–452.

Cohen, S.G., Ledford, G.E. and Spreitzer, G.M. (1996) 'A predictive model of self-managing work team effectiveness', *Human Relations*, vol. 49, no. 5, pp. 643–76.

Cordery, J.L., Mueller, W.S. and Smith, L.M. (1991) 'Attitudinal and behavioural outcomes of autonomous group working: a longitudinal field study', *Academy of Management Journal*, vol. 34, pp. 464–76.

Crawford, N. (1997) 'Bullying at work: a psychoanalytic perspective', *Journal of Community and Applied Social Psychology*, vol. 7, no. 3, pp. 219–25.

Earley, P.C. (1987) 'Intercultural training for managers: a comparison of documentary and interpersonal methods', *Academy of Management Journal*, vol. 30, no. 4, pp. 685–98.

Earley, P.C. (1993) 'East meets West meets Mid-East: further explorations of collectivistic and individualistic work groups', *Academy of Management Journal*, vol. 36, no. 2, pp. 319–48.

Erez, M. and Somech, A. (1996) 'Is group productivity loss the rule or the exception? Effects of culture and group-based motivation', *Academy of Management Journal*, vol. 39, no. 6, pp. 1513–37.

Fiedler, F.E. (1967) *A Theory of Leadership Effectiveness*, New York, McGraw-Hill.

Field, R.H.G. (1982) 'A test of the Vroom–Yetton normative model of leadership', *Journal of Applied Psychology*, vol. 67, pp. 523–32.

Gordon, J. (1992) 'Work teams: how far have they come?', *Training*, October, pp. 59–65.

Hackman, J.R. and Oldham, G.R. (1976) 'Motivation through the design of work: test of a new theory', *Organizational Behaviour and Human Performance*, vol. 16, pp. 250–97.

Hofstede, G.H. (1980) *Culture's Consequences: International Differences in Work Related Values*, Beverly Hills, CA, Sage.

Hollway, W. (1991) *Work Psychology and Organizational Behaviour: Managing the Individual at Work*, London, Sage.

Janis, I.L. (1982) *Victims of Group Think: A Psychological Study of Foreign Policy Decisions and Fiascos* (2nd edn), Boston, MA, Houghton Mifflin.

Kirkpatrick, S.A. and Locke, E.A. (1991) 'Leadership: do traits matter?', *The Executive*, vol. 5, no. 2, pp. 48–60.

Latané, B., Williams, K. and Harkins, S. (1979) 'Many hands make light work: the causes and consequences of social loafing', *Journal of Personality and Social Psychology*, vol. 37, pp. 822–32.

Lawthom, R. (1997) 'What can I do? A feminist researcher in non-feminist research', *Feminism and Psychology*, vol. 7, no. 4, pp. 553–58.

Leymann, H. (1990) 'Mobbing and psychological terror at workplaces', *Violence and Victims*, vol. 5, no. 2, pp. 119–26.

Lord, R.G., DeVader, C.L. and Alliger, G.M. (1986) 'A meta-analysis of the personality traits and leadership perceptions: an application of validity generalization procedures', *Journal of Applied Psychology*, vol. 71, pp. 402–10.

Marx, K. (1985 [1948]) *The Communist Manifesto*, London, Penguin Classics.

Meindl, J.R. (1992) 'Reinventing leadership: a radical, social psychological approach' in Murningham, K. (ed) *Social Psychology in Organizations: Advances in Theory and Research*, Englewood Cliffs, NJ, Prentice Hall.

Meindl, J.R. and Ehrlich, S.B. (1987) 'The romance of leadership and the evaluation of organizational performance', *Academy of Management Journal*, vol. 30, no. 1, pp. 91–109.

Mohrman, S.A., Cohen, S.G. and Mohrman, A.M. (1995) *Designing Team-based Organizations: New Forms for Knowledge Work*, San Fransico, CA, Jossey-Bass.

Morgan, G. (1986) *Images of Organizations*, London, Sage.

Mullen, B. and Copper, C. (1994) 'The relation between group cohesiveness and performance: an integration', *Psychological Bulletin*, vol. 115, pp. 210–27.

Nemeth, C. and Owens, J. (1996) 'Value of minority dissent' in West, M.A. (ed.) *Handbook of Work Group Psychology*, New York, John Wiley.

Olweus, D. (1993) 'Victimization by peers: antecedents and long term outcomes' in Rubin, K.H. and Asendorpf, J.B. (eds) *Social Withdrawal, Inhibition and Shyness in Childhood*, Hillsdale, NJ, Lawrence Erlbaum.

Peiro, J.M. Gonzalez, V. and Ramos, J. (1992) 'The influence of work team climate on role stress, tension, satisfaction and leadership perceptions', *European Review of Applied Psychology*, vol. 42, no. 1, pp. 49–58.

Rayner C. (1997) 'The incidence of workplace bullying', *Journal of Community and Applied Social Psychology*, vol. 7, no. 3, pp. 199–208.

Rayner, C. and Hoel, H. (1997) 'A summary review of literature relating to workplace bullying', *Journal of Community and Applied Social Psychology*, vol. 7, no. 3, pp. 181–91.

Roethlisberger, F.J., Dickson, W.J. and Wright, H.A. (1964) *Management and the Worker*, New York, John Wiley.

Shimmin, S. and Wallis, D. (1994) *Fifty Years of Occupational Psychology in Britain*, Division and Section of Occupational Psychology, British Psychological Society.

Sims, D., Fineman, S. and Gabriel, Y. (1993) *Organizing and Organizations: An Introduction*, London, Sage.

Smith, P.B. and Noakes, J. (1996) 'Cultural differences in group processes' in West, M.A. (ed.) *Handbook of Work Group Psychology*, Chichester, Wiley.

Stogdill, R.M. (1963) *Manual for the Leader Behaviour Description Questionnaire*, Form XII, Colombus, OH, Ohio State University, Bureau of Business Research.

Stogdill, R.M. (1974) *Handbook of Leadership: A Survey of Theory and Research*, New York, Free Press.

Stokes, J. (1994) 'Institutional chaos and personal stress' in Obholzer, A. and Zaiger Roberts, V. (eds) *The Unconscious at Work: Individual and Organizational Stress in the Human Services*, London, Routledge.

Stroebe, W. and Frey, B.S. (1982) 'Self-interest and collective action: the economics and psychology of public goods', *British Journal of Social Psychology*, vol. 21, no. 2, pp. 121–37.

Tajfel, H. (1978) *Differentiation Between Social Groups: Studies in the Social Psychology of Interpersonal Relations*, European Monographs in Social Psychology, no. 14, London, Academic Press.

Tajfel, H. and Turner, J. (1979) 'An integrative theory of intergroup conflict' in Austin, W.G. and Worchel, S. (eds) *The Social Psychology of Intergroup Relations*, Monterey, CA, Brooks/Cole.

Taylor, F.W. (1911) *Scientific Management*, New York, Harper & Row.

Trist, E.L. and Bamforth, K.W. (1951) 'Some social and psychological consequences of the longwall method of coal-getting', *Human Relations*, vol. 4, pp. 3–38.

Unsworth, K.L. and West, M.A. (2000) 'Teams: the challenges of cooperative work' in Chmiel, N. (ed.) *Introduction to Work and Organizational Psychology: A European Perspective*, Oxford, Blackwell.

Vroom, V.H. and Jago, A.G. (1988) *The New Leadership: Managing Participation in Organizations*, Englewood Cliffs, NJ, Prentice Hall.

Vroom, V.H. and Yetton, P.W. (1973) *Leadership and Decision-Making*, Pittsburgh, PA, University of Pittsburgh Press.

West, M.A. and Anderson, N.R. (1996) 'Innovation in top management teams', *Journal of Applied Psychology*, vol. 81, no. 6, pp. 680–93.

Wiersema, M.F. and Bantel, K.A. (1992) 'Top management team demography and corporate strategic chance', *Academy of Management Journal*, vol. 35, no. 1, pp. 91–121.

Zimbardo, P.G. (1975) 'Transforming experimental research into advocacy for social change' in Deutsch, M. and Hornstein, H. (eds) *Applying Social Psychology*, Hillsdale, NJ, Lawrence Erlbaum.

Psychological factors in witness evidence and identification

Helen Westcott and Nicola Brace

Contents

This chapter offers a review of issues relating to the experience of witnessing and reporting upon life events. You may find some personal resonance with criminal events discussed in the chapter, such as violent crime and child sexual abuse. Sometimes the issues require explicit discussion of intimate activities and the associated ethical implications for research concerned with these topics.

Aims

This chapter aims to:

- introduce the field of forensic psychology through work undertaken in one area by forensic psychologists
- identify and explore some of the factors that impact upon witness testimony
- demonstrate some of the difficulties characteristic of applied research, in relation to both ethical issues and ecological validity
- show how psychological research can assist those involved in legal contexts and inform public policy and law reform
- illustrate the link between cognitive and social psychological theories and everyday experiences of events.

1   Introduction

Imagine you are walking through a car park on your way to visit a friend. You see two men running towards you, one chasing the other and shouting something about a bag that the first is carrying. They stop for a moment and have a heated discussion, and then they both run past you and nearly knock you over. Later, at your friend's house you mention the incident to your friend, and wonder what may have been happening.

Perhaps, unknowingly, you have been a witness to a crime. In this chapter, we look at some of the processes that a witness like yourself in the scenario just described might go through in any subsequent investigation. What is seen? What is remembered? How can the police best obtain reliable evidence through questioning? What about identification of the suspects? Once the case has come to court, what factors might influence the evidence a witness gives? Each of these questions has been the subject of psychological research, and that research has drawn on concepts from across the spectrum of psychological theory, including the **constructive nature of memory** and the influence of existing knowledge and stereotypes. In order to consider all of the questions involved, we will not follow the progress of a single case. Rather, we will focus on certain issues at different stages in the process.

Constructive nature of memory
A concept arguing that events are recreated when we try to remember them, rather than being perfectly preserved representations like a video recording. Gaps in the memory may be filled in with things we 'know' rather than remember.

1.1   The relationship between psychology and law

Although both psychologists and lawyers are closely concerned with human behaviour, it may come as something of a surprise that the application of psychology to legal issues is fairly recent. This is because, although their subject matter may overlap, their aims are very different and their approaches vary. The psychologist's concern with scientific rigour contrasts with the lawyer's typically 'common-sense' psychology and the reliance placed on his/her accumulated experience and legal precedents. Whereas psychology is characterised by empirical methods and scientific analyses, law uses its internal systems to scrutinise its legal processes, which have 'evolved'. It has also been the case that law, as a profession, has remained sceptical of the ability of disciplines such as psychology to have anything to offer (e.g. Nijboer, 1995). Increasingly, however, psychologists are working in collaboration with members of the legal profession. Specialist conferences provide a forum for psychologists and members of the legal profession to come together and communicate with each other. In parallel, there has been a growth in both the number of postgraduate courses in **forensic psychology**, and the number of psychology or law degrees that include an option in 'psychology and law'.

Forensic psychology
The application of psychological theories and methods to issues arising in law and legal procedures.

A number of different terms have been adopted to describe the applications of psychology to law, including 'legal psychology', 'criminological psychology', 'psychology and law' and 'forensic psychology'. This is not surprising as the applications are wide-ranging. For instance, there is the work of psychologists who are concerned with the treatment and rehabilitation of offenders, and offender profiling. Additionally, there is research, often conducted in the laboratory, that examines witness testimony, juror decision making and public perceptions and attitudes towards crime and penal sanctions. In this chapter, we are going to focus on just one of these research areas, namely witness testimony, which is one of the more extensively investigated areas.

In some cases, psychologists' research has resulted in changes to the law and legal procedures. For example, reforms to accommodate children's testimony in the courtroom came about largely as a result of research showing that children's evidence was more reliable than had previously been believed, and that also highlighted some of the psychological stresses placed upon child witnesses and how they might be alleviated (Spencer and Flin, 1993). Alternatively, changes that are introduced to legal procedures may prompt new psychological investigations. For example, the need to examine the role of closed circuit television (CCTV) in identification evidence arose from the installation of CCTV systems in many towns and city centres. Thus, while the findings of psychological research may impact upon policy, changes to policy may also prompt research. Therefore the relationship between law and psychology can be viewed as two-way, and influenced also by developments in technology, social policy, and the media (e.g. reporting of public outcry over a particular case or event).

1.2　Factors affecting witness evidence and identification

The nature of the crime is itself significant: witnessing someone stealing from a shop is a different experience from witnessing someone physically assaulting another person, and being a victim of a handbag snatch is very different from being a rape victim. While the findings from research in one particular setting are not necessarily generalisable to all crime scenarios, they have provided information of use to the legal system and have indicated ways in which the reliability of witness testimony can be enhanced, both in the police station and in the courtroom.

The accuracy and reliability of witness testimony can be further affected in a number of ways, some of which are under the control of those professionals conducting the investigation, questioning the witness and obtaining the evidence. The way in which the police question a witness and the procedures for asking a witness to identify a perpetrator in a live identification parade are both open to variation. These are known as **system variables**, and research on such variables can have policy implications (Wells, 1978) – if one set of procedures is found to be more effective in eliciting accurate evidence, then, arguably, it should be adopted as common practice. Other factors that may influence the reliability of testimony, however, cannot be changed – for example, whether the perpetrator was wearing a disguise or positioned too far away from the witness to permit later identification. These are known as **estimator variables**. Although research on estimator variables cannot be used to alter policy, the findings can nevertheless be of assistance, for example in determining whether a witness is likely to be able to identify the perpetrator subsequently.

System variables
Variables that might influence witness testimony and that are under the control of legal professionals, such as interviewing style or identification procedures.

Estimator variables
Variables that might influence witness testimony and that are not under the control of legal professionals, such as the age of the witness.

1.3　Methodological and ethical issues in forensic psychology research

Research carried out in forensic psychology has not gone without criticism. In particular, research that has involved simulations in the laboratory has been questioned on the grounds of its ecological validity. For example, because the law restricts access to real jurors for research purposes, the jury decision-making process has been studied in many cases by asking psychology undergraduates to read a fairly short written description of a criminal case and to make decisions about the guilt/innocence of the defendant and, in the case of guilt, the sentence that should be imposed. The identification of perpetrators has been studied by showing participants a short video of a staged crime scenario and then later asking them to select a picture of the perpetrator from an array of photographs. Psychologists themselves have debated the practical utility of the findings of such studies. Researchers have responded to criticisms by supplementing these rather basic simulations with much more sophisticated ones that have greater ecological validity, and by interviewing real witnesses to crimes and real jurors after they have served in a court case.

Ethical issues are paramount, however, even in more sophisticated approaches to research, and you will be invited to engage with these in activities and boxes throughout the chapter. By its very nature the experience of crime is often frightening and may be painful. Researchers face severe limits, however, on the extent to which they can mimic such aspects of the experience of being a witness or victim.

1.4 Positioning research on witness testimony in different legal systems

Another factor to consider when reviewing the relationship between psychology and law is that there are many different types of law, different systems of justice, and different sorts of legal proceedings from one country to another. Legal systems in the UK, and in other countries in which they are modelled on the English system of common law, are described as adversarial, or accusatorial. Spencer and Flin (1993) summarise such systems thus:

> In an accusatorial system each side presents a case before a court the function of which is limited to deciding who has won. The judges have nothing to do with the preliminary investigations, give no help to either side in presenting its case, and take no active steps to discover the truth, which emerges – or so the theory goes – from the clash of conflicting accounts.

> (Spencer and Flin, 1993, p. 75)

By contrast, in the inquisitorial system found in many European countries and elsewhere in the world,

> The court is viewed as a public agency appointed to get to the bottom of the disputed matter. The court takes the initiative in gathering information as soon as it has notice of the dispute, builds up a file on the matter by questioning all those it thinks may have useful information to offer – including, in a criminal case, the defendant – and then applies its reasoning powers to the material it has collected in order to determine where the truth lies.

> (Spencer and Flin, 1993, p. 75)

In practice, the differences between the two types of system have diminished over the years as each has 'borrowed' from the other (Spencer and Flin, 1993).

The research reported in this chapter, however, is firmly located in the accusatorial system of justice. This is partly due to the accusatorial system posing more problems for witnesses and the reception of their testimony (e.g. placing what may seem to be undue emphasis on oral evidence live in court on the day of the trial), but also because most of the research at the present time stems from the US, which itself has an accusatorial system.

A further important distinction is between *criminal* and *civil* proceedings. In England and Wales, for example, criminal proceedings are *'brought in the name of the Queen for the punishment of wrongdoers'* while civil proceedings are *'brought to settle disputes between one citizen and another, or disputes between the citizen and the State'* (Spencer and Flin, 1993, p. 14). This chapter concerns itself with criminal proceedings, since the research it presents is largely driven by criminal matters such as robberies and sexual offences against children, which are of particular social concern.

One final observation is in order. For the most part, when we refer to 'witnesses' we mean both bystander witnesses and those individuals who are victims as well as witnesses. Intuitively, you may think that there are differences between these groups, especially when the crime is serious or involves physical injury. However, this distinction has not been clearly made by researchers working in this area, and, in many cases, the research agenda has been shaped by issues facing victim-witnesses (e.g. victims of child sexual abuse).

2   Witnessing an event

You might think that we should be better at remembering an event involving a crime than other events. At the time of **encoding**, we would surely realise the importance of attending closely to what is happening and would later rehearse our memory for the event to ensure that it would not be forgotten. However, there are a number of factors that impact on our ability to encode accurately and to retrieve details of the crime in due course. In this section we shall examine these factors and also consider the role of individual differences. Although these are all estimator variables and not controllable, they provide an indication as to what aspects of a crime a witness is likely to be able to report on accurately.

Encoding
Putting information into memory, for example when a crime event is being observed.

Activity 7.1

Think back to the scenario described in the opening paragraph of the Introduction to this chapter. Write down factors that might affect your ability to remember such an incident later. Compare your list with the factors mentioned here in Section 2.

2.1 Remembering different aspects of a crime

There are many factors that can work to our disadvantage as a witness to a crime. As in the scenario described in our opening paragraph, the experience can be very brief – perhaps even a matter of a few seconds – and we may not even realise that what is happening is a criminal event until it is over. Reliable evidence depends upon the witness having the opportunity to observe effectively; for example, accurate face recognition has been found to improve with increases in time spent exposed to the perpetrator's face (e.g. Ellis *et al.*, 1977). Furthermore, the crime may take place in poor lighting and at some distance away. Wagenaar and Van Der Schrier (1996) conducted research demonstrating that, beyond a certain distance and illumination, identification may be problematic. They tested participants' ability to recognise a target's face at seven distances and nine illumination levels. Immediately after seeing the target face, participants were presented with an array of photographs of faces and asked to identify the face they had just seen. As a result, the following guideline emerged regarding the observation conditions that are good enough for the acceptance of identification evidence (the *Rule of Fifteen*): the maximum distance is 15 metres from the event, and the minimum illumination is 15 lux (lux is a measurement of luminance, where 0.3 lux is equivalent to night with full moon, 30 lux to a badly illuminated room and 300 lux to a brightly illuminated room). This research demonstrates that although estimator variables are not under the control of the police/criminal justice system, research can investigate their influence – in this instance providing information relating to the feasibility of an accurate identification.

What about other judgements that witnesses might be asked to make? Research suggests that generally we are not very accurate in our estimates of how long something lasts (temporal duration) or distance. We may overestimate the length of events of short temporal duration, sometimes by as much as 500 per cent. Many studies (e.g. Block, 1978) have shown that a time interval containing unfamiliar, less predictable, complex or many components (as when solving a complex puzzle) is estimated to be significantly longer than an interval of the same duration that contains more familiar, more predictable, simpler or fewer components (as when doing simple arithmetic).

Our ability to provide the correct date for an event may also be poor. Research testing participants' ability to date episodes that they had experienced has shown that their accuracy in dating decreases quite rapidly the longer the time gap between the episode itself and when they try to remember it (the retention interval). When asked about experiences that had taken place in the previous week, participants tended to date accurately only 85–90 per cent of the time, and for experiences that occurred over three months ago this rate dropped to 15–20 per cent (Thompson *et al.*, 1996). Furthermore, many studies have reported a phenomenon known as '**forward telescoping**', a tendency to assign a date to an event that is more recent than the actual date of occurrence. This tendency has been observed as soon as eight weeks after the event occurred. Telescoping is thought to arise because we overestimate the frequency of events occurring during a certain time period, and therefore mistakenly import or bring forward events that actually happened earlier.

    Our estimates of people's height and weight are also often not accurate. Flin and Shepherd (1986) asked 588 participants to estimate the height and weight of 1 of 14 males who had previously asked them for directions in a busy city centre. They found errors for height judgements to range from an underestimate of 14 inches (35.56 centimetres) to an overestimate of 8 inches (20.32 centimetres), and for weight judgements from an underestimate of 98 lb (11.07 kilograms) to an overestimate of 36 lb (4.07 kilograms). Their results showed that the height of all 14 males was underestimated by 6 inches (15.24 centimetres) by at least one participant. Generally, the findings indicated a '*trend of underestimating above-average characteristics and overestimating below-average characteristics ... indicating a general regression to the population mean*' (Flin and Shepherd, 1986, p. 35). Their results also indicated that the participant's own height and weight was used as a norm or anchor against which the height or weight of the male was estimated (although this effect was small in female participants' judgements about height, and absent in their judgements about weight). Therefore, when asking witnesses to estimate such characteristics, it may be helpful to obtain relative judgements. For example, if a perpetrator is seen standing in a doorway, his or her height may be judged by asking how much shorter than the door the perpetrator was.

Forward telescoping
Our tendency to assign a date to an event that is more recent than the actual date of occurrence.

2.2 Direction of attention to an event

If you think back to the scenario outlined in the first paragraph of the Introduction, do you think you could attend to and encode all aspects of the event? There are limits to our attentional capacity and it would not be surprising if, with a criminal event especially, attention is directed towards certain aspects at the expense of others, influencing what is later remembered. In our scenario, for example, you might have attended more to what was being said and to the faces of the two men than to their clothing, and you may not have noticed a car pulling up close by or another person waiting nearby.

    Migueles and García-Bajos (1999) found that, when showing participants a film depicting a kidnapping attempt, actions were remembered better than details. The film contained both central information (the kidnapping itself, which happened suddenly and quickly and involved a young woman being forced into a van), and peripheral information (incidents that were not key to the actual kidnapping, such as a boat arriving at a busy port and passengers getting off). Some of the central and peripheral information was classified as describing *actions* (for example, that a man lifted up the tarpaulin of the van or that a young man who tried to help the girl struggled with the kidnappers) and some was classified as *details* (for example, that the name of the boat was *Samaina* or that the hand of one of the kidnappers was bandaged). Migueles and García-Bajos found that participants viewing the film later reported overall equal amounts of central and peripheral information. However, whereas the peripheral information included similar amounts of actions and details, the central information retrieved contained more actions than details. Such findings suggest that when witnessing a crime our attention may be drawn to central actions at the expense of descriptive details, although in other circumstances our attention may be spread more evenly between actions and details.

Box 7.1 describes another example of how attention may be influenced.

7.1 *Weapon focus*

Weapon focus
Describes a phenomenon in which the presence of a weapon in a crime scenario may impair a witness's memory.

Identification line-up
A procedure whereby the suspect of a crime is presented to the witness along with other individuals who resemble the suspect.

A phenomenon referred to as **weapon focus** has been observed, where the presence of a weapon – a gun or knife, for example – attracts the attention of witnesses, such that their memory for other details, including the perpetrator's facial and physical characteristics, is impaired. This phenomenon is supported by data from a number of experiments using different procedures. For example, in a laboratory experiment, Cutler *et al.* (1987) showed videotaped robberies to participants. In half of these, the robber openly wielded a handgun, whereas in the other half he hid the gun in his jacket. When asked to identify the robber in an **identification line-up**, participants exposed to the gun made 26 per cent correct identifications. By contrast, participants who had viewed the tapes where the gun was concealed made 46 per cent correct identifications. In a study by Maass and Köhnken (1989), an experimenter in a staged event approached participants displaying either a syringe or a pen. Subsequent recognition of the experimenter's face was poorer in the syringe condition than in the pen condition, with 65.9 per cent in the syringe condition making a false identification in a line-up task compared with 45.2 per cent in the pen condition.

2.3 The influence of violence, stress and arousal

In real crimes, the presence of a weapon is likely to be confounded with a higher degree of threat of violence and therefore of stress-induced arousal. One study involving analysis of police records showed that victims of violent crimes, such as rape or assault, provided less complete descriptions of the perpetrator compared to victims of less violent crimes (Kuehn, 1974). However, as we shall see here, the relationship between violence, arousal and witness memory is by no means clear-cut.

Activity 7.2   Ethics of research on violent crime

You may have wondered whether approaching participants with a syringe was ethical. The BPS ethical guidelines on conducting research, revised in 1993 (British Psychological Society, 1993), specify that:

- 'Normally, the risk of harm must be no greater than in ordinary life' (p. 10).

- 'If harm, unusual discomfort, or other negative consequences for the individual's future life might occur, the investigator must obtain the disinterested approval of indepen- dent advisors, inform the participants, and obtain informed, real consent from each of them' (p. 8).

Can you think of a way of simulating a violent crime in a way that conforms to these guidelines? Now see whether you've thought of a method that has been used in the research described below.

Psychologists have investigated the impact of 'violence' on witness memory using a variety of methodologies. Usually, videotaped crime scenarios are shown so that participants do not perceive any threat to themselves, and the degree of violence varies from physical assault to gunshots. Frequently, two crime scenarios are videotaped and matched so that the only difference is the level of violence depicted. There is some evidence suggesting that participants tend to remember the details of the non-violent crime better than those of a violent crime and that identification accuracy is lower for the violent version. For example, Clifford and Scott (1978) showed 48 participants (24 males and 24 females) 1 of 2 videotapes. Both involved a search for a criminal by two policemen, reluctantly assisted by a third person. The beginning and the end of the two tapes were the same but the middle portion of the tape differed. In the non-violent version, the interaction between the police and reluctant third person was mainly verbal, but in the violent version one of the policemen physically assaulted the third person. Using a 44-item questionnaire, the authors found that both male and female participants remembered consistently less of the violent version than of the non-violent one.

The influence of violence on memory could be explained in terms of emotional arousal or stress. Increased violence may result in higher levels of stress, which may then impact negatively on memory. It has been suggested that memory performance may follow the Yerkes–Dodson Law, long established in psychology (after Yerkes and Dodson, 1908), which suggests a rather complex relationship between stress and performance, as shown in Figure 7.1.

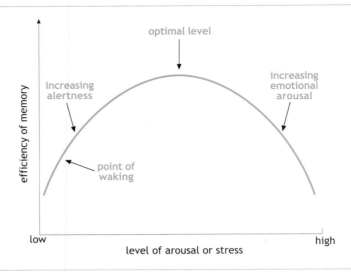

Figure 7.1   The relationship between stress and memory performance (Loftus, 1980)

Activity 7.3

Looking at Figure 7.1, how would you describe the relationship between the two variables?

Comment

Whereas *moderate* levels of arousal are thought to heighten perceptual and attentiveness skills, *low* levels of arousal are linked to lower attentiveness and *higher* levels of arousal (as experienced when in danger) to lower perceptual skills. Thus, when a witness or victim is experiencing extreme stress at the encoding stage, he or she may have a reduced ability to perceive and remember the details of the crime.

You may have noticed that we use the terms 'arousal' and 'stress' as if they are equivalent. There is in fact a lack of clarity surrounding the definition of these two terms and the relationship between them. Chapter 1 of this book describes the complexity of defining stress and how, when some event occurs that you fear you are unable to cope with, there are many different factors that influence your response to that event and whether or not you experience stress.

Other evidence casts doubt on there being such a simple relationship between arousal and eyewitness memory. A study of witnesses to real crime, outlined in Box 7.2, found evidence of good memory, despite high levels of stress and violence.

7.2 Memories of a violent robbery

In a robbery in a Canadian city, a thief entered a gun shop, tied up the owner and took money and guns. The owner freed himself, collected a revolver and left the shop to get the licence number of the thief's car. This led to a confrontation: standing six feet away, the thief fired two shots at the owner, and then the owner discharged six shots, killing the thief. The owner survived severe injury. Of the 21 witnesses who saw the event, 15 were interviewed on the same day and the remaining 6 within 2 days. A detailed account of the incident was constructed on the basis of their accounts, forensic evidence and photographs, etc., so that witness accuracy could be calculated. Yuille and Cutshall (1986) reported high levels of accuracy in the reporting of this traumatic event by witnesses at the original interview and by 13 of these witness who agreed to take part in a research interview 4 to 5 months later (see Figure 7.2).

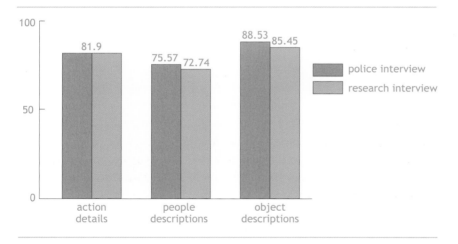

Figure 7.2   Percentage of details accurately recalled

Activity 7.4

What does Figure 7.2 tell us about the recall accuracy of the witnesses' memories of the event?

Comment

The figure shows that the reports of the witnesses were remarkably accurate, even several months after they saw the crime, and despite the presence of both violence and weapons.

With the exception of one witness, all reported event-related stress, but for some this appeared about half an hour after the incident; during the incident itself they were only aware of 'adrenalin effects'. Adrenalin is a hormone that is released in stressful situations and heightens heart rate (refer back to Chapter 1, Stress). The five witnesses who had contact with either the thief, store owner or weapon reported the greatest amount of stress. They showed a mean accuracy of 93 per cent in the first interview and 88 per cent in the research interview, compared with 75 per cent and 76 per cent respectively for the remaining witnesses. However, as these five witnesses were also closer to the event, arousal level and proximity were confounded in this case.

Some psychologists have suggested that there may be a special kind of vivid memory, known as 'flashbulb memory'. This term is used to describe a phenomenon where a detailed and stable memory is formed of the circumstances that people were in when they learned of a traumatic public event. There is, then, a convergence of evidence here, suggesting that intense emotional response or emotional stress can be associated with good retention of certain information.

Yuille and Cutshall's study was based on a single stressful event. Christianson and Hübinette (1993), by contrast, conducted a wider-scale study involving real witnesses to 22 bank robberies. They found no significant relationship between rated degree of emotion and the number of details remembered, and therefore no evidence that high arousal will impact negatively or positively on memory. They approached 110 witnesses, of whom 58 were willing to participate in the study, and of these 20 were victims (bank tellers), 25 fellow employees and 13 customers. The witnesses were interviewed and studied with respect to emotional reactions and memory for detailed information about the robbery. Their accounts – the information provided in the interview – were then compared with that initially recorded in police reports. Like the previous study, the findings revealed relatively high accuracy rates after an extended time interval (between 4 and 15 months) with respect to specific details about the robbery, namely action, weapon, clothing. However, witnesses showed rather poor memory for certain items: footwear, eye colour and hair colour. Findings also revealed that the victims had higher accuracy rates than the bystander witnesses in relation to the circumstances surrounding the robbery (information about date, day, time and number of customers), but this was not related to differential emotional experiences; victims did not report being more emotionally aroused than bystanders. The results as a whole indicate that the specific details directly associated with a highly emotional real-life event are well retained over time.

A bank robbery taking place in Los Angeles

You may remember that the results of the study by Migueles and García-Bajos (1999) suggested that, when witnessing a crime, our attention may be drawn to the central actions at the expense of descriptive details. Generally, studies investigating the effect of emotional arousal on memory have revealed a fairly consistent pattern. Participants' memory for certain central, critical details of emotional or violent events tends to be accurate and persistent over time but their memory for peripheral, irrelevant details or surrounding/circumstantial information tends to be less accurate. Easterbrook (1959) suggested that arousal may *narrow* the focus of attention so that memory for central details will improve, at the cost of memory for peripheral details. The notion of attention narrowing has been used to explain the phenomenon of weapon focus.

Christianson (1997), however, suggests that this narrowing of attention may not be simply a perceptual phenomenon, and that a second stage may mediate this 'tunnelling' effect. A mode of processing may be adopted that assists our memory of central detail information, but inhibits our memory for details that are irrelevant or spatially peripheral to the event. He uses the term '**tunnel memory**' to refer to the process of narrowed attention and heightened psychological focus on certain details of the traumatic event. This has been investigated in studies using a variety of emotional stimuli, including accidents and violent crimes. It is proposed that in order to make sense of these scenes, we process in an elaborate way those details causing us emotional stress. The emotional reaction we experience may then act as a **retrieval cue** for bringing

Tunnel memory
A term used to describe the narrowing of attention and the heightened psychological focus on certain aspects of a traumatic event.

Retrieval cue
A cue or prompt that may help us to find the information we are trying to retrieve from memory.

to mind details about the emotion-provoking event. Tunnel memory effects have been found to lessen over time, possibly as the emotional stress lessens, providing support for the notion that the 'tunnelling' is a memory process rather than solely a perceptual process.

2.4 The influence of witness characteristics

If there are multiple witnesses to a crime, who should the police interview? Might one witness provide more reliable evidence than another witness? Many factors have been explored in relation to the witness, in particular personality, sex and age. Kapardis (1997) reviews the evidence regarding the influence of a range of personality characteristics. Much of this evidence tends to consider performance on face identification tasks and the findings are rather tentative. In many cases, the personality characteristic is thought to influence arousal and as we have seen it is not always clear how this impacts on witness testimony. For example, neuroticism (a concept from personality theory, characterised by such traits as anxiety and emotional instability) may interact with arousal level to influence memory. The identification accuracy of those low in neuroticism has been found to increase as arousal increases from low to moderate, but the reverse was observed for those high in neuroticism.

Might experience matter? Would a police officer provide more complete and accurate testimony, should he or she witness a crime? The weight of the evidence suggests that their testimony is no more reliable than that of members of the public. However, a trained police officer may find witnessing a crime less stressful than other people. Remember also that Chapter 4 of this book looked at research on the ability of police officers to detect lies, and noted that generally they are no better than members of the public.

Two witness factors that have received much attention are sex and age – both of which are easily assessed without the administration of a psychological test. With regards to sex, some studies have shown that female participants provide more reliable 'testimony' than males, whereas others have found the reverse or no difference. Such inconsistent findings suggest that differences between males and females vary or disappear depending on the factors surrounding the event that the witnesses are observing and reporting. For example, males have been found to be better than females at remembering details of a violent incident in several different studies, but no difference has been observed between males and females when shown a non-violent incident (e.g. Clifford and Scott, 1978). Then again, differences can emerge according to the type of details being reported. Some have found that females are more often able to remember or reconstruct the precise date of an event, but exhibit more than males the tendency to overestimate the temporal duration of an event. Therefore, while the sex of the witness may impact upon the evidence provided, its influence is by no means clear-cut.

With regards to age, it is known that our vision and hearing may deteriorate notably from around 70 years of age onwards, and there may also be a decline in attention with ageing. All of these (especially quality of vision) will impact upon the completeness and accuracy of eyewitness accounts. However, the majority of research on the role of age in reliable witnessing has concentrated on children (e.g. Ceci and Bruck, 1993). Generally, young children have been found to provide less information than adults, and are less accurate than adults with regards to precise details of time, temporal order, estimates of distance and speed, and estimates of height and weight of people (so they have greater difficulty with those judgements that adults also find difficult). These findings are consistent with research that suggests an improvement in a variety of cognitive skills with age. However, children as young as six years may perform at adult level in their reporting of an event, and this is dependent on a range of factors, including what they are questioned about and how they are questioned. This will be considered in the next section of this chapter.

We have seen in this section that there are many variables that will influence the accuracy and/or completeness of the testimony of a witness. These variables are estimator variables and thus not under the control of legal professionals – knowing their influence does not provide information on how to improve the reliability of the testimony, although it might be used in court to encourage a jury to place more or less weight on a person's evidence. In the next section, we shall examine how the questioning of witnesses, a system variable that is under the control of the police, can positively influence their memory and testimony.

Summary Section 2

- Many different estimator variables may influence someone's memory of a crime they have witnessed.
- Our memory may be quite poor for certain details, either because we are unable to encode sufficient information because of distance or lighting or because we may not be very good at encoding accurately certain details like height and weight, distance, date and duration.
- Our attention may be allocated in a certain way, because of heightened emotion or arousal, so that we may focus on and remember better certain central, critical details of the event.
- With regard to witness characteristics, only age has emerged as a strong predictor of the reliability of the testimony.

3   Questioning witnesses

Asking questions is part of our daily routine – 'Have you got the time?', 'What did you do at school today?', 'Are you listening to anything I'm saying?' – and yet we may never have stopped to consider the effectiveness of the questions we ask. Many different social, cognitive, motivational and cultural factors can influence both the way in which we ask a question, and the way in which we answer other people's questions. Our focus in this section is on questioning as it occurs in the context of an **investigative interview** designed to elicit an account, or evidence, from a person about an event they have witnessed or experienced themselves.

Investigative interview
An interview that aims to retrieve information from the witness's memory, as distinct from other kinds of interviews where memory retrieval is not the objective, such as therapeutic interviews or job interviews.

3.1   Social and cognitive factors in questioning witnesses

In order for someone to be able to answer a question, they must not only be willing to respond, but also be able to do so. As we saw in the preceding section, not everything we 'see' or 'experience' is automatically encoded and stored in memory. Questions will therefore only be successfully answered if the person involved has relevant information available and accessible in memory. However, the social context is influential, too. Social factors can affect the way an adult or child responds to questions. For example, a witness may try to answer a question by giving an answer that they think the interviewer wants them to. Witnesses may even give a reply to a question that is patently nonsense. Hughes and Grieve (1980) asked five- and seven-year-olds 'bizarre' questions such as 'Is red heavier than yellow?' and found that virtually all of the children answered all of the questions.

Box 7.3 presents a study of one social factor – the role of embarrassment.

7.3	*The role of embarrassment in reports of intimate touching*

Saywitz *et al.* (1991) examined children's memory for a real event that involved intimate touch, in an attempt to mimic some aspects of the experience and reporting of child sexual abuse. Although previous research suggested that older girls (e.g. seven-year-olds) would give more accurate and complete reports of the event than younger peers (e.g. five-year-olds), other studies on embarrassment suggested that five to seven years is a crucial period for developmental changes in embarrassment. Consequently, older girls may be more affected by such social and emotional factors, to the extent that the accuracy and completeness of their reports are inhibited. This would have implications for reports of abuse where it is necessary to talk frankly and precisely about where exactly a child's body has been touched. In the study, therefore, parents of 72 girls aged five and seven years were invited to receive a free doctor's examination for their child. Halfway through the medical, half the children in each age group received an examination of their vagina and anus (the genital condition), while others received an examination of their spine for scoliosis instead (the non-genital condition). One week or one month later, the child was individually interviewed by a female interviewer. The child was asked: 'Tell me everything you can remember about what happened, from beginning to end.' She was then asked to demonstrate what happened in the examination, using anatomical dolls, before being asked some direct and misleading questions about the examination. Saywitz *et al.* predicted that the older girls would provide more complete and accurate information than the younger girls, *except* for their reports of genital touching (due to the inhibiting effects of more advanced social awareness and self-consciousness). The seven-year-olds in the genital condition reported significantly less correct information than seven-year-olds in the non-genital condition, whereas there was no effect of condition on the five-year-olds' reports. Furthermore, the seven-year-olds in the non-genital condition reported significantly more correct details than did five-year-olds in the same condition. There was no significant difference between the two age groups in the genital condition. Thus, both the authors' predictions were supported, and they went on to argue that a 'social-motivational' model of remembering may best explain their findings. Such a model would suggest the possibilities that the older girls were 'editing' their reports, and/or that 'emotional blocking' may have rendered the genital touch information temporarily inaccessible, e.g. due to embarrassment, anxiety or self-consciousness.

We consider the ethical issues raised by this research in Box 7.7.

Cognitive dimensions of questioning have been explored in much more detail than social factors. **Episodic memory** is concerned with specific life events, and for this reason it is episodic memory (or memories) that the interviewer will be trying to access through questioning the witness. For example, in order to pursue particular criminal charges, police interviewers will need to gain sufficiently detailed information about specific elements of the event. This might include details of the identity of an alleged perpetrator and the things that s/he did and said.

In an investigative context, such specifics have further significance, for example in corroborating accounts, and in bolstering the credibility of the witness's account. However, as time goes by, or as we experience an event repeatedly, we tend to lose the contextual information associated

Episodic memory
Memory for specific events (episodes), which includes information about the time and place those events occurred.

with that event such that episodic information is lost whereas semantic information (general information about events without reference to specific contexts or episodes) is retained. It is important, therefore, not to underestimate how difficult it can be for witnesses to retrieve specific information. Furthermore, an **event schema** or **script** has the potential to distort memories, for example by making it very difficult for a person to subsequently distinguish between specific episodes of an event, or by the person relying on inappropriate assumptions about what typically happens. This is especially relevant in the experience and reporting of crimes that follow a common pattern (e.g. repeated child sexual abuse), and special techniques are required in questioning about them. An example of such a technique is asking the witness to begin by describing more notable instances of the repeated event, such as the first or last time, or an occasion that was particularly memorable for some reason (Powell and Thomson, 2001).

One final point to make here is that different sorts of questions can prompt retrieval of information from memory via either *recall* (deliberately bringing something to mind) or *recognition* (recognising that something has been encountered before), depending upon the cues the question contains. **Leading questions**, however, are those that include material that has nothing to do with the witness's actual memory at all, and the respondent may simply repeat the information in the question by way of a response. An example would be asking a witness to a robbery to describe how the perpetrator punched the victim, when the witness has not yet mentioned any physical contact with the victim. Such questions are inextricably linked to the phenomenon of suggestibility, to which we now turn.

3.2 Suggestibility

Suggestibility has been defined by Fundudis (1997) as involving 'the act or process of impressing something (an idea, attitude or desired action) on the mind of another' (p.151). A classic study by Loftus and Palmer (1974) investigated the ability of post-event information (PEI) or, more accurately, *misinformation*, to influence the reports of an event that the witness subsequently gave. Participants were shown a videotaped vehicle accident and were asked questions with a variety of phrasings. For example, some were asked how fast the cars were going when they 'smashed' into each other, whilst others were asked how fast the cars were going when they 'bumped' into each other. Participants gave higher estimates of speed if they were asked the 'smashed' version of the question than if they were asked the 'bumped' version. Remarkably, in a second experiment, 'smashed' participants were also more likely to report seeing broken headlight glass, even though none of the cars' headlights were seen to break on the video.

Event schema/script
Knowledge about particular events or activities which represents what is 'typical' of such events.

Leading questions
Questions that tend to strongly suggest what response is expected, and/or that assume details that have not been provided by the witness.

Suggestibility
Suggestibility involves the act or process of impressing an idea, attitude or desired action upon the mind of another.

The findings of studies such as Loftus and Palmer's relate to the constructive nature of memory (see the Introduction to this chapter) and the concept of an event schema or script. Perhaps the participants could not remember whether there was broken headight glass or not – there were gaps in their memories. These gaps may have been filled in (constructed) with what seemed 'likely' to the participants based on their scripts for car accidents. One would not necessarily expect the headlights to break if the cars had only 'bumped' into each other, but one would certainly expect them to break if the cars 'smashed' into each other.

Note that Loftus and Palmer's experiment was carried out with *adult* witnesses to a videotaped sequence depicting a car accident, yet the term suggestibility has become much more associated with child witnesses, and especially the fallibility of children's memories. Experimental research on suggestibility in adults and children has taken divergent paths: with adults, the issue has become almost a theoretical one, to establish the 'fate' of memory (e.g. 'What is the relationship between the original memory and the suggested information?'); with children, the research questions have been much more practically driven, such as 'What factors affect children's suggestibility in interviews?'

Suggestibility and adult witness research

Elizabeth Loftus has done more than any other psychologist to explore the concept of suggestibility and associated theoretical explanations. After the 1974 study with Palmer, mentioned above, she carried out a second experiment with other colleagues (Loftus *et al.*, 1978) that has also become a classic – see Box 7.4.

7.4 *'Stop/yield' suggestibility study (Loftus et al., 1978)*

Participants viewed a series of slides depicting a car accident at a road junction. The critical slides showed a car moving into a main road that was marked for some participants by a stop sign, and for other participants by a 'yield' (give way) sign. In a subsequent interview with each participant, the sign was described by the interviewer either correctly or incorrectly (i.e. if the participant saw a stop sign it was incorrectly described as a yield sign, and vice versa). Finally, all participants were asked to indicate which slides they had seen originally, choosing between two alternatives – for the critical slides, selecting between slides with a stop or yield sign. When the original slide and the information in the interviewer's questions were consistent, participants selected the correct slide on 75 per cent of occasions. When the PEI in the interviewer's question was misleading (incorrect), witnesses selected the correct slide just 41 per cent of the time.

Critical slides used in the 'stop/yield' suggestibility study

Loftus's studies (and a multitude that followed in a similar vein) pose interesting questions about the mechanism by which such memory failures occur, and the role of misleading PEI. Different interpretations of suggestibility effects are possible:

- The 'new' information from the PEI might *replace* the original memory: the original memory is lost, or had already been forgotten, and the suggestion is accepted as 'true'.
- The 'new' information from the PEI might *merge* with or alter the original memory: what is remembered is a combination of the 'true' original memory and 'false' PEI.
- The 'new' information from the PEI might *coexist* with the original memory: both the 'true' original information and the PEI are remembered separately.

Only the interpretation that both the original and the suggested information *coexist* in memory indicates that it might be possible to retrieve the original correct information from memory with sensitive questioning (subject to other conditions, e.g. the delay between witnessing an event and reporting it). Interestingly, however, recent biological evidence has implied that in fact original memories may be overwritten by, or 'blended' with, newer memories such as the suggested information (Nader *et al.*, 2000). In studies of auditory fear conditioning in rats, researchers demonstrated that even established learned associations (effectively, the rats' memories) between a tone (conditioned stimulus) and a shock (unconditioned stimulus) could be disrupted by injecting an antibiotic into the amygdala of the rats' brains. This injection affects the process of protein synthesis that consolidates or lays down memories in the brain. Until this research, it was thought that once the memories were consolidated, they would be impervious to such injections. However, it now seems, for the fear response in rats at least, that each time a memory is retrieved it becomes 'labile' (unstable and open to change) biologically and susceptible to destruction. Further research is required to fully understand this innovative experimental procedure and, importantly, the implications for other types of memory in other species.

Suggestibility and child witness research

Stephen Ceci has been at the forefront of research into children's suggestibility (e.g. Bruck and Ceci, 1999; Ceci and Bruck, 1993). In a series of studies, Ceci and his colleagues have raised concerns about the particular vulnerability of pre-school children to suggestive questioning. Boxes 7.5 and 7.6 examine two such studies in more detail.

7.5 *The 'Sam Stone' study (Leichtman and Ceci, 1995)*

Two groups of children aged three to six years old received a visit at their school from a stranger called Sam Stone. Prior to the visit, one group (the experimental group) had received stereotypical information about Sam Stone through 12 different stories that depicted him as a very clumsy person. The other group of children (the control group) received no stereotyping information. All children were asked to describe Sam Stone's (non-eventful) visit on four separate occasions over a 10-week period. The experimental group's first interviews contained questions with erroneous suggestions, such as 'When Sam Stone ripped the book, was he being silly or was he angry?' (he didn't rip a book); the control group's questions were non-suggestive. At a fifth and final interview with a new interviewer, all children in both groups were asked about two 'non-events' that involved Sam Stone doing something to a teddy bear and a book.

Only 10 per cent of the control group of three- to four-year-olds claimed that Sam Stone did anything to a book or a teddy bear, a figure which was reduced to 5 per cent when asked if they actually saw him do the misdeeds. In comparison, 46 per cent of three- to four-year-olds in the experimental group spontaneously reported that Sam Stone did one or both of the misdeeds, a figure which rose to 72 per cent in response to specific questions, with 44 per cent stating that they actually saw him do these things.

These findings are interpreted to show that, when questioned suggestively and with a negative stereotype about an individual, pre-schoolers are susceptible to leading questions. In the absence of leading questions or a stereotype, even these three- to four-year-old children were quite accurate in their reports, despite being subjected to repeated interviews.

| 7.6 | *The 'mousetrap study' (Ceci* et al., *1994)* |

Ceci and colleagues interviewed pre-schoolers over 10 consecutive weeks, on each occasion asking the children to think about events that had actually happened to them (e.g. an accident that resulted in stitches) and also about fictitious events they had not experienced (e.g. getting a finger caught in a mousetrap and having to go to hospital to have it removed). At each interview the children were asked if each of the real and fictitious events had ever happened to them (e.g. 'Think real hard, and tell me if this ever happened to you: Can you remember going to the hospital with the mousetrap on your finger?'). After 10 weeks, 58 per cent of the children gave an account of one or more of the fictitious events, with 25 per cent of children giving accounts of the majority of the false events. 'Thus the mere act of repeatedly imagining participation in an event caused these pre-schoolers to falsely report that they had engaged in the fictitious event.' (Ceci *et al.*, 2001, p. 120). This study makes an interesting link to the literature on adults' suggestibility and the mechanisms underlying suggestibility and memory distortion, such as monitoring the source of one's memories (i.e. real or imagined) and social compliance.

In brief, Ceci *et al.* have found that young children can be suggestible in the following circumstances (Bruck and Ceci, 1999; Ceci *et al.*, 2001):

- When the interviewer repeatedly makes false suggestions (through misleading questions) and creates stereotypes about a person (the 'perpetrator').
- When they are asked repeatedly to visualise fictitious events.
- When they are asked about personal events that happened a long time previously and their memory has not been 'refreshed' since.
- When they are asked in a suggestive or leading manner to re-enact an event using anatomically detailed dolls.
- When they are questioned by a biased interviewer who pursues a 'hypothesis' or line of questioning single-mindedly.

Activity 7.5

Before reading on, make two lists: (1) of any methodological issues, and (2) of any ethical issues that you have noted in the child witness studies reported so far in this section of the chapter. When you have finished, compare your lists to the issues that are highlighted in Box 7.7.

7.7 Some methodological and ethical issues in child witness studies of questioning

Earlier we commented on the ethical issues involved when simulating experiences of violent crime. Similar interlinked ethical and methodological issues arise in the study of questioning child witnesses. In general, psychologists want to avoid questioning witnesses about an event portrayed on paper, slides or videotape, for fear that the stimulus is too far removed from the reality of an actual event. Often, as in the Sam Stone study (Box 7.5), researchers will instead set up a staged event, where they can plan exactly what will happen and then videotape it when it does, so that they have a record for later comparison with the witnesses' answers to questions.

Even staged events can be criticised for their lack of ecological validity, however. Psychologists such as Karen Saywitz and Gail Goodman and their colleagues (Box 7.3) have availed themselves of 'naturally occurring' events such as medical examinations, where it is possible to have some record of what has happened. Much research on questioning has been driven by concerns about child sexual abuse, but it is ethically unacceptable and methodologically impossible to record a child being abused for the purposes of research on how that child might later respond to different types of questions.

Certain elements of the abuse experience, however, such as pain, anxiety and bodily touch, are present in experiences such as hospital examinations. Some psychologists have therefore sought permission from children, their parents, and clinical staff to record such examinations (and sometimes to manipulate certain aspects of the examination) and later interview the children involved – think back to the study by Saywitz et al. (Box 7.3), for example. Even here, though, ethical issues arise, such as the appropriateness of recruiting children through offers of free medical examinations, and questioning children who may be stressed by their experience. Indeed, Stephen Ceci once reported having to stop a pilot study that involved his own daughter because she became distressed and vomited when trying to answer questions about secret touching (Ceci, 1992). Additionally, in the Saywitz et al. study (and many others), children were explicitly asked about genital and anal touch, in the context of an interview about their medical. Further concerns that have been highlighted by Ceci et al.'s 'mousetrap' study (Box 7.4) and others like it (Pezdek, 1998) are the potential for researchers to permanently alter children's autobiographical memory, and also to damage participants' self-esteem when they realise later that they have been deceived (e.g. that they really believed something had happened when it had not).

This type of research highlights the dilemmas facing ethical committees who approve or veto such research projects. As well as considering possible problems for participants, committees must also consider the potential benefits of research. For example, it could be argued that the resultant knowledge is essential in order to inform and improve the experience of questioning for genuine child witnesses and victims of abuse. In this respect, it is notable that pioneers like Saywitz, Goodman and Ceci have been at the forefront of policy and practice initiatives in this area.

3.3 Types of questions put to adults and children

Even a very willing and verbally proficient witness will probably need to be questioned at some point. This is because what individuals freely recall about an event tends to be very limited in *quantity*, even if it is typically very high in *quality*. Experimental studies in which adults or children have been questioned about a staged event (i.e. the experimenter knows exactly what the participant witnessed or experienced) reveal that only a small proportion of relevant detail is offered without any sort of prompting (perhaps no more than 20 per cent of the total amount of possible information), but typically it is very high in accuracy (usually 80 per cent or more accurate). In a forensic context it is the specific details that a witness gives that may be vital in identifying a perpetrator or in pursuing a specific criminal charge. Unfortunately, it is precisely this level of detail and completeness that is typically missing from a freely recalled account. However, asking questions has associated costs: the more focused and (especially) the more leading the questions become, the greater the risk of errors and inaccuracies in the witness's account, and the greater the risk of damaging the witness's credibility at court.

A typology of questions

Research on questioning in an investigative context has been largely shaped by the attention on suggestibility, and has therefore mostly been focused on interviewing child witnesses (e.g. Lamb *et al.*, 2001). Before reading on, try Activity 7.6.

Activity 7.6

Below is a short extract from an experimental study in which children aged 9–11 years old were individually interviewed about a videotaped event they had seen a few days previously (Westcott, 1999). Read the extract, and make a note of the different ways in which the questions are phrased (e.g. how general or specific they are). The use of (.) in the transcript denotes a pause in the nine-year-old girl's speech.

Q: What happened on the video?

A: A girl went to school and her mum dropped her off at school and she started drawing a hopscotch and a lady came and she said 'me and my husband are lost' and 'could you show me some directions' and the um the girl told um the directions and um the lady goes um 'could you come in the car and show me the way' and um the girl goes um 'no' and then she saw the lady saw a policeman and then um the lady went in the car and then they drove off.

Q: Okay, what else can you tell me about the video?

A: (.) Don't know.

Q: Anything else?

A: No.

Q: Okay, tell me what the girl looked like.

A: She had browney blondish hair and um (.) she had a dress and then some shoes and socks and um (.)

Q: What colour were her clothes?

A: Red I think.

Q: Were they all red, her shoes and her socks and her dress?

A: Er, her shoes were black I think and her socks were white and her dress was red.

Q: Anything else about her clothes, the girl's clothes?

A: (.)

Q: How young or old was the girl?

A: She looked about eight.

Q: How tall or short was she?

A: She was medium.

Q: What colour was her hair?

A: Blondey brown.

Q: Was she black or white?

A: White.

Q: Anything else about the girl?

A: No.

In Activity 7.6 you should have noted how different questions vary in the degree to which they sought open or focused responses from the child. You may have spotted some poor questioning; how would you interpret a 'yes' response to the question 'Were they all red, her shoes and her socks and her dress?' Fortunately, this child was able to identify and answer all these sub-questions separately. You might like to look back on this activity after you have finished reading the following definitions of different question types.

The first question in Activity 7.6 – 'What happened on the video? – is an example of an **open question** that requires information to be *recalled*. It does not prescribe the witness's response in any specific way, and because of this, is most likely to get the most accurate information. Most of the 'Wh-' questions – what, when, where and who – would be classified as open questions. Lamb and his colleagues (2001) have found throughout their studies of child witness interviews that open-ended questions lead to responses that are three to four times longer, and three times richer in relevant details, than responses to other types of questions. **Facilitators**, such as 'okay', 'hmm', are designed to encourage the witness to continue their account. Since they, too, are non-leading and non-specific, they can also be effective at maintaining the witness's narrative without decreasing the accuracy of the account.

Focused questions direct the witness to search their memory for details or aspects of the event that they have mentioned previously. They may be open-ended or cued invitations to recall *specific* information. For example, 'Tell me what the girl looked like' in the extract above is a focused question (actually, an imperative or order), since the child being interviewed has mentioned the girl already, but not what she looked like. Focused questions may increase the number of details provided by the witness, but usually reduce the accuracy of the witness's account overall (e.g. if the witness relies on an erroneous script to provide specifics, or guesses to please the interviewer). In the study from which the extract is taken, for example, the girl the witness is describing was not wearing a dress nor were any of her clothes red.

Option-posing questions involve recognition, such as 'Was she black or white?' in the extract above. They limit the response the witness can provide (here, to 'black' or 'white'), and are also likely to focus on aspects of the event that the witness has not already mentioned. In this way, they may also be considered 'leading', but the term leading question is usually reserved for questions that strongly suggest what response is sought from the witness, or assume details that the witness has not yet provided. Leading questions (defined at the end of Section 3.1) are those seen as most problematic by both psychologists and lawyers in terms of the limited value they can add (and damage they can do) to a witness's account. They can also damage the credibility of the witness's statement. The possibility that the witness is not answering from memory at all, but is simply repeating information contained in the question, cannot be discounted.

Open questions
Questions that seek an open-ended response from the witness, and that do not limit, focus or direct the witness's response except in the most general way.

Facilitators
Non-suggestive verbal or non-verbal prompts that encourage the witness to continue recalling.

Focused questions
Questions that focus the witness's attention on details or aspects of the event that the witness has previously described.

Option-posing questions
Questions that limit the response the witness can give to specific options, and that usually focus on aspects of the event which the witness has not already described.

Interview questioning in practice

There is a consensus among psychologists and lawyers that, wherever possible, open questions should be used preferentially by investigative interviewers, and that leading questions should be avoided as much as possible. Such advice is contained in many guides to interviewing that can apply to adults or children. So, do investigative interviewers follow this advice in practice?

The answer appears to be 'not really'. Sternberg *et al.* (2001) analysed over a hundred recent investigative interviews carried out by police officers and social workers with child witnesses in England and Wales, and found a similar pattern of results to those from interviews with children in Sweden, Israel and the USA. Trained raters classified the types of questions used in interview transcripts with 119 children aged 4–13 years old. Interviewers asked few open questions (6 per cent), rather more facilitators (13 per cent), many focused questions (47 per cent) and option-posing questions (29 per cent), and some leading questions (5 per cent). More research should assess why it is that interviewers do not question children in the manner advocated by guidance based on psychological research. Emerging evidence suggests that training, monitoring and supporting interviewers requires more attention and resources.

Köhnken (1995) sought to suggest ways of improving investigative interviews with adults by addressing the needs of the interviewer and the interviewee. In asking why interviewers do not perform at their best, Köhnken highlights the need to reduce their **cognitive load**, in order to increase the likelihood that they can process more information in the particular interview with which they are currently involved. He suggests the following ways of reducing cognitive load:

Cognitive load
The burden placed upon a person's resources by various cognitive processes (e.g. memorising, attending) that may be taking place simultaneously during a task.

- Making interviewing skills require automatic as opposed to controlled attentional processing, through appropriate training and practice.

- Audio or video recording the interview to remove the need for the interviewer to take detailed notes contemporaneously.

- Collecting as much detail about the case in hand before the interview, and planning the interview in the light of this information, to reduce the amount of information that has to be processed in the interview itself.

This section has demonstrated the importance of sharing knowledge between psychologists researching from different perspectives. It is also important that professional practising psychologists (e.g. clinical or counselling psychologists), and other practitioners too, contribute. You may have noticed, for example, that we have not touched upon witnesses' experiences of being questioned in this chapter. As you may imagine, ethical issues in approaching and interviewing real witnesses are paramount and can be prohibitive to researchers. However, the input of clinical psychologists and social work practitioners on topics such as the witness's experience has been essential in the collaborative effort to improve the services provided for witnesses, such as the development of sensitive interviewing guidelines and preparation for court programmes (see Section 5 below).

Another positive example of the collaboration between psychology researchers and practitioners is the development of the cognitive interview (CI), which was devised originally around four mnemonic techniques: mental reinstatement of context, reporting everything without editing, recalling events in a variety of orders, and recalling from different perspectives. Fisher and Geiselman (1992) later revised the CI to incorporate more general (and social psychological) interviewer behaviours, such as rapport building and active listening. Most of the enhancements are aimed at improving the witness's experience in the interview, with a view to increasing the quality of the evidence they then provide. Many interviewing protocols resemble the revised CI. For example, police interviewers in the UK are trained in investigative interviewing, which incorporates many aspects of the CI.

3.4 Questioning witnesses in the laboratory and the field – complementary methodological approaches

In this section we have discussed results that stem from both *experimental* and *field studies* of questioning. Both have their advantages and disadvantages. In an experiment, the researcher sets up the event to be witnessed, and usually records it if it is live, so that s/he knows exactly what happened. When witnesses later recall the event, the experimenter is able to record exactly what correct, incorrect and false details the witness reports, so that the accuracy and completeness of different aspects of the event (e.g. person details versus action details) in response to different sorts of questions can be calculated precisely. However, as we have already indicated, this approach is open to criticism on the grounds of ecological validity, which is applied to most experimental work. For example, Ceci's work is designed to mimic aspects of interviews for child sexual abuse. How far can studies such as those of Sam Stone or the 'mousetrap' (Boxes 7.5 and 7.6) contribute to our knowledge of questioning in this area?

The work of Lamb, Sternberg and colleagues (Lamb *et al.*, 2001; Sternberg *et al.*, 2001), in which they have extensively studied transcripts of real interviews (again, mostly for suspected child sexual abuse), is an example of field research. Here, the researchers can be confident that they are describing actual practice in this area. However, Lamb *et al.* do not know what actually happened to any of the children being interviewed, so they are unable to say how accurate, or forensically useful, the child's responses to different sorts of questions are. Lamb *et al.* therefore bolster their statements about the superiority of open questions with reference to experimental studies that have demonstrated that such questions (when asked of staged or videotaped events) lead to greater accuracy in children's reports.

3.5 Some questions about questioning research

Various criticisms could be raised about the approach to researching questioning that has typically been taken by psychologists, emanating most notably from the perspective of social constructionism (the idea that the way we understand the world is constructed between people in social interactions). For example, within the experimental paradigm typically employed, children are portrayed as passive 'responders' rather than as active participants and the role of the interviewer/researcher with regard to the interviewing task is not problematised. In contrast, researchers from a constructionist perspective would argue that any interview is *co-constructed* by both participants, and that the meaning of the interview responses emerges from this interaction. Further, it is essential to consider the wider context within which the interview or interaction takes place.

Let us return to the research on bizarre questions introduced in Section 3.1, wherein children apparently attempted to answer questions which were unanswerable or nonsense (e.g. 'Is red heavier than yellow?'). Waterman *et al.* (2001) recently investigated the original Hughes and Grieve (1980) design in a way that makes the impact of the interview context on child witnesses' apparent competence very clear. Briefly, Waterman and colleagues examined the impact of question type (i.e. open or closed) on both sensible and nonsensical questions. Waterman *et al.*'s refinements revealed that, in fact, children do not answer all nonsensical questions, and that if the question is phrased in an open format (rather than requiring a simple 'yes' or 'no' answer) the majority of children indicate that they do not understand, or do not know the answer. Further, asking children to explain their answers when they did respond to nonsense questions showed that 'no' was often used to indicate that the child thought the question was silly. In many psychological experiments, the researcher does not explore (or at least does not report on) what children thought they were doing in the experimental interview. Offering them such an opportunity affords further insight as this example shows.

The emphasis on children's evidence, which stems partly from public concern about child abuse, is also problematic. Few of the psychologists researching or practising in the field of children's evidence collaborate with those studying or working with adult witnesses, and vice versa.

Thus developmental issues are rarely comprehensively addressed in psychological research on witnessing. Similarly, problems facing older children and young people are overlooked as a result of the preoccupation (especially in US research) with pre-school children's evidence. However, in practice, research findings tend to be treated as applicable to all groups.

There is also the problem that weaknesses in witness memory have come to be linked almost exclusively to children's evidence. This has major implications for the way children are perceived in courts, and for the manner in which the research agenda is shaped for both adult and child witnesses. We know very little, for example, about the individual characteristics of adult or child witnesses who are able to resist suggestions, or about other issues that are highly relevant to forensic practice, such as motivation. For example, much of the concern about children's memory concentrates on their potential to give false evidence (look back to the Ceci studies in Boxes 7.5 and 7.6), yet we know from child witnesses in abuse cases that very often their problem lies in revealing *too little* about what has happened for reasons such as fear or mistrust (e.g. Wade and Westcott, 1997). This can then create problems when other evidence comes to light: child's testimony in court is consequently perceived to be less credible as the defence highlights inconsistencies between what the child originally said and the newer evidence that is now also available.

Summary Section 3

- In this section we have considered the types and impact of different questions as system variables.
- Psychologists have researched cognitive factors in questioning, such as script memory and suggestibility, as well as some social factors, such as embarrassment.
- Suggestibility research with adults has concentrated on theoretical mechanisms that might explain the effects of PEI. Suggestibility research with children has instead concentrated on the importance of questioning in increasing suggestibility effects.
- Different types of questions can influence how accurate and complete a witness' response may be.
- Research on questioning adults and children raises many theoretical, methodological and ethical issues.

4 Identifying perpetrators: the role of the witness

In this section we consider the assistance that a witness may give to the police in revealing the identity of a perpetrator. The procedures that the police employ to elicit this help are system variables, and hence controllable. In some cases, where the available evidence does not suggest a suspect, the witness may be asked to search through mug-shot albums containing photographs of known offenders. Alternatively, a **composite image** of the perpetrator may be constructed with the help of the witness, and this is then publicised in the media in the hope that someone familiar with the perpetrator will see the composite image and identify him or her. In other cases, where the available evidence does suggest a suspect, the witness may be asked to attend a live identification parade and attempt to identify the perpetrator.

Composite image
A likeness of the face of a perpetrator, which is constructed by the witness with a police operator.

The accuracy with which a witness can later identify the perpetrator of a crime has received considerable psychological attention. It is not only a task that can be investigated experimentally, attracting the interest of those already investigating face perception, but also an important issue due to the false convictions that have been uncovered with the introduction of DNA testing. In the period up to March 1994, in 36 of the 40 cases in the US in which people were freed because DNA evidence showed they could not have been the perpetrator, it was eyewitness identification evidence that had led to their convictions (Wells *et al.*, 1999). Huff (1987) suggested that erroneous eyewitness identification is the cause of nearly 60 per cent of cases of mistaken convictions, and Penrod and Cutler (1999), using archival data in the US, estimated that there could be as many as 4500 erroneous convictions per year resulting from mistaken identifications. In this section, we shall examine the procedures used by the police to obtain identification evidence and consider why identification may be problematic.

4.1 Identification procedures: where the identity of the suspect is not known

Eliciting descriptions: the use of composites

In some crime cases, the only lead that the police have is a witness's memory of the perpetrator. The description obtained by the police from the witness can then be publicised and/or used for the purposes of a computer search of a database containing photographic images. If this process does lead to the identification of a suspect, then a live identification parade usually takes place.

The crucial question is: what is the best way to obtain the image the witness has in his or her memory of the face of the perpetrator? While words can be used to describe information about the body, our vocabulary is rather limited when it comes to conveying the physical aspects of the face.

Activity 7.7   Describing a face

Think of someone you know well (but whom you can't see at the moment) and write down a description of his or her face. Then look at this description and see if it also fits the face of anyone else you know or, say, someone you may have seen on television.

To assist in the process of translating the witness's visual memory of the perpetrator's face into an image that can be used to find a suspect, the police have employed artists to obtain a pictorial representation. In the early 1970s, however, a package known as 'PhotoFIT', which someone without artistic skills could use, became available. This system comprised numerous black-and-white prints of facial features (hairlines/ears, eyes/eyebrows, nose, mouth and chin/cheeks). Based on their verbal description, the witnesses would be shown a choice of such features and asked to select the ones that best represented those of the perpetrator. The selected photographed features were then physically blended together, as in a collage. The quality of the end result depended on the skill of the police officer and the extent to which the image was artistically enhanced, rather than being directly related to the witness's memory (e.g. Gibling and Bennett, 1994).

With improvements in technology, computerised versions of composite systems took over from PhotoFIT. These systems, which include E-FIT (Electronic Facial Identification Technique), contain a much larger database of facial features. The procedure usually followed by E-FIT operators starts with an interview of the witness, using the cognitive interview (outlined in Section 3.3). The information given about the face by the witness is entered into the computer, which displays a complete facial image. The witness then suggests alterations to this image until they are unable to improve it any further. The final stage involves transferring the image into an image manipulation package, where minor alterations can be performed such as adding freckles.

The important point to note about this procedure is that it involves the witness working on a whole face, avoiding a feature-by-feature build-up of the composite. Laboratory research on face perception has shown that it is much harder to recognise a facial feature when it is seen on its own than when it is part of the whole face (e.g. Tanaka and Farah, 1993). Also, since we perceive the face as more than simply a collection of individual features, the relative position of the features is very important as well (e.g. Diamond and Carey, 1986).

Activity 7.8

If you have seen films starring Tom Cruise, the American actor, then you may have noticed his rather distinctive nose. Can you spot it below? (See end of chapter for the answer.)

Spot Tom Cruise's nose

It is important to remember that the final composite image is not an exact copy of the face – it is a 'picture description' or 'type-likeness'. The composite is created in the hope that by showing it to the public, someone familiar with the perpetrator will identify the person depicted and provide the police with a lead.

Activity 7.9   Recognising composites of famous faces

The image below shows composite images created using E-FIT of three well-known faces (Brace *et al.*, 2000). Can you identify any of them? (You may not be familiar with all three but you may recognise one or two of the images. See end of chapter for the answers.)

E-FITs of well-known faces

The systems that the police use to create composites will continue to benefit from changes in technology. For example, at some point we are likely to see in the newspapers composites of the same perpetrator but depicting different views (e.g. profile, three-quarter profile and full face). Indeed, on the television or the internet we may even see a moving composite, where the facial image turns to show all viewpoints or is shown to speak. This technology is, at the moment, in development, but its development is being informed by psychological research on how people perceive and remember faces.

Searching through photographs: the mug-shot book

Another procedure that can be used in cases where the suspect is not known is to show the witness photographs of known offenders, collected by the police. If the witness spots a possible suspect, he or she and any other witnesses may be asked to attend an identification parade. Recognising someone from a photograph is not, however, an easy task. A photograph is a two-dimensional image capturing the face in a particular pose and from a particular viewpoint.

Research conducted in the laboratory examining face recognition has shown that pose, angle, expression and lighting can all influence recognition accuracy. Furthermore, a change in medium, for example from seeing someone live to then seeing a photograph of the person, is likely to reduce recognition rate. Kemp *et al.* (1997) found evidence suggesting that when we are not familiar with someone, we may not be good at matching a photograph to them (see Box 7.8).

7.8　*Matching photographs to people*

The experiment carried out by Kemp *et al.* (1997) involved 44 participants who acted as 'shoppers' and presented credit cards depicting a small 2 cm x 2 cm colour photograph etched onto the card. These were identical to real photo credit cards manufactured by certain banks and building societies. For each shopper, four cards were created, each with a different photograph:

- *Unchanged appearance*: the photograph was of the shopper as they appeared during the experiment.
- *Changed appearance*: the photograph was of the shopper after minor modification (different hairstyle, removal of facial hair, or addition/removal of eye-glasses or jewellery).
- *Matched foil*: the photograph was of someone else but of similar appearance.
- *Unmatched foil*: the photograph was of someone who did not look like the shopper but was of the same sex and ethnic group.

An example of four such photographs is shown on the following page. (NB: these photographs are in black and white and not colour as on the credit card.)

unchanged appearance

changed appearance

matched foil

unmatched foil

Photographs chosen for one shopper

The 'shoppers' used their credit cards to 'purchase' a small amount of goods from a supermarket that volunteered to provide access after official closing. Six cashiers and two supervisors participated in the study, and they processed the shopping of the participants in the normal way. The cashiers were briefed to challenge any 'shopper' they thought was showing them a credit card that belonged to someone else and as an incentive to make such a challenge were informed of a bonus depending on the speed and 'accuracy' with which they processed the 'shopping'. The participants were instructed as to which credit card to present to which cashier, but as the cards were in wallets they were 'blind' as to whether or not they were presenting a 'fraudulent' card (i.e. a card with a photograph that was not of themselves). Each cashier was approached by a participant only once.

The results showed that the cashiers were poor at challenging participants showing cards with a photograph of someone else who bore a resemblance to them. The correct decision rate to reject the card showing the *matched foil* was approximately

36 per cent. Even when the photograph was of someone who bore no particular resemblance to the participant but was of the same sex and apparent ethnic group, the *unmatched foil,* the correct decision rate to reject the card was only approximately 66 per cent.

One way of overcoming the limitations of showing photographs would be to start compiling a database of video-frames or video films; advances in computer technology may provide the answer here. With sophisticated compression techniques, it is possible to store, retrieve and play digitised video sequences. However, for the police, the major problem with these 'mug-shot searches' concerns the very large number of images that would be found in the pool from which the subset would be drawn and then shown to the witness. Experimental work (e.g. Laughery *et al.*, 1971) has found that the more photographs participants are exposed to the less likely they are to spot the photograph of a target (someone they had seen previously). Methods are therefore being devised that can sort the photographs so that the image of the perpetrator will be brought close to the beginning of the search (e.g. Levi *et al.*, 1995).

It is worth bearing in mind that the purpose of using photographic images as an investigative tool is to suggest possible suspects (the witness can select more than one image). Below we will see that photographs and video clips can also be used in other identification procedures.

4.2 Identification procedures: where the police have a suspect

While the composite may have no evidential value, other identification evidence may be used in court or to eliminate a suspect from an investigation. There are different kinds of identification evidence, however, and which of them is considered a lawful means of identification may vary from country to country. In England and Wales, at the time of writing, they include the following:

- Live identification parades, where the witness sees the suspect and at least eight other people who, as far as possible, resemble the suspect.
- Group identification, where the witness is given the opportunity of seeing the suspect in a group of people.
- Video film identification, where the witness is shown a video film of the suspect along with video film of eight other people who resemble the suspect.
- Confrontations, where the suspect is confronted by the witness, normally in a room in a police station. In England and Wales, this only takes place if the other procedures described above are not practicable.

A live identification parade

In some countries, where communities are small and widely spaced, it is often impossible for the police to put on a live identification parade. Identifications can instead be made from photo-arrays, where the witness sees a photograph of the suspect and a number of other photographs of people matched to the suspect.

Research conducted in the laboratory has pointed to three factors (system variables) that may influence identification accuracy in live identification parades: instructions, procedure and structure.

First, several studies have shown that indicating through instructions that the perpetrator 'is in' the line-up, rather than saying that he/she 'may be' present, increases the rate of mistaken identification (e.g. Cutler *et al.*, 1987). Second, studies have compared a sequential procedure for presenting the line-up members – where the witness looks at each member one at a time – with the traditional simultaneous line-up method where all members are seen together. Results have revealed that if the target is not in the parade, participants tend to be more likely to identify a **foil** (a member of the parade who is not the suspect) in the simultaneous line-up condition than in the sequential condition (e.g. Cutler and Penrod, 1995).

Third, and perhaps more importantly, the structure of the line-up must be 'fair' so that there is a reasonable degree of resemblance between all parade members. The difficulty here is whether the foils in the line-up should be chosen to resemble the suspect (the procedure used in England or Wales), or whether they should match the general description of the culprit as provided by the witness. Some have argued that to select the foils in the line-up on the basis of their similarity to the suspect creates an unnecessary similarity between the foils and the suspect. Wright and Davies (1999) provide the following example. The witness describes the

Foil
A known innocent stand-in or volunteer, a foil is a member of an identification parade who is not the suspect. Sometimes referred to in research papers as a 'distractor'.

perpetrator as a six-foot tall male with brown curly hair. The police have a *suspect* who fits this description but who also has a scar on his face, something the witness did not mention. If the police select the foils to match the witness's description, and the suspect is innocent, the scar should help safeguard the suspect against being picked out, as the witness has no memory of a scar. Should, however, the suspect be guilty and the witness had failed to mention a scar when providing a description, then this may help the witness correctly identify him as the perpetrator as he is likely to be the only one with a scar (the witness is able to *recognise* the scar, even though they did not *recall* it during their interview). An exception is where this results in the *suspect* 'standing out' in some way. In the above example, should the suspect be five feet six inches tall rather than six feet tall, then choosing the foils all to be six footers would make the suspect stand out.

A survey conducted for the Home Office in 1994 revealed that an estimated 30 per cent of identification parades failed to take place, some of them because a 'fair' parade could not be arranged. Furthermore, of those taking place, over 60 per cent of witnesses stated that less than half the parade members resembled the person who committed the crime (Home Office, 1994). Selection of suitable foils is clearly a problematic issue in real cases. An alternative system called VIPER (Video Identification Parade Electronic Recording) has been developed by the West Yorkshire Police Service (see Box 7.9) in an attempt to address this.

7.9 VIPER (Video Identification Parade Electronic Recording)

The VIPER system allows a sequence of the suspect's face turning slowly from side to side to be digitally captured on videotape. A video parade can then be constructed by allowing the suspect to choose the foils from a suitable selection drawn from a very large database. Research has revealed that the VIPER system overcomes the problem of finding foils, and suffers far fewer cancellations than live parades. In addition, seeing a sequence of moving faces in the absence of body cues has not been found to adversely affect identification rates in laboratory research (Pike *et al.*, 2000). Finally, it is far easier to timetable witnesses to see video parades than live identification parades — if necessary the police can take the videotape of the line-up to the witnesses' homes — and video parades could be potentially far less stressful as the witness is not required to confront a 'live' suspect.

4.3 Factors affecting accurate identification

Disguises and changed appearances

One obvious factor that influences identification is the likelihood that the perpetrator will have changed his or her appearance since committing the crime. It is also likely that an individual will wear some kind of disguise whilst committing a crime. The removal of a wig, hat or spectacles, or a haircut or change to facial hair, will bring about a change in appearance and adversely affect the accurate recognition of unfamiliar faces.

You may have found that you have occasionally failed to recognise someone because of a new hairstyle. However, this is only likely to have happened if you were not very familiar with that person. When we have seen someone on a frequent basis, we often fail to notice such changes; instead sometimes there is just a feeling that the person has changed something about themselves rather than the recognition, say, that they have in fact shaved their beard.

The importance of hair cues was demonstrated in one experiment where participants were shown a videotape of a robbery and then later asked to attempt to identify the 'culprit' in a line-up. In half of the robberies, the robber was not wearing a hat whereas in the other half the robber was wearing a knitted pullover cap that concealed his hair and hairline. Results showed that identification accuracy was significantly impaired when the participants had seen the disguised robber (Cutler *et al.*, 1987).

Although it is possible for a culprit to alter his or her appearance in the period intervening the crime and the identity parade, it is much more difficult for them to alter their voice. Is it possible then that voice identification may be more accurate than face identification? (See Box 7.10.)

7.10 *Voice identification/Earwitness testimony*

Although far fewer studies have been conducted on voice recognition compared with face recognition, research findings suggest that voice identification should only be used with extreme caution in legal contexts. Many factors have been found to influence recognition accuracy, including the length of the utterance, the delay between listening to the voice and making the identification, attempts to disguise the voice by whispering or muffling the speech, familiarity with the voice, the number of other voices in the 'voice line-up' and the position of the target voice in the line-up (Wilding *et al.*, 2000).

Verbal overshadowing

Another issue is whether asking the witness to provide a verbal description of the culprit will make it harder for the witness to subsequently identify him or her in the identification parade. Schooler and Engstler-Schooler (1990) showed participants a video of a crime scenario and then asked one group to provide a verbal description of the face of the perpetrator, a second to form a visual image of the target's face, and a third to do nothing. Those who were asked to produce a verbal description were significantly less accurate in choosing the target than the other two groups, whose results were similar. It was suggested that the verbalisation group was biased towards relying on the memory of how they had described the face rather than on their initial visual memory of the face itself because their verbal memory had over shadowed their visual memory. This effect of **verbal overshadowing** has been replicated in subsequent research and resembles the effect of post-event information (PEI) discussed in the previous section.

Verbal overshadowing
A phenomenon where using words to describe memory for non-verbal stimuli, such as a face, interferes with subsequent recognition of those stimuli.

Unconscious transference

The term *unconscious transference* refers to the situation where a witness may misidentify a suspect who is actually innocent because they had indeed seen the innocent suspect before – but not as the perpetrator of the crime. Ross *et al.* (1994) described a real case where a sailor was picked out from a line-up, not because he had committed the crime but because the victim, a railway ticket clerk, had seen the sailor before when selling a ticket to him. In their experimental work, Ross and colleagues found that participants were three times more likely to 'misidentify' a bystander seen in a film of a robbery, than control participants who had seen a version of the film that did not include the bystander. As participants reported that they had knowingly inferred that the bystander and the assailant were the same person, the term *conscious inference* was used. Research has also considered whether searching through a mug-shot album may negatively impact upon a witness's ability later to identify the culprit in a line-up. Findings suggest that showing participants photographs of 'suspects' will significantly increase the likelihood that they incorrectly pick out an 'innocent suspect' (e.g. Brigham and Cairns, 1988). Rather than identify the 'culprit', they will identify the suspect whose face they had seen before, even though that person may not have been present near the original incident.

The factors that have been outlined here indicate the difficulties witnesses face in providing accurate identification evidence. Box 7.11 considers one possible technological solution.

7.11 *CCTV – a foolproof identification system?*

Can CCTV offer a means of providing irrefutable identification evidence? Is it a technological solution to the error-prone eyewitness identification evidence? Experience suggests that while CCTV cameras may provide invaluable assistance to the police by helping to establish such things as an exact sequence of events, identification from CCTV footage might be problematic for a number of reasons. Usually, identification still involves a human operator who attempts to match the image depicted on the footage with that of a photograph of a known suspect. Although this form of identification does not rely on memory, many of the factors that we have considered in this section will apply here: there may be differences in appearance, lighting conditions, facial expression and viewpoint. Furthermore, the CCTV footage itself may be of very poor quality. Research has found that while these factors will not impede the identification of a familiar person (e.g. Burton *et al.*, 1999), the task is extremely difficult with unfamiliar people (e.g. Bruce *et al.*, 2001) a finding that is consistent with the results of the photo-identity credit card described previously. Bruce *et al.* (1999) have found high error rates, even with good quality images and when viewpoint and facial expressions between the images were as closely matched as possible.

The illustration below shows a full-face target image retrieved from video and an array of full-face photos. This is an example of the type of stimulus material used by Bruce and colleagues. Can you match the target to one of the numbered photos? See the end of the chapter for the answer.

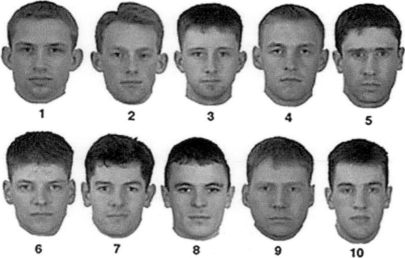

Match the target face to one of the faces in the array

Summary Section 4

- In this section we have focused on one specific aspect of witness testimony, namely perpetrator identification and the procedures used to obtain this evidence – these are system variables.
- We have considered techniques that can be used when the available evidence does not suggest a suspect. Computer technology has assisted in the generation of a composite of the perpetrator, and can help in searching through mug-shots.
- We have also considered the identification procedures that are used when there is a suspect. Research has indicated how instructions, structure and procedure may all influence correct and incorrect identification rates, and we have seen how computer technology has provided an alternative more flexible and faster way of putting together a parade (VIPER).
- Regardless of the identification procedure employed, there are factors that may impinge on the accuracy with which a witness can identify the perpetrator. Neither research on voice identification nor on identifying images from CCTV suggests an alternative more accurate method.

5   Witnesses at court

The particular problems facing witnesses in courts reveal further examples of system variables that can be acted upon through legislative and procedural changes aimed at assisting witnesses. In this section, we shall consider some of the difficulties witnesses encounter in court, and psychologists' involvement in researching and responding to such difficulties. As in Section 3, many of these issues have been highlighted by concerns about the needs of child witnesses in criminal court proceedings, and in adversarial legal systems. First, spend time on Activity 7.10, thinking about whether different groups are likely to experience the same or different problems when appearing as witnesses in court.

Activity 7.10

If you have ever had to appear as a witness at court, did you experience any difficulties in testifying? Perhaps you have acted as a juror, or seen television courtroom dramas. Would you be worried about testifying? Why? Write down what difficulties and fears witnesses might experience in a criminal court. Indicate to what extent you think these would apply to (1) child witnesses, (2) adult witnesses and (3) witnesses who have learning difficulties.

Might they differ further depending on whether the witness is also the victim of the alleged crime?

Come back and evaluate your lists after you have read Section 5.1. Would the special measures described there address concerns you have listed?

The inside of a courtroom

5.1 Witnesses' concerns about appearing in court

Psychologists and welfare professionals have examined witnesses' concerns about their court appearance, especially those reported by children. Spencer and Flin (1993) identified three phases of stress for child witnesses: the experience of the crime itself, the pre-trial period and the trial itself. During the pre-trial period, interviews with children and young people have revealed the following sources of concern (e.g. Freshwater and Aldridge, 1994):

- Repeated delays and rescheduling of cases.
- Lack of knowledge of the legal system.
- Lack of information about, and involvement in, decision making prior to court.

At court, a number of factors were reported as causing anxiety, including:

- Waiting to be called to testify, sometimes for a considerable period of time.
- The formal and unfamiliar layout of the court.
- Seeing the defendant and his/her family and supporters.
- Cross-examination, especially legal jargon ('**legalese**').

Legalese
Lexically and syntactically complicated language that has developed to meet the needs of the legal profession.

Special measures
Specific actions or procedures that may be ordered in respect of some or all categories of eligible witnesses, e.g. use of screens in court, or removal of wigs and gowns.

Following the publication of an influential report, *Speaking Up for Justice* (Home Office, 1998), which documented many of these concerns, the 1999 Youth Justice and Criminal Evidence Act in England and Wales introduced a range of **special measures** to be made available to vulnerable and intimidated child and adult witnesses (subject to certain conditions, such as the nature of the alleged offence). These are listed in Box 7.12.

> **7.12** *Special measures in the 1999 Youth Justice and Criminal Evidence Act*
>
> - Screens to protect the witness from being confronted by the defendant.
> - Live CCTV link to enable the witness to give evidence from outside the court-room.
> - Evidence given in private – press and public may be excluded (except for one named person to represent the press) in cases involving sexual offences or intimidation.
> - Removal of wigs and gowns by barristers and the judge.
> - Video-recorded **evidence-in-chief** taken prior to the court case (i.e. videotape of earlier investigative interview with witness is used instead of requiring the witness to be examined live in court).
> - Video-recorded cross-examination taken prior to the court case (i.e. videotape of previous cross-examination of witness is used instead of requiring the witness to be cross-examined live in court).
> - Examination of the witness through an **intermediary** rather than a barrister.
> - Aids to communication to assist witness, e.g. interpreter or communication aid.
> - Protection of witness from cross-examination by the accused in person.
> - Restrictions on evidence and questions about complainant's sexual behaviour.
> - Provision of **professional social support** to witnesses, both pre-trial and at court.

Evidence-in-chief
The witness's evidence in response to questioning on behalf of the defence or prosecution.

Intermediary
A person approved by the court who communicates to the witness the questions that are put to him or her, and communicates back to the questioner(s) the witness's answers.

Professional social support
Emotional support, information/advice and preparation for court that will assist the witness to give evidence to the best of his/her ability.

These special measures are designed to address social, emotional and cognitive stressors that the witness may face. For example, screens and live links (closed circuit television systems that connect the witness in a room outside the courtroom to the court itself) are used to reduce the anxiety a witness may feel about appearing live in court, either by shielding the witness or by removing them from the courtroom. The permitting of intermediaries and aids to communication recognises that the less developed cognitive abilities of some witnesses (e.g. children and adults with learning difficulties) need to be addressed in order to elicit their testimony appropriately. The underlying assumption is that in prioritising the needs of witnesses (and attending to their welfare) we will increase the likelihood that they will give better-quality evidence in court.

How well do you think such measures address the fears and sources of stress you identified in Activity 7.10 and/or those outlined in Section 5.1? (You may also like to refer back to Chapter 1 on the topic of stress.)

There have been other notable attempts to address witnesses' concerns through preparation for court (e.g. *The Young Witness Pack*, NSPCC/ChildLine, 1998; 'The virtual courtroom', Cooke, 2001). Box 7.13 reports one approach (Saywitz *et al.*, 1993) derived from psychological research on child development and children as witnesses. Saywitz and her colleagues developed a programme of experiments aimed at addressing a number of problems:

- Children's tendency to provide incomplete reports of events.
- Children's failure to comprehend many of the grammatical constructions and vocabulary common in investigative interviews (e.g. legalese, see Section 5.2), and their difficulties in recognising when they do not understand and in asking for clarification.
- Children's susceptibility to misleading questions.
- Children's limited knowledge and experience of the legal system, such that this makes them anxious when testifying.

Saywitz *et al.* developed four separate interventions aimed at addressing each of these problems, using the control possible in experimental settings to evaluate the effectiveness of each. We shall consider the first three in Box 7.13; we have noted some of these problems already in this chapter, and we go on to discuss legalese further in Section 5.2.

7.13 Preparing children for the investigative and judicial process (Saywitz et al., 1993)

Narrative elaboration

Narrative elaboration is a technique to assist children in retelling an event, using five forensically relevant and theoretically driven categories of information: participants; settings; actions; conversations/emotions; and resolution (consequences). The technique aims to make children aware of the type and level of detail required in a forensic context. In the programme of experiments, each of the five categories was represented by a simple drawing on a card. Children practised reporting as much detail as possible about past events, using the cards as a mnemonic device. In the experimental evaluations, children aged six to nine years old experienced a staged event at school, and were then allocated to one of three conditions where they received different training or instructions: narrative elaboration; instruction (instructed to be complete and accurate in retelling, but no category cue cards used); control (no training or instruction). Two weeks after the event, the children were individually interviewed about the event according to their condition. Children receiving narrative elaboration demonstrated a 53 per cent improvement in spontaneous recall over the instruction and control groups (who did not differ from each other), without generating additional errors or negatively affecting their responses to follow-up questions.

Comprehension-monitoring training

This technique was developed to warn children that they may not understand all questions put to them, and to give a rationale as to why some speakers (e.g. lawyers) ask children questions that are difficult to comprehend. Videotaped vignettes were also used to demonstrate negative consequences of trying to answer questions that are not fully understood. In practise sessions, children were taught to identify questions they did not understand and to ask the adult speaker for rephrasing; the children were then given feedback on the accuracy of their reports. Again, six- to eight-year-olds participated in a staged event, and two weeks later were allocated to three conditions before being individually interviewed about the event. The conditions comprised comprehension-monitoring training, rephrase-instructions (children were simply given permission to ask adults to rephrase questions), and control (given only motivating instructions to do their best). Children who received the comprehension-monitoring training were significantly more accurate in their reports than children from either of the other groups.

Resistance training

Resistance training involved a discussion of why children go along with adults' suggestions in questions, as well as teaching children to identify leading questions, mentally compare their memories of an event with the 'guess' put into the leading question by the questioner, answer appropriately after the comparison, and to use self-statements to promote their self-confidence in challenging leading questions (e.g. 'I knew there would be questions like this. I can do it.'). Again, children were individually interviewed two weeks after participation in a staged event, either in a resistance training condition or in a control condition (they received motivating instructions to do their best). As before, the intervention was successful, and children receiving resistance training made significantly fewer errors in response to misleading and other questions than the control (a 26 per cent drop in percentage error). An unanticipated 'side effect', however, was that children in the resistance training condition gave more 'don't know' answers than children in the control group. A subsequent revision to the training, where children were reinforced for telling the answer when they knew it and were warned that the adult interviewer might be disbelieving, eliminated this effect while preserving the superiority of the resistance training.

5.2 Communication in court

A theme that underpins many of the special measures we have outlined above, and, arguably, the whole purpose of a courtroom hearing, is communication – between the barristers and the witness, the barristers and the defendant, the witness and the court, the defendant and the court, the judge and the jury, and so on. We now look at some courtroom communication issues in more detail.

Legalese – how not to question witnesses

In Section 3 we reviewed research that suggested how best to elicit accurate information from witnesses through questioning. However, once the witness enters a criminal courtroom, such guidance appears irrelevant, for the desire to win the case can result in lawyers, especially defence lawyers, asking questions in the least helpful way possible (e.g. Henderson, 2001).

A number of studies (e.g. Brennan and Brennan, 1988) have examined transcripts of lawyers' examinations and cross-examinations of witnesses and have found the language used to be inappropriate to the age and linguistic development of the witness. Legalese is a jargon-laden style, full of complex grammatical structures, formalised vocabulary, and leading questions.

Carter *et al.* (1996) investigated legalese experimentally. Sixty children aged five to seven years old participated in a play session with a research assistant in a laboratory setting. They were then immediately individually interviewed about the session, in experimental conditions that varied the linguistic complexity of the interview questions (simple or complex).

Activity 7.11   *Researching legalese (after Carter et al., 1996)*

Carter *et al.* developed equivalent questions either with 'simple' sentence construction or with a 'complex' construction modelled on lawyers' language as seen in transcripts of court cases. Try constructing a few equivalent questions below, and compare your versions to those produced by the authors (see end of chapter) – one is given complete here as an example:

Simple: Tell me what you did in the balloon room with [research assistant].

Complex: Can you indicate to me whether you played in the balloon room with [research assistant] and what you did while you were there with the aforementioned person?

Write down simple or complex equivalent questions for the following:

Simple:

Complex: Did you engage in any activities involving the blowing of bubbles on the occasion we were speaking of?

Simple:

Complex: Would you say that it's true that crayons were used to colour with?

Simple: Did you sing songs with the person?

Complex:

Simple: What was your prize from the treasure chest?

Complex:

As the researchers expected, when children were questioned in a linguistically complex manner ('legalese') the accuracy of both their free recall and responses to specific questions was diminished. Further, 'very few children spoke up about their lack of understanding of interview questions ... They were also loath to admit their confusion to the interviewer following the conclusion of the interview when asked specifically about their comprehension' (Carter *et al.*, 1996, p.350).

Do you think this is because the children didn't realise that they did not understand the question, or because the children were too embarrassed to appear 'stupid' or 'failures'? Perhaps it is a mixture of both – we have seen in Box 7.13 how preparation can help to alleviate some of these problems.

The use of legalese to bewilder or discredit the witness is, however, only part of the problem. Often legalese is employed by lawyers for the prosecution (who 'called' the witness) or by judges, not because they wish to discredit the witness, but because they are uninformed about the best way to question child witnesses and about associated issues to do with children's cognitive and social development. In addition, they may set up a pattern of responding in which they talk a great deal, and the witness gives very short, one-word answers. This may act as a model for the witness's evidence, so that the witness feels they should not give extended responses. In turn, this may affect the perceived credibility of the witness in the eyes of the jury, as the witness is judged to have poor memory for the event, and to be a less persuasive communicator.

As a result of studies on legalese, psychologists have played an important role in educating judges and lawyers about the best way to question witnesses, and in preparing witnesses about how to cope with such questioning. One less desirable outcome, however, is that defence lawyers can use that same knowledge deliberately to obscure communication with the witness in order to help their case. While legalese research has examined the particular difficulties children face, you may also like to pause and consider what difficulties legalese poses for adult witnesses, too. It is notable that expert witnesses, who appear in court on a regular basis, and who are generally experienced professionals, will undergo training or receive guidance on how to deal effectively with lawyers' questioning techniques.

Juror perceptions of witnesses' testimony

The difficulty faced by those involved in deciding a court case is that they will hear different versions of the event being debated by the prosecution and defence counsels. The 'truth' cannot be verified independently, so the accuracy of witness testimony is assessed by other means, including the way in which witnesses deliver their testimony. Of course, this in turn will be influenced by many factors, including the age of the witness, the conditions under which they witnessed the crime, as well as the type of questions they are asked and the way in which these are phrased. An important factor, influencing how others will perceive the witness, is the internal consistency of the testimony itself and whether there is any contradiction in the answers given by the witness. Indeed, a common way of discrediting a witness is to highlight any inconsistency between what the witness said in their interview with the police with what he or she is saying in court.

Brewer *et al.* (1999) investigated inconsistency as a variable and found that potential jurors reported this to be the strongest indicator of unreliable testimony. 'Inconsistent with previous statement' was considered to be more important than 'pretends not to hear questions', 'exaggerates circumstances', 'inconsistent with other witnesses', 'nervous manner' or does 'not look directly at legal representative' (among several other variables). However, in a study involving participants being interviewed on several occasions about a crime they had seen on videotape, Brewer *et al.* failed to find a strong relationship between consistency and accuracy. While further research is required to examine the relationship further, this study found that virtually all of the 'testimonies' provided contained some inconsistencies and therefore virtually all 'witnesses' were to some extent vulnerable to being discredited.

When deciding who to believe, people will go beyond the content of the communication and consider other indices including non-verbal communication cues (refer back to Chapter 4 where we discussed the clues that we use to detect deception). Research has sought to uncover what these other indices might be, and has looked at witness demeanour. As used by Stone '"demeanour" excludes the content of evidence, and includes every visible or audible form of self-expression manifested by a witness whether fixed or variable, voluntary or involuntary, simple or complex' (1991, p. 822). One important aspect of demeanour that influences the perceptions of witness credibility is witness confidence. A confident witness is considered to be much more believable than one who is hesitant or unsure. Many studies have found that jurors rely on witness confidence, whether stated explicitly or implied nonverbally, to infer the accuracy of witness testimony (e.g. Cutler *et al.*, 1988). The more confident a witness appears, the more likely their testimony will be accepted as an accurate account.

However, research is required here to establish the validity of placing great reliance on a witness's self-reported certainty. Experimental research, looking at the relationship between witness confidence and identification accuracy, has yielded very low correlations. Indeed, if the processes underlying memory and those underlying confidence are to some extent unconscious and independent of each other, then confidence can be increased or reduced while memory is unaffected. In support, Williams *et al.* (1992) found that witnesses' confidence in the accuracy of their own testimony increased as they repeated the same account. This finding highlights that confidence in memory is subject to social influences and is not simply determined by memory accuracy. Thus, witnesses who express solid certainty in their testimony are not necessarily more accurate than those who allow for the possibility that they could be mistaken.

The psychologist as a source of expert knowledge

If you have seen courtroom dramas on television or in films, you will probably be very familiar with the notion of an expert witness: someone, for example a clinician or an academic, being called by the prosecution or the defence to give their opinion on the case. In this final subsection, we will briefly consider the role of the psychologist as an expert witness at court. You may be surprised to learn that the expert witness 'doing battle' in the courtroom is only one of five possible ways that expert assistance may be communicated to a court by a psychologist or other specialist (Spencer and Flin, 1993). These are summarised in Box 7.14.

7.14 *Five methods of giving expert assistance to a court (derived from Spencer and Flin, 1993)*

- *Judicial training.* In England and Wales, for example, the Judicial Studies Board provides initial training for newly appointed judges, and periodic refresher courses for established judges. When a significant piece of new legislation is introduced, specific training programmes may be constructed, or more general topics may be covered. Psychologists can be involved in planning and delivering such training.

- *Specialist courts.* For many years, the main way in which specialist knowledge was applied to the resolution of legal disputes was through the creation of special tribunals. In industrial tribunals, for example, a legal chairperson sits with two non-lawyers (possibly occupational psychologists) who have appropriate specialist experience.

- *Assessors.* These are neutral experts selected by the court to sit as advisors to the judge.

- *Court experts.* These, too, are neutral experts appointed by the court, but instead of sitting with the court, the expert is limited to giving his or her opinion (orally or in writing) on a particular aspect of the case. Such experts (e.g. clinical psychologists) are widely used in childcare cases in civil courts, and in providing reports for sentencing decisions in the criminal courts.

- *Expert witnesses.* Parties to a civil or criminal case may appoint an expert witness (e.g. a psychologist) on any matter that is likely to be outside the knowledge and experience of the judge and jury. Such an expert can give an *opinion*, provided it is within the limits of his/her expertise (in contrast to a 'normal' witness who can only testify about facts as they observed them), but must not usurp the role of the judge and jury. Importantly, they must not give evidence on the 'ultimate issue' (i.e. the veracity of the witness, which is the primary concern of the court). The subject matter of the expert's evidence (information, facts or research results) must be admissible evidence (i.e. evidence that cannot be excluded on legal grounds).

Box 7.14 describes how psychological knowledge and expertise can influence the law. You may like to note that one particular example of psychologists' contribution to judicial training concerns child witness issues, drawing on many of the studies and issues we have discussed in this chapter. A psychologist may occupy one or more of the roles in Box 7.14. For example, s/he may hold an academic position at a university where s/he conducts forensic research, may participate in judicial training sessions, and may also act as an expert witness in criminal or civil court proceedings. You may also have realised reading Box 7.14 that the issue of expert assistance is one of the most complex and contentious intersections of psychology and law, especially in the case of expert witnesses in the courtroom. For example, it is often the case that two 'experts' can be found who interpret the research findings on a particular topic in radically different ways, and who then argue their positions in court (one called by the prosecution, one by the defence). There is also the problem that lawyers generally are sceptical about the contributions psychologists are able to make to issues that arise at court, for example because they feel able to represent psychological knowledge themselves (Nijboer, 1995). Further, it is not easy to determine whether or not evidence offered by a witness is helpful in assisting the jury's deliberations or in influencing the final outcome of the case (e.g. Kapardis, 1997).

Ainsworth (1998, p.161) has summarised the debate on whether or not to admit expert witness testimony (from psychologists or others) as focusing on four issues:

1   The scientific reliability of such testimony.
2   The relevance of the testimony to the facts of the particular case being considered.
3   The effectiveness of traditional safeguards in reducing the danger of misidentifications (e.g. judge's warnings to the jury).
4   Whether such testimony does actually help the jury to understand or determine a fact in issue.

It is beyond the scope of this chapter to go further in identifying these issues. However, you might like to think about them in the light of the research we have presented above, and in the context of associated methodological and ethical issues. For example, you will by now be aware that what one psychologist regards as scientifically acceptable research may be challenged vigorously by a psychologist who has a different perspective (e.g. think back to the discussion of the use of the polygraph in Chapter 4 of this book). What are the implications of exposing jurors to only one, or to both perspectives?

Summary Section 5

- In this section we have highlighted some of the difficulties witnesses encounter when they give evidence in a criminal court, and also some ways in which psychologists have researched and responded to these difficulties (which are system variables).
- Witnesses' concerns include those that are pre-court, e.g. lack of knowledge of the legal system, as well as those at court, e.g. waiting to testify and seeing the defendant. Psychologists have been involved in preparation programmes to address some of these concerns.

- Communication takes place between many different personnel at court. Research on legalese has shown how it impedes communication between the barrister, the witness and the court.
- Jurors may use mistaken cues when evaluating the verbal and nonverbal communicative effectiveness of the witness.
- Psychologists may have a number of roles in providing expert assistance to the court. The role of the expert witness is the most complex and controversial.

6　Discussion

In this chapter we have focused on the experience of witnesses as they progress through the legal process. We started with issues surrounding the encoding of the event, where we found that attention may well be directed to the more central actions of the event and that certain types of information may not be encoded accurately, such as height, weight, distance and temporal information. We considered research showing that the presence of a weapon may negatively impact upon memory of things other than the weapon. However, research on real witnesses has found that the level of stress or arousal they experienced and the violent nature of the crime did not relate to how well they remembered the crime. Age of the witness emerged as an important variable, with younger children tending to remember less than older children and adults.

When questioning a witness about a crime, it is important to consider both the cognitive and the social factors that will influence their memory. Importantly, witnesses will be reconstructing what happened, and the way that questions are phrased can influence responses. Research has shown that younger children are more susceptible to suggestibility and therefore leading questions should be avoided. Several types of questions can be posed by interviewers, and the evidence indicates that open questions and facilitators may assist the witness to provide a more accurate account of the crime than focused and option-posing questions.

One specific aspect of witness memory concerns the identity of the perpetrator. Sometimes the police will require the witness to recall the perpetrator's face and sometimes to identify the perpetrator in an identification parade. Research on face perception has informed the procedures that the police use, while at the same time highlighting the fallibility of this particular type of evidence.

Finally, we considered the experience of witnesses in the courtroom and saw how research has informed the special measures that have been introduced to assist vulnerable witnesses. The way in which the witness is asked questions will influence how well the witness can communicate to the court their memory of the crime. Jurors' perceptions of a witness will be influenced by the confidence the witness displays and the consistency of the account they give. However, neither of these variables are good predictors of the accuracy of the account.

Throughout the chapter we have shown that there are a whole host of variables, at the point at which the crime is witnessed, at the stage of the police investigation and then in the courtroom itself, that all operate to influence the accuracy and completeness of witness testimony. As such, it is extremely difficult to comment on the reliability of the evidence provided by any one witness. Furthermore, sometimes the findings from research are rather tentative or not clear-cut, with those from simulations providing a somewhat different picture to those from cases involving real witnesses. It is important to bear in mind the difficulty that researchers face in conducting research in this area. Ethical issues have to be considered when carrying out simulations: it is simply not possible to manipulate those variables that are thought to be extremely important, such as the fear that the witness may experience and the consequentiality of their testimony – that their evidence may lead to a conviction and a prison sentence. There are also ethical issues in conducting research with real witnesses, who may find it traumatic to recount their experiences to researchers. It is often extremely difficult to draw generalisable conclusions from investigations of real witnesses, as the experience of individual witnesses is so varied, calling into play different variables. Unlike laboratory simulations, it is not possible to control what might be key variables.

This is not to say that the more robust findings have had no positive impact. The unreliability of identification evidence is something brought to the attention of juries in several different countries, and this is based on evidence from simulations as well as evidence from real cases. The susceptibility of recall to suggestive questions has been highlighted in police and interviewing training and there is ample evidence to support the notion of suggestibility from laboratory experiments, field experiments and observational studies. Researchers are aware of the need to use multiple methods and of the dangers of generalising from only one single source of evidence. Those involved in the legal profession are responding to the need for such research and collaborative efforts are now on the increase. Access can be gained to real case data and research questions can be derived from the practitioners themselves.

One issue you may have noticed throughout this chapter is the steadily increasing application of technology in the field of psychology and law. Section 4 described the evolution of E-FIT in the construction of composites, as well as discussing VIPER parades and work on CCTV. In Section 5, we made passing reference to the use of video technology for child witnesses, such as in the use of 'live links' (CCTV systems), which enable a child to testify from a small room outside the courtroom. Videotaped investigative interviews with children are also permitted, subject to certain conditions, to replace the child's evidence-in-chief in some jurisdictions. It is clear, then, that, like almost every other field in psychology, forensic psychologists need to collaborate with other psychologists and practitioners in many different fields in order to make the most of such technological developments.

What is also clear, however, is that technological advances bring with them new research and practice questions that require attention. For example, in the case of CCTV, research is required to see how we can best use this technology to identify perpetrators. In the case of child witnesses, technological hiccups have been virtually eradicated as investigators and courts have become experienced with the technology. Yet, there is still much resistance to videotaped evidence and live links by barristers on both sides, who fear that seeing a child on a TV screen reduces the impact the child witness can make (prosecution), or increases the ease with which a child can be deceptive (defence). Some of these issues and anxieties can be further investigated by psychological research and, indeed, do continue to be.

Finally, while technological advances may address some of the difficulties associated with witness evidence, it should not be seen as an answer to all the problems raised here, and should not be permitted to obscure other systemic issues that can be problematic in witness evidence and identification. There are also other advances that come to mind, such as DNA profiling, as well as developments in offender profiling, interviewing suspects and the analysis of crime patterns (see our suggestions for further reading below). Forensic psychologists have made valuable contributions to such developments, and will continue to be at the forefront of future initiatives concerned with human behaviour in the legal arena.

Further reading

Heaton-Armstrong, A., Shepherd, E. and Wolchover, D. (eds) (1999) *Analysing Witness Testimony*, London, Blackstone Press.
The book is written as a guide for legal practitioners and other professionals and comprises of short papers written by a range of professionals, including forensic psychologists and legal experts.

Jackson, J. and Bekerian, D.A. (eds) (1997) *Offender Profiling*, Chichester, Wiley.
The media has often portrayed offender profiling as an instant device for solving crime. This book provides an account of how offender profiling can be used to assist an investigation.

Karpardis, A. (1997) *Psychology and Law*, Cambridge, Cambridge University Press.
This book is a wide-ranging and detailed text, covering issues such as jury decision making, sentencing and persuasion in the courtroom, as well as many of the topics included in this chapter.

Westcott, H.L., Davies, G.M. and Bull, R.H.C. (eds) (2001) *Children's Testimony: A Handbook of Psychological Research and Forensic Practice*, Chichester, Wiley.
This book offers a comprehensive and review of issues surrounding children as witnesses.

 # References

Ainsworth, P.B. (1998) *Psychology, Law and Eyewitness Testimony*, Chichester, Wiley.

Block, R.A. (1978) 'Remembered duration: effects of event and sequence complexity', *Memory and Cognition*, vol. 6, pp. 320–6.

Brace, N., Pike, G. and Kemp, R. (2000) 'Investigating E-FIT using famous faces' in Czerederecka, A. *et al.* (eds) (2000).

Brennan, M. and Brennan, R.E., (1988) *Strange Language: Child Victims Under Cross-Examination,* Wagga Wagga, NSW, Riverina Literacy Centre.

Brewer, N., Potter, R., Fisher, R.P., Bond, N. and Luszcz, M.A. (1999) 'Beliefs and data on the relationship between consistency and accuracy of eyewitness testimony', *Applied Cognitive Psychology*, vol. 13, pp. 297–313.

Brigham, J.C. and Cairns, D.L. (1988) 'The effect of mugshot inspections on eyewitness identification accuracy', *Journal of Applied Social Psychology*, vol. 18, pp. 1394–1410.

British Psychological Society (1993) *Code of Conduct, Ethical Principles & Guidelines*, Leicester, British Psychological Society.

Bruce, V., Henderson, Z., Greenwood, K., Hancock, P.J.B., Burton, A.M. and Miller, P. (1999) 'Verification of face identities from images captured on video', *Journal of Experimental Psychology: Applied*, vol. 5, pp. 339–60.

Bruce, V., Henderson, Z., Newman, C. and Burton, A.M. (2001) 'Matching identities of familiar and unfamiliar faces caught on CCTV images', *Journal of Experimental Psychology: Applied*, vol. 7, pp. 207–18.

Bruck, M. and Ceci, S.J. (1999) 'The suggestibility of children's memory', *Annual Review of Psychology*, vol. 50, pp. 419–39.

Bull, R. and Carson, D. (eds) (1995) *Handbook of Psychology in Legal Contexts*, Chichester, John Wiley.

Burton, A.M., Wilson, S., Cowan, M. and Bruce, V. (1999) 'Face recognition in poor quality video: Evidence from security surveillance', *Psychological Science*, vol. 10, pp. 243–8.

Carter, C.A., Bottoms, B.L. and Levine, M. (1996) 'Linguistic and socioemotional influences on the accuracy of children's reports', *Law and Human Behavior*, vol. 20, pp. 335–58.

Ceci, S.J. (1992) 'The suggestibility of the child witness', paper presented to the NATO ASI, *The Child Witness in Context: Cognitive, Social and Legal Perspectives*, Lucca, Italy, May.

Ceci, S.J. and Bruck, M. (1993) 'Suggestibility of the child witness: a historical review and synthesis', *Psychological Bulletin*, vol. 113, pp. 403–39.

Ceci, S.J., Crossman, A.M., Scullin, M.H., Gilstrap, L. and Huffman, M.L. (2001) 'Children's suggestibility research: implications for the courtroom and the forensic interview' in Westcott, H.L. *et al.* (eds) (2001).

Ceci, S.J., Huffman, M.L., Smith, E. and Loftus, E.F. (1994) 'Repeatedly thinking about a non-event: source misattributions among preschoolers', *Consciousness and Cognition*, vol. 3, pp. 388–407.

Christianson, S-Å. (1997) 'On emotional stress and memory: we need to recognize threatening situations and we need to "forget" unpleasant experiences' in Payne, D.G. and Conrad F.G. (eds) *Intersections in Basic and Applied Memory Research*, Mahwah, NJ, Lawrence Erlbaum.

Christianson, S-Å. and Hübinette, B. (1993) 'Hands up! A study of witnesses' emotional reactions and memories associated with bank robberies', *Applied Cognitive Psychology*, vol. 7, pp. 365–79.

Clifford, B.R. and Scott, J. (1978) 'Individual and situational factors in eyewitness testimony', *Journal of Applied Psychology*, vol. 63, pp. 352–9.

Cooke, P. (2001) 'The virtual courtroom: a view of justice', *Ann Craft Trust Bulletin*, no. 35, pp. 2–5.

Cutler, B.L. and Penrod, S.D. (1995) *Mistaken Identification: The Eyewitness, Psychology and the Law*, New York, Cambridge University Press.

Cutler, B.L., Penrod, S.D., and Martens, T.K. (1987) 'The reliability of eyewitness identifications: the role of system and estimator variables', *Law and Human Behavior*, vol. 11, pp. 223–58.

Cutler, B.L., Penrod, S.D. and Stuve, T.E. (1988) 'Juror decision making in eyewitness identification cases', *Law and Human Behavior*, vol. 12, pp. 41–55.

Czerederecka, A., Jaśkiewicz-Obydzińska, T. and Wójcikiewicz, J. (eds) (2000) *Forensic Psychology and Law*, Kraków, Institute of Forensic Research Publishers.

Diamond, R. and Carey, S. (1986) 'Why faces are and are not special: an effect of expertise', *Journal of Experimental Psychology: General*, vol. 115, no. 2, pp. 107–17.

Easterbrook, J. (1959) 'The effect of emotion on cue utilization and the organization of behavior', *Psychological Review*, vol. 66, pp. 183–201.

Ellis, H.D., Davies, G.M. and Shepherd, J.W. (1977) 'Experimental studies of face identification', *National Journal of Criminal Defense*, vol. 3, pp. 219–34.

Fisher, R.P. and Geiselman, R.E. (1992) *Memory-Enhancing Techniques for Investigative Interviewing: The Cognitive Interview*, Springfield, IL., Charles C. Thomas.

Flin, R.H. and Shepherd, J.W. (1986) 'Tall stories: eyewitnesses' ability to estimate height and weight characteristics', *Human Learning*, vol. 5, pp. 29–38.

Freshwater, K. and Aldridge, J. (1994) 'The knowledge and fears about court of child witnesses, school children and adults', *Child Abuse Review*, vol. 3, pp. 183–95.

Fundudis, T. (1997) 'Young children's memory: how good is it? How much do we know about it?', *Child Psychology and Child Psychiatry Review*, vol. 2, pp. 150–8.

Gibling, F. and Bennett, P. (1994) 'Artistic enhancement in the production of photo-fit likenesses: An examination of its effectiveness in leading to suspect identification', *Psychology, Crime and Law*, vol. 1, pp. 93–100.

Henderson, E. (2001) 'Persuading and controlling: the theory of cross-examination in relation to children' in Westcott, H.L. *et al.* (eds) (2001).

Home Office (1994) *Identification Parades: A Scientific Evaluation*, London, Home Office Research, Development and Statistics Directorate.

Home Office (1998) *Speaking Up for Justice: Report of the Interdepartmental Working Group on the Treatment of Vulnerable or Intimidated Witnesses in the Criminal Justice System*, London, Home Office Procedures and Victims Unit.

Huff, C.R. (1987) 'Wrongful conviction: societal tolerance of injustice', *Research in Social Problems and Public Policy*, vol. 4, pp. 99–115.

Hughes, M. and Grieve, R. (1980) 'On asking children bizarre questions', *First Language*, vol. 1, pp. 149–60.

Kapardis, A. (1997) *Psychology and Law: A Critical Introduction*, Cambridge, Cambridge University Press.

Kemp, R., Towell, N. and Pike, G. (1997) 'When seeing should not be believing: photographs, credit cards and fraud', *Applied Cognitive Psychology*, vol. 11, no. 3, pp. 211–22.

Köhnken , G. (1995) 'Interviewing adults' in Bull, R. and Carson, D. (eds) (1995).

Kuehn, L.L. (1974) 'Looking down a gun barrel: person perception and violent crime', *Perceptual and Motor Skills*, vol. 39, pp. 1159–64.

Lamb, M.E., Orbach, Y., Sternberg, K.J., Esplin, P.W. and Hershkowitz, I. (2001) 'The effects of forensic interview practices on the quality of information provided by alleged victims of child abuse' in Westcott, H.L. *et al.* (eds) (2001).

Laughery, K.R., Alexander, T. and Lane, A. (1971) 'Recognition of human faces: effects of target exposure time, target position, and type of photograph', *Journal of Applied Psychology*, vol. 55, pp. 477–83.

Leichtman, M.D. and Ceci, S.J. (1995) 'The effects of stereotypes and suggestions on preschoolers' reports', *Developmental Psychology*, vol. 31, pp. 568–78.

Levi, A.M., Jungman, N., Glinton, A., Aperman, A. and Noble, G. (1995) 'Using similarity judgements to conduct a mugshot album search', *Law and Human Behavior*, vol. 19, pp. 649–61.

Loftus, E.F. (1980) *Memory*, Reading, MA, Addison-Wesley.

Loftus, E.F., Miller, D.G. and Burns, H.J. (1978) 'Semantic integration of verbal information into visual memory', *Journal of Experimental Psychology: Human Learning and Memory*, vol. 4, pp. 19–31.

Loftus, E.F. and Palmer, J.C. (1974) 'Reconstruction of automobile destruction: an example of the interactions between language and memory', *Journal of Verbal Learning and Verbal Behavior*, vol. 13, pp. 585–9.

Maass, A., and Köhnken, G. (1989) 'Eyewitness identification: simulating the "weapon effect"', *Law and Human Behavior*, vol. 13, pp. 397–408.

Migueles, M. and García-Bajos, E. (1999) 'Recall, recognition and confidence patterns in eyewitness testimony', *Applied Cognitive Psychology*, vol. 13, pp. 257–68.

Nader, K., Schafe, G.E. and Le Doux, J.E. (2000) 'Fear memories require protein synthesis in the amygdala for reconsolidation after retrieval', *Nature*, vol. 406, pp. 722–6.

Nijboer, H. (1995) 'Expert evidence' in Bull, R. and Carson, D. (eds) (1995).

NSPCC/ChildLine (1998) *The Young Witness Pack*, London, NSPCC.

Penrod, S.D. and Cutler, B.L. (1999) 'Preventing mistaken convictions in eyewitness identification trials: the case against traditional safeguards' in Roesch, R. *et al.* (eds) (1999).

Pezdek, K. (ed.) (1998) *Applied Cognitive Psychology Special Issue*, vol. 12, no. 3.

Pike, G., Kemp, R., Brace, N. and Allen, J. (2000) 'Video identification parades: an investigation of VIPER' in Czerederecka, A. *et al.* (eds) (2000).

Powell, N. and Thomson, D. (2001) 'Children's memories for repeated events' in Westcott, H.L. *et al.* (eds) (2001).

Roesch, R., Hart, S.D. and Ogloff, J.R.P. (eds) (1999) *Psychology and Law: The State of the Discipline*, New York, Kluwer Academic/Plenum Publishers.

Ross, D.F., Ceci, S.J., Dunning, D. and Toglia, M.P. (1994) 'Unconscious transference and mistaken identity: when a witness misidentifies a familiar but innocent person', *Journal of Applied Psychology*, vol. 79, pp. 918–30.

Saywitz, K., Goodman, G.S., Nicholas, E. and Moan, S. (1991) 'Children's memories of a physical examination involving genital touch: implications for reports of child sexual abuse', *Journal of Consulting and Clinical Psychology*, vol. 59, pp. 682–91.

Saywitz, K., Nathanson, R., Snyder, L. and Lamphear, V. (1993) *Preparing Children for the Investigative and Judicial Process: Improving Communication, Memory and Emotional Resiliency*, Final Report to the National Center on Child Abuse and Neglect (Grant No. 90CA1179).

Schooler, J.W. and Engstler-Schooler, T.Y. (1990) 'Verbal overshadowing of visual memories: some things are better left unsaid', *Cognitive Psychology*, vol. 22, pp. 36–71.

Spencer, J.R. and Flin, R. (1993) *The Evidence of Children: The Law and the Psychology*, London, Blackstone Press.

Sternberg, K.J., Lamb, M.E., Davies, G.M. and Westcott, H.L. (2001) 'Memorandum of good practice: theory versus application', *Child Abuse and Neglect*, vol. 25, pp. 669–81.

Stone, M. (1991) 'Instant lie detection? Demeanour and credibility in criminal trials', *Criminal Law Review*, pp. 821–30.

Tanaka, J.W. and Farah, M.J. (1993) 'Parts and wholes in face recognition', *Quarterly Journal of Experimental Psychology: Human Experimental Psychology*, vol. 46A, pp. 225–45.

Thompson, C.P., Skowronski, J.J., Larsen, S.F. and Betz, A. (1996) *Autobiographical Memory: Remembering What and Remembering When*, Mahwah, NJ, Lawrence Erlbaum.

Wade, A. and Westcott, H.L. (1997) 'No easy answers: children's perspectives on investigative interviews' in Westcott, H.L., and Jones, J. (eds), *Perspectives on the Memorandum. Policy, Practice and Research in Investigative Interviewing*, Aldershot, Arena.

Wagenaar, W.A. and Van Der Schrier, J.H. (1996) 'Face recognition as a function of distance and illumination: a practical tool for use in the courtroom', *Psychology, Crime and Law*, vol. 2, pp. 321–32.

Waterman, A., Blades, M. and Spencer, C. (2001) 'How and why do children respond to nonsensical questions?' in Westcott, H.L. *et al.* (eds) (2001).

Wells, G.L. (1978) 'Applied eyewitness research: system variables and estimator variables', *Journal of Personality and Social Psychology*, vol. 36, pp. 1546–57.

Wells, G.L., Wright, E.F. and Bradfield, A.L. (1999) 'Witness to crime: social and cognitive factors governing the validity of people's reports' in Roesch, R. *et al.* (eds) (1999).

Westcott, H.L. (1999) *Questioning Child Witnesses: Questions About Questioning Research*, unpublished manuscript.

Westcott, H.L., Davies G.M. and Bull, R.H.C. (eds) (2001) *Children's Testimony: A Handbook of Psychological Research and Forensic Practice*, Chichester, Wiley.

Wilding, J., Cook, S. and Davis, J. (2000) 'Sound familiar?', *The Psychologist*, vol. 13, pp. 558–62.

Williams, K.D., Loftus, E.F. and Deffenbacher, K.A. (1992) 'Eyewitness evidence and testimony' in Kagehiro, D.K. and Laufer, W.S. (eds) *Handbook of Psychology and Law*, New York, Springer.

Wright, D.B. and Davies, G.M. (1999) 'Eyewitness testimony' in Durso, F.T. (ed.) *Handbook of Applied Cognition*, Chichester, Wiley.

Yerkes, R.M. and Dodson, J.D. (1908) 'The relation of strength of stimulus to rapidity of habit-information', *Journal of Comparative Neurology of Psychology*, vol. 18, pp. 459–82.

Yuille, J.C. and Cutshall, J.L. (1986) 'A case study of eyewitness memory of a crime', *Journal of Applied Psychology*, vol. 71, pp. 291–301.

Answer to Activity 7.8

Tom Cruise's nose is third from left.

Answer to Activity 7.9

Mel Gibson, Sean Connery, Paul McCartney.

Answer to Box 7.11

Number 3.

Answer to Activity 7.11

Our suggestions are:

Simple: Did you play with bubbles?

Complex: Did you engage in any activities involving the blowing of bubbles on the occasion we were speaking of?

Simple: Did you colour with crayons?

Complex: Would you say that it's true that crayons were used to colour with?

Simple: Did you sing songs with the person?

Complex: On that same occasion, were any songs sung by you and [RA name]?

Simple: What was your prize from the treasure chest?

Complex: Please try to recollect what, if anything, it was that you received as a prize from the treasure chest.

Epilogue

Andy McBurnie

Now that you have finished working through DSE232 *Applying Psychology*, it may be useful to reflect on what you have covered. To assist you in doing this, this section of the book revisits some of the main issues and themes that have arisen in the course. Hopefully you will have derived a lot of pleasure from working through the course and the chapters in this book will have broadened your psychological horizons. You will have seen that psychology is rarely straightforward when dealing with real-life issues and problems. Throughout the course each chapter has illustrated a different topic in applied psychology and, while each one is very different, one thing that is common to them all is the complexity of the issues and problems being addressed.

Complexities of approaches

Dealing with such complexity requires applied psychologists to adopt an eclectic approach. By eclectic we are referring to the need to utilise different methodologies and to draw on different theories and perspectives, often integrating these to address a specific issue. For example, in Chapter 1 'Stress' you came across some of the problems of defining and assessing stress, one result of which was the requirement for the use of different methodologies. These difficulties were exacerbated by a number of different mediators such as personal control (locus of control, self-efficacy), personality and social support, each of which originated from different theoretical stances and perspectives. To understand the effects of mediators like these, psychologists have to incorporate ideas from different perspectives and theoretical stances into their thinking, analysis and subsequent design of research, therapy or interventions. Similarly, Chapter 2 'Post-traumatic stress disorder' highlighted the different antecedents to PTSD and the fact that different people react differently to similar situations, often presenting with different symptoms. This again demonstrated the requirement for adopting different methodologies. It also showed how different theories can lead to different treatments and interventions. Just to add to the complexity, this chapter also raised other aspects that need to be considered, such as medico-legal or forensic issues. Other chapters threw up different complexities. For example, Chapter 4 'Telling and detecting lies' explained how attempts to apply psychology to this area can be affected by various factors, including situational factors, the fact that there are verbal, nonverbal and cognitive indicators (among others) of lying, difficulties in measuring nonverbal indications, the motivations for lying and the replication of such motivations in research. Chapter 5 'The autistic spectrum' again raised the problems of definition, particularly with the wide range of symptoms that can constitute autism, and diagnosis. This chapter also highlighted how theories that originated in other areas of psychology have informed research in this area. Chapter 6 'Relationships at work' drew from areas of psychology that were informed by occupational and organisational contexts. This chapter showed how issues that occur in the 'field', for example the need to improve teamworking, influence what and how psychologists research. You will have noticed that certain issues, such as labelling, diagnosis and definition are present across much of applied psychology as are other aspects such as ethical issues and the adoption of pragmatism. Chapter 7 'Psychological factors in witness evidence and identification' not only demonstrated the problems of dealing with complexity, for example in the form of a large number of variables (level of arousal, memory limitations, estimator variables) and conflicting theories regarding the issue of questioning, but also how the subject matter that is being researched can throw up its own set of complications; in this case, the issues of child witnesses raised particular ethical and practical problems.

Connections between chapters

You should also have observed that some of the areas could, on occasion, be connected. As an example, the chapters on stress, post-traumatic stress disorder, relationships at work and computer-mediated communication between them could apply to the stress caused by the use of communication media by 'cyber bullies', both at work and at school. Indeed, at the time of writing, this is rapidly becoming an issue that education policy makers are considering in more detail. Another example of a cross-chapter connection that you might have considered stems from the roles of deception and relationships at work. Considering the difficulties in detecting lies, how might relationships at work be affected by deception? Related to this might be some work exploring the impact of emotional labour in work situations. For example, Grandey (2003) has focused on the issue of displaying emotions that are different from how an individual actually feels and the different ways in which people manage to keep up the act. No doubt you will have made some of your own connections and we hope that you will continue to think about applied psychology as being characterised by strong links between different fields and areas of psychology and an eclectic approach. Indeed, this eclecticism provides a fertile ground for developing new solutions to existing problems, as well as driving the development of theory.

Ethical considerations

Throughout the course it has been emphasised that adherence to ethical principles is paramount when researching psychology. Each field and topic throws up its own set of issues and problems in this area, for example: dealing with the problem of researching the effects of abuse in children (Chapter 7); the issue of revisiting traumatic events when dealing with PTSD (Chapter 2); the use of deliberate deception, such as threats, when investigating lying (Chapter 4); the issue of consent when researching online communities (Chapter 3). As the various chapters show, such ethical considerations are taken very seriously and can lead to modifications (sometimes ingenious) in the design of the research. However, you will also have seen that it is often necessary to adopt a pragmatic approach to real-life issues and problems. Realistically, a pragmatic approach is both inevitable and desirable, given that it is the *practical application* of psychology that is under consideration. It is also important to recognise that the benefits of research or interventions are always carefully considered and weighed up against any misgivings that may arise in terms of ethics or acceptable practice. Only then are decisions made as to how to proceed with the research or intervention.

Remember, though, that ethical considerations are not solely confined to issues regarding research participants or clients, but are also important when considering psychological best practice and/or the efficacy of any treatment, therapy or intervention. This was perhaps best highlighted in Chapter 5 'The autistic spectrum', where the 'myth of miracle cures' was discussed, but the principle applies equally to the other topics and is one that runs through all of applied psychology.

When considering ethics in applying psychology, we must also look to the longer-term implications that psychological knowledge may have on a situation. We must also guard against the misuse of psychological ideas: remember that the BPS *Code of Ethics and Conduct* requires that psychologists strive to prevent 'misuse or abuse' of psychological knowledge. Similarly, we must ensure that we adhere to common values, such as equal opportunity and non-discriminatory elements of practice, as well as people's personal and cultural values, such as cultural mores. For all of these reasons, actually practising in psychology requires intensive study of psychology to at least MSc level, typically with a further period of practise supervised by an already-qualified Chartered Psychologist who has expertise in an appropriate field. In the UK, the BPS charters eligible members to be accredited as practitioners, and since 2008 it is illegal for unqualified people to lay claim to the title of 'Psychologist'. An understanding of ethics is an important component of the competency requirements that someone must meet in order to become a psychologist.

Throughout DSE232 *Applying Psychology* the focus has been on the 'active' and 'practical' application of psychology to a variety of real-life issues, and, indeed, you have considered how psychology could be applied to practical problems in your assessed work. Such application is an accurate reflection of the type of areas in which professional applied psychologists work. Whilst you will be aware that research is a key element of applying psychology, and all of the fields endorse that view, you will also have seen that it is not purely research that applied psychologists are concerned with. They also apply psychology to the design and implementation of appropriate treatments, therapies or interventions that are to the benefit of individuals, groups, organisations or society as a whole. This work may focus on everyday aspects of modern life that affect the majority of people, for example the issues discussed in the chapters about computer-mediated communication, relationships at work or stress. Alternatively it may be work in an area that only affects a very small percentage of the general population, for example on the autistic spectrum, or work that affects particular individuals under certain circumstances, for example post-traumatic stress disorder. Some of the work done by applied psychologists could be said to be concerned with informing policy and procedures for the benefit of society, for example some of the work discussing psychological factors in witness evidence and identification. On the other hand, you may consider that some of the work is in an area that overlaps between societal benefit and personal relevance, for example the issues around telling and detecting lies and in relationships at work.

DSE232 *Applying Psychology* has covered a broad range of topics, but there are still many more subjects that are left unexplored, both in the fields covered and in other fields of psychology. In this Epilogue we would like to take the opportunity to briefly introduce you to some of these additional topics and fields.

Additional topics in the fields covered in DSE232

Health psychology

Health psychologists can work in a variety of settings, including hospitals, academic health research facilities, health authorities and university departments. Areas that they cover include:

- investigating health-related cognitions (the processes which can explain, predict and change health and illness behaviours)
- communication between healthcare practitioners and patients that may influence healthcare delivery
- psychological interventions to prevent damaging behaviours such as smoking, drug abuse and poor diet
- encouraging health promoting behaviours such as exercise, good dietary choice and regular health checks
- looking at the psychological impact of illness on individuals, families and carers
- investigating the use of interventions to facilitate coping with pain or illness, such as promoting self-management, improving quality of life and reducing disability and handicap.

Forensic psychology

In addition to the aspects covered in the course, forensic psychologists are also active within the prison and probation systems as well as informing police procedures and legal policy. Key tasks undertaken include piloting and implementing treatment programmes and modifying offender behaviour, for example:

- anger management, social and cognitive skills training, and treatment for drug and/or alcohol addiction
- responding to the changing needs of prison staff and prisoners and reducing stress for staff and prisoners, for example the delivery of stress management or training on how to cope with understanding bullying
- informing techniques for hostage negotiation
- providing hard research evidence to support policy and practice in policing, prisons, probation services and youth offending teams
- undertaking statistical analysis to explore offender and prison populations
- giving expert evidence in court
- undertaking offender risk analysis
- advising parole boards and mental health tribunals
- assisting the police with crime analysis and offender profiling.

Clinical psychology

Clinical psychologists can deal with a wide range of psychological difficulties including (but not limited to) anxiety, depression, relationship problems, learning disabilities, child and family problems, and serious mental illness. Clinical assessment may use a variety of methods including psychometric testing, interviews, and direct observation of behaviour. Such assessments may lead to therapy, counselling or advice. Clinical psychologists usually work as part of a multidisciplinary team, which may include social workers, medical practitioners and other health professionals, and can work with individuals or groups of people.

Occupational psychology

Occupational psychologists address a broad spectrum of areas in the workplace. Examples of these include:

- personnel selection and assessment for recruitment, appraisal or promotion requirements (this can involve a variety of assessment tools such as psychometric tests, structured interviews, individual/group exercises and work sample exercises)

- training – identification of needs, training design and delivery
- design of environments and work in order to produce optimum performance and/or address health and safety requirements
- personal development including counselling and career development
- organisational development and change facilitation.

(Source: adapted from the BPS website, 2007)

Additional fields not covered in DSE232

Educational psychology

Educational psychologists tackle the problems encountered by young people in education, which may involve learning difficulties and social or emotional problems. They carry out a wide range of tasks, with the aim of enhancing children's learning and enabling teachers to become more aware of the social factors affecting teaching and learning. The work of an educational psychologist can be either directly with a child (assessing progress, giving counselling) or indirectly (through their work with parents, teachers and other professionals). Reports may be written about children for allocation of special educational places, or as part of court proceedings or children's panels. There is also a growing field of 'teaching and learning' psychology, which extends the psychological contribution by including further and higher education (including exploring university students' learning!).

Sport and exercise psychology

It is relatively rare for individuals to practise in both sport and exercise psychology; typically, though some exceptions exist, they specialise in one or the other.

Sport psychologists work with sports participants across a range of both team and individual sports and from amateur to elite levels of competition. The aim is predominantly to help athletes prepare psychologically for competition and to deal with the psychological demands of both competition and training. Examples of the work they carry out include counselling referees to deal with the stressful and demanding aspects of their role, advising coaches on how to build cohesion within their squad of athletes, and helping athletes to deal with the psychological and emotional consequences of sustaining an injury.

An exercise psychologist is primarily concerned with the application of psychology to increase exercise participation and motivational levels in the general public. Examples of the work they do include optimising the benefits that can be derived from exercise participation, and helping individual clients with the implementation of goal-setting strategies.

Neuropsychology

Neuropsychologists work with people of all ages with neurological problems, which might include traumatic brain injury, stroke, toxic and metabolic disorders, tumours and neuro-degenerative diseases. Neuropsychologists require not only general clinical skills and knowledge of the broad range of mental health problems, but also a substantial degree of specialist knowledge in the neurosciences. Specialist skills are required in the assessment of neurological patients, and rehabilitation encompasses a broad range of specialist behavioural and cognitive interventions not only for the client, but also for the client's family and carers.

Counselling psychology

Counselling psychologists are a relatively new breed of professional applied psychologists, concerned with the integration of psychological theory and research with therapeutic practice. The practice of counselling psychology requires a high level of self-awareness and competence in working with intra- and inter-personal dynamics within therapeutic contexts. The work carried out includes the assessment of mental health needs and risk assessment, the formulation of a psychological explanation of the genesis and maintenance of the psychological problem, and the planning, implementation and evaluation of therapy. Counselling psychologists may work directly with individuals, couples, families and groups, or act as consultants.

(Source: adapted from BPS website, 2007)

Other fields of psychology

There are many other fields of psychology which do not yet have a separate division within the BPS, such as environmental psychology, traffic psychology, consumer psychology, community psychology, coaching psychology, media psychology and political psychology. Of course, as these areas grow they may in future become divisions in themselves: as you have learned, psychology is dynamic and continues to develop and expand to explore new areas and address new issues. In the UK these are often located in the larger areas described above, but may have a higher profile in some other countries.

Looking forward

We hope that DSE232 *Applying Psychology* has enriched and expanded your knowledge of psychology and has encouraged you to broaden your psychological horizons further by getting you to consider the applied dimension. However, applying psychology is not necessarily restricted to professional psychologists. Indeed, there are many examples of theories and ideas stemming from psychology that have been adopted by other disciplines and fields. For example, police officers involved in training using investigative interviewing techniques draw on psychological knowledge about memory (e.g. the cognitive interview) and communication (e.g. conversation management techniques). Human resources professionals employ insights and techniques developed by occupational psychologists when selecting people for leadership positions. Computer programmers, computer games designers and software engineers utilise techniques developed by human factor psychologists when constructing new displays and controls. Specialist teachers and social workers are trained with psychological knowledge to enable them to work effectively with children with autistic spectrum disorders. There are many more examples like this.

Your understanding of and interest in this course has hopefully developed your skills at identifying knowledge that is relevant to particular contexts, and in communicating that knowledge to others. This is an important skill for graduates of all disciplines, and one which we hope you have enhanced by studying this course.

Thinking ahead, you might consider taking psychology further. Perhaps DSE232 has whetted your appetite for a future career as an applied psychologist? If this is the case, you should probably consider learning more about professional training in psychology by exploring the BPS website for further information. You can also find useful information on the Open University Psychology Programme website. In addition, the Open University Careers Advisory Service will be able to provide you with some information on possible career training opportunities. You can find links to all of these sites from the DSE232 course website. On the other hand, you may have perceived the links that psychology has to many other careers, such as education, social work, healthcare, business, human resources, or creative professions. As a result you may be able to see more clearly what you might want to do in the future. Since many students are already working professionals, it is also possible that you will be able to apply some of the ideas you encountered to your existing work.

Whatever your future holds, we hope that the understanding you have gained of this subject will benefit you for many years to come.

References

BPS (2007) The British Psychological Society website [online], http://www.bps.org.uk/home-page.cfm (Accessed 21 November 2007).

Grandey, A.A. (2003) 'When "the show must go on": Surface acting and deep acting as determinants of emotional exhaustion and peer-rated service delivery', *Academy of Management Journal*, vol. 6, no. 4, pp. 86–96.

Index

Acknowledgements

Grateful acknowledgement is made to the following sources for permission to reproduce material in this book:

Chapter 1

Text
p. 28: Sarafino, E.P. (1994) *Health Psychology: Biopsychosocial Interactions*, John Wiley & Sons, Inc. Copyright © 1994 by John Wiley & Sons, Inc. This material is used by permission of John Wiley & Sons, Inc.

Figures
Figure 1.1: Sheridan, C.L. and Radmacher, S.A. (1992) *Health Psychology: Challenging the Biomedical Model*, John Wiley & Sons, Inc. Copyright © 1992 by John Wiley & Sons, Inc. This material is used by permission of John Wiley & Sons, Inc.; Figure 1.3: Summers, T.P., De Cotiis, T.A. and Denisi, S.A. (1995) 'Sources of consequences of occupational stress' in Crandall, R. and Perrewé, P.L. (eds) *Occupational Stress: A Handbook*, Taylor & Francis.

Tables
Table 1.1: Sutherland, V.J. and Cooper, C.L. (1990) *Understanding Stress: A Psychological Perspective for Health Professionals*, Manchester School of Management, University of Manchester, Institute of Science and Technology; Table 1.2: Sanders, C.M. (1989) *Grief: The Mourning After*, John Wiley & Sons, Inc. Copyright © 1989 by John Wiley & Sons, Inc. This material is used by permission of John Wiley & Sons, Inc.; Table 1.3: Reprinted from *Journal of Psychosomatic Research*, vol. 11, Holmes, T.H. and Rahe, R.H. 'The social readjustment rating scale', 1967, with permission from Elsevier Science; Table 1.4: Zitzow, D. (1984) 'The college adjustment rating scale', *Journal of College Student Personnel*, March 1984, American College Personnel Association; Tables 1.5 and 1.6: Carver, C.S. *et al.* (1989) 'Assessing coping strategies: a theoretically based approach', *Journal of Personality and Social Psychology*, vol. 56, no. 2. Copyright © 1989 by the American Psychological Association, Inc. Adapted with permission; Table 1.8: Schaufeli, W. (1999) 'Burnout' in Firth-Cozens, J. and Payne, R.L. (eds) *Stress in Health Professionals: Psychological and Organisational Causes and Interventions*, John Wiley & Sons Ltd. Copyright © 1999 by John Wiley & Sons Ltd. Reproduced with permission.

Illustrations

p. 8: *The Attack* by William Strutt (1825–1915) Photo: © Whitford & Hughes, London/The Bridgeman Art Library; p. 39: Photo: CNRI/Science Photo Library.

Chapter 2

Figures

Figure 2.1: McFarlane, A.C. and De Girolamo, G. (1996) 'The nature of traumatic stressors and the epidemiology of posttraumatic reactions' in van der Kolk, B.A., McFarlane, A.C. and Weisaeth, L. (eds) *Traumatic Stress: The Effects of Overwhelming Experience on Mind, Body and Society,* The Guilford Press; Figure 2.3: Eysenck, M. (1998) *Psychology: An Integrated Approach,* © Addison Wesley Longman Limited, 1988, reprinted by permission of Pearson Education Limited.

Tables

Table 2.1: Reprinted with permission from the *Diagnostic and Statistical Manual of Mental Disorders,* Fourth Edition, Text Revision. Copyright 2000 American Psychiatric Association; Table 2.3: Bird, M.B., Spizer, R.L., Gibbon, M. and Williams, J.B. (1997) *Structured Clinical Interview for DSM-IV Axis I Disorders (SCID-I) – Clinician Version, Administration Booklet,* American Psychiatric Press; Table 2.5: Foa, E.B., Keane, T.M. and Friedman, M.J. (eds) (2000) *Effective Treatments for PTSD,* The Guilford Press; Table 2.6: Van der Kolk, B.A., McFarlane, A.C. and Weisaeth, L. (1996) *Traumatic Stress: The Effects of Overwhelming Experience on Mind, Body and Society,* The Guilford Press.

Illustrations

p. 81: Judith Hawkins/Rex Features; p. 100: Courtesy of Gerardo Herreros.

Chapter 3

Figures

Figure 3.1: Loftus, E.F. (1980) *Memory,* Addison-Wesley. Copyright © 1980 by Elizabeth F. Loftus.

Illustrations

p. 34 *(bottom)* and p. 36: Reprinted by permission of Nicola Brace, Richard Kemp and Graham Pike; p. 42: Home Office Police Information Technology Organisation.

Chapter 4

Figures

Figures 4.1, 4.2, 4.3, 4.4, 4.5: Vrij, A. (2000) *Detecting Lies and Deceit,* 2000 copyright © John Wiley & Sons Limited. Reproduced with permission.

Illustrations

p. 201: Paul Ekman; p. 204: Dieter Endlicher/Associated Press; p. 205: *(top)* Charles Tasnadi/Associated Press, *(bottom)* Lana Harris/Associated Press; p. 227: Richard T. Nowitz/Science Photo Library.

Chapter 5

Text

Box 5.1: Reprinted with permission from the *Diagnostic and Statistical Manual of Mental Disorders*, Fourth Edition, Text Revision. Copyright 2000 American Psychiatric Association; Box 5.15: Robinson, S. (1997) 'TEACCH in adult services: the practitioner's eye view', *Communication, The Journal of The National Autistic Society.*

Figures

Figure 5.1: National Autistic Society; Figure 5.2: Happé, F. (1999) 'Understanding assets and deficits in autism: why success is more interesting than failure', Spearman Medal Lecture, *The Psychologist,* vol. 12, no. 11, November 1999; Figure 5.3: *(top)* A. Chumichyov/Novosti (London), *(bottom)* Wiltshire, S. (1991) *Floating Cities,* Michael Joseph; Figure 5.4: Frith, U. (1989) *Autism: Explaining the Enigma,* Basil Blackwell Ltd; Figure 5.6: Happé, F. (1994) *Autism: An Introduction to Psychological Theory,* Psychology Press Ltd; Figure 5.7: Gillberg, C. (1991) 'Clinical and neurobiological aspects of Asperger syndrome in six family studies', in Frith, U. (ed.) *Autism and Asperger Syndrome,* © Cambridge University Press; Figure 5.8: Slim Films; Figure: 5.9: Baron-Cohen, S. *et al.* (1999) 'Social intelligence in the normal and autistic brain: an fMRI study', *European Journal of Neuroscience,* vol. 11, pp. 1891–8, © 1999 European Neuroscience Association. Photo courtesy of Autism Research Centre, Cambridge; Figure 5.10: Howlin, P., Baron-Cohen, S. and Hadwin, J. (1999) *Teaching Children with Autism to Mind-Read,* reproduced by permission of John Wiley & Sons Limited.

Tables

Table 5.1: Bailey, A., Le Couteur, A., Gottesman, I., Bolton, P., Simonoff, E., Yuzda, E. and Rutter, M. (1995) 'Autism as a strongly genetic disorder: evidence from a British twin study', *Psychological Medicine,* vol. 25, pp. 68–77, © Cambridge University Press.

Chapter 6

Figures
Figures 6.2 and 6.4: Adapted from Spears, R. and Lea, M. (1992) *Contexts in Computer-mediated Communication*, Harvester Wheatsheaf. Reprinted by permission of Russell Spears.

Illustrations
p. 324: Copyright © Bletchley Park Trust/Science and Society Picture Library.

Chapter 7

Figures
Figure 7.1: Adapted from The Leadership Grid Figures for *Leadership Dilemmas – Grid Solutions*, by Robert, R. Blake and Anne Adams McCanse (formerly the Managerial Grid figure by Robert R. Blake and Jane S. Mouton), Houston: Gulf Publishing Company, pages 29–30. Copyright Grid International, Inc. Reproduced by permission of the owners; Figure 7.3: adapted from Vroom, V.H. and Yetton, P.W. (1973) *Leadership and Decision-Making*, University of Pittsburgh Press. Copyright © 1973, University of Pittsburgh Press. All rights reserved.

Illustrations
p. 7: From Roethlisberger, F.J. (1966) The Relay Assembly Room, *Management and the Worker*, Harvard University Press; p. 15: Copyright © Rex Features; p. 33: Photo: US Defense Department handout/Associated Press AP.

Every effort has been made to trace all copyright owners, but if any has been inadvertently overlooked, the publishers will be pleased to make the necessary arrangements at the first opportunity.

For enquiries or renewal at
Ardleigh Green LRC
Tel: 01708 462758